LIFE OF AESOP THE PHILOSOPHER

WRITINGS FROM THE GRECO-ROMAN WORLD

General Editor
Clare K. Rothschild

Editorial Board
Theodore de Bruyn
Andrew Cain
Margaret M. Mitchell
Teresa Morgan
David T. Runia
Karin Schlapbach

Number 50
Volume Editor: John T. Fitzgerald

LIFE OF AESOP THE PHILOSOPHER

Introduction, Text, and Commentary by

Grammatiki A. Karla

Translation by

David Konstan

SBL PRESS

Atlanta

Copyright © 2024 by SBL Press

All rights reserved. No part of this work may be reproduced or transmitted in any form or by any means, electronic or mechanical, including photocopying and recording, or by means of any information storage or retrieval system, except as may be expressly permitted by the 1976 Copyright Act or in writing from the publisher. Requests for permission should be addressed in writing to the Rights and Permissions Office, SBL Press, 825 Houston Mill Road, Atlanta, GA 30329 USA.

Library of Congress Control Number: 2024934933

CONTENTS

Preface vii
Abbreviations ix

Introduction 1
   Plot   3
   Structure   4
   Textual Tradition   6
   Life of Aesop as an Open Text   8
   Reception   9

The MORN Recension and Its Textual Tradition 15
   Manuscripts   15
   Recensio   19
      Contamination in M   24
   Lolliniana   25
   The Relationship of the MORN Recension to the G Version   34
      Language and Style   35
      Religion: Gods   37
      Narratological Changes   39
   The Relationship of the MORN Text to the BPThSA Recension   44
      Omission of Episodes/Chapters   44
      The Transposition of Chapter 131   46
      Additional Episodes   46
      Content   47
      Style and Language   50
   The Relationship of MORN to the Papyrus Fragments   53
      PSI 156   54
      Oxyrhynchus Papyrus XVII 2083   55
      Papyrus Berolinensis 11628   55
      The Golenischeff Papyrus   56

Oxyrhynchus Papyrus XLVII 3331	57
Oxyrhynchus Papyrus LIII 3720	57
Conclusions: The Redactor of the MORN Recension, Date, and Place	58

Editorial Methodology..61

Translator's Note..64

Sigla Codicum..65

Text and Translation..67

Commentary..167

Bibliography..221

General Index..235

PREFACE

My acquaintance with the Life of Aesop dates from my early years as an undergraduate student at the Philology Department of the National and Kapodistrian University of Athens; I have fond recollections of the months spent in the front rows of an amphitheater packed to capacity, trying to keep notes during the unforgettable lectures of my teacher and renowned Aesop specialist, I.-Th. A. Papademetriou. Since then, the Life of Aesop has been a constant companion of my academic career. In my next, graduate, steps at universities in Germany (Hamburg and Berlin), I agreed with great pleasure to the proposal to work on the Life of Aesop for my PhD degree. The result was my published thesis, *Vita Aesopi: Textüberlieferung, Sprache und Edition einer frühbyzantinischen Fassung des Äsopromans* (Serta Graeca. Beiträge zur Erforschung griechischer Texte 13 [Wiesbaden: Reichert, 2001]), which offers an edition of one of the two recensions of the version Westermanniana, the recension BPThSA. Therefore, I felt that the edition of the other recension (MORN) was a real desideratum that I owed the scholarly public.

The colleagues and friends who encouraged and assisted me in this major endeavor were numerous. My dear friend David (Konstan) was one of the first with whom I discussed this plan. With his innate optimism and enthusiasm, he prompted me to continue my research on the Life and was kind enough to undertake an English translation of the edition, something that I consider a great honor. To him I also owe the proposal to publish the edition in SBL Press's acclaimed series Writings from the Greco-Roman World. My collaboration with David was for me a true lesson in life, scholarly ethics, humanity, and incredible efficacy and productivity. I count myself really lucky to have had the opportunity to work with him. The contribution of my close friend Io Manolessou at all stages of this project, the wealth of her knowledge, and the generous offering of her time and patience are beyond words. My colleague Ioannis Konstantakos urged me on to work on recension MORN and was always more than willing to offer his assistance whenever I sought it. My colleague Mari Yosi read a first draft of this book and contributed greatly to its improvement with her perceptive remarks.

I owe a great debt of gratitude to the British School at Athens, which granted me a Centenary Bursary Award (2011/2012), thus funding my field trip to Oxford in order to study the manuscript Baroccianus 194 (O) at first hand. In Oxford, I benefited greatly from the assistance of Regius Professor Chris Pelling and from the always-enlightening discussions with Mr. Nigel Wilson. My research was also partly funded by the Special Account for Research Grants (SARG) of the National and Kapodistrian University of Athens, thanks to which I was able to visit Munich in order to study the manuscript Monacensis gr. 525 (M) at first hand. I would also like to express my gratitude to the General Editors of Writings from the Greco-Roman World series, Professor John Fitzgerald and Professor Clare K. Rothschild, who accepted this edition for publication and contributed considerably to its improvement with their wide knowledge and experience. Last but not least, I would like to express my deepest thanks to the Director of SBL Press, Bob Buller, for his patience and the professional editing at the final stage of this book. Of course, the responsibility for all errors or omissions remains exclusively mine.

This book is dedicated to my family: my husband Manolis and my children Symeon-Dimitris and Eirianna. Their love and patience inspire my scholarly work and make my life beautiful.

Grammatiki Karla
National and Kapodistrian University of Athens

ABBREVIATIONS

Primary Sources

Acta Monast. Lemb.	Acta Monasterii Lembiotissae
Add.	Additional Manuscripts
Ber.	Berakhot
Bib. hist.	Diodorus Siculus, *Bibliotheca historica*
Cant. dub.	Romanus Melodus, *Cantica dubia*
Comm. ad Hom. Il.	Eustathius, *Commentarii ad Homeri Iliadem*
Conv. soppr.	Conventi soppressi
Decl.	Libanius, *Declamationes*
Ecl.	Stobaeus, *Eclogae*
Ecl. nom.	Thomas Magister, *Ecloga nominum et verborum Atticorum*
EM	Gaisford, Thomas. *Etymologicum magnum*. Oxford: Oxford University Press, 1848.
Ep.	*Epistulae*
Epid.	Hippocrates, *Epidemiae*
Eup.	Dioscorides, *Euporista*
Geop.	Geoponica
Hist.	Herodotus, *Historiae*
Il.	Homer, *Ilias*
Nub.	Aristophanes, *Nubes*
Od.	Homer, *Odyssea*
Oed. tyr.	Sophocles, *Oedipus tyrannus*
Onom.	Pollux Grammaticus, *Onomasticon*
Or.	*Orationes*
P.Apoll.	Papyrus Apollonopolites
Paris. gr.	Parisinus graecus
Part.	Herodian, *Partitiones*
P.Berol.	Papyrus Berolinensis

P.Col.	Papyrus Columbia
P.Oxy.	Papyrus Oxyrhynchus
P.Ross.Georg.	Papyri russischer und georgischer Sammlungen
PSI	Papiri della Società Italiana
Rhet.	Aristotle, *Rhetorica*
Th	Thessalonicensis Bibliothecae Universitatis
Thaum.	Sophronius, *Thaumata*
Vat. gr.	Vaticanus graecus
Vesp.	Aristophanes, *Vespae*
Vit. Euth.	Vita Euthymii patriarchae Constantinopolitani
Vit. phil.	Diogenes Laertius, *Vitae philosophorum*
Vindob. theol. gr.	Vindobonensis theologicus graecus
Vulc.	Collectio Bonaventura Vulcanius
y.	Jerusalem Talmud

Secondary Sources

AJP	*American Journal of Philology*
BETL	Bibliotheca Ephemeridum Theologicarum Lovaniensium
Bib	*Biblica*
BNP	Hubert, and Helmuth Schneider, eds. *Brill's New Pauly: Encyclopaedia of the Ancient World*. 22 vols. Leiden: Brill, 2002–2011.
ByzZ	*Byzantinische Zeitschrift*
CP	*Classical Philology*
CR	*Classical Review*
DGE	Adrados, Francisco Rodríguez, ed. 1980–. *Diccionario Griego-Español*. Madrid: Consejo Superior de Investigaciones Científicas. http://dge.cchs.csic.es/xdge/.
DNP	Cancik, Hubert, et al., eds. *Der Neue Pauly: Enzyklopädie der Antike*. Stuttgart: Metzler, 1996–.
EBR	Klauck, Hans-Josef, et al., eds. *Encyclopedia of the Bible and Its Reception*. Berlin: De Gruyter, 2009–.
ILNE	Ἱστορικὸν Λεξικὸν τῆς Νέας Ἑλληνικῆς (Historical Lexicon of Modern Greek). http://www.xanthi.ilsp.gr/mnemeia/en_default.aspx.
JBL	*Journal of Biblical Literature*

JGRChJ	*Journal of Greco-Roman Christianity and Judaism*
LNTS	Library of New Testament Studies
LBG	Trapp, Erich, ed. 1994–2017. *Lexikon zur byzantinischen Gräzität besonders des 9.–12 Jahrhunderts*. 8 vols. Veröffentlichungen der Kommission für Byzantinistik VI/1–8. Vienna: Verlag der Österreichischen Akademie der Wissenschaften.
LSJ	Liddell, Henry George, Robert Scott, Henry Stuart Jones. 1996. *A Greek-English Lexicon*. 9th ed. with revised supplement. Oxford: Clarendon.
LSJSup	supplement section to LSJ
MIOF	*Mitteilungen des Instituts für Orientforschung*
MSG	Montanari, Franco. *The Brill Dictionary of Ancient Greek*. Edited by Madeleine Goh and Chad Schroeder. Leiden: Brill, 2015.
NovT	*Novum Testamentum*
NTS	New Testament Studies
OCD	Hornblower, Simon, and Antony Spawforth, eds. *Oxford Classical Dictionary*. 3rd ed. Oxford: Oxford University Press, 2003.
Pack	Pack, Roger A. *The Greek and Latin Literary Texts from Greco-Roman Egypt*. 2nd ed. Ann Arbor: University of Michigan Press, 1965.
PG	Migne, Jacques-Paul, ed. Patrologia Graeca [= Patrologiae Cursus Completus: Series Graeca]. 161 vols. Paris: Migne, 1857–1886.
PRSt	*Perspectives in Religious Studies*
QUCC	*Quaderni Urbinati di Cultura Classica*
REG	*Revue des études grecques*
R&T	*Religion and Theology*
SCO	*Studi Classici e Orientali*
Stephanus	Stephanus, Henricus. 1831–1865. *Thesaurus graecae linguae*. 8 vols. Paris.
SymS	Symposium Series
TAPA	*Transactions (and Proceedings) of the American Philological Association*
TLG	Thesaurus Linguae Graecae. http://stephanus.tlg.uci.edu.
WD	*Wort und Dienst*

WUNT	Wissenschaftliche Untersuchungen zum Neuen Testament
ZPE	*Zeitschrift für Papyrologie und Epigraphik*

INTRODUCTION

The Life of Aesop (hereafter Life) is a literary work dealing with the adventurous fictional life of the fabulist Aesop, the legendary and possibly historical personality of the seventh/sixth century BCE. It is written in Greek by an anonymous author and probably dates between the first century BCE and the first or second century CE.

The Life deals primarily with Aesop's status as a slave, his Phrygian origin, his sojourn on Samos under a master, his efforts to exonerate himself from the accusation of the Delphians, and his death in Delphi, events already known from literary and other sources of the classical period.[1] At another level, many stories about Hesiod, Diogenes, Socrates, the Seven Sages, and other philosophers found their way into the Life from a number of earlier sources,[2] while oral popular traditions such as anecdotes, novellas, fables, jokes, and riddles were also incorporated in this fascinating piece of "light" literature. For example, the old story of Ahiqar was a work of Middle Eastern and perhaps Babylonian or Persian origin, which, in the light of a papyrus fragment from Elephantine, would seem to have been in circulation in Aramaic as early as 500 BCE and was probably available in Greek from the early Hellenistic period. It, too, was embedded in the Life (chs. 101–123).[3]

It seems, therefore, that the anonymous author of the Life was hardly interested in using authentic sources to depict the life of the real Aesop.

---

1. See, for example, Herodotus, *Hist.* 2.134–135; Aristophanes, *Vesp.* 1446–1448; and Aristotle, *Rhet.* 2.20. The testimonia on Aesop are published by Perry 1952, 211–41.

2. Holzberg 1993, 7; Jouanno 2005, 419–23; Hägg 2012, 112–13. In particular on the influence of the traditions regarding the Seven Sages on the Life, see Konstantakos 2004, with full bibliography at 102–3.

3. Konstantakos 2013 investigates the incorporation of the Aramaic Story of Ahiqar into the Life and illustrates the anonymous author's compositional technique.

Instead, his aim was to compose a work at once didactic, amusing, and thrilling. Since it displays the features typical of the biographical genre (it follows the hero's life from a certain point onward[4] until his death) but also includes fictional elements, one might call it a fictional biography. Its inclusion in the biographical genre is congruent with the titles found in the Byzantine manuscripts which preserve the text of the Life. The manuscripts of the so-called Westermanniana version (recension MORN and recension BPThSA) give the title Βίος ("Life"), Διήγησις ("Narrative"), or both (Βίος καὶ Διήγησις, "Life and Narrative"), while the oldest manuscript (tenth–eleventh century), that of version G, bears the title Βίβλος Ξάνθου Φιλοσόφου καὶ Αἰσώπου δούλου αὐτοῦ. Περὶ τῆς ἀναστροφῆς Αἰσώπου ("The Book of Xanthus the Philosopher and of Aesop His Slave. Concerning the Course of His Life"); at the end of the work one may find the amplified title Αἰσώπου γέννα, ἀνατροφή, προκοπὴ καὶ ἀποβίωσις ("Aesop's Birth, Upbringing, Career, and Death").[5] The word Βίος in the title is also transmitted by the manuscripts of the Planudean version (at least those used in Eberhard's edition). It is likely, then, that the textual tradition mirrors the reception of the Life as biography.

David Konstan and Robyn Walsh characterize the Life as "subversive biography" in order to differentiate it (and other works such as the Alexander Romance and the gospels) from "civic biography" (to which belong works such as Plutarch's *Parallel Lives*) (Konstan and Walsh 2016, 28). Moreover, if we wish to focus on the novelistic elements of the Life and so include it in a larger category of similar literary works, we might call it a novel on the fringe. To this category belong works such as the Acts of the Apostles or Apuleius's *The Golden Ass*, and if we prefer to associate it with a narrower subgroup of "subversive" biographical works, we may mention not just the Alexander Romance but more especially the Life of Homer.[6]

---

4. Strangely enough, the Life, instead of beginning with the hero's birth, starts with an episode from his adult life. It has been suggested by several scholars (Dillery 1999, 279; Jedrkiewicz 2009, 196), and my own research corroborates this, that the incubation in the first chapters dealing with Aesop's healing by Isis and the Muses is of crucial importance. It signals for Aesop the beginning of his real life as the protagonist of the Life of Aesop; as such, it is the equivalent of the episode dealing with the birth of the protagonist (Karla 2014, 94–95 with bibliography).

5. See the comment on the title in Hägg 1997, 183–84.

6. See Perry 1936, 1–2; Papademetriou 1989, 11–14; Hägg 2012, 99–147; Rigopoulou 2012; Karla 2009b.

Among the gospels, the one closest to the Life from a literary and narrative point of view is Mark.[7]

Plot

At the beginning of the Life, Aesop is described as an exceedingly ugly slave who is also dumb (in the sense of speechless). Because of his ugliness, he is compelled to work in the fields. The episodes that follow illustrate two of Aesop's characteristics. He is clever and pious. When the priests of Isis lose their way, Aesop looks after them and helps them to find their way again. Tyche repays this good deed by giving him "the finest language and quickness of speech and the invention of ready arguments with colorful fables" (ch. 7).

Aesop is sold off to a slave trader and ends up on Samos as a slave in the house of the philosopher Xanthus. A number of humorous stories featuring master and slave demonstrate Aesop's intelligence and intellectual superiority both to Xanthus, who is a professor of philosophy, and to his students. After a while, Aesop manages, thanks to his acumen, to interpret an obscure omen for the people of Samos and so avert an imminent attack on the city by King Croesus. The grateful Samians grant him his freedom and proclaim "the spot where he was turned over to King Croesus" a hallowed place dedicated to him, which they name the Aesopeum after him. After leaving Samos, he travels around the world, earning money and glory thanks to his public lectures.

Eventually Aesop reaches Babylon, where his special gifts earn him a high administrative position at the court of King Lycurus (or Lycurgos in G). There, however, he is falsely accused by his adoptive son and sentenced to death by the king. The executioner, however, instead of performing his duty, hides Aesop. Later, when the king regrets having put Aesop to death, the executioner brings him out of hiding. Aesop is sent to Egypt, to the

---

7. See Wills 1997, 29–31; Andreassi 2015; Elliott 2005; Shiner 1998; Grottanelli 1987; Watson 2010; Hägg 2012, 147. For other studies involving the ancient traditions of Aesop's life and fables in relation to biblical literature, see Beavis 1990, 1992; Froelich and Phillips 2019; Harnisch 1985, 97–105; Hauge 2016; Hedrick 2004, 18–22; Parsons 2007, 21–22; Parsons and Martin 2018, 45–70; Pervo 1998; Pesce and Destro 1999; Reece 2016; Ross 2016; Scott 1989, 313–16; Stigall 2012; Strong 2021, 2022; Vouga 1992, 1999, 2001; Wills 2008; Wojciechowski 2008; Zimmerman 2014 (I owe the references on this subject to Prof. John T. Fitzgerald).

court of King Nectenabo, where he solves a series of riddles to the benefit of the Babylonians. Lycurus honors his wisdom by dedicating to him a golden statue.

Aesop decides to continue his travels around the world and proceeds to Delphi. Since the Delphians fail to show him any special honor, he makes some highly offensive remarks against them. As a result, they hide a golden cup from the temple of Apollo in his baggage and accuse him of theft. Aesop tries to prove his innocence and, in the attempt to talk some sense into them, narrates various myths as a warning against committing unjust acts, but in vain. He is executed by being thrown off a cliff.

> And so while the Delphians were afflicted by an unremitting and violent plague, they received an oracle to propitiate the death of Aesop, for they were stricken by conscience for having slain Aesop treacherously. So they built a temple and set up a stela in his honor. Afterwards, when the leaders of Greece and the other teachers heard what had been done to Aesop, they went to Delphi and formed an assembly and avenged the death of Aesop. (ch. 142)

Structure

The views of scholars who have considered the structure of the text display two general trends. One school of thought divides the Life into five sections and the other one into three.[8] In my opinion, the text can be divided in three large units that in turn may be divided into smaller subsections as follows:

Chapters 1–100: Aesop as slave
   1: prooemium (origin, social status, and physical description of Aesop)
   2–9: (miracle of Isis, restitution of justice): "birth" of the logopoios
   10–20
      10–11: Aesop is handed over to Zenas, a kind of first sale for Aesop
      12–20: Aesop is sold to a slave trader (Aesop is sold for a second time)

---

[8]. Holzberg 1992, 41. The five-section division of the Life has been accepted by several critics, who have, however, proposed a number of minor changes. Cf. for instance Merkle 1996, 212–13, 217–19; Jouanno 2006, 28; Hägg 2012, 112; Ruiz Montero 2014, 259. Papademetriou (1989, 21–22) also suggests a tripartite structure for the Life.

21–100: Aesop in Samos
    21–27: Aesop is sold to Xanthus (third sale for Aesop)
    28–80: Various humorous episodes involving Aesop and Xanthus
    81–98: Aesop and the Samians; Aesop earns his freedom
    99–100: Aesop and Croesus; Aesop returns to Samos (conclusion of the first part: deification of Aesop)

Chapters 101–123: Aesop in the service of the Babylonian king Lycurus
    101–111: Aesop at the court of Lycurus, in Babylon
    112–123: Aesop at the court of Nectenabo in Memphis; his return to Babylon (conclusion of the second part: deification of Aesop)

Chapters 124–142: Aesop at Delphi and his death
    124–127: The cause (the insult and the reaction of the people of Delphi)
    128–131: Aesop imprisoned and condemned to death
    132–141: Aesop's various attempts to save himself (narration of fables, supplication at the sanctuary of the Muses)
    142: Aesop's death and deification

The first unit (chs. 1–100) may have originally been an independent narrative[9] that the author of the Life incorporated into his own composition, having made the necessary changes. This view rests on external (title, closure) and internal elements (transformation of the figure of the protagonist, setting, fables, register of language/style).[10] This first part is an early (if not the earliest) Greek literary example of the comic-picaresque narrative, a genre that is the Greek ancestor of the Latin *Satyrica* of Petronius and *The Golden Ass* of Apuleius.[11]

The second part (chs. 101–123) comes from a version of the story of Ahiqar that was circulating in Aramaic as early as the fifth century BCE, in demotic Egyptian since at least the Ptolemaic period, and in Greek perhaps since the fourth century BCE.[12]

---

    9. Ludwig 1997, 17; Holzberg 1992a, 64–65, esp. on chs. 92–100; Kurke 2011, 12–4; Hägg 1997, 183.
    10. Further analysis of this view in Karla 2016b, 318–20.
    11. Karla 2016b, 321–22.
    12. See p. 1, above. On this, see Konstantakos, 2008a, 23–36, 158–66; 2008b,17–81, 225–70; also Kussl 1992; Marinčič 2003; and additional bibliography in Beschorner and Holzberg 1992, 177–78.

The third part (chs. 124–142), which draws on a historical nucleus concerned with the death of Aesop, includes many fables and is based on the pattern of *pharmakos*.[13]

Textual Tradition

The textual tradition of the Life is particularly rich. Six papyrus fragments ranging from the second/third century CE to the sixth/seventh century CE have come down to us:[14]

- P.Berol. 11628 (= Pack 2074) from the second/third CE, which transmits chapters 121–124
- P.Oxy. XLVII 3331 and P.Oxy. LIII 3720 (Addendum to 3331) from the third CE, which transmit passages from chapters 18, 75–76, and 107–111
- PSI II 156 (= Pack 2072) of the fourth century CE, which contains passages from chapters 1–3
- P.Oxy. XVII 2083 (= Pack 2073) dated to the fourth/fifth century CE, which transmits text from chapters 59–62
- P.Ross.Georg. I 18 (= Pack 2075) from the sixth/seventh century CE, which transmits text from chapters 124–133

Furthermore, the manuscript tradition of the text consists of the following versions:

1. Version G, or Perriana (named after its first editor, Ben Edwin Perry 1952, 35–77), is transmitted in a single manuscript, Codex 397 of the Pierpont Morgan Library New York (G) from the early eleventh century CE.[15] This is the most ancient manuscript of the Life, and in all likelihood the text transmitted therein is the one closest to the archetype.[16] This version was also edited by Papathomopoulos (1990, 2009) and Ferrari (1997).

---

13. Wiechers 1961, 31–42; Nagy 1980, 279–316; Jedrkiewicz 1989, 99–107.
14. Perry 1936, 39–70; Haslam 1980, 53–56; 1986, 149–72; Ferrari 1995, 296.
15. According to Husselman (1935, 104) and Perry (1933, 198), the manuscript dates to the tenth/eleventh century CE.
16. Karla 2009a. Perry's edition of version G was translated into English by Daly 1961, 29–90, who also included in brackets supplementary material derived from Version W and other sources. It is reprinted in Hansen 1998, 111–62, along with Hansen's

2. Version W, or Westermanniana (named after its first editor Westermann 1845), consists of two recensions, MORN and BPThSA.[17] The text transmitted in this version is shorter than that in the Perriana (G) but in some cases includes material from the archetype that does not appear in G. It also survives in more manuscripts, which implies that it had a wider transmission. It was probably from this version, more specifically from recension MORN, that the Latin translation of the Life, the so-called Lolliniana, named after the Lolliniana library of Belluno in Italy (where the fourteenth-century Codex 26 transmitting chapters 1–88a is kept), originated.[18] Another Latin translation of the Life and the *Fables* of Aesop was produced by Rinuccio da Castiglione of Arezzo in 1448, who apparently used a Greek manuscript belonging to the recension BPThSA (perhaps an immediate ancestor of manuscript P; Perry 1934). Perry (1952, 81–107) also edited the Westermanniana, while Papathomopoulos (1999a) edited both recensions (MORN and BPThSA) separately and Karla (2001) the recension BPThSA.

3. The Byzantine version of the Life, the Accursiana (named after the first editor, Bonus Accursius, 1479/1480) or Planudean version, also derives from the Westermanniana and, to be more precise, from a manuscript of recension BPThSA (Karla 2001, 58–61). This redaction is a transposition of the Life into a more erudite linguistic register by the monk Maximos Planudes (fourteenth century).[19] It is transmitted in at least thirty manuscripts, although there is only one edition (based on seventeen manuscripts), produced by Eberhardt in 1872.

4. There are also four *metaphrases* (translations), in a low register, dating to the early Modern Greek period (sixteenth–seventeenth centuries) There are two editions of these early Modern Greek translations: Papathomopoulos 1999b and Eideneier 2011.

---

introduction (106–11). For an English rendering of Papathomopoulos's edition of G, see Wills 1997, 180–215.

17. Both recensions are named after the manuscripts: M (Monacensis gr. 525, fourteenth century), O (Baroccianus 194, fifteenth century), R (Vaticanus gr. 1192, fourteenth century), N (Parisinus gr. 2894, thirteenth century), B (Londinensis Add. gr. 17015, fifteenth century), P (Vaticanus Palatinus gr. 269, fifteenth century), Th (Thessalonicensis Bibliothecae Universitatis 86, eleventh century) S (Mosquensis G.I.M. 436, thirteenth century), A (Atheniensis, Benaki Museum 53) (TA 72, thirteenth/fourteenth century).

18. Edition in Perry 1952, 111–30.

19. For the ascription of this version to Planudes, see Karla 2003.

Life of Aesop as an Open Text

The existence of many versions is one of the main features of so-called open texts. The differentiation between open and closed texts is due to Umberto Eco: "According to Eco, a 'closed' text is one which encourages a particular interpretation, whereas an 'open' text invites a diversity of readings."[20] Konstan (1998) and Thomas (1998) have adapted this terminology in order to characterize ancient (postclassical) literary texts such as the Life of Aesop, the Alexander Romance, the Historia Apollonii regis Tyri, and the Life of Homer, which share some common elements: they survive without an author's name or are assigned to a pseudonym, and they are notable for the stratification of the various sources, the concentration of the narrative on a central figure or protagonist, the fluidity of the narrative structure, the abundance of translations and versions, and the chameleon-like fashion in which they have come down to us.[21]

The Life is transmitted anonymously. It is remarkable that no author's name or even a pseudonym is mentioned in any of the manuscripts that transmit this work.

As we have already mentioned above, the Life is based on various literary sources enriched with material from popular oral tales. In particular, the Life consists, first, of legends about Aesop's life as a slave and his death at Delphi, which were circulating from the fifth/fourth century BCE onward, and, second, of incorporated tales and anecdotes about other literary figures, such as Hesiod, Diogenes, Socrates, or the Seven Sages, which circulated orally or in writing, in historical works, treatises, biographies, and anthologies.[22] It is characteristic of such compositions that a whole work, the story of Ahiqar, ends up embedded in the Life as an entire unit, with Ahiqar replaced by Aesop (detailed in Konstantakos 2013). Third, the Life includes popular oral tales such as the story of the widow of Ephesus (ch. 129) or "Aesopic" fables that are also incorporated in the Life.[23]

The structure of the Life, at a superficial level at least, is not complex. The whole work concentrates on the life of a single personage and offers a selection of his deeds up to his death. The reader follows the life of an

---

20. Cuddon 2013, 494. See also Hawthorn 2000, 245–46.
21. Fusillo 1994, 239; Konstan 1998; Thomas 1998; Karla 2009b, 26–28; Hägg 2012, 99–101.
22. Merkle 1996; Konstantakos 2004.
23. Karla 2009b, 24–25.

antihero, a trickster, a picaro, rather than a hero who succeeds in achieving what he needs or truly desires, such as freedom, recognition, and honors, either by divine intervention (such as the miracle by which he regains his voice and vocal abilities generally) or, chiefly, by means of his own intelligence (Karla 2016a, 55).

Konstan writes, "The episodic form is to some degree a function of the armature: the story of an individual's life serves as the pole on which to hand an indefinite string of adventures and encounters" (1998, 124). The Life is an episodic narrative, a "string of pearls narrative."[24] It consists of various episodes that have narrative autonomy.[25] Each one is a short story with a beginning, middle and end.[26] The recording of parallel action is exceptional (e.g., ch. 46). Actions are usually not interrupted by other actions because they unfold in chronological sequence (see, e.g., chs. 65–66; for additional details on the structure of the Life, see Karla 2016a, 55–56).

The textual fluidity of the Life, in combination with the simple language of the work, means that author(s), compilers, redactors, or translators of the Life felt free to intervene and alter the text, tampering with the details of various narratives and editing the content through the addition or elimination of self-contained stories. This in turn resulted in the transmission of several different revised narrations (*versiones* and *recensiones*).[27]

Reception

The Life spread widely in both East and West, from the Middle Ages to the present time.[28] It was probably the didactic character of the Life that secured its survival up to late antiquity and the Byzantine era.[29]

---

24. Hawthorn 2000, 338.

25. On episodic narrative in the Life of Aesop and a comparison with the Gospel of Mark in this aspect, see Shiner 1998.

26. Fusillo (1996, 289) compares this structure with that of television serials, especially soap operas.

27. Karla 2016a, 62. On different versions of the Life, see Perry 1933, 198–200; and pp. 6–7, above.

28. See, for example, in modern German literature the novels Bronnen 1956; Schädlich 1999. On the first novel, see Beschorner 1992. A general bibliographical survey on the reception of the Life can be found at Beschorner and Holzberg 1992, 179–87; and Holzberg 2021, 17.

29. On the reception of the Aesopic fables in Byzantium, see Papademetriou 1989, 105–25; and Adrados 1999, 559–629.

In his "Testimonia de Aesopo Fabulisque Aesopiis" (Perry 1952, 211–41), Perry notes references to Aesop recorded in the Suda (T3, T6, T31, T37), in works of the Patriarch Photius (T14, T17, T37, T47), and even in the work of Constantine Porphyrogennitus (T4). These passages, however, do not prove the existence of any direct interaction with the Life at the level of vocabulary or meaning, because they report views on the fabulist that were widely accepted in antiquity or alternative versions of the Aesop narrative different from the story recorded in the Life. Possible exceptions to this are the references in the works of the late antique authors, Julian (T58) and Himerius (T30, 56).[30] The phrase δοῦλος οὐ τὴν τύχην μᾶλλον ἢ τὴν προαίρεσιν ("slave not by chance but by choice"), recorded in Julian's text, probably indicates knowledge of a similar phrase of the Life, τὴν μὲν τύχην <ἦν> δοῦλος ("he was slave by chance"), found in the prologue of the work (ch. 1). The reference to the ugliness of Aesop in the speeches of Himerius (*Or.* 13.5, Perry T56)[31] and more specifically the phrase ἀλλ' ἤδη καὶ αὐτὸ τὸ πρόσωπον καὶ τὴν φωνὴν γέλωτα καὶ χλεύην ἥγηντο ("his face and his voice provoked laughter and mockery") seem to point to corresponding expressions attested in the Life.[32]

In addition, the works of two other scholars, from the Late Byzantine period this time, attest to the knowledge and study of the Life. The prolific scholar and monk of the Palaeologan era, Maximos Planudes (1255–1305), "translated" the Life and the fables into Atticizing prose,[33] while Andreas

---

30. To Perry's testimonia on the Life, Avlamis (2011, 74 n. 26) adds one more, by Himerius (*Or.* 66; Colonna 1951), where, in the phrase τῶν πάνυ Φρυγῶν ("the very Phrygians"), Avlamis notes a definite allusion to the opening of the Life of version G Φρὺξ τῆς Φρυγίας ("a Phrygian from Phrygia"). To be sure, Perry includes the same fragment in his testimonia on the type of the fables (*de generibus*) (T92).

31. φασὶ δὲ καὶ Αἴσωπον ... οὐ μὴ ὅτι τοὺς λόγους τινές, ἀλλ' ἤδη καὶ αὐτὸ τὸ πρόσωπον καὶ τὴν φωνὴν γέλωτα καὶ χλεύην ἥγηντο, γενέσθαι μὲν πάνσοφον....

32. ἦν δὲ καὶ νωδός ("he was dumb," ch. 1 G), ἦν καὶ βραδύγλωσσος καὶ βομβόφωνος ("he stammered with a booming voice," ch. 1 W), οὗτος τῆς γερανομαχίας σαλπιστής ἐστιν. οὗτος ῥιζοκάλαμός ἐστιν... ("Is this the trumpeter in the battle between pygmies and cranes [*Il.* 3.3–6]? Is this a man or a turnip?," ch. 14, G), οἱ δὲ Σάμιοι, ἰδόντες τὸν Αἴσωπον καὶ γελάσαντες, ἐπεφώνουν 'ἀχθήτω ἄλλος σημειολύτης, ἵνα τοῦτο τὸ σημεῖον διαλύσηται' ("But when the Samians saw him, they began to laugh, and shouted, 'Bring us some other interpreter of omens to explain this sign,'" ch. 87 G).

33. For arguments in favor of the identification of the translator of the Life (this Byzantine version has been named Accursiana or Planudea) as Planudes, see Karla 2003.

Libadenos (fourteenth century CE) wrote the Life in the codex Monacensis gr. 525.³⁴ There is also indirect testimony in the work of Nicephoros Gregoras (1290/1293–1358/1361), which suggests that this scholar of the Palaeologan period probably knew some version of the Life.³⁵ In *Ep.* 1 (τῷ ἐπὶ τῆς τραπέζης, PG 149:649, 652; and Leone 1982–1983) there is a passage in which the Phrygian origin of Aesop and his wisdom contrary to nature seem to testify to knowledge of one of the recensions of the Life.³⁶ In the early Modern Greek period (sixteenth–seventeenth centuries), the Life was transmitted in a low register, and there are four Modern Greek translations.³⁷

The Life spread to the West, in countries such as Italy, Germany, the Netherlands, England, Spain, and France, in the following versions (Papademetriou 1997, 61–62): (1) the Latin translation of the fourteenth century called Lolliniana (see above), which is transmitted in only one manuscript; (2) the Latin translation by Rinuccio da Castiglione, which was produced in circa 1448 and was widely diffused in the West (Perry 1934); (3) the Planudean version, published in 1479 in Milan by Bonus Accursius; this version offered both the Greek text and a Latin translation by Rinuccio da Castiglione.

An Aesopic collection (known as Ulmer Aesop), compiled by the German humanist Heinrich Steinhöwel and published in a bilingual Latin-German edition by Johann Zainer in Ulm (1476/1477), was prefaced by a

---

34. Perry 1933, 200. On this codex, see below.

35. This excerpt is not included in Perry's testimonia but is mentioned in Papademetriou 1997, 8 n. 3.

36. ἐγένετό τις ἀνὴρ ἐν Φρυγίᾳ πάλαι σοφός, τοὔνομα Αἴσωπος, οὐ κατὰ τὴν Πυθαγόρου σοφίαν καὶ Πλάτωνος, οὐδὲ κατὰ τὴν Ἀκραγαντίνου Ἐμπεδοκλέους ... ἀλλ' ἦν Αἰσώπῳ τῷ Φρυγὶ τὸ ἐξαίρετον τῆς σοφίας, ὡς ἦν αὐτοδίδακτος καὶ φύσει σοφός, οὐκ ἀνθρώπων σοφῶν ὁμιλίαις, οὐδὲ τέχνης ἀνάγκαις, ... ἀλλὰ ξένῃ φύσεως ἀνὴρ ἐκεῖνος δυνάμει χρησάμενος τέρας ἔδοξε τοῖς ἔπειτα σοφοῖς οὐ μικρόν ("there was once a very wise man in Phrygia called Aesop, and his wisdom was not that of Pythagoras or Plato nor that of Empedocles..., but this Aesop the Phrygian possessed the highest wisdom, since he was self-taught and wise by nature, not through intercourse with wise men or through artificial means, ... but possessing a strange innate power he seemed a great marvel to the wise men of later times") There is no edition of this letter in Guilland 1927, only a brief summary of the content, a date (1325–1330), and a catalog of the sources (p. 16). For more details on the reception of the Life in Late Byzantine times, see Karla 2016b, 329–32.

37. On published editions of these texts, see p. 7, above.

Life of Aesop based on Rinuccio's Latin translation.[38] A year later, in 1478, Günter Zainer reprinted the German text in Augsburg, and in 1479/1480 Anton Sorg published one Latin and two German editions, again in Augsburg. Julien Macho, an Augustinian monk, translated the collection in French and published it in 1480 in Lyon. This translation was reprinted ten times by 1534. Macho's translation was also the basis for the English translation by William Caxton (1484), a Dutch translation produced in Gouda (1485), a Spanish translation in Toulouse (1488), and a Czech version in Prague by J. Kamp in the same year. The German printer Johann or Hans Hurus published another Spanish version of the text that was translated from a German edition and produced in Saragossa (1489). In the same year there was an edition in Cologne and in 1492 a Low German version produced in Magdeburg. Catalan and Danish translations were published from the mid-sixteenth century onward.[39]

In addition, literary motifs and novellas derived from the Life found their way into later literature in the West, for example, in Boccaccio's *Decameron*, Balzac's *Contes Drolatiques*, the picaresque novel, upon which it exercised a decisive influence, and, possibly, the Italian novel *Bertoldo* (*Le sottilissime astuzie di Bertoldo*, 1606), by Giulio Cesare (dalla) Croce, and *Don Quixote*, by Miguel de Cervantes.[40]

In Slavonic literature there is the work The Story of Iosop the Wise and How He Lived, dated to the fifteenth century CE. The life of the protagonist displays some similarity to the adventures of Aesop of the Life, and it is not impossible that the Slavonic text is based on the Greek. Iosop is depicted in the introduction as mute, deaf, and wise. God rewards one good deed, his benefaction, with eloquence and hearing. He becomes the slave of a nobleman named Xanthio in Constantinople. The clever slave plays tricks on his master. In the second part of the story of Iosop, Emperor Digin (a word akin to the Greek Digenis, "born of two races") poses a riddle, and

---

38. See the detailed study in Hilpert 1992, 131–54.

39. This paragraph is based on Wheatley 2000, 19. See also Dicke 1994.

40. The Life was particularly influential on the chief representative of the picaresque genre in Spain, "La vida de Lazarillo de Tormes y de sus fortunas y adversidades," which was first published in 1554 (Holzberg 1993, 1–2; Papademetriou 1997, 58–72). On its influence on *Bertoldo*, see Papademetriou 1997, 43–57. Regarding *Don Quixote*, Adrados writes, "It is even possible that Quijote, whose Sancho could have taken his name from the Sanctius of the Latin versions of the *Life* (the Ξάνθος of the Greek *Life*) … has been influenced by this work" (1979, 93).

Xanthio is called upon to solve it. He proves unable to do so and hands the matter over to Iosop. Iosop impresses the emperor and becomes a palace counselor. After considerable success at court, he is captured and executed by his own nephew.[41]

The figure of Aesop is expanded in Eastern literature.[42] An interesting case is the Uyghur Book of Yosipas. In the ancient town of Qočo, fragments written in the Manichaean Uyghur script were found on a ninth-century CE codex. The book bears the title in red ink on the top margin: "The Good and Beautiful Book of Yosipas." The published fragments of this book indicate that there are some similarities with the Life, especially regarding the stories set on Samos.[43] Yosipas here seems to be in the service of a master named Kidinus (an equivalent to Xanthus).[44] A Syriac translation, of the seventh or eighth century, probably lies behind the Uyghur Book of Yosipas (Rásonyi Nagy 1930, 440–43).

There is also evidence for a Syriac translation of the Life; as Pavlos Avlamis notes:

> in a letter to John the Stylite of Litarb dated to 715 CE, George, bishop of the Arab tribes, provides a Syriac paraphrase of the *Life of Aesop*, which has remained unacknowledged by classicists. George provides John the Stylite with a commentary concerning the literary characters of Aesop and Xanthus by paraphrasing the *Life of Aesop*, especially chs. 20–31. This is the first episode of the Samos section, in which Xanthus strolls around the agora with his entourage of students and buys Aesop at the slave market. (Avlamis 2013, 278–79)

---

41. A detailed comparison between the Greek Life and the Story of Iosop may be found in Toth 2005, 118–24.

42. On the late antique translations of the Life into Syriac and into Uyghur (a Turkic Language of central and eastern Asia), see also Perry 1959, 14–15 and 21; Zeitz 1935, 24–25; Zieme 1968; Avlamis 2013.

43. See the comprehensive examination of the interaction between the Greek Life and the Uyghur translation via linguistic and cultural reencodings in Avlamis 2013, esp. 269–84.

44. Le Coq (1922, 33; frag. 14) published one fragment of the Book of Yosipas and identified it as an Aesopic fable. But the Hungarian Turkologist László Rásonyi Nagy (1930) identified the fragment as an Uyghur version of chapters 47–48 of the Greek Life of Aesop. Zieme (1968) edited further eight fragments of the Book of Yosipas and suggested that they corresponded to various chapters of the Life. Jens Wilkens (2000) reedited these fragments and added two further fragments (all information in Avlamis 2013, 269–72).

THE MORN RECENSION
AND ITS TEXTUAL TRADITION

Manuscripts

The MORN recension is one of the two redactions of the Westermanniana version and probably represents the oldest text of this version (Perry 1936, 40). It is transmitted in the following manuscripts.

M is the codex Monacensis gr. 525 of the fourteenth century.[1] It transmits the entire text of the Life in folios 154r, 154v, 6, 1-4, 9, 5, 10-17, 8, 7v, 7r, 18-20. The manuscript has been damaged, mainly by humidity. Occasionally words, phrases, or whole sentences of the text of the Life are not easy to read.[2] The manuscript was written by the scholar Andreas Libadenos and contains texts of considerable thematic variety deriving from many different periods. It begins with the Life of Aesop (Βίος Αἰσώπου τοῦ φιλοσόφου is the title of the manuscript) and continues with Aesop's *Fables* (Μῦθοι τοῦ Αἰσώπου σοφιστοῦ καὶ λογομυθοποιοῦ μεταποιημένοι μὲν ὡς ἐν παραδείγμασιν, ὀνησιμώτατοι δὲ τῷ ἀνθρωπείῳ βίῳ ταμάλιστα). This is followed by the *proverbiorum syllogae* of Aesop (Αἰσώπου κωμικαὶ κωμῳδίαι κατ' ἀλφάβητον), the fables of Syntipas (Συντίπα του φιλοσόφου ἐκ τῶν παραδειγματικῶν αὐτοῦ λόγων), a letter by the philosopher Diocles (Διοκλέους φιλοσόφου καὶ ἀρχιητροῦ ἐπιστολὴ προφυλακτικὴ πρὸς Ἀντίγονον βασιλέα Περσίδος), the story of Stephanites and Ichnelates (ἐκ τῆς τῶν Ἀράβων διαλέκτου μετένεξις Συμεὼν μαγίστρου καὶ φιλοσόφου τοῦ Σὴθ μυθικὴ διήγησις τὸ κατὰ Στεφανίτην καὶ Ἰχνηλάτην λεγόμενον Σαρακηνῇ διαλέκτῳ Κυλλιλὲ καὶ Δημία), a fragment of the Book of Syn-

---

1. See a detailed description of the manuscript in Bühler 1987, 170-79; Hinterberger 2005.

2. Autopsy in October 2012. Comparison with the *apparatus criticus* of Perry and Papathomopoulos suggests that over the years some sections of the manuscript have become harder to read.

tipas, and the third poem of Ptochoprodromos (Hinterberger 2005, 27). Other texts follow. In the view of Hinterberger, the texts transmitted in Monacensis gr. 525 belong to four different categories, while Bühler distinguishes five different groups.[3] Hinterberger's four categories consist of: (1) the texts mentioned above, which are λαϊκότροπα (popular), texts written in a popular style and intended to offer entertainment and advice; such texts were popular at the Byzantine court (Hinterberger 2005, 39–40); (2) Libadenos's autobiography and other works by him; (3) works of other authors, such as the poem "Europa" by the Hellenistic poet Moschos, compositions by Leon Grammatikos, some passages from the geographical work by Dionysios Periegetes accompanied by commentary by Eustathius, bishop of Thessalonike (twelfth century CE), a collection of Greek proverbs, and a text on grammar; and (4) astrological and medical pieces and some sections of theological works.

O is the codex Baroccianus 194 of the fifteenth century CE, which is preserved in the Bodleian Library in Oxford and belongs to the Barocci collection.[4] It preserves the text of the Life (chs. 1–104) in folios 1r–7r.[5] "This [manuscript] is a large quarto written on paper in a very small and somewhat ornate hand" (Perry 1933, 201). It is remarkable that the Life is the first text in this codex (as in M) and bears no title. It starts with folio 1r Κατὰ πάντα τὸν βίον γενόμενος βιοφιλέστατος and ends in the middle of folio 7r followed by a lacuna. Folio 7v is also blank. The scribe makes several grammatical errors, is occasionally careless, and does not seem concerned about the clarity of the text (see, e.g., ch. 2). The codex may have been compiled for didactic reasons. The Life is followed by texts such as Distichs or Sententiae Catonis (in a Greek translation by Planudes), *sententiae* of Pythagoras (Πυθαγόρου ἔπη τὰ καλούμενα χρυσά, *Golden Verses*),

---

3. Bühler 1987, 170–79. Bühler considers the Proverbs at folios 146r–153v as a separate category, thereby adding one group to those proposed by Hinterberger (see Hinterberger 2005, 27 n. 9).

4. The collection is named after "Giacommo Barocci, a Venetian" who collected Greek manuscripts. In 1628 they were "bought into England by Mr. [Henry] Feathorstone, the stationer," according to Ussher (quoted in Macray 1890, 68). On 26 January 1628/1629 "they were deposited with Laud at London House.... They consist at present of 244 volumes" (Madan and Craster 1922, 3). On the collection, see also Holton 1991, 7–8, with citations of Panagiotakis 1974 and Bancroft-Marcus 1982.

5. Autopsy in summer 2012. I am grateful to the British School at Athens for granting permission to access the manuscript.

Pseudo-Nonnus's mythological stories (*Scholia mythologica*), grammatical treatises, rhetorical works and commentaries, as well as theological texts.[6]

R is housed in Rome, in the Vatican Library, and is known as Vaticanus Graecus 1192. It was written in the fifteenth century. The text of the Life spreads over folios 189r–198r (chs. 88a–141). Perry observes that the text of this manuscript begins where the Latin Life of Lolliniana (Cod. 26) ends and believes that "Lo and R come from the same manuscript after it had been broken into two parts and separated. If so, R would seem to be a fragment of the original manuscript itself rather than a copy of thereof" (Perry 1933, 201). The codex contains no fables. It is not included in some modern catalogs of manuscripts; as a result, no paleographical or codicological description of it is available; my research is based on the digital publication of the codex by the Vatican Library and the information in the Pinakes project published online at the CNRS website.[7] Vat. gr. 1192 (MS R) begins with a grammatical treatise (folios 1–8v), followed by some theological works (such as apocrypha, speeches, and hagiographical texts) up to folio 176v. Folios 177r–188v contain an *akephalon* (i.e., mutilated at the beginning) text on grammar, probably the notes of some grammarian. It starts with a brief passage followed by grammatical notes on the text.[8] A blank page follows, and then, at folios 189r–198v, the title appears, Ὁ βίος τοῦ Αἰσώπου ("The Life of Aesop"), written by a different scribal hand. At the top of the page, in the margin, a different hand has

---

6. See the observation by Avlamis 2013, 284 n. 70: "A parallel example in the Byzantine context would be the codex Bodleianus Baroccianus 194, which includes the *Life of Aesop* and places it among improving stories and grammatical scholarship. The context at the beginning of the manuscript, where the *Life of Aesop* is found, is didactic: distichs of Cato, the *Golden Verses* attributed to Pythagoras. The rest of the codex is occupied by grammatical and rhetorical treatises and commentaries. And yet this is the only medieval manuscript that includes the risqué episode of Aesop's sexual wager (chs. 75-6), which is otherwise attested only in *P.Oxy.* 3331 fr. 2 (third century CE), while it was evidently torn and removed in other Byzantine codices."

7. For the Vatican Library digital images, see http://digi.vatlib.it/view/MSS_Vat.gr.1192. See also the Pinakes website: http://pinakes.irht.cnrs.fr/notices/cote/67823/.

8. As in 178v, ἀρετὴ καὶ παιδεία καὶ γνῶσις ἀγαθῶν ἁπάντων εἰσὶ τὸ κεφάλαιον. Ταῦτα οὖν κτῆσαι καὶ σὺ -ὦ παιδίον ὡς χρηστῶν ἁπάντων κρείττονα καὶ ὑψηλότερα αἴρουσι καὶ γὰρ ταῦτα τὸν κεκτημένον πρὸς ὕψος αἰνετῆς θεωρίας (*sic*), and then up to folio 18r grammatical notes (declination, compounds, synonyms). Or in folio 181r the short text Ἀριστοτέλης ἔφη. Οὐδὲν μεῖζον ἀγαθὸν ἀρχῆς. ἡ γὰρ ἀναρχία μέγιστον πάντων κακῶν is followed by grammatical notes. In parts the space between the lines is somewhat large, appropriately for recording grammatical comments.

inscribed: ... αἰσώπου βίος καὶ μῦθοι ("Life of Aesop and Fables"); the text concludes at the end of 198v with the phrase ἀνήρ τις ἐρασθεὶς τῆς ἰδίας ("A certain man fell in love with his own"). The last line of the main text is placed at the bottom margin inside an almost rectangular frame, and next to it the scribe has added one more line (θυγατρὸς καὶ εἰς ἔρωτα τρωθείς, "daughter and wounded by passion").[9] In folios 199r–199v the names of early Byzantine emperors are noted,[10] and in folios 200r–201r a text that I cannot identify. It begins as follows: Ἄφες τὰ ἀπὸ τῆς κτίσεως κόσμου καὶ λάβε τὴν κοντυτέραν τῶν ἐτῶν τῶν χειρίστων.[11] A section with theological texts follows folios 202r–233v. These texts include hagiographical works, the baptismal service with brief explanatory comments on the different stages of the priest's acts during the service,[12] the text of the Divine Liturgy with annotations,[13] and, at the end, in folios 233r–233v, some gospel parables (παραβολαί). These texts seem to be mutilated at the beginning and at the end.

N: Paris. gr. 2894 (thirteenth/fourteenth century). This codex transmits the section comprising chapter 90 (χάρισαι τῇ πόλει τὴν ἐλευθερίαν) to chapter 98 (καὶ τὰ μὲν τραύματα) of the Life.[14] The section takes up only one folium, the first, at the beginning of the codex. The text that comes next was probably written by a different hand dating from the same era and employing the same style (*minuscola Fettaugen*); it certainly displays a different ruling. The text entitled Anonymi Prolegomena in rhetoricam (folios 2–11v) is next, followed by Libanius's declamation entitled Δύσκολος γήμας λάλον γυναῖκα ἑαυτὸν προσαγγέλλει" (*incipit* ἔδει μὲν ὦ βουλὴ τεθνάναι...

---

9. See also Perry 1933, 201.

10. *Incipit*: Κωνσταντῖνος πρώτιστος εὐσεβοκράτωρ. Κωνστάντιος παῖς οὐ καλός ... Ἰουλιανὸς δ' ἀσεβὴς παραβάτης, Ἰουβιανὸς ἀσεβέστατος λίαν....

11. 201v. This folio must have been left blank originally, before a later hand wrote on it. The scribe tried two or three times to write the phrase εἰς τὸν ἀδελφόν μου τὸν κύριον..., before producing a brief text beginning with a crux †τιμιόταται περ εἰς το του κυρίου θαρῶ αἴλαιος... (sic).

12. In folios 220r–227v: inc. τὸ ἅγιον επαυτό συναπτόμενον ἐν καιρῷ εὔθετο τῇ ἁγίᾳ σου ἐκκλησίᾳ καὶ τελοῦμεν ... καὶ ἀγαθῷ καὶ ζωοποιῷ σου. Ἀκολουθία τοῦ βαπτίσματος: αλάσει ο ιερεύς τὴν ιερατικὴν του στολήν... (sic).

13. In folios 229r–232v: *inc.* ζωῆς ἡμᾶς ὁ Θεὸς ἡμῶν ... *des.* οἱ ὀφθαλμοὶ ἡμῶν καὶ ἐπὶ σοὶ ἠλπίσαμεν.

14. As already observed by Perry (1933, 202), "in Omont's catalogue the fragment in question is erroneously assigned to the Planudean Life." The same error is preserved in modern bibliographies (e.g., Pontani 2005, 321–23; Pinakes project).

desinit abruptum πῶς ἔχει τὰ τῶν ἀγρῶν καὶ διεξέρχεται, Libanius, *Decl.* 26.17.3) (folios 11v–12v). There follow parts of the *Iliad* and *Odyssey* with scholia (folios 13–333) and various medical texts (folios 334–335), a fragment of the work *De hominis generatione* by Libanius Alchemista (folio 336), and excerpts from the Cyranides (folios 336v–337).[15] Two leaves of an eleventh-century manuscript with theological texts were used for the binding (Perry 1933, 202). Evidently the texts of this codex were intended to be used for teaching purposes, as they contain material, such as Homeric texts, typically used in the instruction of students and items (e.g., medical texts) that deal with practical disciplines.

Lo: Biblioteca Lolliniana (Belluno), cod. 26 (fourteenth century) is a Latin translation of the Life transmitted in folios 48v–62v. The translation covers chapters 1–88a. It begins "Incipit vita acta qualiter Esopus nomine gessit, eo quod omnia in parabolis posita sunt acta illius, quia amator sapientie fuit" and ends "sed gustant vinum si bonum est aut non." According to Mazzatinti (1892, 123), the codex includes the following texts: *Summa poenitentialis* (folios 1–40); *Expositio missae* (folios 41–43); *De Sibillis* (folios 44–48); and *Vita Aesopi* (folios 48–64). Perry (1933, 202) claims that the Life is "followed by a series of *sententiae* not mentioned by Mazzatinti."

Recensio

The entire text of the Life (chs. 1–142) is transmitted in only one manuscript: MS M. A large part of the text (chs. 1–104) has survived in MS O as well. The Latin translation contains chapters 1–88a, and MS R contains chapters 88a–141. N has only chapters 90–98. The present *recensio* will be based on these five texts, three of which are fragmentary and the fourth is the Latin translation.

The manuscripts of the MORN recension can be split into two families. The first (φ) includes MSS ORN(Lo) and the second (χ) only MS M. The latter forms its own family, in that it is distinct from the others, in view of certain peculiarities found only in MS M but not in the φ family.

---

15. See Omont 1888, 3:56 (https://tinyurl.com/SBLPress1658a1); Pontani 2005, 321–23; http://pinakes.irht.cnrs.fr/notices/cote/52532.

For example, chapters 75 and 76, which refer to the affair between Aesop and the wife of Xanthus, exist only in O and Lo.[16] In G, the inclusion of certain phrases (διακινήσωμεν ἅμα δὲ καὶ τὸ ὑπόλοιπον τινάξεις κοκκύμηλον καὶ ἐνέγκῃς τῇ κυρίᾳ σου, ἵνα τὰ ἱμάτια λάβῃς) attests to the fact that the episode was part of the text both in the ancestor of G and in G itself. Moreover, the same phrases are attested in certain papyrus fragments (P.Oxy. XLVII 3331; P.Oxy. LIII 3720, addendum to 3331; see Haslam 1980, 1986), which suggests that the adultery episode was also present in the archetype of the Life. These chapters do not appear in M or in the archetype of the BPThSA recension. Perry argues that the survival of Aesop's response, Ἐγώ σε ἀνταμυνοῦμαι, in MS M is an indication that the wager story did exist in an earlier stage of the tradition of this particular manuscript.[17]

On the other hand, M transmits chapters 50a, 77a, and 77b, which are not in MSS O or Lo (nor in G). In 50a Xanthus's wife abandons her husband and returns to her parents. Thanks to a clever trick, Aesop reconciles the couple. In 77a Aesop deliberately misinterprets the metaphorical phrase of his mistress "even my arse has eyes" and strips off the woman's clothes as she is sleeping, so "that the eyes in her arse might watch the table." Xanthus, on entering the room with his visitor, finds the mistress with her posterior bare. In 77b Xanthus has invited some philosophers for dinner and has ordered Aesop to stand guard at the gate and to allow entrance only to sages. Aesop asks everyone the question "What does a dog shake?," a phrase that in Greek sounds similar to "Who are you, you dog?" The philosophers feel insulted, and all leave except one, who answers correctly. When Xanthus discovers the reason why only one of his guests has appeared, he becomes furious with Aesop. These stories seem to have been a later addition[18] and are found in the BPThSA recension. Their presence in M is perhaps to be explained either by the fact that chapters 77a and 77b were already part of an ancestor of the family χ, dated to before the arche-

---

16. The omission of these chapters in the text tradition could have been accidental or deliberate, in view of the obscenity of the story told in them. On this issue, see Perry 1933, 209; 1936, 7–11.

17. In the archetype of the BPThSA, Aesop's reply is only partially preserved.

18. See detailed argumentation, based on a structural analysis, in Perry 1933, 226; 1936, 35–37; Holzberg 1992a, 59–61. Merkle (1996, 222) argues instead that these episodes were part of the text in the archetype.

type of the BPThSA recension (Perry 1952, 28) or by the possibility that they were a product of contamination in an ancestor of M.

Furthermore, some variants or errors in MS M are not present in MSS ORN and consequently are absent from the family φ as well:

Chapter	MS M	MSS ORN (recte)
16	ἀνήβων	προυνικῶν O
16	δύο παῖδας πρῶτον εὑρίσκει	εὑρίσκει παῖδας O plures servos Lo
24	λῦδος	Λυδός
26	καλόδουλος, οὐ δραπετεύσω· ἐὰν δὲ om.	OLo habet
35	κύρι	κύριε O
52	ἐπειδὰν ἑνωθεῖ	ἐπιδέξηται O
64	θαμβεῖται	θυμοῦται O tanto furore est repletus Lo
79	ἀναπηδήσας	ἀνεπόδισεν O
83–85	ἔχεις	ἔξης O
86	εἶπεν	ὑπέδειξεν O
86	συνιδεῖν τὸν Αἴσωπον	ἐλθεῖν τὸν οἰκέτην αὐτοῦ O
89	πολῖται	σάμιοι καὶ τίμιοί μου OR
92	τιμωρήσομαι	βλάψω ORN
109	συμφέροντα	συμβαίνοντα R
114	εἰσελθὼν	εἰσελθόντος R
117	ζητοῦντες	ἀπαιτοῦντες R
131	θυγάτριον	θυγατέρα R
133	ἐκδικήσειε (-ε *supra lin.*)	ἐκδικήσωσι R

We may postulate, then, that MS M derives directly from a source χ, which is its ancestor.

The codices O and R share some common errors and some readings not found in MS M, such as:

Ch.	MSS ORN	M (recte)
7	Φιλοξενία O (*Dei* Lo)	Τύχη
18	διὰ κελόμενος O	διακλώμενος
26	ἔπεισε O	ἔστησε
95	γνῶντες ORN	γνόντες
96	πρεσβύτας ORN	πρεσβευτάς
	τοῦτο OR : τούτου N	τότε
	οἱ δὲ λέγε add. ORN	non habet
104	ἵνα OR	τοῦτον
104	λόγους OR	ψευδέσι λόγοις
104	ἀπέλαβεν τὴν τοῦ ἐσώπου διοίκησιν καὶ δουλείαν OR	τὴν τοῦ Αἰσώπου διοίκησιν παρέλαβεν

Moreover, although Codex N transmits only a small part of the text (chs. 90–98), there are some common errors between O and R (Lo) that are not found in N:

Ch.	MSS OR	MS N (recte)
90	ἐλεύθερον OR	ἀπελεύθερον
90	δέδωκε OR	ἔδωκε
91	ἐπειδὴ OR	ἐπεὶ
91	νυνὶ om. OR	νῦν
92	γίνεσθαι om. OR	habet
95	δεινή OR	πεδινή (πεδηνή N)
	ὑπάρξεις OR	γενέσθαι

On the other hand, O and R exhibit their own distinct errors; this excludes a direct relationship between them. Among such errors in MS O that are not present in MS R are the following:

Ch.	MS O	MS R cum cett. recte
97	εὐχαρίστους	εὐχρήστους (εὐχρίστους R)
97	(συμμαχησάντων) τῶν προβάτων	τοῖς προβάτοις
90	ἐλευθελοκαλεῖ	ἐλευθερικά

| 97 | διασπαράξαντες | διέφθειραν |
| 98 | ἀκούσαντες | νοήσαντες |

Further, MS R manifests a set of readings that are not found in MS O, such as:

Ch.	MS R	MS O
95	ἐγκρατεῖς	ἐγκρατής
98	μεῖναι om.	habet
99	(ἄνθρωπός) τις om.	habet
100	γράψας	συγγράψας
100	δεδομένης	γενομένοις
101	ἐθαυμαστώθη καὶ post σοφίαν add.	om.

We can assume, therefore, that MSS O and R, which are independent of each other, derive from a common source, which we can term φ2:

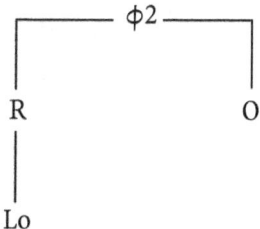

MS N belongs to this family, as is clear from the errors common to it and OR, but because it also exhibits errors of its own (see below), it cannot derive directly from φ2 and probably derives from a source φ1, which constitutes a separate branch of the φ family.

Ch.	MS N	MSS OR (recte)
90	σου (ὁμότιμος)	σοί
90	συμβουλεύονται	συμβουλεύοντες
92	ἑλληνίδι διαλέκτω	ἐν χλανίδι διαλεύκω

94	δούς	ὁδούς
	ὁμαλόν	σκληρόν
96	πόθεν	πόθος

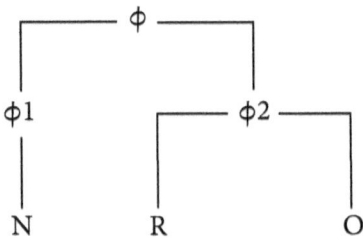

In the light of the above observations, the relationship of MSS M, O, R, and N can be schematized as follows:

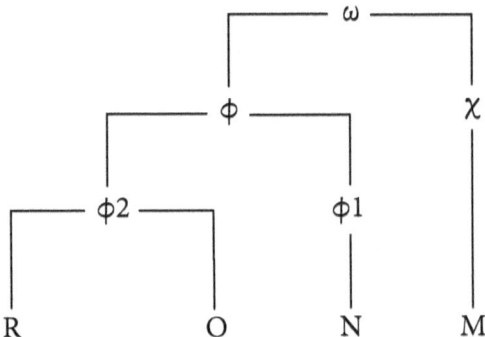

Contamination in M

It is important to note some common errors or readings between MSS M and λ (mainly MS L) and similarly between MSS M and W.[19]

---

19. λ is the common ancestor of MSS LFV (see Perry 1933, 204–5), which, like MS W (Conv. soppr. 627), represent the so-called mixed texts; i.e., the transmitted texts of the Life in these manuscripts have many contaminations from both redactions (MORN and BPThSA) of the Westermanniana version (Perry 1933, 203–7).

The episodes in chs. 50a, 77a, and 77b are attested in all three witnesses (M, λ, and W). Furthermore, there are some common errors and/or peculiar readings between MS M and λ (mainly MS L), such as the following:

Ch.	Mλ	cett. recte
97	ὁμοίως M(L)	ὁ μῦθος
98	ἀναγκάζουσι M(LW)	ἀνακράζουσι
104	ἔθετο (ML)	ἔκρυψεν
105	ἐπειδὴ θέλω (MLV)	βούλομαι γάρ R
106	ὅλους (τοὺς φίλους) (ML)	πάντας R
107	συνοχήν ML	κάθηρξιν BVR
108	ἀποκριθησόμενον MLV	ἀπολογούμενον R
128	τὸ στρῶμα ML	τὰ σκεύη R

In Perry's view, the three stories (50a, 77a, and 77b) are "undoubtedly ancient" (1936, 30), and "it is much more probable that these episodes were absent in the archetype of the Westermann recension and that they were interpolated for the first time into the archetype of the SBP, and thence into λM" (1933, 223). Their absence from MSS OLo and G may be due either to the fact that the branch of the textual tradition preserved in these two manuscripts never exhibited the contamination observed in MS M or to the possibility that these three stories were included in the archetype of Westermanniana but were omitted later on by the scribe of the common hyparchetype, who took into consideration the tradition of the G version.

Lolliniana

The Latin translation of the Life that is transmitted in a fourteenth-century codex comes from a text that must be an ancestor of the MO recension. Perry (1933, 231) argues that "the fact that R, which is a fragment and not an excerpt, begins in the very next sentence after that with which Lo, a contemporary text, leaves off, can hardly be a mere coincidence," adding that Lo and R may be regarded as representing the same manuscript after it had been split into two separate parts (1933, 201).

Notably, the wager story (chs. 75 and 76) is extant only in O and Lo, and the *dubia* chapters 50a (reconciliation of Xanthus and his wife through the intervention of Aesop), 77a (naked mistress), and 77b (the single guest) are omitted only in O and Lo. For these reasons, Perry assumes that a close relationship existed between the two manuscripts. Before agreeing or disagreeing with this view,[20] we must examine the *usus scribendi* of the translator of Lolliniana, to uncover his peculiar translation style and scribal poetics.

Sometimes the translator summarizes the Greek text by omitting what he considers to be superfluous details. Usually he does so in order to speed up the narrative development and to give a faster pace to the plot. For example in chapters 2 and 3, when the slaves who work with Aesop eat the figs that belong to their master and have to find an excuse to explain why the figs have disappeared, one of them suggests that they blame Aesop: "Esopus laborat foras in campum, nos autem comedemus hos fructus et cum dominus noster quasierit hos fructus dicemus quia Esopus, invento hostio aperto, intravit et manducavit eos" ("Aesop labors outside in the field, so we will eat those fruits [the figs], and in the case that our master asks about those fruits we will say that Aesop found the cellar open, went inside, and devoured them"). In the Greek text (MORN) the same story is reported in considerably more detail:

"Καὶ ὁ Αἴσωπος βραδύγλωσσος ὢν πρὸς ἀπολογίαν δαρήσεται, ἡμεῖς δὲ τὴν ἐπιθυμίαν ἐκπληροῦμεν." Καὶ παρακαθεσθέντες τοῖς σύκοις ἓν ἓν τρώγοντες, ἔλεγον "οὐαί σοι, Αἴσωπε." Συμφωνήσαντες εἰς ἑαυτοὺς ἵνα, εἴ τι ἀπόληται ἢ ἐκχυθῇ, εἴπωσι ὅτι ὁ Αἴσωπος ἐποίησε, κατέφαγον τὰ σῦκα. Ὁ δὲ κύριος αὐτῶν μετὰ τὸ λούσασθαι καὶ ἀριστῆσαι, "Ἀγαθόπου," φησί, "δός μοι τὰ σῦκα." Κἀκεῖνος ἔφη "δέσποτα, Αἴσωπος εὐκαιρήσας καὶ εὑρὼν τὸ ταμεῖον ἀνεῳγμένον εἰσελθὼν κατέφαγε τὰ σῦκα.[21]

---

20. It is difficult to disagree with Perry's views regarding the relationships among the various manuscripts and the textual tradition of the Life, although he does not seem to have been interested in the relationship of Lo to the Greek manuscripts that preserve the text of the Life.

21. "'Aesop, stammering in his defense, will be beaten, while we will sate our appetite.' Sitting down by the figs, they gulped them down one by one and said, 'Woe to you, Aesop!' Agreeing between themselves that, if anything should be spoiled or spill out, they would say that Aesop did it, they ate up the figs. After washing and having his lunch, the master said, 'Agathopus, give me the figs.' And he said, 'Master, Aesop had the chance, found the storehouse open, went inside, and ate the figs.'" The English translations of Lolliniana are provided by me.

In the Latin text, this passage is summarized in just three words: "Et sic fecerunt" ("And that is how it happened"). The story then moves on to the anger of the master against Aesop, omitting the dialogue between the slaves, their decision to put the blame on Aesop, and the exchange between Agathopous and the master, leading to the accusation of Aesop.[22] It is also notable that the scribe of Lo leaves out chapter 67 (the etiological story about looking at one's own excrement while defecating), probably because of its scatological content.

Occasionally, however, the Latin translation records additional material, as in chapter 29. In the Greek versions of the narrative recorded in this chapter, Xanthus misleadingly announces to his wife that he has bought her a slave so handsome that she has never seen any other like him before. The Latin translator then decides to give in detail the description of the "handsome" slave: "Ego modo comparavi tibi iuventulum optimum, habentem occulos grandes, statum excelsum, faciem albam, capillos russos, et omnia splendidum qualem numquam vidisti" ("I brought over for you just now the most handsome youth, one who has big eyes, tall stature, white face, red hair, and everything on him is so splendid, as nothing of the sort you have ever seen"). In general, the Latin translator is fond of displaying his own good taste when he has the opportunity to describe people.[23] For example in the episode of the sale of the three slaves (the musician, the teacher, and Aesop), in chapter 21, the attributes of these slaves are slightly changed from those given in the Greek texts. Since the musician in the Greek versions "had fine legs, the merchant dressed him in a white tunic and sandals and combed his hair and set him on the selling block," whereas in Latin: "musicus qui erat rusticus[24] capilis et alba facie, induit eum vestibus albis et unxit capillos eius et possuit eum in foro" ("The musician who was rustic concerning his hair and his white face, he [the merchant] dressed him in white garments, combed his hair, and led him in the market place"). In the Greek text, the teacher, "who was second best to look at, he dressed in a long tunic and sandals, combed his hair, and giving him a neckerchief he set him on the selling block." In the Latin text, however, "Grammaticus qui fuscus erat, induit vestibus tinctis et calciamenta in pedibus eius et

---

22. See also chs. 1, 16, 18, 19, 28, 34, 43, 45, 47, 50, 52, 54, 59, 66, 70, 72.

23. Concerning the aesthetic values of the Latin translator, it would be interesting to investigate, for example, how the Greek word σαπρός has been translated. In ch. 26 it is translated as *niger*.

24. The proposed reading by Perry, *russis*, seems to me more appropriate.

possuit illum in foro." ("The school teacher who was dark-skinned, he [the merchant] dressed him in bright-colored garments, put shoes on the man's feet, and led him in the marketplace").

In the same way in chapter 32 Aesop accuses the wife of Xanthus because she would like to have "a young slave, with pretty eyes, curly hair, light-skinned." In the Latin translation, this kind of slave is described as "bonum, formosum, lucidum, sapientem, amabilem" ("good, handsome, brilliant, smart, loveable").

In general, the translator follows the Greek text and intentionally changes or omits things such as the names of gods. In fact, nowhere in the Latin text names of gods are mentioned. Not only is the conspicuous reference to Isis, a typical feature of both MORN and BPThSA, missing,[25] but even the few references to other gods by name in MORN have been removed. In chapter 4, for example, "the priests of Isis" have been substituted by just *sacerdotes*, whereas in chapter 7 the goddess who heals the mute Aesop is not Isis (G), or Tyche (M), or Philoxenia (O) but simply *Deus*. In chapter 68, even though there is a textual problem with the reference to Dionysus in MORN, the translator omits the name of Dionysus altogether.[26] We do not know what happened to the mention of Apollo because the Latin text breaks off before the section where references to Apollo appear in the Greek text (chs. 100, 127).

The translator, or scribe, of manuscript Lo seems to have had limited geographical knowledge. Some place names are omitted or incorrect; for example, instead of εἰς Ἔφεσον (ch. 20) in the Greek text, Lolliniana has *ibi*. The intention of the merchant to depart to Asia to sell the slaves (ch. 17) is omitted as well. In chapter 24, the reading *bidbia* (Lo) is found instead of *Lydia* (corr. Perry);[27] the Greek text reads Λυδία. The reference to Samos seems to require explanation, as one infers from the context in which the name first occurs: "Si vis vendere hos pueros, perge in civitate quae dicitur Samo. ... et multi alii de illa provincia et de ipsa insula" ("If you want to sell your slaves, go on to the city called Samos ... and many others from the

---

25. See Karla 2009a, 446–49.

26. However, in ch. 79, where there is a reference to the king of Byzantium, Dionysios, the name of the king is noted in Latin text as well: "quia aurum istud dabitur imperatori Bysancio qui dicitur Dionisius" ("because that gold will be handed over to the emperor Bysantius, who is called Dionysius").

27. In this case the false reading could have been caused by the writer of the manuscript Lo or an ancestor thereof.

same region and from the island itself," ch. 20).[28] The translator seems to be more familiar with Phrygia, or at least with its name. In the first chapter he mentions correctly that Aesop comes from Phrygia, whereas he omits the city of Amorion ("natus de partibus Frigie" where the original has τῷ δὲ γένει Φρὺξ ἐξ Ἀμορίου τῆς Φρυγίας). In the episode describing the sale of Aesop, when Xanthus asks Aesop about his origin, no reply is found in the Greek text. Only in the Lolliniana, in reply to Xanthus's question "ex quali gente es tu," Aesop says, "De Frigia" (ch. 25).

As for rendering personal names in general, the translator omits them or transliterates them in Latin or renders them as seems right to him. Aesop is transmitted as Esopus,[29] Xanthus as Sanctus, Agathope (Ἀγαθόπους ch. 2), Tyrum (Τύρος ch. 24), and Philocalum (Φιλόκαλος ch. 24), but the name (Λύκαινα) of Xanthus's dog is rendered as Linge (ch. 45). The translator paraphrases Euripides's passage but omits the name of the poet (ch. 32). This means either that he did not know the author Euripides, which seems the most likely possibility, or that he thought there was no point in mentioning the poet's name to his audience. Interestingly, the translator always converts references to currency and coins used in trade into their Latin equivalents. The trade price for the teacher, τρισχιλίων δηναρίων ("three thousand dinars"), is transmitted as "ducentos soldos" ("two hundred soldi," ch. 24); the trade price for Aesop, ἑξήκοντα δηνάρια ("sixty dinars"), as "decem solidos" ("ten soldi," ch. 27); and the trade price of the wood, ἀσσαρίων δώδεκα ("twelve cents"), as "xii follares" ("as twelve follares," ch. 59).

On the other hand, sometimes the translator offers Latin transliterations of Greek words, for example, *antilogiam* in chapter 34, *phylosophya* in chapter 51, *stradigo* in chapter 65, and in "homo aperiergus est, hoc est obendiens" in chapter 61; the translator even prints terms and phrases in Greek (ἐπιτάφια γράμματα) in chapters 79 and 80 in order to preserve the acrostic. Occasionally, however, he makes mistakes, as he does, for example, in chapter 30, where he seems not to know the meaning of the word καπριῶσα (in high heat) and to take it to be a personal name: "Una autem ex ancillis, Kapriosa nomine." Likewise, in chapter 81 he fails to recognize the classical meaning of the word ἐκκλησία ("assembly") and translates it in the Christian sense, thus producing "venerunt in templum" ("they went to the temple").

---

28. See also Capadotia instead of Cappadocia.
29. A reading that reproduces the Greek original ἔσωπος (as in MS O).

As for its relationship to other manuscripts, Lo agrees with some peculiar readings of MS O, as in chapter 35, where the erroneous reading οἰκεῖται (MS O), instead of διοικεῖται (MS M), seems to have been translated as "est locutus."[30] Even so, Lo does not have the corruptions (or the additional material) recorded in MS O.[31] On the other hand, there are errors in Lo that are not found in MS O; for instance, in chapter 55, Lo has "Tunc discipuli dixerunt," whereas all Greek versions identify Xanthus as the speaker. At the end of chapter 62, cake (πλακοῦς) is offered in all Greek manuscripts, but fish ("appossuerunt pisces") is offered in Lo, even though fish has already been served.[32]

Moreover, Lo occasionally agrees with mistakes or peculiar readings of MS M, as in chapter 10, where the sentence "nullum bonum est nobis hoc signum" is attributed to the "steward." This occurs because the phrase Καὶ ὁ δεσπότης, which signals the change of the speaker, is omitted in MS M.

In rare cases Lo combines readings from MSS M and O, as in chapter 9, where the reaction of the steward upon hearing Aesop speaking is described as ἐθαμβήθη ("He was stunned") in M, with the same meaning, if not wording, occurring in all other manuscripts, but in MS O alone the servant is reported to have felt fear: ἐφοβήθη ("He was afraid"). Lo translates "miratus est, et timore perterritus" ("he was stunned and outright terrified").[33]

Only seldom does Lo agree with the BPThSA recension against the MORN recension; for instance, in chapter 46 Aesop's response to the reaction on the part of his mistress in Lo, "sed in corde suo orabat valde tibi" ("but in her heart she was praying for you to be well"), is closer to the text recorded in the BPThSA recension (τῷ δὲ νοΐ αὐτῆς ηὔχετό σοι).[34] In

---

30. See also ch. 21's *calciamenta in pedibus*, where εἰς τοὺς πόδας is found only in O; similarly in chs. 24 (*et faciem eius tenebrosam*), 25 (*aut in terra aut in lectus pannis*) 30 (*et dixit "quis nobis clamabit..."*), 31 (*Iste est quem laudabas?*), 61 (*ait intra se*), 72 (*potest bibere mare totum*), and 87 (*cum manu*).

31. For example, in ch. 32 the phrases of MS O, ἐπὶ πολὺ δὲ λέγοντος τοῦ ἐσώπου στραφεῖς ἡ κυρία αὐτοῦ πρὸς τὸν ξάνθον ἔφη, are not to be found in Lo. In ch. 69 also the phrase μὴ θέλων ἡττηθῆναι καὶ ἐκ τοῦ οἴνου κεκαρομενος ὤν, which MS O reports, is missing in Lo. In ch. 49 Lo has *Sanctus ait intra se* (like most Greek manuscripts), in contrast to MS O, which has ὁ δὲ πρὸς αὐτήν.

32. See also the lacuna at the end of ch. 56 or in ch. 80.

33. See also ch. 10's "Domine, novam rem in pomero tuo factam" ("Master, something new/strange happened in your orchard"), where the reading *domine* is found in MS O and *tuo* in MS M.

34. MSS MO have τοῖς δὲ νεύμασιν ἐν ἑαυτῇ ηὔχετό σοι.

rare cases Lo has common readings with the G version, as in chapter 60, where Aesop and the nonmeddler greet each other. Lo has "Gaude et tu, frater." The reading *frater* may be traced to the reading πατερίων of MS G and of P.Oxy. 2083. In the same episode (ch. 62), when the nonmeddler eats the served fish, he is compared to *delfinos*.[35] Only MS G preserves this form of the word (δελφῖνος) in contrast to almost all other Greek manuscripts, which have δελφίς.[36] Moreover, in chapter 72, when Xanthus's opponent seeks to collect his bet, Aesop in Lo replies, "Dico tibi, da omnia tua domino meo et noli fiscare" ("I told you that all your property belongs to my master, so don't blabber"). The phrase *noli fiscare* seems to be drawn directly from MS G καὶ μὴ φλυάρει, because the other Greek manuscripts have no corresponding reading.[37]

The translator of Lo follows the plot of the narrative and in general does not alter the original by adding characters or by changing the outcome of the stories. In a few cases he retells the story in his own way, and only rarely does he intervene drastically and alter the Greek text. Such rare occasions involve the rephrasing of sentences or clauses (as in ch. 72),[38] something that affects only the style, rather than the content, of the narrative.

The most important change takes place in the episode involving the citizens of Samos and Xanthus (chs. 81–86), who cannot interpret an omen: an eagle flies away after seizing a ring to be worn by whoever was to be elected as "guardian" of the city's laws; the eagle then comes back and drops the ring of the city in the lap of a slave. In chapter 82, the Greek text of MOR has simply: Ὁ δὲ Ξάνθος διαπορῶν καὶ αἰτήσας διωρίαν εἰς τὸν ἴδιον ἦλθεν οἶκον ("Xanthus was at a loss, so he asked for time and went to his house"). In Lo, instead of this, one finds: "Sanctus autem cum no potuit solvere hoc signum, dixerunt omnes qui ibi aderant una cum praeside 'Vadat Sanctus et habeat inducias usque ad tres dies et inveniat nobis interpretationem; quod si non, interficiemus illum'. Sanctus, ut audivit, tristis factus est" ("Then, since Sanctus could not solve the omen, everyone present

---

35. According to Perry's *apparatus criticus* (1952, 124), Lo has the reading *delfinos*, which Perry corrected to *delfinus*.

36. δελφὶς (MLF), δέλφις (O), ἀδελφός (WV).

37. See Perry's *apparatus criticus* (1952, 127): "*fiscare significat fraudare vel illudere*; cf. Du Cange s.v. *fiscatio*. παράδος – καὶ μὴ φλυάρει solus G inter codd. gr."

38. The Greek text MORN seems to have τὸ δὲ πλῆθος τῆς πόλεως συνέδραμον ἰδεῖν, whereas Lo has "Multitudo populi civitatis venerunt videre hoc miraculum, quo modo debuisset bibere mare."

there along with their leader said: 'Let Sanctus go away, and let him have up to three days time to interpret the omen for us. Otherwise we shall kill him.' When Sanctus heard this, he became sad"). The suggestion in direct speech that the priest turn to Xanthus for an interpretation of the *signum* (sign) can be traced to version G (ch. 81):

> ἀναστάς τις ἐκ τοῦ πλήθους πρεσβύτης ἔφη· "ἄνδρες Σάμιοι, τούτοις μέλλομεν προσέχειν οἵτινες ταῖς ἀπαρχαῖς γαστέρα πληροῦνται <καὶ> εὐσχημόνως τὸν βίον διακυβεύουσιν. ἀγνοεῖτε δὲ ὅτι οὐκ ἔστιν εὔκολον σημεῖον ἐπιλύσασθαι· εἰ μὴ γάρ τίς ἐστιν ἔμπρακτος παιδείας, σημεῖον οὐ καταδιαιρεῖται. παρ' ἡμῖν δέ ἐστιν Ξάνθος ὁ φιλόσοφος, ὃν ὅλη ἡ Ἑλλάς οἶδεν· αὐτοῦ δεηθῶμεν ἵνα τὸ σημεῖον διαλύσηται." καθεζομένου δὲ τοῦ Ξάνθου ἐπεφώνουν καὶ ἐδέοντο παρακαλοῦντες ὅπως διακρίνῃ τὸ σημεῖον.
>
> An old man of the city got up and said, "Fellow Samians, we are about to give heed to men who fill their bellies with the cult offerings, and though they appear respectable enough, they gamble away their own fortunes. Are you not aware that it is no easy feat to interpret an omen? If a person is not well versed in these matters, he cannot correctly analyze a portent. But among us we have Xanthos the philosopher, known to all of Greece. Let us ask him to interpret the sign." When the old man sat down, they all called out and appealed to Xanthos to interpret the sign.

It is clear that the text of G in Lo has been abbreviated, for the theoretical prologue is missing, and the citizens, instead of appealing to Xanthus, in fact threaten him. Furthermore, the philosopher is given a deadline of three days to come up with an interpretation. Later in the narrative, in all Greek versions (given summarily in MOR and BPThSA, in detail in G), Xanthus attempts to commit suicide (G mentions specifically that the philosopher plans to use a rope to hang himself). In Lo, he tries to interpret the sign but in vain; as a result, he decides to abstain from food and drink: "Ivit domum suam et cepit perscrutari <et>, pro eo quod non poterat interpretari signum, neque manducavit neque bibit" ("He went home and set out to decipher it, and because he could not interpret the omen, he neither ate nor drank"). In Planudes's version, the desperate suicide attempt by Xanthus is omitted as well. It may well be that there is no explicit mention of suicide in either the Lo or in Planudes because of the strict prohibition of suicide by the Christian church.[39] Furthermore, in the Greek versions Xanthus speaks about his problem to Aesop directly, without any inter-

---

39. See my comment in Karla 2006, 222–23.

mediary. In Lo, however, a maid-servant tells Aesop of Xanthus's terrible psychological situation and subsequently carries a message from Aesop to Xanthus: "Nunciavit Esopo una ancilla quae panem ei ferebat, et dixit Esopus 'Vade et nuntia domino meo ut excuciat me de isto loco, et ego dabo sibi consilium ut non moriatur dominus meus'" ("A maidservant, who brought bread to Aesop, announced this to him, and Aesop replied: 'Go and tell my master to take me to that location, and I will give him resolution so that my master may not die,'" chs. 83–85).

To conclude, the translator of the Lolliniana evidently had no broad education in Greek or Roman culture, nor did he have any accurate knowledge of geography. Overall, the translation leaves out redundant information and opts for brevity, but it does pay special attention to the plot and the liveliness of the narrative. This explains the use of direct discourse in places where the Greek original probably used indirect speech.[40] The translator seems not to have functioned in a purely mechanical fashion, which would explain why, when he removes something from the story, he is still careful to maintain coherence of plot and a smooth transition to the next episode. The translator is attentive to the text and subtly revises it to read as a contemporary piece of literature: various names of ancient gods have been removed, the monetary units in the financial transactions have been changed, and the prose displays a different aesthetic. Furthermore, the translator tries to emphasize the morally instructive character of the narrative, so scatological stories do not appeal to him. His implied audience seems to be unsophisticated and interested less in morality than in entertainment or even in picking up some useful advice. They may also have derived pleasure by identifying with the antihero, a man of the people, who outsmarts his master, the renowned philosopher Xanthus.

The archetype of the Greek manuscript that the translator used indeed seems to belong to the MORN recension, and even more closely to the family ORN. Two theories have been suggested to explain the readings that seem to derive from the M family or the G version: either the translator had at his disposal more than one manuscript, or his original was contaminated. It is quite difficult to infer that Lo and R represent the same manuscript "after it had been broken into two parts and separated" (Perry 1952, 29–30). The evidence indicates only that Codex R picked up where Lo

---

40. Notably, almost all cases of direct speech in Lo are also to be found in G. The Greek text of version G comes from the edition by Ferrari 1997, while the English translation is by Wills 1997, 178–224.

ends and that both come from the fourteenth century. No other common elements are to be found, as their content is different.

The Relationship of the MORN Recension to the G Version

To describe precisely the relationship of the MORN recension to G version is no simple matter. No definite answer to the question as to which of the two recensions is closer to the archetype has been offered to date, and critics still argue about it (see Karla 2009a). It seems, however, that Perry's view has prevailed. Perry thinks that the text of the G version is closer to the archetype in language and content, when compared with the text of the Westermanniana version, and by extension, of the MORN recension. The latter, in Perry's opinion, must be a version revised by a fifth- or sixth-century grammarian who wished to purify the language and style of the text and to produce an abbreviated form unencumbered by confusing details. In similar fashion, the pivotal role of the Muses and Apollo in the narrative of the G version either drops out completely or is to be inferred from scant traces in the plot.[41]

Luzzatto has expressed the opposite view, but her arguments are clearly problematic,[42] since she suggests that, in terms of content, the Westermanniana version is the one closest to the archetype and is not simply an abbreviated version of the G text. Scholars such as La Penna, Haslam, and Holzberg have taken the view that the G version seems to be closer to the original text and that the Westermanniana, rather than being a direct compendium of the latter, draws on some other text not known today that preserved material from the original. This material is not found in the G text, as comparison with the papyrus fragments shows.

In what follows I investigate the differences between the two versions in order to illuminate aspects of style in the MORN recension.

---

41. Perry 1936, 11–12, 25–26; 1952, 1–3.

42. Luzzatto 1996, 359. She produces two main arguments. The first is that there are no references to the relationship between Aesop and the Muses in the Westermanniana and in the oldest papyrus fragments, as is the case in the G version and in the Golenischeff Papyrus of the seventh century (P.Ross.Georg. I 18). The second is that in authors of the fourth century such as Himerius and Libanius, there are no references to the hostility between Aesop and Apollo.

Language and Style

The language of both versions is the koine, and the style is of "an intermediate layer."[43] Even so, to the trained reader the language of version G seems more colloquial, since it contains several words of Latin origin (λακινάριον, 21; πριμιπιλάριος, 87),[44] diminutive forms (σκευάριον, 17; ἀνδραπόδιον, 27; πατερίων, 60),[45] words known from earlier usage in the texts of Old or New Comedy (βούπαις, 20; ἐνεδρεία, 55),[46] words with postclassical usage and meaning (γενέσια, 42; λόγιος, 33),[47] and vulgarisms (ἀπόμαγμα, 14; πρασόκουρον, 35).[48] Sentences set in direct speech in G are often found in indirect speech in MORN (e.g., in chs. 61, 72, 77, 90, 106, 107), while the verb of some clauses in the G text has been replaced by a participial construction in the corresponding passage in the MORN version (e.g., in ch. 50 the G text has Αἴσωπος εἰσῆλθεν. ὁ Ξάνθος λέγει; the MORN, ἐλθόντος δὲ αὐτοῦ λέγει).[49] The overall style of the G text is more vivid, with questions in direct speech (ch. 66), rhetorical figures (ch. 71), and rhetorical questions (ch. 130).

Moreover, some obscenities in the G text are omitted in the MORN recension. For example in chapter 30 both the G and the MORN texts record an episode where a slave girl sees the ugly Aesop and insults him with the words ποῦ σου ἡ κέρκος; ("Where is your tail?"). The MORN recension, however, omits both the comment of the narrator and Aesop's reply recorded in the G text ("replying to her joke about his dog's head,

---

43. The term *Zwischenschicht* in Rydbeck 1967, 177.
44. See more examples in Stamoulakis 2016, 460–62.
45. More examples in Stamoulakis 2016, 463–66.
46. Stamoulakis 2016, 449–53.
47. Stamoulakis 2016, 416–33.
48. According to Adrados (1999, 674), "The vulgarism of the *Life* is expressly sought, on one hand, as a resource for its diffusion, on the other, as a further element of the derision of the learned society, as was customary."
49. See also ch. 54 (G: τῇ ἐπαύριον οἱ σχολαστικοὶ ἐμέμψαντο τὸν Ξάνθον. ὁ Ξάνθος λέγει…; MORN: Τῇ δὲ ἑξῆς ἡμέρᾳ μεμφθεὶς ὑπὸ τῶν φίλων ὁ Ξάνθος ἔφη) and in ch. 123 (G: ὁ δὲ Αἴσωπος παραγενάμενος εἰς Βαβυλῶνα διηγήσατο τῷ Λυκούργῳ πάντα τὰ πραχθέντα ἐν Αἰγύπτῳ, καὶ ἀποδέδωκεν αὐτῷ τὰ χρήματα; MORN: Ὁ δὲ Αἴσωπος παραγενόμενος εἰς Βαβυλῶνα διηγήσατο … ἀποδοὺς καὶ τὰ χρήματα). The style of the text in the G version, the frequent usage of the conjunction καί, and the direct speeches are common features of orality.

Aesop replied, 'My tail does not grow behind, as you would expect, but here in front'").

The author/redactor of the G version seems to have been better educated than the redactor of the MORN text, since the Homeric passages (ch. 124) and other intertextual references (ch. 28)[50] recorded in full in G are not extant in the corresponding sections in the MORN text.[51]

The changes in geographical names are also remarkable. For example, in chapter 20, in reference to the origin of the students of Xanthus, G mentions that πολλοὶ τῶν ἀπὸ τῆς Ἀσίας καὶ τῆς Ἑλλάδος παρ' αὐτῷ σχολάζουσιν ("many people come from Asia Minor and Greece to study with him"), whereas MORN has instead καὶ πολλοὶ τῆς Ἑλλάδος καὶ τῶν νήσων πρὸς αὐτὸν φοιτῶσι ("and many people from Greece and the islands..."). Sometimes names of cities or countries are omitted in MORN, such as the name of Memphis in chapter 112 or that of the Lydians in chapter 133. In the final scene of the killing of Aesop in G, Aesop tells the Delphians that ἠβουλόμην Συρίαν, Φοινίκην, Ἰουδαίαν μᾶλλον κυκλεῦσαι ἢ ἐνθάδε παρ' ὑμῶν ἀναγκασθῆναι ἀποθανεῖν ("I would rather wander through Syria, Phoenicia, and Judea than be killed by you here," ch. 141). In the corresponding passage in MORN "Sicily" has replaced all these countries (προηρούμην Σικελίαν ὅλην κακοπαθῶν κυκλεῦσαι ἢ ἐνθάδε παραλόγως ὑφ' ὑμῶν ἀποθανεῖν).[52]

In chapter 142 the people who avenge Aesop's death in G are οἱ ἀπὸ τῆς Ἑλλάδος καὶ οἱ ἀπὸ Βαβυλῶνος καὶ οἱ Σάμιοι ("from Greece, Babylon, and Samos"), whereas in MORN they are οἱ τῆς Ἑλλάδος ἔξαρχοι καὶ οἱ λοιποὶ διδάσκαλοι ("the leaders of Greece and the other teachers"). In short, from the dissonance of the two versions in topographical information it may be possible to locate with some precision the geographical region of origin for the author of the MORN text, in Greece or in the western Mediterranean (Sicily). If this is so, then it is hardly by coincidence that the last sentence of chapter 102 in G, ὥστε οὐ μόνον τὰ βάρβαρα τῶν ἐθνῶν κατειληφέναι, ἀλλὰ καὶ τὰ πλείονα μέρη ἕως Ἑλλάδος ὑποτέτακται ("so that it included not only

---

50. Papademetriou 1989, 53–57. See also Karla 2011 on the interpretation of a scene (the meeting between Aesop and his mistress, chs. 29–33) of the Life as a Homeric parody.

51. See also the omission of the phrase ἐπεὶ ὄψει Αἴσωπον Δημοσθένην καθαρόν (ch. 32).

52. "I would prefer to suffer circling all of Sicily than to die here unreasonably at your hands." See the remarks on the audience in La Penna 1962, 272–73.

the barbarian peoples but most of the lands up to Greece"), is altogether omitted in the MORN text.

Religion: Gods

Another distinctive feature of the MORN that is linked to the identity of the redactor of the text is the omission of Isis, the rare references to gods by their names, and the absence of any reference to the hostility between Aesop and Apollo.

Isis is present in G as the healer goddess who "removed from Aesop's tongue the impediment that had prevented him from speaking and gave him back his voice." She is the agent who "also persuaded each of the Muses in turn to grant Aesop something of her own gifts. They bestowed upon him the power to compose elaborate Greek tales. The goddess prayed further that Aesop might achieve fame, and then she withdrew" (ch. 7). As I have argued elsewhere,[53] the epiphany of Isis and the miracle of the restitution of Aesop's voice have a pivotal role in the introductory chapters of the Life in the G version, from a narratological point of view. The author skillfully introduces references to the worship of Isis to stress the bond between Aesop and the goddess and to enhance the narrative texture of the introduction. Most references to Isis have disappeared in MORN, which has retained the core of the narration as recorded in G, but the plot has undergone drastic change: Aesop helps the priests of Isis who have wandered off the highway (ch. 4); in turn, they pray to Isis to help him for his kindness (ch. 5); Aesop falls asleep (ch. 6). Suddenly, Tyche "stood over his slumbers and granted him the finest language and quickness of speech and the invention of ready arguments with colorful fables, since he was kind to gods and kind to guests" (ch. 7). In G there is only one priestess of Isis who, after receiving help from Aesop, prays to Isis. A full chapter (ch. 5) in G (instead of just the one sentence in MORN)[54] is dedicated to the prayer to Isis mentioning the goddess's cult titles and elements of her worship (Karla 2014, 86–87). Also, in chapter 6 of the MORN recension only one sentence

---

53. See Karla 2014 and the essays by Mignogna 1992, Dillery 1999, and Robertson 2003.

54. Οἱ δὲ ἐπάραντες τὰς χεῖρας εἰς τὸν οὐρανὸν καὶ εὐξάμενοι αὐτῷ ὡς ὑπ' αὐτοῦ εὐεργετηθέντες ὑπεχώρησαν ("They raised both their hands to heaven, and, praying for him on account of his kindness toward them, they went on their way").

is devoted to the physical aspect of the spot where Aesop and Isis meet.[55] By contrast, a detailed ekphrasis (a *locus amoenus*) is to be found in G.[56] In what follows, Isis is not mentioned again either in version G (except in the address μὰ τὴν Ἶσιν in ch. 15) or in MORN.

However, the Muses continue to have a significant, perhaps key, role in the narration of G. In chapter 100, when Aesop returns to Samos and announces the decision of Croesus to offer the Samians peace for the sake of Aesop, the Samians name after him the spot "where he was turned over to King Croesus" (the Aesopeum), and Aesop "erected a shrine for sacrifices to the Muses and set up in the middle a statue of himself as a memorial, but not one of Apollo, the head of the Muses. As a result, Apollo was angered, just as he had once been with Marsyas." This hostility of Apollo will bring about the death of Aesop,[57] as will become clear at the end of the story.[58] In MORN, there is no mention of the shrine of the Muses in Aesop's speech and consequently no reference to the anger of Apollo.

The Muses are mentioned also in chapter 123 in the G text, where the king Lycurus (or "Lycurgos" in G) orders a golden statue of Aesop together with the Muses to be erected "and held a great festival in honor of Aesop's wisdom." The MORN text instead simply states that "Lycurus ordered a gold statue to be dedicated to Aesop." In chapter 134 of G, when the Delphians "were leading him away to the cliff, he took refuge in the temple of the Muses," whereas in MORN, Aesop "took refuge in the temple of Apollo."[59] The pivotal role of the anger of Apollo in G has disappeared in the MORN, and this disappearance is perhaps due to the religious beliefs of the redactor of the MORN recension. It is not a coincidence that in MORN reference both to Apollo and to almost all the other gods is missing. These omissions include short references and address forms, such as μὰ τὴν Ἶσιν

---

55. Αἴσωπος δὲ στραφεὶς καὶ ὑπὸ τοῦ καύματος χαυνωθεὶς εἰς ὕπνον ἐτράπη ("Aesop turned back, and, enervated by the heat, he betook himself to sleep").

56. Karla 2014, 87–90; 2019a, with relevant bibliography.

57. On this issue, see La Penna 1962, 268–73; Nagy 1979, 289–308; Papademetriou 1989, 28; Jedrkiewicz 1989, 83–107; Dillery 1999, 268–80; Robertson 2003, 247–66.

58. See ch. 127, where the narrator claims that "Apollo was also angry, because Aesop had slighted him in Samos by not including him with the statues of the nine Muses."

59. See also ch. 139, where Aesop begs the Delphians to respect Apollo, since he has taken refuge with the god (MORN). In version G, he invokes Zeus, god of hospitality to strangers and of Olympus, who is more appropriate to the fable of the beetle and the eagle mentioned before.

(ch. 15), νὴ τὴν Νέμεσιν (ch. 16), and μὰ τὴν Ἥραν (ch. 26; only νὴ τοὺς θεούς is found in MORN), as well as entire incidents, such as the mention of the dream sent by Aphrodite to the wife of Xanthus (ch. 29) and the fable of the true and false dreams narrated by Aesop (ch. 33). In chapter 94, Aesop narrates to the Samians the fable of the two different paths, the way of freedom and the way of slavery, one of which they are to follow. In G, Zeus orders Prometheus[60] to show people the two paths; in MORN, by contrast, it is Tyche who "has revealed the two paths for our lives."

Narratological Changes

G has more descriptions of scenery that enrich the story with vividness and theatricality. For example, in chapter 6 the detailed description of the *locus amoenus*,[61] wherein Aesop falls asleep in G, is omitted in MORN, and so is the foreshadowing (prolepsis) of the miracle that occurs in the next chapter.[62] In chapters 81 and 82, G refers in detail to the gathering of the Samians in the theater to hold elections (ch. 81),[63] and similarly detailed are the descriptions of the two appearances of the eagle, in the first of which the eagle seizes the official ring and in the second of which it gives it back (ch. 82). None of these details is found in MORN, and their absence brings about major changes in the plot: the Samians in MORN simply "gathered and a show was going on," while the eagle appears only once.[64]

---

60. The G text has αὐτοῖς εὐθέως instead of Prometheus, and the reading Προμηθεύς is proposed by Perry.

61. On the style of this *locus amoenus* and its dialogue with other texts, see Mignogna 1992; Perry 1936, 13–14.

62. The detailed, step-by-step narrative in ch. 70, when Xanthus is about to realize his fault and the terrible damage that the bet has caused his property, is summarized in a short reference in MORN. Similarly abbreviated is the dialogue between the captain of the king's guard and the king Lycurus in ch. 107.

63. "At about that time there was an election in the city, and the populace gathered into the theater. The keeper of the laws brought in the city constitution and the official ring of the city and placed them in the middle, saying, 'Fellow citizens, now you must elect a new keeper of the laws who will uphold the constitution and use the official ring to transact all the business of the city'" (G, ch. 81).

64. "While they were deliberating over whom they would entrust with this position, an eagle swooped down, took the ring in its talons, and flew away…" (G, ch. 81), "But as the crowd was about to disperse, the eagle swooped down again and dropped the ring into the lap of a slave who belonged to the city…" (G, ch. 82).

Narrative details of minor importance, such as μετὰ δὲ τὸ πιεῖν αὐτοὺς δύο ἢ τρία ποτήρια ("And after two or three drinks," ch. 52), ὁ ἄγροικος τῷ ὀναρίῳ ἐπικαθήμενος ("the crude man was riding the donkey," ch. 59), and μέλλων δὲ προστιθέναι ὁ Ξάνθος τὸ πόμα πρὸς τὸ στόμα ("But when Xanthos was about to put the cup to his lips," ch. 73), also are absent from the MORN text, and so are various comments of the narrator, such as δέρεται ὁ ταλαίπωρος μάγειρος ("the unfortunate cook was whipped," ch. 62).

The redactor of the MORN text avoids in-depth depiction of the psychology of the characters. Detailed points of human psychology, such as that included in chapter 78, τοῦ δὲ Ξάνθου ζητοῦντος τίς ἡ ὑπογραφὴ καὶ τί δηλοῖ, μὴ εὑρίσκων δεινῶς ἔπασχεν, ἠθύμει, ἐν ἀπορίᾳ καθιστήκει ὅτι φιλόσοφος ὢν τὴν τῶν στοιχείων οὐχ εὕρισκεν λύσιν ("Xanthus tried to discern the meaning of the letters but could not. He was quite perplexed and troubled, because although he was a philosopher, he could not decipher their meaning," ch. 78), are not part of the MORN narrative, which in turn reads: Ὁ δὲ ἐπιμελῶς καταμαθὼν καὶ πολλὰ στρεβλωθεὶς ("Although Xanthus studied them carefully and strained much"). Similarly omitted are phrases such as (ὁ Ξάνθος) στυγνὸς γενόμενος ("Xanthus's countenance fell," ch. 40), ἀποχλωριαίνει ("Xanthus's face went white," ch. 43),[65] μένει περίλυπος ("she was sad," ch. 46),[66] πολὺς οὖν ἐγένετο γέλως καὶ πλεῖστος γογγυσμὸς εἰς τοὺς σχολαστικούς ("There was much laughter and not a little whispering among the students," ch. 47), ὑποσχόμενος δὲ ἐξῆλθεν σκυθρωπός ("he agreed, but left with a troubled look on his face," ch. 82), and (ὁ δὲ νεανίσκος) ... ἐπιχαρὴς ἐγένετο ... ὁ δὲ Αἴσωπος ἰδὼν καὶ ἀγανακτήσας... ("the young man ... was reveling in the affair. When Aesop learned what was going on, he became angry...," ch. 103).

Moreover, in the MORN recension details of characterization, mainly regarding Aesop, are omitted, whereas they are found in G. In the latter text, Aesop is bold toward his master Xanthus, toward the latter's wife, and toward Xanthus's students. For example, Aesop torments his master before helping him solve the omen of the eagle and ring (chs. 83–86). Even though in chapter 83 Aesop promises to solve the omen, in chapter 84 it is mentioned explicitly that "Aesop decided to turn the screws on him [Xanthus]" (ὁ Αἴσωπος θέλων αὐτὸν λυπῆσαι) and announces that he cannot help his master, because he is not a seer. Only when he sees that Xanthus is

---

65. See also in G, ὁ Ξάνθος ἀποχλωριᾷ (ch. 54).
66. Αἴσωπος λυπηθείς (G, ch. 74).

ready to commit suicide does he decide to help him. In the MORN text, on the other hand, Aesop is described from the beginning of the story as wise and fond of his master (ἤδη σοφὸς καὶ φιλοδέσποτος ὤν) and offers to assist him (chs. 83–85). In chapter 32 of G, he boldly expresses his indignation by warning his mistress: μή σοι δείξω ἀνδρὸς νεωνήτου θυμόν, ἱπποπόρνη ("Be careful, or I'll show you the righteous indignation of a new slave, you whore!"). This warning is not found in MORN. Finally, in chapter 42 Aesop "cut the foot off a pig that was being fattened" (MORN), whereas in G the pig "was being kept for the birthday of Xanthus's wife."

Furthermore, the detailed characterization in version G and missing from the MORN text is not restricted to the protagonist alone. Actorial motivation on the part of secondary characters in G is not to be found in MORN.[67] For example, the details in chapters 81–86, which refer to Xanthus's reaction upon realizing that he cannot interpret the omen involving the official ring, gradually reveal his embarrassment, his self-consciousness, his cowardice, and his inability to respond efficiently in difficult circumstances. The drastic abbreviation of these chapters in the MORN versions does not allow his character to emerge.[68]

The motif of the ugliness of Aesop has a key function throughout the entire Life.[69] In G, this motif receives special emphasis, in contrast to MORN. In chapters 87–88, for example, the reaction of the Samians upon seeing Aesop is described in MORN relatively briefly, as follows: κατανοήσαντες οἱ Σάμιοι τὴν τούτου μορφὴν ἐμπαίζοντες αὐτῷ ("the Samians seeing his ugly form made fun of him," ch. 87). In G, their insulting words are reported in detail: Οἱ δὲ Σάμιοι εἶπον· "οὗτος τοῦτο τὸ σημεῖον δύναται διαλύσασθαι; τὸ τέρας τῆς ὄψεως αὐτοῦ· βάτραχός ἐστιν, ὗς τροχάζων, ἢ στάμνος κήλην ἔχων, ἢ πιθήκων πριμιπιλάριος, ἢ λαγυνίσκος εἰκαζόμενος, ἢ μαγείρου σκευοθήκη, ἢ κύων ἐν γυργάθῳ;" (ch. 88).[70]

---

67. According to Irene de Jong's glossary (2001, xi), "actorial motivation" is "the analysis of the 'why' in the story in terms of the aims and intentions of a character. An actorial motivation is usually explicit." Such actorial motivations are missing in MORN in chs. 9, 62, 86, 88, 93, 99.

68. See, for example, also the gutlessness of King Croesus's councilors in ch. 95 or the detailed portrait of King Lycurus in ch. 106 of G that are absent in MORN.

69. See Papademetriou 1997, 13–42; Jouanno 2005, 399–400; Karla 2016b, 328.

70. "But the Samians said, 'Look how ugly he is! He must be a frog, or a hedgehog, a misshapen jar, the captain of the monkeys, a flask, a cook's pot, or a dog in a wicker basket!'"

Another characteristic example involves Croesus's reaction to Aesop as he enters his palace; the episode is presented in detail in G: ὁ δὲ βασιλεὺς ἰδὼν τὸν Αἴσωπον ἠγανάκτησεν καὶ εἶπεν "ἴδε τίς ἐκώλυσέν με πόλιν ὑποτάξαι, καὶ τέλη λαμβάνειν οὐκ εἴασεν. καὶ εἰ μὲν ἄνθρωπος οὐ χαλεπόν, ἀλλ᾽ αἴνιγμα καὶ τέρας τῶν ἀνθρώπων" (ch. 98).[71] In MORN, the reference to Aesop's ugliness is absent.[72]

The narrative structure of the two texts displays some other differences besides those revealed in matters of character portrayal. In version G, the narration runs more smoothly than in the MORN recension. For example, in chapter 80 Xanthus puts Aesop in jail, "fearing Aesop's tongue."[73] In the chapters that follow (chs. 83–85), in MORN, Aesop immediately offers to help his master.[74] By contrast, in chapter 83 of the G text, Aesop refuses to help his master, even though Xanthus offers to free him in exchange for his services. The exchange between the two displays notable rhetorical vividness:

εἰσελθὼν οὖν φησίν "κάλει τὸν Αἴσωπον." καὶ εἰσῆλθεν δέσμιος. ὁ δὲ Ξάνθος λέγει "λύσατε αὐτόν." Αἴσωπος λέγει "οὐ βούλομαι λυθῆναι." Ξάνθος· "ἀλλὰ λύω σε ἵνα καὶ σύ τι λύσῃς. Αἴσωπος· "οὐκοῦν ἰδίας μου χρείας ἕνεκα λύεις με." Ξάνθος λέγει "παῦσαι, Αἴσωπε, τὸ λεγόμενον ἐπίλυσον, λῆξον τῆς ὀργῆς." Αἴσωπος λυθεὶς εἶπεν....[75]

---

71. "When the king saw Aesop, he was angry and said, 'Just look at the man who prevented me from subjugating the city and kept me from collecting my tribute! If he were a man, it would not be so bad, but he is an enigma, a monstrous portent among men!'"

72. "When the king saw Aesop, he was displeased and said, 'Look at who prevented me from subjugating so numerous a people.'" In ch. 121 the phase διὰ τὸν σαπρόμορφον καὶ κατάρατον τοῦτον ("on account of this unsightly and accursed fellow," G) is replaced by διὰ τὸν Αἴσωπον τοῦτον ("because of this Aesop," MORN).

73. Ἐλθόντων δὲ αὐτῶν, φοβούμενος ὁ Ξάνθος τὴν γλῶσσαν αὐτοῦ ἐκέλευσε αὐτὸν εἰς φυλακὴν βληθῆναι ("But when they arrived, Xanthus, fearing Aesop's tongue, ordered him to be thrown into prison," MORN); γενάμενος δὲ ἐν τῷ οἴκῳ, καὶ φοβούμενος μὴ ποθεν λαβὼν τῷ βασιλεῖ μηνύσῃ τὸν θησαυρόν, ἐκέλευσεν αὐτὸν δεθέντα συγκλεισθῆναι ("But when they reached home, Xanthos was afraid that Aesop would look for some opportunity to inform King Dionysius that they had the treasure and commanded that Aesop be bound and locked up," G).

74. For this incongruence, see Perry 1936, 19 n. 29; Karla 2009a, 445–46.

75. "He called for Aesop, who entered in chains, and said, 'Release him.' But Aesop said, 'I don't want to be released.' 'I am releasing you so that you may in turn release

In some episodes in G, an interlacing technique can be observed at work, providing a motivation, as it were, that connects the different stories. In the MORN recension, however, the episodes are only loosely connected to each other.[76] For example, Aesop and Xanthus receive vegetables as a gift from the gardener when Aesop solves the man's riddle (ch. 34–37). Still, as the next chapter shows, Xanthus's wife angrily tramples on the vegetables and ruins them, leaving Xanthus with nothing to serve the friends he has invited but humble lentils: καὶ ἐπειδὴ διὰ τὴν μανίαν τῆς γυναικός μου συνεπατήθη τὰ λάχανα, ἀπελθὼν φακὸν ἕψησον ἡμῖν ("since my wife trampled the vegetables in a fit of rage, cook lentil for us"). Then, when Xanthus orders Aesop to give the best portions to his "favorite one" (τῇ εὐνοούσῃ), implying his wife, Aesop acquires one more reason to take revenge on Xanthus's wife, as his monologue in the G text reveals:

νῦν καιρός ἐστιν τοῦ μετελθεῖν με τὴν μῆνιν τὴν πρὸς τὴν κυράν, ἀνθ' ὧν με ἀγορασθέντα ἔσκωψεν καὶ ἐκακολόγει, καὶ ὅτι τὰ δωρηθέντα μοι ὑπὸ τοῦ κηπουροῦ λάχανα σκορπίσασα συνεπάτησεν, καὶ οὐκ ἀφῆκέν μου τὴν δωρεὰν εὐχαρῆ τῷ δεσπότῃ μου γενέσθαι. ἐγὼ αὐτῇ δείξω ὅτι πρὸς εὔνουν οἰκέτην οὐδὲν ἰσχύει γυνή· ἐπὰν γὰρ ὁ δεσπότης εἶπέν μοι ὅτι 'δὸς τὰ μέρη τῇ εὐνοούσῃ', νῦν ὄψεται τίς αὐτῷ εὐνοεῖ.[77]

In the MORN recension, there is no mention of the episode of the trampled vegetables, thus robbing the stories concerned of any interconnection.[78]

In general, the jokes and humorous incidents present in many episodes in version G are missing in the MORN recension.[79] For example, in chapter 30, much of the dialogue between the slave girls who are competing among themselves to marry the new slave (that is, Aesop), even though

---

me from a problem.' 'Then it is for your own interest that you are releasing me.' 'Stop, Aesop. Get over your anger and solve this problem.' And Aesop, now released...."

76. Perry 1936, 21: "Incidents which are abrupt or poorly motivated in W take on a new meaning when read in the older context preserved in G."

77. "Now is my chance to exact my revenge on my mistress. I'll pay her back for the way she mocked me and made fun of me when I had just been purchased. She also tore up and trampled the vegetables the gardener gave me and would not allow my gift a chance to please my master. I'll show her that a woman cannot compete with a household slave for the affections of his master. My master said, 'Give the portions to the one who adores me'; well, now he is going to find out who really adores him."

78. On this example, see Perry 1936, 6–7; Karla 2009a, 446; more examples in Perry 1936, 21–24.

79. See Jouanno 2005.

they have not seen him, is not found in the MORN text. Equally missing from MORN is the episode involving the surprise of Xanthus upon being informed by Aesop that his "favorite" (εὐνοοῦσα) has eaten all the portions of food. Xanthus's surprise is justified, because for him "favorite" means his wife, but for Aesop it means Xanthus's dog. The comic scene of the diarrhea in chapter 53 is also omitted in the MORN recension, and so is Aesop's kick to the ankle of his master (ch. 69).[80]

Only rarely do we encounter in the MORN recension additional material not found in the G version. Chapters 50a, 77a, 77b, which are preserved only in Codex M, must have been inserted at some later phase of the textual tradition of the Life, for they were not in the original text.[81] The *gnomae* that Aesop recites to his son (chs. 109–110) take up more space in the MORN recension, but this could be due to the material having been drawn from a different source with a didactic content, such as a florilegium of sentences. Moreover, fewer of the fables narrated by Aesop in the Life are missing in the MORN recension, perhaps because of the shortness of the fables themselves.

The Relationship of the MORN Text to the BPThSA Recension

The most important differences between the two recensions (MORN and BPThSA) are the omission of several episodes (chapters), the transposition of chapter 131, and the insertion of additional episodes.

Omission of Episodes/Chapters

When Aesop describes one of Xanthus's friends as a "meddler" (περίεργος) in chapter 55, Xanthus, in an attempt to find a reason to punish his slave, asks him to find a person who is a nonmeddler (ἀπερίεργος). The MO(RN) recension describes two attempts by Aesop to find such a person. The first attempt, involving a man who is reading in the marketplace, is unsuccessful (chs. 57–58), but the second, involving an uncultivated, uneducated man who is talking to his ass, is successful. In the BPThSA recension, there is only one attempt, involving a person who is sitting somewhere, who reminds us of the figure in the first attempt in the MORN recension.[82]

---

80. See Karla 2009a, 446.
81. See bibliography below in note 86.
82. See Perry 1933, 208: "The words ἐν ἑνὶ τόπῳ and καθεζόμενον seem to be taken

The episode involving the man talking to the ass is present also in G[83] and in P.Oxy. 2083 (as well as in Wλ), which means that "in this instance the redactor of the SBP archetype has intentionally, and I may add characteristically, abridged the text found in MO" (Perry 1933, 208). To the arguments offered by Perry, I would add that, from a narrative perspective, the two unsuccessful attempts in MSS MO reflect the central structural core of this unit, namely, the antithesis between the learned and the uncultivated man, which proves their authentic character.

Moreover, chapters 75 and 76, which refer to the affair between Aesop and his mistress, are omitted in BPThSA. The episode is transmitted in MS O and in the Latin translation Lo but not in MS M. In MS G there is some textual evidence (from the last part of chapter 76); likewise, only part of the text from chapter 76 is preserved in a papyrus fragment (P.Oxy. 3331). It has consequently been argued that this episode was part of the archetype text of the Life.[84]

When Aesop appears in front of the Samians to explain the omen of the ring and the eagle, he begins his performance with a long speech on how deceitful external appearance can be when judging a person's character. In G and MORN, there are two such rhetorical prologues (chs. 88 and 88a). In G, these prologues are more detailed (Perry 1952, 18); in MORN, the main difference between the two chapters is the simile, in the first (ch. 88), of the quality of the ceramic pots and the taste of the wine inside, and in the second (ch. 88a), of the beautiful roses and their thorns. In the BPThSA recension, the second prologue (ch. 88a) is missing: either the redactor of BPThSA omitted it intentionally, or the prologue was not in his copy (Karla 2001, 42).

In chapters 112–115, Aesop finds himself in the court of Nectenabo as special emissary of King Lycurus, sent there to solve certain riddles. These involve Nectenabo and his friends putting on various costumes and Aesop guessing what they enact or whom they represent. In BPThSA, chapter 113

---

from the description of the man in the first episode who was sitting παρ' ἑνὸς μέρους of the crowd in the market place and reading."

83. In G there are only some traces from the first episode (ἀπελθὼν εἰς τὴν ἀγορὰν ἐζήτει ἄνθρωπον ἀπερίεργον), and according to the *apparatus criticus* by Perry (1952, 54) "post ἄν. ἀπερ. quae sequebantur usque ad initium cap. 59 (ἄνθρωπον ἀπερίεργον W) e cod. exciderunt."

84. Perry 1933, 209; 1936, 7–11; Karla 2001, 41. On the connection of this story with similar ribald tales of antiquity, see Konstantakos 2006, 565–80.

and the beginning of chapter 114 are missing. As a result, the leading men, who are wearing white robes, and the king, who has "donned a priestly robe and on his head a tiara and diadem that had horns set with gems, sitting in state on a high throne," are erroneously likened to the sun in spring, while those around the king are likened to the fruits of the earth. "Here again the original text, preserved in MR, has been abbreviated and corrupted by SBP" (Perry 1933, 210).

Chapter 126, in which Aesop reports in detail the bad reputation of the Delphians, in that they are descended from slaves, is omitted in the BPThSA recension. Its existence in MS S is perhaps due to contamination from the MORN recension (Karla 2001, 42).

The Transposition of Chapter 131

Chapter 131, which deals with a foolish girl, is misplaced in the BPThSA recension. In the MORN recension, this story follows the question asked by Aesop's friend, who has visited Aesop in prison: "But why did you get it into your head to insult the people of Delphi, and above all in their own country?" In the BPThSA recension, this question seems to be merely rhetorical, but the transposition of the story after chapter 140, when the Delphians have led Aesop forcibly to the edge of the cliff, is obviously wrong for two reasons. First, the story is not related to the context, and, second, Aesop has told the Delphians two fables, one after the other, a narrative technique not used anywhere else in the Life. The inclusion of this story in G, in the Golenischeff Papyrus, and also in MORN, in the same place in all three sources, proves that this was the story's original position.[85]

Additional Episodes

As mentioned above, chapters 50a, 77a and 77b are transmitted only in the manuscript M (as well as in the MSS W, LFV) and in the BPThSA recension; they are not part of the text in manuscripts G, Lo and O. As Perry (1933, 226) observes "someone at a later date, very probably the author of the SBP archetype, interpolated them from an earlier source." Their presence in MS M could be interpreted as result of contamination with the BPThSA recension (Karla 2001, 40–41). Moreover, in regard to

---

85. Perry 1933, 210; Van Dijk 1995, 143–44; Karla 2001, 40.

narrative structure, these three episodes seem to be superfluous and out of context.[86]

Finally, there are some differences between the MORN and BPThSA recensions on the level of content and language.

Content

In comparison to the MORN recension, the BPThSA recension omits details that have no impact on the main plot.[87] For example, regarding the episode of the merchant's preparations for the sale of the three slaves (ch. 21), the MORN recension gives a detailed description of how the lyre player and the teacher are dressed. The redactor of the BPThSA recension simply reports that both are dressed in new costumes. In chapter 22, in the MORN recension, Xanthus is reported to have gone first to work, then to the marketplace ("Xanthus first went to his school and made his lecture stronger and then came with his friends to the marketplace to look around"), whereas the BPThSA recension simply states that "Xanthus went out and came to the marketplace." In chapter 23, Xanthus explains why he was impressed by the intelligence of the merchant: "The merchant did not set the two handsome slaves on the outside and the misshapen one in the middle for the sake of a sale; it was rather so that, by placing the ugly alongside the beautiful, he might show off their excellence more conspicuously" (MORN). In the BPThSA recension Xanthus does not provide any explanation but simply exclaims "what knavery!" (βαβαὶ τῆς πανουργίας!).[88]

Sometimes personal names or titles are missing in the BPThSA recension, as in chapter 79, where the name of the king of the Byzantians, Dionysius, the name of Xanthus's father, Dexicrates (ch. 90), or Lycurgus's title, "king of the Babylonians" (ch. 121) have been omitted. In some cases, certain personal comments by the narrator that are present in the MORN recension are missing in the BPThSA recension, such as the phrase "but

---

86. Perry 1936, 35–37; Holzberg 1992a, 59–61. However, Merkle (1996, 222) believes that chapters 77a and 77b were present in the archetype of the Life.

87. On the omissions in BPThSA, see Karla 2001, 49–52.

88. See also in chs. 47, 48, 51, 55, 72, 79, 81, 88, 90, 103, 108. In ch. 90, for example, Xanthus's friends advise him as follows in the MORN recension: "Free him yourself, for if he becomes a freedman of Hera, he will have all the rights of a free man." In the BPThSA recension, however, it is merely noted that "the friends counseled Xanthus to do it."

none of them realized what had happened" at the end of chapter 42.[89] In other cases, psychological details that are included in the MORN recension are omitted in the BPThSA recension, as, for example, in chapter 43 the phrase "Aesop grew pale." More widespread is the omission from the BPThSA recension of minor information, such as topographical details or personal attributes; for example, the text in chapter 92 does not mention the place where the Samians were gathered ("in the theater") or the beauty of the costume of the letter-carrier ("a bright white mantle").[90]

Additionally, some general theoretical observations are not found in the BPThSA recension, such as the *epimythium* (the moral of certain fables),[91] similes or exempla,[92] and pieces of advice by Aesop to his stepson Aenus (chs. 109, 110; see Karla 2001, 50–51). In a few cases statements of warning are omitted in the BPThSA recension, such as the warning of Aesop to Xanthus in chapter 74: Αἴσωπος δὲ ἀχαριστηθεὶς ἐλυπήθη καί φησι "μεῖνον με. Ἐγώ σε ἀνταμυνοῦμαι" ("Aesop was hurt by this ingratitude and said, 'You wait; I will get back at you'").[93] Some phrases in the MORN recension that give emphasis or add a humorous touch are not found in the BPThSA recension, such as the phrase ὁλονυκτὶ δυσφορήσαντες ("and were indisposed the entire night") in chapter 53 or the phrase Μετὰ δὲ τὸ δειπνῆσαι τῆς γαστρὸς νυξάσης ("After dining, at the urging of his belly") in chapter 67. It might not be coincidental that certain passages in the MORN recension that display textual problems are omitted in the BPThSA

---

89. See also in ch. 107 the omission of the phrase "he [Hermippus] desired to prove to him [King Lycurus] that his error was a fortunate one."

90. Likewise in ch. 81 the phrase καὶ τῶν θυμελικῶν παιζομένων ("and a show was going on"), in ch. 128 περιβομβίζοντες αὐτόν ("buzzing around him"), in ch. 137 Καὶ ἔθηκεν αὐτὰ ἐπὶ τοῖς τοῦ Διὸς γόνασιν ("and he placed them upon the knees of Zeus"), and in ch. 140 καὶ ἔστησαν αὐτὸν ἐπὶ τοῦ ἄκρου ("and placed him at the edge") are omitted in the BPThSA recension.

91. In ch. 67, Ἀπ' ἐκείνου οὖν οἱ ἄνθρωποι φοβούμενοι, διαβλέπουσι τὰ ἴδια ἀφοδεύματα μὴ καὶ αὐτοὶ τὰς ἰδίας χέσωσι φρένας ("From then on, in fact, people have been afraid and look at their own excrement so that they, too, don't shit out their brains"); in ch. 97, Ὁ μῦθος οὖν ἔδειξε μὴ εἰκῇ τοὺς εὐχρήστους προδιδόναι ("So, what the fable shows is not to betray casually those who are useful to you").

92. In ch. 98, a significant part of Aesop's reply to Croesus is missing in the BPThSA recension: Ὅμοια δὲ πάσχετε οἱ ἐξ ἀκοῆς ὀργιζόμενοι … ὥσπερ τὰ κενὰ τῶν ἀγγείων τοῖς ὠταρίοις εὐβάστακτοι εὑρίσκονται.

93. See also in ch. 100. The foundation of Aesopeum (Αἰσώπειον) by the Samians is not mentioned in the BPThSA recension.

recension. For example, in chapter 68, instead of the corrupt text δέσποτα, Διόνυσος <εὑρὼν> τὸ οἰνικὸν πόμα †τρεῖς κράσεις τῷ ἀνθρώπῳ διὰ πόματος χρήσασθαι εἶπεν†· (MORN); the BPThSA recension has simply: δέσποτα, ὁ Διόνυσος, τὸ οἰνικὸν πόμα, τρεῖς κράσεις ἔχει ("Master, Dionysus, the drink of wine, has three mixings").[94]

In many cases several words attested in the BPThSA recension have been replaced in the MORN recension by synonyms, such as κύριε instead of δέσποτα (ch. 50a and elsewhere),[95] τύψον instead of δεῖρον (ch. 50), κενόδοξον instead of καθαρόν (ch. 24), εὔσωμον, εὔκοσμον instead of εὐόμματον, οὐλόκομον (ch. 32), and (ἐκκλησίαν) ποιήσας instead of (ἐκκλ.) συναγαγών (ch. 96).[96]

Sometimes the two recensions present a markedly different narrative content. For example, in chapter 11 the MORN recension records Xanthus's announcement to Aesop, Συνεῖδον οὖν πιπράσαι σε ("I have resolved, then, to sell you"), while in the BPThSA recension Aesop's reply is recorded instead: ὁ δέ (sc. Αἴσωπος) φησι· ὃ βούλει πρᾶξον ("Aesop said, 'do what you want'"). In chapter 15 of the MORN recension, the merchant said to Aesop: Ἄφες με! Μηδέν σοι τῶν ἀγαθῶν γένοιτο. Ὅ,τι προσεκαλέσω με, παρατήρημα; ("Let go of me! May nothing good happen to you. Why have you called out to me, you piece of rubbish?"). In the BPThSA recension, the merchant's words are: ἔξελθε ἀπ' ἐμοῦ, ῥερυπωμένε κύον ("Go far away from me, filthy dog!"). In chapter 47 the MORN recension transmits the following riddle: πῶς ἔσται μεγάλη ταραχὴ ἐν ἀνθρώποις; ("How will the greatest disturbance among human beings occur?"), whereas the BPThSA recension gives ἀνάγκη (necessity) instead of ταραχή.[97] In chapters 121–122 the two recensions transmit two different deadlines for Aesop's reply: in the MORN recension, Aesop asks for an additional three days in which to respond; in the BPThSA recension, he promises to give a response the next day.

In some cases, the setting is different in the MORN recension from the one presented in the BPThSA recension. For example, in chapter 77, Aesop sees the crows in front of the gate (πρὸ τοῦ πυλῶνος) in the MORN

---

94. See also chs. 10, 26, 52.
95. See also κυρία (in BPThSA) and δέσποινα (in MORN) in ch. 45 and elsewhere.
96. See also chs. 34, 48, 62, 72, 77a, 77β, 78, 79, 80, 81, 83–85, 86, 90, 91, 93, 94, 100.
97. See also chs. 16, 20, 44, 54, 77, 80, 106–107, 109, 111, 117, 128, 133.

recension, whereas he sees the crows sitting on a tree (ἐπί τινος δένδρου καθεζομένας) in the BPThSA recension.⁹⁸

Only rarely does the BPThSA recension offer more detail than the MORN recension.⁹⁹ One of those rare occasions occurs in chapter 45, when Aesop calls the dog to feed it. In the MORN recension, the dog's response is described: Ἡ δὲ ποππύσασα προσέδραμεν αὐτῷ ("The dog smacked its lips and ran to him"), whereas the BPThSA recension adds one more detail: τὴν κέρκον ὧδε κἀκεῖσε περιστρέφουσα ("wagging its tail here and there"). Chapter 73, in which Xanthus calls off the bet to drink the sea, closes in MORN with the student imploring Xanthus to recall the bet. The BPThSA recension prints a more explicit text: δυσωποῦντος δὲ τοῦ ὄχλου ἐπείσθη ὁ Ξάνθος ("the crowd put Xanthus out of countenance, and he was convinced"). In chapter 30 an extra phrase in the BPThSA recension adds a touch of obscenity to the scene. Both recensions tell of a slave girl who mocked the ugliness of Aesop and said to him: "Bless you! Where is your tail?" Yet only in BPThSA does the redactor have Aesop replying: ὁ δέ (Αἴσωπος)· εἰ κέρκον χρῄζεις, ἔχω ("and Aesop replied, 'If you have need of a tail, I have one'").¹⁰⁰

Style and Language

The MORN recension also presents some differences from the BPThSA recension in terms of style and language, although there seems to be no systematic effort to maintain a consistent style in one or the other. Each version may opt for a different word to express the same notion, choosing a synonym or some colloquial or more elevated expression to do so. For example, in chapter 65 (Aesop's meeting with the governor) the following differences between the two versions occur:

MORN γνωρίσας– BPThSA γνούς
MORN δόξας– BPThSA νομίσας
MORN παρῆκεν– BPThSA κατέλιπεν

---

98. See also the differences reported in the situation between Xanthus and his wife in ch. 61.
99. These details are not found in MS G.
100. See also in ch. 131 the more detailed description of the intercourse between the foolish girl and the man in the recension BPThSA.

In the first example the MORN recension adopts a more colloquial form, while the BPThSA recension employs a second aorist participle. In the other two examples, the MORN recension prints the more elevated form. There are many other examples of this type of stylistic discrepancy between the two recensions. Here I limit myself to noting only a few: in chapter 20 πιπράσας τὰ σωμάτια (MORN) – πωλήσας τὰ ἀνδράποδα (BPThSA); in chapter 36 διοικούμενα (MORN) – γινόμενα (BPThSA); in chapter 37 γεννηθέντα (MORN) – κυηθέντα (BPThSA); in chapter 40 ἠγόρασα (MORN) – ὠνησάμην (BPThSA); and in chapter 50 δεῖρον (MORN) – τύψον (BPThSA).[101]

Changes in morphology are also frequent. Sometimes the point of divergence between the two recensions is just one word. Such a word may be a conjunction, as in chapter 47: ἐὰν (οἱ νεκροὶ ἀνιστάμενοι τὰ ἴδια ἀπαιτήσωσι) (MORN) – ὅταν ... (BPThSA); it may also be a different form of the same word, as in chapter 110: εἰδὼς ὅτι καὶ τῷ κυνὶ ἡ κέρκος ἄρτον προσπορίζεται ("knowing that the dog's tail, too, provides it with bread," MORN) – εἰδὼς ὅτι καὶ τὸ κυνάριον ἄρτον ἡ οὐρὰ πορίζει (BPThSA). In the last example we encounter various types of divergence: first, the same word appears in different form in each recension: τῷ κυνὶ – τὸ κυνάριον;[102] then a word occurs in two different but synonymous forms: ἡ κέρκος – ἡ οὐρά; finally, the same verb is used in the middle voice as a compound in one recension and in the active voice without a preposition in the other recension: προσπορίζεται (compound in the middle voice), πορίζει (active voice without a preposition).[103] In chapter 105, the future tense is expressed differently in each recension: τοὺς οἰκοδομήσοντας (MORN) – τοὺς μέλλοντας οἰκοδομεῖν (BPThSA).

In some cases the prefix of a compound verb is either different or omitted: in chapters 104 παρέλαβεν (MORN) – ἀπέλαβεν (BPThSA), 106

---

101. See Karla 2001, 47.
102. See also in ch. 77a ἡ κύων (MORN) – ἡ κύνα (BPThSA).
103. See also in ch. 71 μὴ ἀρνοῦ (MORN) – μὴ ἄρνησαι (BPThSA); in ch. 77a ἄπελθε καὶ περὶ τούτου μηδὲν φρόντιζε (MORN) – ἄπελθε μηδὲν περὶ τούτων φροντίζων (BPThSA); in ch. 77b ἐγὼ δὲ ἱστάμενος ἔσωθεν, ἠρώτων (MORN) – ἐμοῦ ἔσωθεν ἑστῶτος (ἱσταμένου SA) ἠρώτων (BPThSA); in ch. 80 ἄκουε (MORN) – ἄκουσον (BPThSA); in ch. 87 ἐλθόντος (MORN) – ἐληλυθότος (BPThSA); in ch. 95 ἀπεπέμψαντο (MORN) – ἀπέπεμψαν (BPThSA); in ch. 110 (Αἰσχρὸν) ἀτυχοῦντα ἐπιγελᾶν (MORN) – ἀτυχοῦντι (BPThSA); in ch. 116 μύστρας (MORN) – μύστρα (BPThSA); in ch. 133 φιλιωθεὶς (MORN) – φιλιάσας (BPThSA); in ch. 134 δραμόντος (MORN) – δεδραμηκότος (BPThSA); and in ch. 137 τὴν κόπρον (MORN) – τὰ κόπρια (BPThSA).

συγκαλέσας (MORN) – προσκαλεσάμενος (BPThSA),[104] and 112 προκαθίσας (MORN) – καθεσθείς (BPThSA).[105] The recensions may also introduce the same prepositional construction with different prepositions: thus in chapter 123 εἰς Βαβυλῶνα (MORN) – ἐν Βαβυλῶνι (BPThSA) or in chapter 132 ἐπὶ τῷ κρημνίσαι αὐτόν (MORN) – εἰς τὸ κατακρημνίσαι (BPThSA).

In some cases, a main or a subordinate clause is found in the BPThSA recension in the place of a participle in the MORN recension. For example in chapter 32 the MORN recension prints the participial construction ἡ δὲ ἀκούσασα ταῦτα, whereas the BPThSA recension in the same place has the subordinate clause ὡς ταῦτα ἤκουσε.[106] In chapter 77 the phrase ἐγὼ ἰδὼν τὸ δικόρωνον is found in MORN, whereas in the corresponding passage BPThSA has εἶδον τὸ δικόρωνον. In the same chapter one reads εἰσῆλθε καὶ ἀνήγγειλε (two verbs) in M but εἰσελθὼν ἀνήγγειλεν (a participle before a verb) in BPThSA and MS O.[107] In chapter 86 MORN has πεισθεὶς οὖν ὁ Ξάνθος, whereas BPThSA has τότε ἐπείσθη ὁ Ξάνθος.[108] In chapter 104, instead of ὡς ἐκείνοις βοηθοῦντος (MORN), BPThSA has ὡς ὅτι αὐτοῖς βοηθεῖ.

On one occasion (ch. 107), there is a participle in the BPThSA recension (ῥερυπωμένου) but a prepositional construction (ἐν ῥύπῳ) in the MORN recension. A participle in the MORN recension (συνέδραμον ... ἀπαιτοῦντες τὸν αἴλουρον) corresponds to an infinitive (συνέδραμον τοῦ ἐξελέσθαι τὸν αἴλουρον) in the BPThSA recension (ch.117). In another passage (ch. 80), in the place of a genitive absolute in the MORN recension (ἐλθόντων δὲ αὐτῶν) stands a participle in the nominative in the BPThSA recension (ἐλθὼν οὖν).

In some passages the MORN recension has a bare infinitive, while the BPThSA recension gives an infinitive with article (μὴ εὑρὼν λῦσαι – μηδόλως εὑρηκὼς τοῦ λῦσαι, ch. 35),[109] a prepositional construction

---

104. Exactly the same example in ch. 111.

105. Even the prefix of a compound adjective may be different from one recension to the other, as in ch. 107 κατάλυπος (MORN) – περίλυπος (BPThSA).

106. A participle in MORN may be rendered with a conditional clause (δυνάμενος λέγειν – εἴ τι δύνασαι τῇ πόλει, λέγε, ch. 88) or a relative clause (καὶ τοὺς ἐπιρρέοντας ποταμούς – καὶ τοὺς ποταμούς, οἵτινες εἰς αὐτὴν ἐπιχέονται, ch. 71) in BPThSA.

107. See also in ch. 101 ἐπορεύετο τὴν οἰκουμένην καὶ ἐν τοῖς ἀκροατηρίοις διελέγετο (MORN) – παρεπορεύετο τὴν οἰκουμένην διαλεγόμενος πανταχοῦ (BPThSA) and in ch. 141 ἐκράτησε καὶ ἐβιάσατο (MORN) – κρατήσας ἐβιάσατο (BPThSA).

108. See also in ch. 111 εὐτρεπίσας (MORN) – ηὐτρέπισεν (BPThSA).

109. See also in ch. 109 ἵνα ἀδυνατῶσι βλάπτειν σε (MORN) – ἵνα ἀδυνατῶσι τοῦ βλάπτειν σε (BPThSA).

(συνέδραμον ἰδεῖν – συνέδραμεν ἐπὶ τὴν θεωρίαν, ch. 72), or a final clause (καὶ ὑβρίσαι ἡμᾶς καὶ κύνας ἀποκαλέσαι – ὅπως ὑβρίσῃ καὶ κύνας ἡμᾶς ἀποκαλέσῃ, ch. 77b).

Of great interest, too, are those cases in which the dative in the MORN recension is replaced by a prepositional construction or an accusative in the BPThSA recension, such as: τῷ ἐμπόρῳ (ἔφη) – πρὸς τὸν ἔμπορον (ch. 16),[110] κοχλιαρίῳ – τὸ κοχλιάριον (ch. 41).[111] However in chapter 77b the MORN recension has a prepositional construction or an accusative where a dative is used in the BPThSA recension: (μὴ ἐάσῃς) τινα – τινί, εἰς τὸν πυλῶνα (κρούσας) – τῷ πυλῶνι. Also, instead of the (adverbial) dative (ὡς φύσει φιλεῖ) used in the MORN recension, a substantival adjective (ὡς φυσικά) has been chosen in the BPThSA recension.

Sometimes when the MORN recension has direct speech (πόθεν εἶ), the BPThSA recension has indirect speech (ἐπυνθάνετο) πόθεν ἄρα τυγχάνει (ch. 24). Or, vice versa, where MORN has indirect speech (λογισάμενοι ὅτι καὶ εἰς ἑτέρας πόλεις ἀπελθών...) the BPThSA recension has direct speech (εἶπον πρὸς ἀλλήλους· ἐὰν οὗτος εἰς ἑτέρας πόλεις ἀπέλθῃ, ch. 127).

In some cases, finally, a single phrase may appear in two different versions, with the order of the words shuffled, as in chapter 131: Καὶ γὰρ ἡ μήτηρ μου πολλά σοι πρὸς τοῦτο εὐχαριστήσει (MORN) – Καὶ γὰρ ἡ μήτηρ μου πρὸς τοῦτο πολλά σοι εὐχαριστήσει (BPThSA).

The Relationship of MORN to the Papyrus Fragments

As mentioned above (p. 6), the Life is attested in six papyrus fragments, their dates ranging from the second/third century CE to the sixth/seventh century CE.[112] However, because they transmit different passages of the Life, it is difficult to determine exactly from which part of the textual tradition each one derives. Perry (1936, 38) gave a diagram with the main

---

110. See also in ch. 51 τῷ Αἰσώπῳ ἔφη (MORN) – πρὸς τὸν Αἴσωπον (BPThSA) and the same in chs. 65 and 129.

111. See also in ch. 88 κακίστῃ μορφῇ ... ἔδωκε (MORN) – κακίστην μορφήν (BPThSA).

112. P.Berol. 11628 (= Pack 2074) transmits chapters 121–124 (second/third century CE) and P.Oxy. XLVII 3331 and P.Oxy. LIII 3720 (addendum to 3331) chapters 18, 75–76, 107–111 (third century CE); PSI II 156 (= Pack 2072) has text from chapters 1–3 (fourth century CE); P.Oxy. XVII 2083 (= Pack 2073) transmits text from chapters 59–62 (dated to the fourth/fifth century CE). P.Ross.Georg. I 18 (= Pack 2075) transmits text from chapters 124–133 (sixth/seventh century CE).

branches of the ancient tradition of the text in which he included three papyrus fragments: the Oxyrhynchus Papyrus 2083, the Berlin Papyrus 11628, and the Golenischeff Papyrus. He did not take account of PSI 156 because the corresponding text in the recensions MORN/BPThSA "is very unreliable in this part of the Life, and there is a considerable lacuna in the corresponding part of G" (1936, 40).[113] Perry's diagram makes P.Oxy. 2083 an ancestor of the common tradition of G and Westermanniana, whereas the Berlin Papyrus and the Golenischeff draw upon a tradition that "had some kinship with the version from which SBP extracted the three episodes above described, and probably also a considerable number of smaller variants."[114]

In my view, it is difficult to categorize the papyrus fragments in terms of either of the two main traditions (G version or Westermanniana version). Comparison shows that their texts either agree with the texts of these traditions (mostly with G, but often their text is identical to the text of the Westermanniana) or record forms unattested elsewhere. I am not convinced that we should ascribe the papyrus fragments to one tradition alone, and I would be reluctant to assume that they belong to a common source, the one Perry terms π;[115] I am inclined, rather, to regard them as independent witnesses of the tradition behind the text of the Life, typical samples of the open transmission process behind it. More specific comments about the papyri follow.

PSI 156 (= Pack 2072)

In line 18 the reading of the papyrus ετερου γευσα[μενος corresponds only to the MO(RN) reading (οὐδενὸς γὰρ ἦν) ἐτέρου γευσάμενος (ch. 3). G has (οὐδαμῶς γὰρ ἦν) γευσάμενος, whereas the BPThSA recension has the reading νῆστης οὖν ἦν. In line 21 again the phrase θ]αυμασας αυτου το νοερον[

---

113. Perry did not have at his disposal P.Oxy. XLVII 3331 and P.Oxy. LIII 3720 (addendum to 3331) because they were published later.

114. Adrados (1999, 682) expresses a similar opinion: "The papyri align themselves with one or the other of these two recensions: POxy. 2083 agrees with G; the Golenishef Papyrus is closely related; the PSI 156 is, in contrast, of the W type; the position of PBerol. 11628 is more doubtful."

115. See also Haslam's criticism (1986, 152): "But the hypothesis of a unitary source for all the various non-GW witnesses is hardly in keeping with the realities of textual transmission as evidenced by the papyri, and receives specific confutation in the discrepancies between the present papyrus and the Vienna codex."

corresponds exactly to the reading MO(RN): Ὁ δὲ θαυμάσας αὐτοῦ τὸ νοερὸν (ch. 3); G has θαυμάσας δὲ ὁ δεσπότης τὸ ἐνθύμημα αὐτοῦ. The word αὐτομάτως on line 26 of the papyrus is recorded also in MSS (M)OSB.

However, the phrase κατω μη χαλάσωμεν (verso 23) is closer to the direct statement of G (καὶ μὴ κάτω τοὺς δακτύλους βάλωμεν) than to the indirect one of the MO(RN) recension (Οἱ δὲ δοῦλοι ἐβουλεύσαντο τοὺς δακτύλους ... καὶ κάτω μὴ χαλάσαι).

In general, PSI 156 (fourth century) seems to belong to the tradition of the MORN recension.

Oxyrhynchus Papyrus XVII 2083 (= Pack 2073)

This fragment displays many similarities to MS G. There are only a few readings in it that are found only in the MORN recension:

In line 12 the arrangement of the words [ειτα λέγει Ξάνθο]ν οιδας τον φιλόσοφο in the papyrus is paralleled more closely by a phrase in the MORN recension (Ξάνθον οἶδας τὸν φιλόσοφον;) than by the corresponding phrase in G (οἶδας Ξάνθον τὸν φιλόσοφον; [ch. 60]). The variant κυρι[α in line 38 is found also in MORN (and in BPThSA), whereas G has κυρά (ch. 61). Similarly, in the phrase η δε θελουσα τω Α[ισωπω κακα γενεσθαι] in line 46, the participial construction ἡ δὲ θέλουσα is a reading found only in the MORN recension. G in this place gives a completely different phrase: ἡ γυνὴ τοῦ Ξάνθου διὰ τὸ μῖσος τὸ πρὸς τὸν Αἴσωπον (ch. 61). The imperative δοθήτω in line 60 of the papyrus agrees with the MORN recension (and BPThSA), whereas G has the infinitive δοθῆναι (ch. 62).

Papyrus Berolinensis 11628 (= Pack 2074)

The Berlin fragment, which is the earliest textual evidence for the Life, seems to preserve readings that occur both in G and in MORN. It is striking that only the papyrus and G mention a three-year tribute paid by Lycurus; all other manuscripts mention a ten-year tribute. The common readings between the Berlin fragment and the MORN recension that differ from G are the following:

The reading in lines 34–35 (α]πέπεμψε ο δε Αισωπ[ος) is similar to the corresponding phrase in the MORN recension (ch. 123), whereas G gives ἔπεμψεν αὐτόν. The infinitive ανατεθη[ναι] in line 42 occurs in exactly the same form in the MORN recension (and BPThSA), but MS G has ἀχθῆναι (ch. 123). In lines 45–47, βουλ[ο]μενος την Ελλάδα [εκ]πλευσαι in the papyrus corresponds more closely to the variant in MORN (ἐβουλεύσατο εἰς τὴν Ἑλλάδα ἀποπλεῦσαι, ch. 124)[116] than to the phrase in G (ἀπελθεῖν θέλων εἰς Δελφούς), which in addition gives a different location, as it has Delphi instead of Greece.

Of great interest, too, is the reading in lines 52–53: επεδεικνυετο την α[υτου] παιδείαν (ch. 124). G has ἐπεδείκνυτο τὴν ἑαυτοῦ σοφίαν καὶ παιδείαν, and the MORN recension has καὶ τὴν ἑαυτοῦ ἐπιδεικνύμενος σοφίαν (BPThSA: καὶ τὴν ἑαυτοῦ σοφίαν ἐπιδεικνύμενος). It is clear that G preserves the original reading of the papyrus (παιδείαν), while the variant σοφίαν seems to be drawing upon the tradition of the Westermanniana version, which is the common source of both the MORN and the BPThSA recensions.

Perry (1936, 53) claims "that the Berlin papyrus does not belong to the ancient tradition typified by GW, but to that which we have described above … as the source of SBP's interpolations." He draws this conclusion from the reading given by the papyrus, Λυκωρος, "which seems to be the source of SBP's Λυκοῦρος, as contrasted with Λυκοῦργος in GW."

The form Λυκοῦργος is also written in MS R, whereas Λυκοῦρος is transmitted by MS M. In my opinion, the Berlin papyrus once again gives the reading of MORN (and BPThSA), as it does in many other cases, and differs from the text in MS G. In general, this papyrus fragment agrees with the tradition of the MORN recension but not consistently so, since readings that belong to the text tradition of G are to be found here as well.

The Golenischeff Papyrus (P.Ross.Georg. I 18 = Pack 2075)

The Golenischeff Papyrus fragment mentions Apollo and the Muses (lines 15, 22–23), who are absent from the MORN and the BPThSA recensions. The negative comparison of the citizens of Delphi with vegetables and the link to the Homeric quotation (*Il.* 6.146) are likewise recorded only in G (ch. 124) and in the Golenischeff Papyrus. Moreover, in the papyrus the story involving the foolish girl (ch. 131) seems to come after the story of the widow (of Ephesus), when Aesop's friend asks him some rhetorical questions (ch. 130), as in G and the MORN recension.[117] In at least one

---

116. ἐβουλεύσατο εἰς τὴν Ἑλλάδα πλεῦσαι in BPThSA.

117. In contrast to the BPThSA recension, in which the story of the foolish girl is located after ch. 140 (see above). There are many rhetorical questions in G and Golenischeff Papyrus (ch. 130), whereas the MORN recension has only one.

case (the mention of the place at line 69), the papyrus is more detailed than the other versions,[118] even though in other sections (lines 29–30) the account in the text of the papyrus is shorter.

Oxyrhynchus Papyrus XLVII 3331

This fragment preserves a passage from chapters 75–76 that refers to the affair between Aesop and Xanthus's wife. This story is to be found only in codices O and Lo, while traces are found also in G (Perry 1936, 7–8; Haslam 1980, 53–54). Since the text comparable to the fragment is only in MS O, all comments are based on a comparison between these two. The vocabulary of the fragment looks quite similar to that of MS O (see the underlined words in the edition of Haslam, such as ἱμάτια, σκάπτειν, μεσότοιχον, κυρίας, ἓν ἐξ αὐτῶν), even though variants are to be observed as well, such as κλ]αδον γεμοντα (3331) – κλάδον ἕνα πλήρη (MS O); χαριζομαι σοι (3331) – παρέχω σοι (MS O); ευστοχησας (3331) – εὐστόχως (MS O); different morphological forms are also attested, as in βαλε (3331) – βαλεῖν (MS O). In two parts of the papyrus (lines 8–9, 13), the text seems to be longer than the corresponding text in MS O.

Oxyrhynchus Papyrus LIII 3720

Haslam, who edited this papyrus, offers a detailed commentary, along with a comparison of the papyrus with the G and W textual traditions, and offers the following important remarks:

> While the papyrus is generally closer to G than to the W tradition (see e.g., 1, 2–4, 12–14, 106), it not infrequently agrees with the W tradition against G (e.g., 1–2 κληθῆναι, 4 ἐδάκρυσεν, 8f. ὑπὲρ ὧν κατηγόρησεν αὐτοῦ ὁ Αἶνος, 112 πρὸς τὸ ἐκείνων βούλημα). Perhaps rather more in the W recension is inherited than might have been thought, and correspondingly less to be assigned to later rewriting. At 10 there is an agreement with SBP against all the other witnesses: this in conformity with Perry's recognition that SBP, while basically W manuscripts, occasionally draw on another source. And at 19 an apparent tense-agreement with MW

---

118. In line 75 the papyrus has a phrase in direct discourse, as does G, and contrary to the MORN recension (and BPThSA), which give the same phrase in indirect discourse. Then in line 53, the papyrus and the MORN recension give an indirect statement, while the corresponding phrase in G is in direct discourse.

shows that M may preserve original W readings against R, as well as confirming the independent value of the pure (non-SBP) W tradition. But often the papyrus stands alone. It is more distant both from G and from W than they are from each other. Its narrative is rarely shorter, and sometimes gives circumstantial detail not to be found in G or W (e.g., the phrases at 8 and 22). For all the suspicion that properly attaches to longer texts in general (especially perhaps in the case of a popular quasi-biographical work of no fixed constitution, cf. the Gospels), the papyrus' text gives little impression of having been padded; rather, the versions of G and W appear abridged in relation to 3720, much as W is itself abridged in relation to G" (Haslam 1986, 152).

Conclusions: The Redactor of the MORN Recension, Date, and Place

Because of the fluidity of the text and the open textual tradition of the Life, it is not easy to determine with certainty the scribal poetics of its different versions. However, it is possible to make some assumptions concerning the profile of the redactor of the MORN recension on the basis of the comparisons and remarks that I have noted above.

The place names in chapters 133 and 144 (see above) may relate to the origin of the redactor of the MORN recension.[119] He came either from Greece or from some place in the western Mediterranean and possessed a limited knowledge of the Eastern world. He was probably not a pagan, since there are no references to the pagan gods in this version, and he is familiar with the gospels, or with early Christian literature and the language of the gospels in general. In chapter 53, for example, the phrase γλῶσσα ἄνδρα ταπεινοῖ καὶ πάλιν ὑψοῖ is taken from LXX 1 Kgs 2:1–10.[120] He was not highly educated, since the Life lacks intertextual associations

---

119. Ch. 141 προῃρούμην Σικελίαν ὅλην κακοπαθῶν κυκλεῦσαι ἢ ἐνθάδε παραλόγως ὑφ' ὑμῶν ἀποθανεῖν ("I would prefer to suffer circling all of Sicily than to die here unreasonably at your hands"); ch. 142 οἱ τῆς Ἑλλάδος ἔξαρχοι καὶ οἱ λοιποὶ διδάσκαλοι ("the leaders of Greece and the other teachers"). On the basis of the first passage (ch. 141) in versions G and Westermanniana, La Penna (1962, 271–72) claims that the archetype of version G was written in Syria and that the archetype of the Westermanniana version was produced in Sicily.

120. See also the similarities in ch. 64's εἰς Ἅιδου καταβαίνεις with Matt 11:23 or Luke 10:15 and ch. 87's καὶ τὰς χεῖρας τῷ ὄχλῳ κατασείσας ᾔτησεν ἡσυχίαν. Σιγῆς δὲ γενομένης ἔφη ("Aesop … waved his hands at the crowd and demanded silence. When there was silence, he said") with Acts 21:40. All examples are discussed in Karla 2009a, 451–52.

with other literary works of classical antiquity, and he is not interested in employing rhetorical arguments. In fact, he has purposely omitted them in some cases.

The differences between the MORN and the BPThSA recensions suggest that the main intention of the redactor of BPThSA was to produce an abridgement of the original Life, although the changes are not made at random, which may very well indicate an educated author. Abridgements and morphological, syntactical, or semantic variations (e.g., synonyms) may have served a didactic function. Similar variations are observed in the text of G and of the MORN recension. It may therefore not be wrong to attribute these variants to an intention on the part of the redactor to use the text of the Life for educational purposes. Indeed, both the *Fables* and the Life of Aesop are texts appropriate for use in schools, with content fitting for instruction at various levels, and attractive to teachers and students alike. Moreover, the didactic function of the many variations of the Life is supported by the fact that one basic detail, in addition to the tendency to abridge, that differentiates the various texts seems to be linguistic, as may be surmised from the morphological, syntactical, and semantic differentiation of individual forms, words, and phrases.

As for dating, in his last article on the Life, Perry (1966) revised his earlier hypothesis that the Westermanniana version was to be dated in the tenth century and expressed the view instead that the archetype of SBP came from the sixth century, while that of the MORN recension was earlier. One of the reasons for this revision of his views was the discovery of one folium of the eleventh-century manuscript Thessalonicensis Bibliothecae Universitatis 86 (Th), which is the oldest source attesting the tradition of the Westermanniana recension. The discovery of this manuscript alone, however, does not justify so considerable a change of date. Perry did not produce additional arguments for his new and much earlier date (fifth–sixth century), and this is an issue that has troubled several later critics, including Papathomopoulos (1999a, 33), although no satisfactory answer has so far been offered, and, indeed, there has been no adequate discussion of the issue to date. It is possible that the close relationship of the MORN recension to the papyrus fragments supports the date offered by Perry. As we have seen, comparison with the papyrus fragments reveals that the MORN recension bears many similarities to them (see, e.g., P.Berol. 11628 or P.Oxy. 3720, both from the third century), and this may serve as evidence for an earlier date of the MORN recension.

EDITORIAL METHODOLOGY

The Life of Aesop is a popular prose text written in the Hellenistic Koine.[1] The nature of the text (description of the adventurous life of an antihero, in simple language) was such that scribes/redactors felt "free" to proceed to interventions, such as changes, additions, and deletions; as a result, there have come about several versions and translations of the Life that have enjoyed great popularity and vast dissemination.[2]

The MORN recension is a (main) branch in the manuscript tradition of an open text.[3] Its edition, therefore, should take into consideration two major parameters: the text itself and the particularities of the manuscript tradition. It is obvious that the application of the standard editorial methodology for ancient high-register texts would be anything but suitable. *Open* texts, due to the multiplicity of interventions (both in content and linguistic form) by scribes/redactors, do not allow the stemmatic restitution of an archetype. Each recension, each version, almost each manuscript constitutes a valuable witness to the history of the text; more important, each one can stand on its own. For this reason, an edition based on a single manuscript (*Leithandschrift*) seems to be indicated in the case of such texts, although of course it cannot be applied in all of them in the same way; each version, each recension, has its own particularities and needs to be treated individually and autonomously depending on the conditions of textual transmission.

This line of reasoning has already been discussed for the edition of the corresponding recension BPThSA of the Westermanniana. In that case, the

---

1. For the Life as popular literature, see Karla 2016a, as well as Avlamis 2011 from an anthropological/sociological viewpoint. For the language of the older version G, see Ruiz Montero 2010 and Stamoulakis 2016, with relevant bibliography. For the language of version BPThSA, see Karla 2001, 69–126.

2. On the reception of the Life, see pp. 9–13, above.

3. On the notion of open text, see pp. 8–9, above, with relevant bibliography.

method I adopted was the copy-text/*Leithandschrift* one, and the edition was based not on a single manuscript but on a family of manuscripts: BPTh (Karla 2001, 127–29). For the edition of the MORN recension, it is not feasible to adopt exactly the same methodology, due to the special features of the manuscript tradition (see pp. 15–25, above). In fact, in the case of MORN, the choice is limited between manuscripts M and O, since R transmits only a small part of the text (chs. 88a–141) and N an even smaller one (it consists of a single folio containing chs. 90–98). Of course, there is also the Latin translation preserved in MS Lo, which, according to Perry, is a rendition in Latin of the lost MS R (for details, see pp. 25–34, above). This text could be of assistance in the edition of recension MORN, but inevitably only to a limited degree, due to the difference in language.

The selection between MS M and MS O as the *Leithandschrift* for the MORN recension proved difficult (see pp. 19–25, above). MS M is the only one to provide a complete text. However, it is the only witness for its family branch, and therefore it is not possible to verify whether its readings are an innovation by the specific scribe or represent the whole family (χ) or even recension MORN in general. Furthermore, the copyist of MS M is known: the learned Byzantine writer Andreas Libadenos, which makes the above distinction even harder. An additional difficulty is that MS M is contaminated (see, e.g., chs 77a, 77b).

On the other hand, MS O transmits a large part of the work (chs. 1–104), though not all of it. Furthmore, MS O, or the common descendant of OR, is characterized by great sloppiness in writing: lipographies (e.g., ch. 102 OR; ch. 113 R; ch. 126 R), misreading or miscopying of words (e.g., ch. 20 ἐν ἀπορίᾳ instead of εὐπορίᾳ; ch. 32 ὁλόκαλον instead of οὐλόκομον; ch. 128 περιμείζοντες R instead of περιβομβίζοντες), incomprehensible expressions (see ch. 1 MS O), interpolations ranging from a small phrase (e.g., ch. 25 ἢ ἐν κατωγείῳ; ch. 28 διὰ τῶν πλατιῶν; ch. 62 ὑποψηθηρίζων; ch. 125 τοῖς προύχουσιν ὑμῶν καὶ τοῖς προγόνοις R) to a whole sentence (e.g., ch. 66; chs. 83–85, 87, 102 OR; chs. 105 R, 123 R; ch. 139 R). Moreover, in many places the text of O/OR omits details that are found both in M and in version G (e.g., chs. 21.2–4; 98.8–12).[4]

On the basis of these considerations, the general procedure followed in the present edition is as follows: MS M has been considered the most representative of the MORN recension and has served as *Leithandschrift*, but

---

4. Version G seems to be closer to the original text of the Life (Karla 2009a).

not all of its readings have been blindly adopted. The aim was to provide a text representative of the whole MORN recension and not only of MS M or one of its immediate ancestors.

Chapter division follows that of Perry (as all other editions of the Life). Orthography follows standard rules of traditional grammar (in issues such as accentuation, clitics, iota subscriptum, etc.), as does punctuation. The apparatus criticus is mixed: the readings adopted in the text are given only in order to ensure clarity. It does not list all orthographic variants of the manuscripts but only those where orthographic variation affects morphology, syntax, or semantics.

The commentary that follows the edition is not literary-hermeneutical but serves mainly to explain and justify editorial choices and focuses on words and phrases that are of interest for the history of the Greek language.

TRANSLATOR'S NOTE

The reader will observe that the translation accompanying the text is literal and in places may seem less than graceful. There are two reasons why I have preferred a rougher style. First, the original itself is not highly polished, so rendering it in elegant prose would convey a wrong idea of its texture. Second, and more important, the text being translated is one of several versions of the Life that survive; these versions differ in small ways from one another, sometimes as minor as the substitution of a participial phrase for an infinitive or a different prefix for a given verb. The present edition makes one of these recensions available, and I felt that the task of the translator was to be as faithful to the text, as constituted by Grammatiki Karla, as possible, so that the reader might be able to note where it departs from other versions, even in slight details.

I would like here to express my profound gratitude to Grammatiki Karla, with whom it has been a privilege and a pleasure to collaborate on this work, and to Io Manolessou, who went over the entire translation and improved it both for accuracy and style in more ways than I can say. I would have happily placed her name alongside mine as cotranslator.

David Konstan
New York University

SIGLA CODICUM

Recension MORN(Lo)

    M Monacensis graecus 525 (fourteenth century)
    O Baroccianus 194 (fifteenth century)
    R Vaticanus graecus 1192 (fourteenth century)
    N Parisinus graecus 2894 (thirteenth century)
    Lo Bellunensis Lollinianus 26 (fourteenth century)

Recension BPThSA

    B Londinensis Add. graecus 17015 (fifteenth century)
    P Vaticanus Palatinus graecus 269 (fifteenth century)
    Th Thessalonicensis Bibliothecae Universitatis 86 (eleventh century)
    S Mosquensis, Gosudarstvennyj Istoričeskij Musej 436 (thirteenth century)
    A Atheniensis, Benaki Museum 53 (TA 72) (thirteenth/fourteenth century)

λ (consensus librorum LFV, vel LV, vel L)

    L Leidensis Vulc. 93 (fifteenth century)
    F Laurentianus LVII 30 (sixteenth century)
    V Vaticanus graecus 695 (fifteenth century)

    W Laurentianus Conventi soppressi 627 (thirteenth century)

Version G

    G Pierpont Morgan Bibliotheca 397 (tenth/eleventh century)

TEXT AND TRANSLATION

Βίος Αἰσώπου τοῦ φιλοσόφου

1. Ὁ κατὰ πάντα τὸν βίον βιωφελέστατος γενόμενος Αἴσωπος, ὁ λογομυθοποιός, τῇ μὲν τύχῃ γέγονεν δοῦλος, τῷ δὲ γένει Φρὺξ ἐξ Ἀμορίου τῆς Φρυγίας, κακοειδὴς μὲν εἰς ὑπερβολήν, προκέφαλος, κοντοτράχηλος σιμός τε, μέλας καὶ μουστάκων, προγάστωρ δὲ καὶ γαλιάγκων, στρεβλός, ὑπόκυρτος, ἡμερινὸν ἁμάρτημα. Πρόσεστιν τούτοις δὲ ἦν βραδύγλωσσος καὶ βομβόφωνος φαῦλός τε καὶ δεινὸς πανουργίᾳ.

2. Τοῦτον οὖν ὁ δεσπότης ὡς ἄχρηστον τῆς πολιτικῆς ὑπηρεσίας ἐξέπεμψεν αὐτὸν εἰς ἓν τῶν κτημάτων αὐτοῦ σκάπτειν. Καὶ δή ποτε παραγενομένου αὐτοῦ ἐπὶ τὸν ἀγρόν, γεωργός τις κάλλιστα τρυγήσας σῦκα προσήνεγκεν αὐτῷ καί φησι «δέσποτα, λάβε ἀπὸ τῶν σῶν καρπῶν ὀπώραν πρώιμον.» Ὁ δὲ τερφθεὶς ἔφη «νὴ τὴν σωτηρίαν μου, καλὰ σῦκα.» Καί φησι τῷ οἰκέτῃ «Ἀγαθόπου, λάβε καὶ φύλαξόν μοι αὐτά. Μετὰ δὲ τὸ λούσασθαι καὶ ἀριστῆσαι παράθες μοι τὴν ὀπώραν.» Συνέβη δὲ κατὰ τὴν ὥραν ἀνανεῦσαι τὸν Αἴσωπον ἀπὸ τοῦ ἔργου καὶ εἰσελθόντα ζητεῖν τὸν ἐφήμερον ἄριστον. Ὁ δὲ Ἀγαθόπους λαβὼν τὰ σῦκα καὶ λιμανθείς, φαγὼν ἓν καὶ δύο λέγει πρός τινα τῶν συνδούλων αὐτοῦ «ἤθελον κορεσθῆναι τῶν σύκων καὶ δέδοικα». Ὁ δὲ πρὸς αὐτόν· «ἐὰν κἀγὼ φάγω μετὰ σοῦ, δώσω γνώμην ἵνα φαγόντες μὴ δαρῶμεν.» Καὶ ὁ Ἀγαθόπους φησί «πῶς;» Ὁ δέ· «φάγωμεν οἱ δύο τὰ σῦκα

Βίος ... φιλοσόφου : titul. om. O ‖ **1.1** Ὁ : om. O | γενόμενος βιοφιλέστατος O 1–2 ὁ λογομυθοποιός : evan. in M **2** τῷ ... γένει : γένει δὲ O | Φρὺξ ... Ἀμορίου : Φρὺξ ἐξ Ἀμύρου (?) evan. in M **3** κακοειδὴς : σκακοειδὴς O (κακοειδὴς leg. Perry, Papath.) | μὲν : om. O | προκέφαλος : προ- evan. in M | κοντοτράχηλος : κοντοδείρης O **4** τε : om. O | μέλας : μέγας O | καὶ¹ ... καὶ² : om. O | προγάστωρ : lit. π, ρ, ο evan. in M | δὲ καὶ : evan. in M | γαλιάγκων : corr. Perry, iter. Papath. : γαλλιάγκων M : γελιακόν O **5** ἡμερινὸν ἁμάρτημα : evan. in O | Πρόσεστιν : correxi ex πρὸς ἔστιν M : πρὸς ἐπὶ in M leg. Perry et Papath. : evan. in O | τούτοις : evan. in O | δὲ ... βραδύγλωσσος : καὶ βραδύγλωττος ἦν O | καὶ ... **6** δεινὸς : τὰν ὅπαν βληχος ωςδῖν .βα ... O **6** πανουργίᾳ : ... ουργίας O ‖ **2.1** Τοῦτον ... **2** σκάπτειν : ὀνούμενος τοίνυν αὐτός γε ἀπεστάλθη παρὰ τοῦ δεσπότου ὡς ἄχρηστος παντα ... τῆς τοῦ ταμείου ὑπηρεσίας εἰς ἱμερὴν γεωργεῖν O **3** παραγενομένου : παρα- evan. in M | αὐτοῦ : om. O | ἐπὶ ... ἀγρόν : ἀπ' ἀγροῦ O | κάλλιστα : -λλιστα evan.

Life of Aesop the Philosopher

1. Aesop, the writer of fables, who throughout his entire life was most beneficial for the lives of others, was a slave by chance, but by birth he was a Phrygian from Amorion in Phrygia. He was ugly in the extreme, long in the head, short-necked, snub-nosed, swarthy, and mustached, a protruding belly and shortened arms, misshapen, humpbacked, a failure all the livelong day. In addition to this, he stammered with a booming voice and was loutish and terribly wily.

2. And so, his master sent him out to dig in one of his properties, since he was useless for service in the city. In fact, once, when the master had gone out to the field, a farmer who had gathered in some excellent figs brought them to him and said, "Master, take some early fruit from your harvest." He was delighted and said, "By my salvation, they are fine figs," and to his slave he said, "Agathopus, take them and keep them for me. After I have washed up and had lunch, set the fruit before me." It happened that at this hour Aesop was returning from work and went in seeking his daily lunch. Agathopus took the figs and, since he was hungry he ate one or two and said to one of his fellow slaves, "I wanted to glut myself on the figs, but I was afraid." The other said to him, "If I too eat them with you, I'll give you some advice so that we won't be beaten even though we've eaten them." "How?" said Agathopus, and the other said, "Let's both of us

---

in M | κάλλιστα ... σῦκα : ἰσχάδας πάνυ ὡραίας O 4 ἤνεγγεν τὸ τοῦ ἐσώπου δεσπότῃ O | δέσποτα ... 5 σῦκα : εἰ γὰρ ἐρά ... οιέ ... ρ ὀπώραν πρόιμον, σφόδρα τῶν εὐδμήων αὐτῇ γε πέλει. ὁ δὲ γε δεσπότης ερ ... τὴν τῶν ἰσχάδων ὥραν, ἔφησε θειμύρει πάμπαν ἐμοῖ ταυτά γε τυγχάνουσι κἀκτούτ. .. ρὸς φυλακήν O | λάβε ... τῶν : evan. in M 5 ἔφη ... μου : evan. in M | Καί ... 6 Ἀγαθόπου : τῷ οἰκέτει ἀγαθόπῳ δέδωκεν τὰς ἰσχάδας φήσας O 6 λάβε καὶ φ evan. in M | λάβε ... 7 ὀπώραν : μετὰ τὸ ἐξελ ... ... ου καὶ ἀριστῆσαι παράθες μοι ταῦτα O 7 παράθες μοι : evan. in M 8 τὸν Αἴσωπον : om. O | ἀπὸ : ἐκ O | ζητεῖναι O | ἄριστον : lit. evan. in M (αὐ ... in M leg. Perry, Papath.) 9 λιμανθείς : corr. Perry : λιμπισθείς corr. Papath : λιπανθείς O : evan. in M | φαγών : O : evan. in M 10 αὐτοῦ ... σύκων : evan. in M | δέδοικα : φοβοῦμαι O 11 εἶπεν post πρὸς αὐτόν add. O | ἐὰν : evan. in O | ἐὰν ... γνώμην : evan. in M 12 φησί ... 13 ἐάν : evan. in M

καὶ ἐὰν ὁ δεσπότης ζητήσῃ, εἰπὲ αὐτῷ ὅτι ὁ Αἴσωπος ἄδειαν εὑρὼν κατέφαγε τὰ σῦκα. Καὶ ὁ Αἴσωπος βραδύγλωσσος ὢν πρὸς ἀπολογίαν δαρήσεται, ἡμεῖς δὲ τὴν ἐπιθυμίαν ἐκπληροῦμεν.» Καὶ παρακαθεσθέντες τοῖς σύκοις ἓν ἓν τρώγοντες, ἔλεγον «οὐαί σοι, Αἴσωπε.» Συμφωνήσαντες εἰς ἑαυτοὺς ἵνα, εἴ τι ἀπόληται ἢ ἐκχυθῇ, εἴπωσι ὅτι ὁ Αἴσωπος ἐποίησε, κατέφαγον τὰ σῦκα.

3. Ὁ δὲ κύριος αὐτῶν μετὰ τὸ λούσασθαι καὶ ἀριστῆσαι, «Ἀγαθόπου», φησί, «δός μοι τὰ σῦκα.» Κἀκεῖνος ἔφη «δέσποτα, Αἴσωπος εὐκαιρήσας καὶ εὑρὼν τὸ ταμεῖον ἀνεῳγμένον εἰσελθὼν κατέφαγε τὰ σῦκα.» Ὁ δὲ θυμωθεὶς ἔφη «Αἴσωπόν μοί τις καλεσάτω.» Ὁ δὲ παρεγένετο καί φησιν ὁ δεσπότης «λέγε μοι, κατάρατε, οὕτω μου κατεφρόνησας ὅτι εἰς τὸ ταμεῖον εἰσελθὼν τὰ ἐμοὶ ἡτοιμασμένα σῦκα κατέφαγες;» Ὁ δὲ ἀκούσας, λαλεῖν δὲ μὴ δυνάμενος διὰ τὸ τῆς γλώσσης βραδύ, θεωρῶν δὲ τοὺς κατηγόρους αὐτοῦ εἰς ὄψιν ἑστῶτας, μέλλων δέρεσθαι, πεσὼν παρὰ τοὺς πόδας τοῦ δεσπότου, παρεκάλει μικρὸν ἀνασχεῖν. Καὶ λαβὼν ξέστην καὶ ὕδατι χλιαρῷ συγκεράσας, λεκάνην τε παραθεὶς καὶ πιών, ἐχάλασε τοὺς δακτύλους ἐπὶ τὸ ἴδιον στόμα καὶ σπαράξας ἑαυτὸν ἀνέβαλε τὸ ὕδωρ μόνον ὃ ἐπεπώκει. Οὐδενὸς γὰρ ἦν ἑτέρου γευσάμενος. Ἐδέετο δὲ καὶ τοὺς κατηγόρους ποιῆσαι ὁμοίως καὶ «ἐπιγνώσῃ τὸν βεβρωκότα τὰ σῦκα.» Ὁ δὲ θαυμάσας αὐτοῦ τὸ νοερὸν ἐπέταξε καὶ τοῖς ἄλλοις ποιῆσαι ὁμοίως. Οἱ δὲ δοῦλοι ἐβουλεύσαντο τοὺς δακτύλους πέμψαι παρὰ τὰς γνάθους καὶ κάτω μὴ χαλάσαι. Ἅμα δὲ τῷ πιεῖν αὐτοὺς τὸ χλιαρὸν ὕδωρ καὶ συγκύψαι, τὰ σῦκα χολοποιὰ ὄντα προσανέβλυσαν καὶ αὐτομάτως ἀνέδραμον. Τότε ὁ δεσπότης εἶπεν «τί καταψεύδεσθε τοῦ μὴ δυναμένου λαλεῖν;» Καὶ ἐκέλευσεν αὐτοὺς γυμνωθέντας τύπτεσθαι. Ἔγνωσαν δὲ σαφῶς
 ὅστις καθ' ἑτέρου δόλια μηχανᾶται,
 αὐτὸς καθ' ἑαυτοῦ τοῦτο λανθάνει ποιῶν.

2.13 ὅτι : om. O | εἰσελθὼν post εὑρὼν add. O 14 Αἴσωπος ... πρὸς : evan. in M | ἡμεῖς ... 15 δὲ : καὶ ἡμεῖς O 15 τοῖς σύκοις : τῆς συκῆς O 16 τρώγοντες : ἐσθίοντες O | οὐαί : οὐαὶ οὐαὶ O | εἴ ... 17 τι : ὅτι O 17 ἀπόληται : corr. Perry, iter. Papath. : ἀπόληται M : ἀπόλυται O | ὁ : ante Αἴσωπος om. O | κατέφαγε O ‖ 3.2 φησί : λέγει post ἀριστῆσαι O 3 ἔφαγε O 5 κατάρατε : ἐπικατάρατε δοῦλε O | τὰ ... 6 ἡτοιμασμένα : τὰ ἡτοιμασμένα μοι O 6 ἔφαγες O | λαλεῖν δὲ : καὶ λαλεῖν O 7 αὐτοῦ post ὄψιν add. O 8 δαίρεσθαι M | τοῦ δεσπότου : τοῦ κυρίου αὐτοῦ O | αὐτὸν post παρεκάλει add. O 9 τὸν ξέστην O | καὶ ... συγκεράσας : καὶ θερμὸν χλιὸν κεράσας O 10 τε : om. O | ἰδίους ante δακτύλους add. O | εἰς

eat the figs, and if the master asks for them, tell him that Aesop found a safe opportunity and ate the figs. Aesop, stammering in his defense, will be beaten, while we will sate our appetite. Sitting down by the figs, they gulped them down one by one and said, "Woe to you, Aesop!" Agreeing between themselves that, if anything should be spoiled or spill out, they would say that Aesop did it, they ate up the figs.

3. After washing and having his lunch, the master said, "Agathopus, give me the figs." And he said, "Master, Aesop had the chance, found the storehouse open, went inside, and ate the figs." The master grew angry and said, "Have someone summon Aesop to me." Aesop appeared, and the master said, "Tell me, you abominable thing, did you feel such contempt for me that you went into the storehouse and ate the figs that had been prepared for me?" When he heard this but was not able to talk because of his stammer, and when he saw his accusers standing before his eyes and being himself on the point of being beaten, he fell before the feet of his master and begged him to hold off for a bit. Then he took a pitcher mixed in warm water, put a basin next to it and drank, then stuck his fingers into his own mouth, and, making himself retch, he threw up only the water he had drunk, since he had not tasted anything else. He begged that his accusers, too, do likewise and said, "You will know the one who ate the figs." The master was amazed at his intellect and ordered the others, too, to do likewise. The slaves planned to shove their fingers alongside their jaws and not stick them down, but as soon as they drank the warm water and bent forward, they spurted out the figs as well, since they are bilious, and they spontaneously got up and ran. Then the master said, "Why did you falsely accuse someone who could not talk?" and he ordered that they be stripped and thrashed. They clearly recognized that

    Whoever plots deceits against another,
    Unbeknownst he does it to himself.

τὸ στόμα αὐτοῦ O **11** ἀνέβαλε : ἐξέμεσε O | πεπώκει O **12** ὁμοίως ποιῆσαι inv. O | πάντως post ἐπιγνώσῃ add. O **13** ἐπετάξε O **15** παρὰ : περὶ O | τὸ πιεῖν O | χλιαρὸν : om. O **16** καὶ συγκύψαι : καὶ συγ lit. evan. in M | προσανέβλυσαν : corr. Perry, iter. Papath. : προσ ἀνέβλυσαν O : προσ ... M (προσαν in M leg. Perry, Papath.) **17** ἑστὼς ante εἶπεν add. O | καταψεύδεσθαι O | τὸ μὴ δυναμένῳ O **18** ὅτι post σαφῶς add. O **20** ἑαυτοῦ : αὐτοῦ ex Westermann corr. Perry, iter. Papath. | τοῦτο ... ποιῶν : ex SG corr. Papath. : τοῦτο ποιῶν λανθάνει ex Eberh. (*Fab. Rom.*, p. 231) corr. Perry : τὸν δόλον δρᾶν O | λανθάνει : evan. in M

4. Τῇ δὲ ἐπιούσῃ ἡμέρᾳ ὁ δεσπότης ζευκτῷ καθίσας εἰς τὴν πόλιν εἰσῄει. Τοῦ δὲ Αἰσώπου εἰς τὸν ἀγρὸν σκάπτοντος οἱ ἱερεῖς τῆς Ἴσιδος πλανηθέντες τῆς λεωφόρου ἦλθον εἰς τὸν ἀγρὸν καὶ παρεκάλουν τὸν Αἴσωπον δεῖξαι τὴν ἀπάγουσαν ὁδὸν εἰς τὴν πόλιν. Ὁ δὲ ἀγαγὼν αὐτοὺς ὑπὸ σύσκιον δένδρον παρέθηκεν αὐτοῖς ἄρτον καὶ ἐλαίας καὶ ἰσχάδας καὶ ἠνάγκασε φαγεῖν. Καὶ δραμὼν εἰς τὸ φρέαρ ἀνιμήσατο ὕδωρ καὶ ἤνεγκεν αὐτοῖς πιεῖν. Καὶ κρατήσας τῆς χειρὸς ἐξήγαγεν αὐτοὺς εἰς τὴν εὐθεῖαν καὶ τετριμμένην ὁδόν.

5. Οἱ δὲ ἐπάραντες τὰς χεῖρας εἰς τὸν οὐρανὸν καὶ εὐξάμενοι αὐτῷ ὡς ὑπ' αὐτοῦ εὐεργετηθέντες ὑπεχώρησαν.

6. Αἴσωπος δὲ στραφεὶς καὶ ὑπὸ τοῦ καύματος χαυνωθεὶς εἰς ὕπνον ἐτράπη.

7. Ἡ δὲ Τύχη ἐπιστᾶσα καθ' ὕπνους ἐχαρίσατο αὐτῷ λόγον ἄριστον καὶ τὸ ταχὺ τῆς γλώττης καὶ ἐτοιμολογίας εὕρεσιν διὰ ποικίλων μύθων ὡς φιλοθέῳ ὄντι καὶ φιλοξένῳ.

8. Ὁ δὲ Αἴσωπος τοῦ ὕπνου ἐξεγερθεὶς φησιν «οὐᾶ! Πῶς ἡδέως κεκοίμημαι! Ἀλλὰ καὶ καλὸν ὄναρ ἐθεασάμην. Νῦν ἰδοὺ ἀκωλύτως λαλῶ καὶ τὰ βλεπόμενα ὀνομάζω· δίκελλα, ὄνος, βοῦς, ἅμαξα. Νὴ τοὺς θεούς, πόθεν ἔλαβον τὴν χάριν; Νενόηκα,» φησίν, «εὐσεβήσας εἰς τοὺς ἄνδρας τοὺς ξένους. Ὥστε εὐπρόσδεκτον παρὰ θεῷ τὸ ἀγαθοποιεῖν. Ὁ δὲ καλῶς πράσσων λήψεται καλὰς ἐλπίδας.»

9. Περιχαρὴς οὖν γενόμενος ὁ Αἴσωπος καὶ πάλιν λαβὼν τὴν δίκελλαν ἤρξατο σκάπτειν. Ὁ δὲ τῶν ἀγρῶν οἰκονόμος εἰς τὸ ἔργον παραγενόμενος ἕνα τῶν οἰκετῶν ῥάβδῳ κατέξαινεν. Ὁ δὲ Αἴσωπος προσπαθήσας ἔφη «ἄνθρωπε, τί τὸν μηδέν σε ἀδικήσαντα οὕτως εἰκῇ καὶ μάτην κατὰ πᾶσαν ἀποκτείνεις ἡμέραν μηδὲν ἐργαζόμενος; Ἀλλ' ἐγὼ τῷ δεσπότῃ ἀναγγελῶ ἅπαντα.» Ὁ δὲ Ζηνᾶς ἀκούσας (τοῦτο ἦν τῷ οἰκονόμῳ ὄνομα) τοιαῦτα τοῦ Αἰσώπου λέγοντος, ἐθαμβήθη καὶ φησιν «Αἴσωπος λαλεῖν ἀρξάμενος ἐμὲ κέκρουκε. Προκαταλάβομαι αὐτοῦ, ἐπεὶ τοῦ δεσπότου ἐλθόντος κατηγορήσας μεταστήσει με τῆς οἰκονομίας.»

4.1 αὐτοῦ πάλιν post δεσπότης add. O | ζευκτῷ καθίσας : corr. Papath. : ζεύγῳ καθ. Perry : ζ ... θίσας M : ζευτω καθήσας O | εἰς : ἐπὶ O | εἰσῄει : εἴσιση O **2** οἱ ... **3** ἦλθον : συνέβη τοὺς τῆς Ἴσιδος ἱερεῖς πλανηθέντας τῆς λεωφόρου ἐλθεῖν O **3** καὶ : οἳ καὶ O **4** ὁδὸν ... τὴν : evan. in M | ἔσωπος post ὁ δὲ add. O **6** ἀνιμήσατο : ἠντλήσατο O | αὐτοῖς : αὐτοὺς O ‖ **5.**1 τὰς ... τὸν : τὼ χεῖρε εἰς M | αὐτῷ : αὐτὸν O | ὡς : om. O ‖ **6.**2 ἐτράπετο M | **7.**1 Τύχη : φιλοξενία O | αὐτῷ : αὐτὸν O | ἄριστον λόγον inv. O **2** ἐτυμολογίας M | ὡς ... **3** φιλοξένῳ : ὡς φιλόθεον ὄντα καὶ φιλόξενον O ‖ **8.**1 ἐκ τοῦ ὕπνου ἐγερθεὶς O **2** καὶ ἰδοὺ νῦν O **3** λαλῶν καὶ ante νὴ add. O **4** ταύτην post χάριν add. O | εἰς ... ἄνδρας : om. O **5** εὐπρόσδεκτον : δεκτ

4. On the following day the master, seated on a two-horse carriage, went into town. While Aesop was digging in the field, priests of Isis who had wandered off the highway came into the field and asked Aesop to point out the road into the town. He led them beneath a shady tree and set bread and olives and dried figs before them and obliged them to eat; then he ran to the well and drew up water and brought it to them to drink, and he grabbed their hand and led them to the straight and trodden road.

5. They raised both their hands to heaven, and, praying for him on account of his kindness toward them, they went on their way.

6. Aesop turned back, and, enervated by the heat, he betook himself to sleep.

7. But Fortune stood over his slumbers and granted him the finest language and quickness of speech and the invention of ready arguments with colorful fables, since he was kind to gods and kind to guests.

8. Aesop awoke from his nap and said, "Wow! How pleasantly I slept!" And what a fine dream I had. Look now, I am talking unimpededly, and I'm naming what I see: pitchfork, ass, ox, wagon. By the gods, whence did I obtain this gift? I know," he said, "because I was pious toward those men, those strangers. So, doing good deeds is well-received by the god. Whoever acts benevolently will be granted excellent prospects."

9. Aesop was overjoyed, and, taking up the pitchfork again, he began to dig. The steward of the fields, overseeing the work, hit one of the slaves with his staff. Aesop was affected by this and said, "Fellow, why are you tormenting in this way, randomly and arbitrarily, all day long a man who has in no way wronged you, when you yourself are not working? I am going to report everything to the master." When Zenas (for this was the steward's name) heard Aesop saying these things, he was stunned and said, "Aesop has begun to talk and has knocked me. Let me anticipate him, since, if he accuses me when the master arrives, he will remove me from my stewardship."

… O | τῷ ante θεῷ add. O | τὸ ἀγαθὸν ποιεῖν O ‖ **9.1** τὴν δίκελλαν λαβὼν inv. O **2** μετὰ πόνου post ἤρξατο add. O | Ὁ … τῶν : evan. in M **3** ἕνα τῶν οἰκε evan. in M | ῥαύδῳ κατέξενεν O : τύπτει ῥάβδῳ M **4** σε : σοι O | οὕτως … **5** ἐργαζόμενος : ποιεῖς ταῦτα O | μάτην … πᾶσαν : evan. in M **5** ἀποκτείνῃς M | ἀπαγγελῶ O **6** ζήνας O | γὰρ post τοῦτο ex SB suppl. Papath. | τοῦτο … ὄνομα : om. O : post Ζηνᾶς trans. Papath. | τοιαῦτα … **7** λέγοντος : τοῦ ἐσώπου οὕτως λαλοῦντος O **7** ἐθαμβήθη : ἐφοβήθη O | ἐσώπου λαλεῖν ἀρξαμένου O | ἐμὲ … **8** κέκρουκε : corr. Perry, iter. Papath. : -ρουκε evan. in M : ἐμοὶ κεκρούκῃ O **8** αὐτοῦ : αὐτὸς O **9** μεταστήσῃ O

10. Καὶ ταῦτα εἰπὼν ὑποζυγίῳ ἐπιβὰς εἰς τὴν πόλιν εἰσῄει. Παραγενόμενος δὲ πρὸς τὸν δεσπότην εἶπε «χαίροις!» Ὁ δέ φησι «τί τεταραγμένος παρῇς;» Καὶ ὁ Ζηνᾶς· «πρᾶγμα τι τερατῶδες ἐν τῷ ἀγρῷ σου συνέβη.» Ὁ δὲ «τί;», φησι. «Μὴ δένδρον ὄψιμον παρὰ καιρόν τινα καρπὸν ἤνεγκεν ἢ κτῆνος τετράπουν
5 παρὰ φύσιν ἐγέννησεν;» Ὁ δέ· «οὔ,» φησι, «ἀλλ' Αἴσωπος ὁ σαπρὸς λαλεῖν ἤρξατο στωμύλως.» Καὶ ὁ δεσπότης· «μηδέν σοι τῶν ἀγαθῶν γένοιτο! Τοῦτο νομίζεις τερατῶδες εἶναι σημεῖον;» «Καὶ μάλα», φησίν· <ὁ δεσπότης·> «οἱ θεοὶ χολωθέντες ἀνθρώπῳ πρὸς ὀλίγον <χρόνον ἀφείλαντο τὴν φωνὴν αὐτοῦ, νῦν δὲ> πάλιν διαλλαγέντες ἐχαρίσαντο.» Ὁ δὲ Ζηνᾶς· «δέσποτα, λαλεῖν
10 ἀρξάμενος Αἴσωπος πάντα ὑπὲρ ἄνθρωπον φθέγγεται· εἰς ἐμὲ γὰρ ὕβρεις τραχείας φέρει, εἰς σὲ δὲ καὶ τοὺς θεοὺς μεγάλα βλασφημεῖ.»

11. Ὁ δὲ κύριος ὀργισθεὶς λέγει τῷ Ζηνᾷ «ἰδού, ἀπὸ τοῦ νῦν κεχάρισταί σοι. Πώλησον, χάρισον, ἀπόλυσον, ὃ βούλει εἰς αὐτὸν πρᾶξον.» Ὁ δὲ Ζηνᾶς λαβὼν αὐτοῦ τὴν ἐξουσίαν, ἐλθὼν εἰς τὸν ἀγρὸν τῷ Αἰσώπῳ ἔφη «ἐχαρίσθης
15 μοι παρὰ τοῦ δεσπότου ἵνα ὃ δοκήσει μοι εἰς σὲ διαπράξωμαι. Συνεῖδον οὖν πιπράσαι σε.»

12. Ἔτυχεν οὖν σωματέμπορον διὰ τοῦ ἀγροῦ παριέναι, καὶ ὃς ζητῶν μισθώσασθαι κτήνη, συναντήσας τῷ Ζηνᾷ, γνωστῷ αὐτῷ ὄντι, ἠσπάσατο αὐτὸν καί φησιν «ἔχεις μοι κτήνη μισθώσασθαι ἢ πωλῆσαι;» Ζηνᾶς εἶπεν
20 «οὔ, σωμάτιον δὲ ἔχω ἀρρενικὸν εὔωνον. Εἰ θέλεις, ἀγόρασον.» Ὁ ἔμπορος ἔφη «δεῖξόν μοι αὐτό.»

13. Ὁ δὲ Ζηνᾶς στείλας ἤνεγκε τὸν Αἴσωπον καί φησι τῷ ἐμπόρῳ «ἰδοὺ ὁ παῖς· καταμαθὼν ἀγόρασον.»

14. Στραφεὶς δὲ ὁ ἔμπορος καὶ τὸν Αἴσωπον ἰδών, γελάσας εἶπεν «πόθεν
25 σοι ἡ χύτρα αὕτη; ῥοιζοκάλαμός ἐστι ἢ ἄνθρωπος; Οὗτος τῆς τερατομαχίας σαλπιστής ἐστιν. Εἰ μὴ φωνὴν εἶχεν, εἰρήκει τις ὅτι ἀσκοκήλη ἐστίν. Ὦ Ζηνᾶ, μόνον τῆς ὁδοῦ με ἐπλάνησας ἕνεκα τοῦ καθάρματος τούτου, δοκῶν τι ἀγαθὸν πιπράσκειν.» Καὶ ταῦτα εἰπὼν ἐπορεύετο.

10.1 ἐπιζυγίῳ O 2 δὲ¹ : om. O 3 δέσποτα ante πρᾶγμα add. O | τι : om. O | σου : om. O 4 τινα : τι O 6 Καὶ … δεσπότης : om. M 7 εἰκότος post μάλα add. O | φησίν : om. O | ὁ δεσπότης : scripsi : ὁ δεσπότης· διὰ τί; εἰ ex G corr. Perry 8 θεοὶ : om. M | χολωθέντες ἀνθρώπῳ : σχολασθέντες ἐν ἀνθρώπῳ O | χρόνον … 9 δὲ¹ : ex G rest. Perry, iter. Papath. 10 ἀρξαμένου O | Αἴσωπος : om. O | γὰρ : δὲ O 11 φέρει : ἐκφέρειν O | εἰς : om. O ‖ **11.**1 κύριος : om. O | κεχάρισθαι O 2 πρᾶσσε M | Ὁ … Ζηνᾶς : ὁ δὲ ζῆνας ἀκούσας καὶ O 4 ἵνα : om. O | δοκήσῃ M | διαπράξω O 5 πιπράσαι σε : πιπράσσεσαι O ‖ **12.**1 τινά post σωματέμπορον

10. With these words he mounted an ass and proceeded to the town. When he arrived at the master, he said, "Greetings!" The master said, "Why did you show up so disturbed?" And Zenas said, "A very strange thing happened in your field." "What?" said the other; "Was it a tree that bore late fruit out of season or a four-footed animal that gave birth unnaturally?" "No," said the other, "it's rather that misshapen Aesop has begun to speak fluently." The master: "May nothing good happen to you! You think this is a monstrous sign?" "Certainly," he said. <And the master:> "The gods were angry at the man and for a short while took away his voice, and now they have become reconciled and given it back again." But Zenas said, "Master, Aesop, now that he has begun to talk, he speaks above himself. For he levies coarse insults against me and blasphemes greatly against you and the gods."

11. The master grew angry and said to Zenas, "See here, from now on, he's given to you: sell him, give him away, set him free, do whatever you want to him." Zenas, having gained this authority from him, went to the field and said to Aesop, "You have been handed over to me by the master, so that I can do to you whatever I shall decide. I have resolved, then, to sell you."

12. A slave merchant happened to arrive at the field, who was looking to rent some animals, and he met Zenas, who was an acquaintance, and greeted him and said, "Can you rent or sell me some animals?" Zenas replied, "No, but I have a male slave at a good price; buy him, if you like." The merchant said, "Show him to me."

13. Zenas sent for and brought Aesop and said to the merchant, "Look, here is the slave; examine and buy him."

14. When the merchant turned round and saw Aesop, he laughed and said, "Where did you get this crock? Is he a whistling reed or a human being? This one is the bugler for a monster war. If he didn't have a voice, one would say that he was a wineskin made out of a hump. O Zenas, you only diverted me from the road on account of this trash here, thinking to sell me something good." And having said this, he went on his way.

---

add. O | παριέναι : παρειέν O | ὅς : om. O **2** καὶ ante συναντήσας add. O **3** αὐτὸν : αὐτῷ O | μοι : post μισθώσασθαι trans. O **5** αὐτό : αὐτῷ O ‖ **13.1** Ζηνᾶς : om. O | τῷ ἐμπόρῳ : om. O ‖ **14.1** τὸν ... ἰδών : om. O | εἶπεν : ἔφη O **2** ῥοιζοκάλαμός : corr. Stamoulakis, iter. Papath. : ῥιζοκάλαμος O : ῥιζοκάλαμον M **3** εἰρήκει : εἴρηκα O : εἰρήκειν ἂν corr. Perry ex G, iter. Papath. : εἰρήκοι Westermann | τις : om. O | ἀσκοκύλη O **4** εἵνεκα O | τούτου : τοῦδε M | ἀγαθόν τι inv. O

15. Καταδραμὼν δὲ αὐτὸν Αἴσωπος ἔφη «μεῖνον». Ὁ δὲ πρὸς αὐτόν φησιν· «Ἄφες με! Μηδέν σοι τῶν ἀγαθῶν γένοιτο. Ὅ τι προσεκαλέσω με, παρατήρημα;». Αἴσωπος ἔφη «ἕνεκα τίνος ἐνθάδε ἐλήλυθας;» Ὁ ἔμπορος «δοκῶ τι ἀγαθὸν ὠνήσασθαι. Σαπρὸς εἶ πάνυ καὶ κακοῦ οὐ χρῄζω.» Αἴσωπος λέγει «ἀγόρασόν με καὶ πολύ σε ὠφελήσω.» Ὁ δὲ πρὸς αὐτόν· «Τί δύνασαι σὺ ὠφελῆσαί με;» Αἴσωπος ἔφη· «Οὐκ ἔχεις ἐν τῷ σωματεμπορείῳ σου παιδία κλαίοντα ἢ ἀτακτοῦντα; Ἀγόρασόν με καὶ κατάστησόν με παιδαγωγόν. Καὶ ἔσομαι αὐτοῖς ἀντὶ μορμολυκίου φοβέριστρον.» Ὁ δὲ ἔμπορος πεισθεὶς τῷ λόγῳ καὶ στραφεὶς λέγει τῷ Ζηνᾷ· «Πόσου τὸ κακὸν τοῦτο πωλεῖς;» Ζηνᾶς λέγει «δὸς τριώβολον». Ὁ δὲ ἔμπορος γελάσας ἔδωκε τὸ τριώβολον, λογισάμενος ὅτι οὐδὲν τοῦ μηδενὸς ἠγόρακεν.

16. Ὁδεύσαντες δὲ εἰς τὴν πόλιν εἰσῆλθον εἰς τὸ σωματεμπορεῖον. Δύο δὲ παιδία ὑπὸ μητέρα ὄντα, ὡς εἶδον τὸν Αἴσωπον, ἀνέκραξαν καὶ κατεκρύβησαν. Ὁ δὲ Αἴσωπος τῷ ἐμπόρῳ ἔφη· «Ἔχεις μου ἤδη τῆς ἐπαγγελίας ἀπόδειξιν, ὅτι κατὰ παιδίων προυνικῶν ἕτοιμον ὤνησω μορμολύκιον.» Ὁ δὲ γελάσας λέγει «Αἴσωπε, εἴσελθε εἰς τὸν ἐνδότερον τρίκλινον καὶ ἄσπασαι τοὺς συνδούλους σου.» Εἰσελθὼν οὖν εὑρίσκει παῖδας καλλίστους καὶ ἀμώμους καὶ ἀσπάζεται αὐτοὺς λέγων «χαίρετε, σύνδουλοι.» Οἱ δὲ ὁμοφώνως εἶπον «σαπρόν, νὴ τὸν Ἥλιον! Τί γέγονε τῷ δεσπότῃ; Ὅτι οὐδέποτε κακοπινὲς ἠγόρασε σωμάτιον. Πλὴν πρὸς βασκανίαν τοῦ σωματεμπορείου αὐτὸν ὠνήσατο.»

17. Ὁ δὲ ἔμπορος πρὸς τοὺς παῖδας εἰσελθὼν ἔφη· «Στενάξατε τὴν ἑαυτῶν τύχην. Κτήνη γὰρ οὔτε ἀγοράσαι οὔτε μισθώσασθαι εὗρον. Διέλεσθε οὖν τὰ ἐφόδια σκεύη. Αὔριον γὰρ ἀπαίρομεν εἰς τὴν Ἀσίαν.» Οἱ οὖν παῖδες σὺν δύο γενόμενοι ἐμερίζοντο τὰ σκεύη. Ὁ δὲ Αἴσωπος ὑποπεσὼν εἶπε· «Καλοὶ σύνδουλοι, ἐπεὶ νεώνητος καὶ ἀσθενής εἰμι, παραχωρήσατέ μοι τὸ

15.1 αὐτὸν : om. O | ὁ αἴσωπος O | περίμεινον O **2** φησιν : post ἄφες trans. O | με : om. O | τὸ ἀγαθὸν O | γένοιτο : M^sl : γένησαι M : γενήσεται O | Ὅ τι : MO : τί Perry corr. "cum G" : <τί> ὅτι Papath. | προσεκαλέσω με : προσκαλέσομαι O **3** παρατήρημα : παρατήρημα ὤν O : del. Perry : περίτριμμα Papath. | Αἴσωπος … ἔφη : om. O | καὶ ὁ ἔμπορος φησί O **4** ὠνήσεσθαι O | δὲ post σαπρὸς add. O | κακὸν O **5** με : μοι O | σὺ : om. O **6** με : μοι O | Αἴσωπος … ἔφη : Καὶ ὁ ἔσωπος O | σωτεμπορίῳ O | σου : om. O **7** με² : om. M **8** φοβέριστρον : om. O **9** πόσον O **10** Ζηνᾶς … λέγει : καὶ ὁ ζηνᾶς O | ἔμπορος : om. O **11** λογιζόμενος O | ὅτι … ἠγόρακεν : ὅτι οὐδὲν τῶ ὄντων μηδὲν ἠγόρακί O |

15. Aesop ran after him and said, "Wait!" The merchant said to him, "Let go of me! May nothing good happen to you. Why have you called out to me, you piece of rubbish?" Aesop said, "Why have you come here?" The merchant said, "Because I thought to purchase something good. You are thoroughly misshapen, and I don't need some miserable thing." Aesop declared, "Buy me and I will be of great use to you." The merchant answered him, "How can you be of use to me?" Aesop said, "Don't you have in your slave market crying or disorderly children? Buy me and make me their tutor, and I will be more terrifying to them than the boogeyman." The merchant was persuaded by this argument and turned and said to Zenas, "How much are you selling this miserable thing for?" Zenas said, "Give me a three-obol coin." The merchant laughed and gave him a three-obol coin, reasoning that he had bought nothing for nothing.

16. As they were traveling to the town they entered the slave market. When two children who were right by their mother saw Aesop, they cried out and hid. Aesop said to the merchant, "You now have the proof of my promise, that you have bought a ready boogeyman against mischievous children." The merchant laughed and averred, "Aesop, go into the inner dining room and greet your fellow slaves." So Aesop went in and found the finest slaves, without a blemish, and he greeted them, saying, "Hello, my fellow slaves." They replied with one voice, "You misshapen thing, by the Sun! What's happened to the master? He's never yet purchased a loathsome slave, but he's bought this one as as a charm against the evil eye for the slave market."

17. The merchant came up to the slaves and said, "Groan over your own fortune! For I did not find any animals to buy or to rent, so distribute the baggage to carry among yourselves. Tomorrow we depart for Asia." The slaves in pairs divided up the baggage, but Aesop fell to his knees and said, "Excellent fellow slaves, since I am newly purchased and weak, let me

---

πλέον post οὐδὲν add. Papath. ‖ **16.**1 σωματεμπόριον O (ν evan.) | δὲ² : μέντοι M 4 προυνικῶν : ἀνήβων M | ἑτοίμων O | ὠνήσομαι O | μορμολύκιον corr. Perry : μόρμυκα M : μέρμυκα O 5 καὶ : om. O 6 οὖν : δὲ O | εὑρίσκει παῖδας : δύο παῖδας πρῶτον εὑρίσκει M 7 σαπρόν νὴ : σαπρὸς ἦν O 8 ἦ ante τί add. O | τὸ οὐδέπω M | τοιοῦτον post κακοπινὲς add. O | ἠγόρακεν O 9 πρὸς βασκανίαν : πρὸς ἀβασκανίαν corr. Papath. : προβασκάνιον corr. Westermann | σωματεμπορίου O ‖ **17.**1 πρὸς ... ἔφη : πρὸς αὐτούς O 2 ἑαυτούς O | ἀγοράσαι : ἠγόρασα O 3 καὶ post οὖν add. M 3 Αὔριον ... 4 σκεύη : om. O 5 νεώνητος ... εἰμι : νεώνητός εἰμι καὶ ἀσθενής O

ἐλαφρότερον φορτίον.» Οἱ δέ φασιν «ἐὰν οὐ δύνῃ, μηδὲν ἄρῃς.» Αἴσωπος λέγει· «ἀπόπληκτόν ἐστι πάντων κοπιώντων ἐμὲ μόνον ἀχάριστον τῷ δεσπότῃ φαίνεσθαι.» Οἱ δέ φασιν «ὃ θέλεις ἆρον».

18. Ὁ δὲ περιβλεψάμενος ὧδε κἀκεῖσε θεωρεῖ σκεύη καὶ ἀγγεῖα διάφορα τὰ πρὸς ἐκδημίαν, σάκκους, στρώματα καὶ γοργάθους. Ἰδὼν δὲ ἕνα γόργαθον μεστὸν ἄρτων, ὃν ἐβούλοντο δύο ἆραι, εἶπεν· «ἐμοὶ τοῦτον φορτώσατε.» Οἱ δὲ λοιποὶ ἔλεγον· «τί μωρότερον τοῦ ἀνθρώπου τούτου; Παρεκάλει τὸ πάντων ἐλαφρότερον φορτίον ἆραι καὶ τὸ βαρύτερον πάντων ἐξελέξατο. Τὴν ἐπιθυμίαν αὐτοῦ πληρώσωμεν.» Ἐπιτιθέασιν οὖν αὐτῷ τὸν γόργαθον καὶ ἐκίνησε διακλονούμενος. Ὁ δὲ ἔμπορος ἰδὼν αὐτὸν ἐθαύμασε καί φησι «Αἴσωπος πρόθυμος εἰς τὸ κοπιᾶν καὶ τοὺς λοιποὺς προτρεπόμενος γενναίως φέρειν. Ἤδη αὐτοῦ τὴν τιμὴν ἔσωσε· κτήνους γὰρ φορτίον ᾖρεν.»

19. Οἱ δὲ λοιποὶ σύνδυο βαστάζοντες κατεγέλων αὐτοῦ. Ἐκεῖνος δὲ εἰς τὴν ὁδὸν ἐλθών, τὸν γόργαθον θεὶς περιπατεῖν ἐδίδασκεν. Εἰ γὰρ εἰς ἀνάβασιν ἐληλύθει, ταῖς χερσὶν καὶ τοῖς ὀδοῦσιν ἕλκων ἀνεκύλιε τὸν γόργαθον. Εἰ δὲ εἰς κατάβασιν, συντομώτερον ἐκύλιε αὐτόν. Καὶ οὕτως ἐκοπία ἕως εἰς πανδοχεῖον ἦλθον. Ὁ δὲ ἔμπορος θέλων τὰ σωμάτια ἀναλαβέσθαι ἐκέλευσεν αὐτὰ ἀναπεσεῖν. Καί φησι τῷ Αἰσώπῳ «ἀρτοδότησον.» Ὁ δὲ ἑκάστῳ ζεύγει ἄρτον παρέθηκε. Πολλῶν δὲ ἀρτοδοτηθέντων ἡμίκενος ὁ γόργαθος γέγονε. Μετὰ δὲ τὸ ἀναλαβέσθαι τὰ σωμάτια, πάλιν ὁδοιπορούντων ὁ Αἴσωπος προθυμότερος εἰς τὴν μονὴν παρεγένετο. Ἀρτοδοτήσας δὲ τῇ ἑσπέρᾳ τὸν γόργαθον κατεκένωσε. Τῇ δὲ ἐπαύριον κενὸν αὐτὸν ἐπὶ τῶν ὤμων περιβαλόμενος ἔμπροσθεν προέτρεχεν. Οἱ δὲ σύνδουλοι εἰς ἀλλήλους ἔλεγον· «τίς ἐστιν ὁ ἔμπροσθεν τρέχων; Ξένος ἡμῶν ἐστιν;» Ἄλλος ἔφη· «ὁ σαπρὸς ἐκεῖνός ἐστιν.» Ἄλλος λέγει· «οὐκ οἴδατε τὸ ἀνθρωπάριον τοῦτο πῶς φρονίμως ἔδρασεν ὑπὲρ πάντας ἡμᾶς; Ἡμεῖς γὰρ στρώματα καὶ τὰ λοιπὰ σκεύη τὰ μὴ δυνάμενα δαπανηθῆναι ἄραντες κοπιῶμεν, ἐκεῖνος δὲ τοὺς προχείρως δαπανωμένους ἄρτους ὡς πανοῦργος ᾖρεν.»

17.7 ἐστι : absc. in M | ἀχάριστον ... 8 φαίνεσθαι : τῷ δεσπότῃ ἀχάριστον φαίνεσθαι inv. O ‖ **18.**1 καὶ : om. O 2 καὶ ante στρώματα add. O 4 λοιποὶ : om. O | ποῖον ante τί add. O 6 πληρώσωμεν : ποιήσωμεν M | ἐπιτιθέασιν O | αὐτῷ : αὐτὸν O 7 διακλονούμενος : ex GSA corr. Perry, iter. Papath. : διακλώμενος M (fort. recte) : διὰ κελόμενος O 8 εἰς post καὶ add. O 9 ἔσωσα O ‖ **19.**1 κατεγέλων αὐτοῦ : κατέλεγον αὐτῷ καὶ κατεγέλουν O 2 διελθὼν O 3 ταῖς ... ἕλκων : καὶ τοῖς ὀδοῦσιν καὶ ταῖς χερσὶν εἷλκων O | ἀνεκύλιε O 4 Εἰ : ἐὰν M | κατάβασι O | ἐκύλιε O | αὐτόν : τὸν γόργαθον O 5 ἦλθον : ἐλθὼν O 6 αὐτὰ : αὐτοὺς O |

have the lighter burden." And they said, "if you are unable, don't pick up anything." Aesop replied, "It's terrible that when everyone is working hard I alone should appear thankless to the master." And they said, "Pick up what you wish."

18. Aesop looked around here and there, and he saw baggage and various jugs for travel abroad, sacks, bedding, and baskets. Noticing one basket that was full of breads, which one pair wished to pick up, he said, "Load this one on me." The others exclaimed, "What is dumber than this fellow? He asked us if he could pick up the lightest burden of all, and he has selected the heaviest of all. Let's fulfill his desire." So they put the basket on his back, and he started walking unsteadily. When the merchant saw him, he was amazed and said, "Aesop is eager for hard work, and he motivates the others to bear their load with dignity. He has redeemed his price, since he has picked up the burden of an animal."

19. The other pairs carried theirs and laughed at him, but he started on the road and, putting down the basket, taught it to walk. For if he was going uphill, he pulled the basket with his hands and teeth and rolled it up, but if he was going downhill, he rolled it more quickly. He toiled in this way until they arrived at an inn. The merchant wished to refresh the slaves and ordered them to lie at ease, and he said to Aesop, "Give them bread!" Aesop served a loaf to each pair, and after many loaves had been distributed the basket was half-empty. Once the slaves were refreshed, as they resumed their journey Aesop arrived still more eager at the stopover. In the evening, he distributed the loaves and emptied the basket, and the next day he tossed it, empty, on his shoulders and was running up ahead. His fellow slaves said to one another, "Who is that running up ahead? Is it some stranger among us?" But another said, "It's that misshapen fellow," and another said, "Don't you realize how cleverly that little fellow put one over on all of us? We picked up the bedding and the rest of the baggage that could not be consumed, and we toil carrying it, while he, the wily fellow, picked up the bread, which was immediately consumed."

ζεύγει : ex WPLF corr. Perry, iter. Papath. : ζεύ^γ M : ζευγαρίῳ O **7** ἄρτων M | περιέθηκε O | ἄρτων δοθέντων O | ἐγένετο O **8** ὁδοιποροῦντες O **9** τὴν : om. O **10** ἐκένωσεν O fort. recte (cf. WLF) | ἐπὶ ... περιβαλόμενος : exsp. ἐπὶ τῶν ὤμων ἀναλαβὼν (cf. SBW) : ἐπὶ τῶν ὤμον περιβαλλόμενος M : ἀνέλαβεν ἐπὶ τῶν ὤμων καὶ O **11** ἔμπρ. πάντων διέτρεχεν O **11–12** ὁ ... τρέχων : ὁ προπορευόμενος ἡμῖν O **12** ἔφη : ἔλεγεν O **13** Ἄλλος : ἕτερος O

20. Ὁδοιπορήσαντες οὖν ἦλθον εἰς Ἔφεσον. Καὶ πιπράσας ἐκεῖ τὰ σωμάτια ἐκέρδησε. Κατελείφθησαν δὲ αὐτῷ τρία· γραμματικός, ψάλτης καὶ ὁ Αἴσωπος. Τὶς δὲ φίλος λέγει τῷ ἐμπόρῳ· «ἐὰν θέλῃς τὰ σωμάτια πιπράσαι, πέρασον εἰς τὴν Σάμον. Ξάνθος γὰρ ὁ φιλόσοφος ἐκεῖ οἰκεῖ καὶ πολλοὶ τῆς Ἑλλάδος καὶ τῶν νήσων πρὸς αὐτὸν φοιτῶσι ἐν εὐπορίᾳ ὄντες.» Πεισθεὶς οὖν ὁ ἔμπορος τῇ τοῦ φίλου γνώμῃ παρεγένετο εἰς τὴν Σάμον.

21. Καὶ τὸν μὲν ψάλτην εὔκνημον ὄντα λευκοὺς ὑπέδυσε χιτῶνας καὶ ὑποδήματα καὶ τὴν τρίχα κτενίσας, ἔστησεν ἐπὶ τοῦ πρατείου. Τὸν δὲ γραμματικὸν δεύτερον ὄντα προσβλεπτέον βαθεῖς ἐνέδυσε χιτῶνας καὶ ὑποδήματα· κτενίσας δὲ τὴν τρίχα καὶ σουδάριον δοὺς ἔστησεν ἐπὶ τοῦ πρατείου. Τὸν δὲ Αἴσωπον μὴ ἔχων τί ἀποκρύψαι ἢ τί κοσμῆσαι, ἐπείπερ ὅλως ἦν ἁμάρτημα, ἐνέδυσεν αὐτὸν σακκοχίτωνα καὶ τῶν καλῶν ἔστησεν εἰς μέσον. Πολλοὶ δὲ κατανοοῦντες τὰ σωμάτια, ὁρῶντες τὸν Αἴσωπον πρὸς ἀλλήλους ἔλεγον· «πόθεν τὸ κακὸν τοῦτο; Οὗτος καὶ τοὺς ἄλλους ἀφανίζει.» Ὁ δὲ Αἴσωπος ὑπὸ πολλῶν σκωπτόμενος τολμηρῶς εἰστήκει.

22. Ὁ δὲ Ξάνθος εἰς τὴν σχολὴν προελθὼν καὶ τὴν μελέτην στερεώσας ἧκε σὺν τοῖς φίλοις ἐπὶ τῆς ἀγορᾶς θεάσασθαι.

23. Ὡς δὲ εἶδε τοὺς δύο παῖδας εὐπρεπεῖς, τὸν δὲ μέσον σαπρόν, ἐθαύμασεν τοῦ ἐμπόρου τὴν ἐπίνοιαν καί φησι πρὸς τοὺς φίλους· «ὁ ἔμπορος οὐ χάριν τῆς πράσεως τοὺς μὲν εὐειδεῖς παῖδας ἔξωθεν ἔστησε, καὶ μέσον τὸν σαπρόν, ἀλλ' ἵνα τὸ ἀειδὲς τῷ κάλλει παρατεθὲν τὴν τούτων ἀρετὴν ἐμφανεστέραν δείξῃ.»

24. Ἐπιστὰς οὖν τῷ πρώτῳ παιδὶ εἶπε· «πόθεν εἶ καὶ τί σου τὸ ὄνομα;» Κἀκεῖνος ἔφη· «Καππάδοξ εἰμί, Τύρος καλοῦμαι.» «Τί οὖν οἶδας ποιεῖν;» Ἐκεῖνος ἔφη «πάντα». Ὁ δὲ Αἴσωπος ἐγέλασεν. Οἱ δὲ σχολαστικοὶ ὡς εἶδον αὐτὸν ἐξαίφνης γελάσαντα, μόνον δὲ τοὺς ὀδόντας αὐτοῦ φανεροὺς ὄντας, τέρας ἐδόκουν θεωρεῖν. Ἔλεγον δὲ πρὸς ἀλλήλους· «οὐχὶ κήλη ἐστὶν

20.2 τρεῖς O | γραμματικοί, ψάλται O 3 τοῦ ἐμπόρου post φίλος add. O | τῷ ἐμπόρῳ : αὐτῷ O 4 ἐκεῖσε O 5 φοιτῶντες O | ἐν ... ὄντες : ἐν ἀπορίᾳ O | ἀγοράσωσιν αὐτούς post ὄντες add. O 6 ὁ ἔμπορος : om. O ‖ 21.1 ἅμα τῷ γραμματικῷ post ψάλτην add. O | εὐκνήμους ὄντας O | ὑπέδησε M : ὑπενέδυσε O : ὑπενέδυσε corr. Perry, iter. Papath. 2 εἰς τοὺς πόδας post ὑποδήματα add. O | καὶ νήψας post κτενίσας add. O | πρατηρίου O | Τὸν ... 4 πρατείου : om. O 3 προσβλεπτέον : corr. Papath. : πρόβλεπτον M 5 ἀποκρύψαι ... κοσμῆσαι : κοσμῆσαι ἢ εὖ ... σαι (εὐτρεπῆσαι leg. Papath.) ἢ ἀποκρύψαι O | ὅλως : ὅλος ex P corr. Papath. 6 σακκοχίτωνα : σάκκον O | καὶ ... μέσον : καὶ ἔστησεν μέσον τῶν δύο εὐειδῶν παίδων O 7 κατανοοῦντες : καὶ ἀγνοοῦντες O | αὐτῶν post σωμάτια add. O |

20. And so they proceeded and arrived at Ephesus, where the merchant sold the slaves and made a profit. Three were left: a teacher, a lyre player, and Aesop. A friend of his said to the merchant, "If you wish to sell your slaves, take them over to Samos, since Xanthus the philosopher lives there, and many people from Greece and the islands who are well-to-do resort to him." The merchant heeded the opinion of his friend and went to Samos.

21. Since the lyre player had fine legs, the merchant dressed him in a white tunic and sandals and combed his hair and set him on the selling block. The teacher, who was second best to look at, he dressed in a long tunic and sandals, combed his hair, and giving him a neckerchief he set him on the selling block. But since he had no way to conceal or adorn Aesop, since he was an utter failure, he dressed him in a sack-like tunic and set him between the handsomer ones. Many people were inspecting the slaves, and seeing Aesop they said to one another, "Where's this thing from? He eclipses even the others." Though he was mocked by many people, Aesop stood there courageously.

22. Xanthus first went to his school and made his lecture stronger and then came with his friends to the marketplace to look around.

23. When he saw the two good-looking slaves, with the misshapen one in the middle, he was impressed by the intelligence of the merchant and said to his friends, "The merchant did not set the two handsome slaves on the outside and the misshapen one in the middle for the sake of a sale; it was rather so that, by placing the ugly alongside the beautiful, he might show off their excellence more conspicuously."

24. And so, standing next to the first slave, he said, "Where are you from, and what is your name?" And he answered, "I am a Cappadocian, and I am called Tyros." "And what can you do?" And he said, "Everything." And Aesop laughed. When the students saw him suddenly laughing, with only his teeth visible, they thought they were seeing a monster, and they

---

πρὸς ... ἔλεγον : ἔφασκον O 8 τὸ κακὸν : om. M 9 ἱστήκει O ‖ **22.1** Ὁ ... προελθὼν : Ξάνθος δὲ ὁ φιλόσοφος εἰς τὴν σκόλην εἰσελθών O 2 ἐπὶ ... θεάσασθαι : εἰς τὴν ἀγοράν O ‖ **23.1** Ὡς ... εἶδε : θεασάμενος O | μὲν post τοὺς add. O | ἔνθεν κἀκεῖθεν ἱσταμένους post εὐπρεπεῖς add. O | τὸν ... σαπρόν : τὸν δὲ σαπρὸν μέσον inv. O 2 βαβαὶ τῆς πανουργίας post φίλους add. O | ὁ ἔμπορος : om. O 3 μὲν : om. O | ἔστησεν O | ἀλλ' : om. O 4 τῷ : om. O ‖ **24.1** εἶπε : ἐπυνθάνετο O | εἶ : ἦ O | καὶ ... ὄνομα : καὶ τί αὐτοῦ ὄνομα O 2 τῆρος O | φησίν post οὖν add. O 3 Ἐκεῖνος ἔφη : ὁ δὲ O | Ὁ δὲ : om. O | ἑστὼς post Αἴσωπος add. O | Οἱ : ὁ O 4 καὶ τὸ πρόσωπον τυγρὸν καὶ σκυθρωπὸν γεγονώς post γελάσαντα add. O | αὐτοῦ : om. O 5 ὄντας : γενέσθαι O

82 Life of Aesop the Philosopher

ὀδόντας ἔχουσα;» Ἄλλος ἔφη· «τί ἰδὼν ἐγέλασεν;» Ἕτερος λέγει· «οὐ γελᾷ, ἀλλὰ ριγᾷ. Γνώσωμεν δὲ τί λαλεῖ.» Ἐλθὼν οὖν ἐξ ὄπισθεν εἵλκυσεν αὐτὸν καί φησι· «κομψότατε, τί ἐγέλασας;» Ὁ δὲ ἐπιστραφεὶς ἔφη· «ὑποχώρει, θαλάσσιον πρόβατον.» Ὁ σχολαστικὸς διαπορηθεὶς ἐπὶ τὸ ῥηθὲν ὑπεχώρησεν.
5 Ὁ Ξάνθος τῷ ἐμπόρῳ ἔφη· «πόσου ὁ ψάλτης οὗτος;» Ὁ δὲ λέγει, «χιλίων δηναρίων». Ὁ δὲ ἀκούσας ἐν ὑπερβολῇ τὸ τίμημα πρὸς τὸν ἕτερον ἦλθεν καί φησι· «σὺ πόθεν εἶ;» Ὁ δὲ ἔφη «Λυδός.» «Ὄνομα δέ σοι τί;» Ὁ δέ, «Φιλόκαλος». Ξάνθος λέγει «τί οἶδας ποιεῖν;» Ὁ παῖς λέγει «πάντα.» Ὁ δὲ Αἴσωπος πάλιν ἀνεγέλασεν. Οἱ δὲ σχολαστικοὶ ἰδόντες ἔλεγον· «τί ἄρα
10 πάνυ προσγελᾷ;» Ἕτερος εἶπεν· «ἐὰν θέλω πάλιν θαλάσσιος τράγος ἀκοῦσαι, ἐπερωτήσω αὐτόν.» Ὁ Ξάνθος τῷ ἐμπόρῳ ἔφη· «πόσου τὸν γραμματικὸν πωλεῖς;» «Τρισχιλίων δηναρίων», ἐκεῖνος ἔφη. Ὁ Ξάνθος ἀκούσας ἠκηδίασε καὶ στραφεὶς ἐπορεύετο. Οἱ δὲ σχολαστικοὶ εἶπον· «καθηγητά, οὐκ ἤρεσάν σοι τὰ σωμάτια;» «Ναί,» φησι, «ἀλλὰ δόγμα ἐστὶ πολύτιμα μὴ ἀγοράζειν
15 παιδάρια, δι' εὐτελῶν δὲ σωματίων δουλεύεσθαι.» Εἷς δὲ τῶν σχολαστικῶν φησι· «εἰ παράγγελμά ἐστι πολυτελῆ μὴ ὠνεῖσθαι, ἀγόρασον τοῦτον τὸν ἀειδῆ. Τὴν γὰρ αὐτὴν παρέχεται διακονίαν. Ἡμεῖς δὲ κατὰ κοινοῦ δώσομεν τὸ τίμημα.» Ὁ δέ φησι «γελοῖόν ἐστιν ὑμῶν τὴν τιμὴν διδόντων ἐμὲ δοῦλον ἀγοράσαι. Καὶ καθαρὸν ὂν τὸ γύναιον οὐκ ἀνέξεται ὑπὸ αἰσχροῦ δουλεύεσθαι
20 σωματίου.» Οἱ δὲ σχολαστικοὶ εἶπον· «καθηγητά, αἱ πλείονές σου διδαχαὶ εἰσι γυναικὶ μὴ πείθεσθαι.»

25. Ὁ Ξάνθος ἔφη· «ἐπιγνῶμεν εἰ οἶδέ τι, μὴ καὶ τὸ τίμημα κενῇ χάριτι προσαπόληται.» Προσελθὼν οὖν τῷ Αἰσώπῳ ἔφη· «χαῖρε.» Ὁ δέ φησι «διὰ τί γάρ; Λυποῦμαι;» Ὁ Ξάνθος ἔφη «ἀσπάζομαί σε.» Ὁ δέ, «κἀγὼ σέ.» Ὁ Ξάνθος
25 ἅμα τοῖς λοιποῖς καταπλαγεὶς ἐπὶ τὸ τῆς ἀπολογίας ἕτοιμον πάλιν πρὸς αὐτὸν ἔφη· «ποταπὸς εἶ;» Ὁ δέ, «σάρκινος.» Ἔφη ὁ Ξάνθος· «οὐ τοῦτο λέγω, ἀλλὰ ποῦ ἐγεννήθης;» «Ἐν τῇ κοιλίᾳ τῆς μητρός μου,» ἔφη. «Οὐ τοῦτο ἐρωτῶ,

---

24.6 Ἄλλος ... ἔφη : ἄλλος ἔλεγεν O | λέγει : ἔφη O 7 εἷς post οὖν add. O | εἵλκυσεν αὐτὸν ἐξ ὄπισθεν inv. O 8 Ὁ ... ἔφη : ὁ δὲ στραφεὶς πρὸς αὐτὸν λέγει O 9 Ὁ ... σχολαστικὸς : ὁ δὲ σχολαστικὸς O 10 Ὁ ... Ξάνθος : ὁ δὲ Ξ. O | λέγει : om. O : εἶπεν atramento rubro in margine sinistra in ms. M 11 Ὁ ... ἀκούσας : ὡς οὖν ἤκουσεν O | ἐν : om. O 12 λῦδος M | τί σοι inv. O | Ὁ δέ : καὶ ἀπεκρίνατο O 13 Ξάνθος ... τί : τί φησίν O | Ὁ¹ ... λέγει² : καὶ ὁ παῖς O | Ὁ² ... 14 δὲ¹ : καὶ ὁ O 14 ἐγέλασεν O 15 πάνυ : om. O | προσγελᾷ : πρὸς πάλιν γελᾷ O | ἐπερωτῆσαι αὐτὸν post πάλιν add. O | θαλλάττιος O 16 ἐπερωτήσω αὐτόν : μέλλω O | Ὁ : om. O 17 ὁ δὲ ante τρισχιλίων add. O | ἐκεῖνος ἔφη: om. O | ἀκηδίασεν O 19 δόγματα O | ἀγοράζειν : ὠνεῖσθαι O 20 χρὴ post σωματίων add. O 21 πολυτελῆ : πολύτιμα O 22 αὐτὴν : αὐτοῦ O 24 Καὶ καθαρὸν : ἀλλὰ καὶ σπαστρικὸν καὶ κενόδοξον O 25 πλείοναί O

said to one another, "Is that some tumor with teeth? And another said, "What did he see that made him laugh?" And another said, "He isn't laughing; he's shivering. Let's find out what he says." So coming up to him from behind, he drew him aside and said, "My clever fellow, what did you laugh at?" Aesop turned round and said, "Back off, you sea goat." Disconcerted by this remark, the student backed away. Xanthus said to the merchant, "How much is this lyre player?" and the merchant said, "A thousand dinars." When he heard the excessive price, he went up to the other and said, "Where are you from?" He replied, "I am a Lydian." "And what is your name?" And he said, "Philocalus." Xanthus said, "What can you do?" And the slave said, "Everything." Again, Aesop laughed. Seeing him, the students said, "What on earth is he laughing at?" The other said, "If I want to hear 'sea goat' again, I'll ask him." Xanthus said to the merchant, "How much are you selling the teacher for?" "Three thousand dinars," he said. When Xanthus heard this, he was discouraged, and he turned and was on the point of leaving. But the students said, "Professor, didn't the slaves please you?" "Yes," he said, "but it is my principle not to buy expensive young slaves but to be served by cheap slaves." One of the students said, "If it is your precept not to purchase expensive slaves, buy this ugly one, since he provides the same service. We'll give you the amount jointly." But Xanthus said, "It's ridiculous that I should buy a slave and you give me the compensation. My wife is classy and will not put up with being served by an ugly slave." The students said, "Professor, most of your teachings say: do not obey a woman."

25. Xanthus said, "Let us find out if he knows anything, so that the cost isn't wasted in addition to an empty favor." So he approached Aesop and said, "Cheers!" And he answered, "Why so? Am I suffering?" Xanthus said, "I greet you." And Aesop answered, "And I you." Xanthus, along with the others, was amazed at his readiness of speech, and he said to him once more, "What are you?" And he replied, "Flesh." Xanthus said, "I don't mean that, but where were you born?" "In my mother's womb," he said.

---

26 μὴ πείθεσθαι γυναικί inv. O | καὶ ὡς σὺ γυναίου λόγον (λ. supra lin.) πληρεῖς post πείθεσθαι add. O ‖ **25.1** ποτε post τι add. M **2** προσαπόληται : corr. Perry, iter. Papath. : προσαπολῆται M : πρὸς ἀπόλυται O | Προσελθὼν οὖν : καὶ προσελθὼν O | ἔφη : εἶπε O | φησι : om. O | διά : om. O **3** ἐλυπώμην O | ἔφη : om. O | Ὁ δέ : ὁ Αἴσωπος λέγει O | Ὁ Ξάνθος² : ὁ δὲ Ξ. O **4** ἅμα ... λοιποῖς : om. O | ἐπὶ τὸ ἕτοιμον τῆς ἀπολογίας inv. O | πάλιν : om. O **5** ἔφη : λέγει O | σαρκίνος O | Ἔφη ... Ξάνθος : om. O | λέγω : ἐρωτῶ λέγει ὁ φιλόσοφος O **6** ἐρωτῶ : λέγω O

ἀλλὰ ποίῳ τόπῳ ἐγεννήθης;» Αἴσωπος ἔφη· «οὐκ ἀνήγγειλέ μοι ἡ μήτηρ μου πότερον ἐν κοιτῶνι ἢ ἐν τρικλίνῳ.» Ὁ Ξάνθος ἔφη· «τί οἶδας ποιεῖν;» Ὁ δὲ ἔφη «παντελῶς οὐδέν.» «Διὰ τί;» φησι. «Ὅτι οὗτοι πάντα εἰδέναι σοι ἐπηγγείλαντο.» Οἱ δὲ σχολαστικοὶ θαυμάσαντες εἶπον· «καλῶς ἀπελογήθη. 10
5 Οὐκ ἔστιν γὰρ ἄνθρωπος πάντα εἰδώς. Διὰ τοῦτο γοῦν καὶ ἐγέλασε.»

26. Ξάνθος εἶπε· «θέλεις ἀγοράσω σε;» Ὁ δέ φησιν· «ἐμοῦ εἰς τοῦτο συμβουλίας δεῖ σοι; Θέλεις ἀγόρασον, θέλεις πορεύου. Οὐδείς σου βίαν ποιεῖ. Τῆς σῆς ἐστιν ἐξουσίας. Καὶ εἰ μὲν βούλει, λύσας θύρας βαλαντίου, ἀργύριον ἀρίθμει. Εἰ δὲ οὐ βούλει, μή με σκώπτῃ.» Ξάνθος εἶπε· «τί οὕτω πολύλαλος εἶ;»
10 Αἴσωπος εἶπεν· «εἰ πτηνὸν λαλοῦν πολύτιμον εὑρίσκεται, τί με ἐξουθενεῖς;» 5
Οἱ σχολαστικοὶ «καλῶς, νὴ τοὺς θεούς, ἔστησε τὸν καθηγητὴν» ἔφησαν. Ὁ Ξάνθος εἶπεν· «ἐάν σε ἀγοράσω, μὴ δραπετεύσῃς;» Αἴσωπος γελάσας εἶπεν· «τοῦτο εἰ θελήσω πρᾶξαι, οὐ λήψομαι σὲ σύμβουλον ὡς σὺ ἐμέ. Τὸ δραπετεύειν ἐν σοί ἐστιν, οὐκ ἐν ἐμοί. Ἐὰν γὰρ ᾖς καλόδουλος, οὐ δραπετεύσω· ἐὰν
15 δὲ κακόδουλος καὶ φθορὰν ἐργάζῃ τῶν ἀναγκαίων μὴ φροντίζων, ὥραν μίαν 10
οὐ μένω πρὸς σέ.» Ὁ Ξάνθος ἔφη· «καλῶς λαλεῖς, ἀλλὰ σαπρὸς εἶ.» Αἴσωπος ἔφη· «εἰς τὸν νοῦν δεῖ ἀποβλέπειν καὶ οὐκ εἰς τὴν θέαν.»

27. Προσελθὼν οὖν ὁ Ξάνθος τῷ σωματεμπόρῳ λέγει· «πόσου τοῦτον πωλεῖς;» Ὁ δὲ ἔφη· «σκῶψαί μου πάρει τὴν ἐμπορίαν;» Ὁ Ξάνθος «διὰ τί;»
20 φησιν. «Ὅτι ἀφεὶς τοὺς ἀξίους σοι παῖδας τὸν σαπρὸν ᾑρετίσω. Ἕνα ἐκείνων ὤνησαι καὶ τοῦτον λάβε πρόσδομα.» Ὁ Ξάνθος· «εἰπὲ τὴν τούτου τιμήν.» Ὁ δὲ πρὸς αὐτόν· «δὸς ἑξήκοντα δηνάρια καὶ λάβε αὐτόν.» Οἱ δὲ σχολαστικοὶ 5
δέδωκαν μὲν τὸ τίμημα, Ξάνθος δ' ἠγόρασεν. Μαθόντες οἱ τελῶναι τὴν πρᾶσιν

25.7 τόπῳ : τρόπῳ O | ἐγεννήθης : om. O | Αἴσωπος ἔφη : καὶ ὁ Αἴσωπος O 8 ἢ ἐν κατωγείῳ post τρικλίνῳ add. O | ἔφη : φησί O 9 ἔφη : om. O | φησι : ὁ δέ rubro atramento add. M^sl | πάντα εἰδέναι : πάντες οὐδένα O ‖ δυνάμενοι rubro atramento in marg. add. M 10 θαυμάσαντες εἶπον : μὰ τὴν ἄνω πρόνοιαν rubro atramento add. M^sl 11 Οὐκ ἔστιν : οὐ γάρ ἐστιν rubro atramento M^sl | γάρ : om. O | εἰδώς : εἰδέναι M | Διὰ ... γοῦν : διὰ γὰρ τοῦτο O | ἐγέλασεν O : ἐγέλα rubro atramento M^sl ‖ **26.**1 ὁ ante Ξάνθος add. O | Ὁ ... φησιν : καὶ ὁ ἔσωπος O 2 σοι : σε O 3 ἐστιν : om. O | τοῦτο post ἐξουσίας add. O | λύσαι M | βαλάντιον O 4 σκόπτει O | ὁ ante Ξάνθος add. O 5 Αἴσωπος εἶπεν : ὁ δέ O | εἰ ... λαλοῦν : ἀπό τινων λάλων M : εἰ πετεινὸν λαλεῖ corr. Perry, iter. Papath. | με : ἐμέ O 6 Οἱ σχολαστικοί : οἱ δὲ σχολαστικοὶ εἶπον O | καλῶς νὴ : καλὸν ἡ O | ἔστησε : ἔπεισε O | ἔφησαν : om. O |

"I'm not asking you that, but in what place were you born?" Aesop said, "My mother didn't tell me whether it was in the bedroom or the dining room." Xanthus said, "What can you do?" And Aesop said, "Absolutely nothing." "Why?" said Xanthus. "Because these others declared that they know how to do everything." The students were impressed and said, "He has made an excellent defense, for no human being knows everything. This, then, is why he laughed."

26. Xanthus said, "Do you want me to buy you?" Aesop said, "Do you need my advice for this? Buy if you like, leave if you like; no one is forcing you; it is up to you. But if you wish, loosen your purse strings and count out the money, and if you don't wish, stop mocking me." Xanthus said, "Why are you so talkative?" Aesop said, "If people find a talking animal valuable, why do you make nothing of me?" The students said, "By the gods, he has checked the professor neatly." Xanthus said, "If I buy you, you won't run away?" Aesop laughed and said, "If I wish to do that, I will not take you for advisor the way you did me. Running away is up to you, not me. If you treat your slaves well, I won't run away, but if you treat your slaves badly and produce a failure of bare necessities because you don't care, then I won't stay an hour with you. Xanthus said, "You speak well, but you're misshapen." Aesop said, "You should look to the mind, not the appearance."

27. So Xanthus approached the slave dealer and said, "How much are you selling this one for?" And he replied, "Are you here to mock my business?" "Why so?" said Xanthus. "Because you dismissed the slaves who were worth something to you and have chosen the misshapen one. Buy one of those others and take this one as an extra." Xanthus said, "Tell me the price of this one." And the merchant said to him, "Give me sixty dinars and take him." The students gave the money, and Xanthus bought him. When

---

Ὁ ... 7 εἶπεν : καὶ ὁ Ξάνθος πρὸς τὸν ἔσωπον Ο 8 θέλω Ο | γὰρ post τὸ add. Ο
9 οὐκ : οὐχὶ Ο | καλόδουλος ... 10 δὲ : om. Μ 10 παρεργάζει Ο 11 μείνω Ο | Ὁ
... ἔφη : καὶ ὁ Ξάνθος Ο | λαλεῖς : λέγεις Ο | ὁ ante Αἴσωπος add. Ο 12 καὶ οὐκ :
οὐχ Ο || **27.**1 τότε ὁ Ξάνθος προσελθὼν Ο | λέγει : ἔφη Ο 2 ἔφη : φησὶ Ο | σκόψαι
Ο | πάρει : corr. Perry : παρῇ Μ : παρεῖς Ο : πάρεις ex S corr. Papath. | καὶ ante
ὁ Ξ. add. Ο 3 ὁ δὲ ante ὅτι add. Ο | σοι : σου Ο | τούτων post ᾑρετίσω add. Ο
4 πρὸς δῶμα Ο | καὶ ante ὁ Ξ. add. Ο | εἰπὲ : φράσον post τιμήν Ο | τὴν ... τιμήν
: τούτου τὴν τιμήν inv. Ο 6 δέδωκαν : δεδώκασι rubro atramento Μ^{sl} | τὸ τίμημα
rubro atramento in marg. add. Μ : om. Ο | ὁ ante Ξάνθος rubro atramento in marg.
sinistra add. Μ | δ' ἠγόρασεν : ἠγόρακεν Ο : δὲ ὠνήσατο Μ^{sl} | δὲ post μαθόντες add.
Ο : οὖν rubro atramento Μ^{sl}

παρεγένοντο ἐρωτῶντες τίς μὲν πέπρακεν, τίς δὲ ἠγόρασε. Διετρέποντο οὖν ἀμφότεροι εἰπεῖν διὰ τὸ ἐλάχιστον τίμημα. Ὁ δὲ Αἴσωπος ἀνακέκραγεν· «ὁ πραθεὶς ἐγώ, ὁ πωλήσας οὗτος καὶ οὗτος ὁ ἀγοράσας. Εἰ δὲ οὗτοι σιωπῶσιν, ἐγὼ ἐλεύθερός εἰμι.» Οἱ δὲ τελῶναι γελάσαντες ἐχαρίσαντο τῷ Ξάνθῳ τὸ τέλος. Ἀλλήλοις δὲ συνταξάμενοι ἐχωρίσθησαν.

28. Ὁ δὲ Αἴσωπος ἠκολούθει τῷ Ξάνθῳ. Καύματος δὲ μεσημβρινοῦ ὄντος καὶ τῆς ὁδοῦ ἐκκαείσης ὁ Ξάνθος περιπατῶν, τὰ ἱμάτια ἀνασυράμενος οὔρει. Ὁ δὲ Αἴσωπος θεασάμενος καὶ ἐκ τῶν ὄπισθεν τὸ ἱμάτιον δραξάμενος εἵλκυσε καί φησι «πώλησόν με ταχύ, ἐπεὶ δραπετεύω.» Ὁ Ξάνθος ἔφη· «τί ἔχεις;» Ὁ δέ φησιν «οὐ δύναμαι τοιούτῳ ἀνδρὶ δουλεύειν.» Ὁ Ξάνθος «διὰ τί;» φησιν. Αἴσωπος ἔφη «σὺ δεσπότης ὢν καὶ μηδένα φοβούμενος εἰ καὶ τύχοι βραδῦναί σε, ἐξουσιαστὴς ὤν, οὐκ ἔδωκας ἄνεσιν τῇ φύσει, ἀλλὰ περιπατῶν οὐρεῖς. Ἐμὲ γοῦν τὸν δοῦλον ἐπὶ διακονίᾳ ταχῦναι σταλέντα, ἀνάγκη πετόμενον χέζειν.» Ὁ Ξάνθος· «τούτου ἕνεκεν ἐταράχθης; Τρία βουλόμενος ἐκφυγεῖν κακὰ περιπατῶν οὔρησα.» Ὁ δέ· «ποῖα ταῦτα;» Ὁ Ξάνθος· «ἑστῶτός μου, τὴν κεφαλὴν ὁ ἥλιος κατέφλεξε. Τοὺς πόδας μου, ἐν τῷ οὐρεῖν ἑστῶτος, ἡ γῆ κατέκαυσεν. Ἡ δὲ τοῦ οὔρου δριμύτης τὰς ὀσφρήσεις μου ἔβλαψεν ἄν. Ταῦτα οὖν τὰ τρία φεύγων φαῦλα περιπατῶν οὔρησα.» Ὁ δέ·«περιπάτει», λέγει, «πέπεικάς με.»

29. Ξάνθος ἔφη· «Αἴσωπε, ἐπεὶ καθάριόν μοι τὸ γυναιόν ἐστι μὴ θέλον ὑπὸ αἰσχροῦ σωματίου δουλεύεσθαι, μεῖνον πρὸ τοῦ πυλῶνος ἕως οὗ εἰσελθὼν πρὸς τὴν κυρίαν, ἐγκώμιόν τι γελοίου ἀπαγγείλω, ἵνα μή σου ἐξαίφνης τὴν σαπρίαν ἰδοῦσα, ἀπαιτήσασα τὴν προῖκα φύγῃ». Αἴσωπος εἶπεν «ἄπιθι καὶ ταχὺ ποίει.» Εἰσελθὼν δὲ ὁ Ξάνθος πρὸς τὴν γυναῖκά φησι «κυρία, οὐκ ἔτι με ὀνειδίσεις ὅτι ὑπὸ σῶν δουλεύομαι παιδαρισκαρίων. Ἴδε κἀγὼ σοὶ παῖδα ἠγόρασα, καὶ ὄψει κάλλος οἷον οὐδέ πω τεθέασαι.»

27.7 μὲν : om. O | δὲ : om. O | ἠγόρακεν O | Διετρέποντο οὖν : Καὶ δὴ ἐντρέποντο O 8 ἀνακεκράγει O 9 δὲ : μὲν O | σκοπῶσι καὶ ante σιωπῶσιν add. M 11 ἀλλήλως O ‖ 28.2 διὰ τῶν πλατιῶν post Ξάνθος add. O | ἀνασυρόμενος O 4 τάχυον O | καὶ ante ὁ Ξάνθος add. O | ἔφη: om. O 5 φησιν² : om. O 6 καὶ ὁ ante Αἴσωπος add. O | ἐπειδὴ ante σὺ add. O | εἰ ... 7 σε : εἰ καὶ τύχη σε βραδῦναι O 7 τῇ φύσει ἄνεσιν inv. O 8 γοῦν : om. O | ἐπὶ τῇ διακονίᾳ O | ταχῦναι : ex W corr. Perry : ταχεῖναι M : ταχύνῃ O 9 χέζειν : τὰ τῆς κύστης περιττὰ διὰ τῆς ἕδρας τῇ γῇ πέμπειν O | Ὁ ... Ξάνθος : ὁ δὲ πρὸς αὐτὸν O 9-10 κακὰ ἐκφυγεῖν inv. O 10 Ὁ δέ : ὁ ἔσωπος λέγει O | καὶ ante ὁ Ξ. add. O | φησί post ὁ Ξ add. O | ἑστῶτός μου : ἂν post ἑστῶτός μου add. O : post κατέφλεξε trans. Papath. 11 κατέφλεξε : κατέκαυσεν O |

the tax collectors learned of the sale, they came by and asked who sold him and who bought him. Both were reluctant to say because of the minimal price, but Aesop shouted out, "I am the one who was bought, this is the one who sold me, and this the one who bought me. If they keep silent, I myself am free." The tax collectors laughed and forgave Xanthus the tax. Agreeing among themselves, they departed.

28. Aesop followed Xanthus. It was in the heat of midday, and the road was sweltering, and Xanthus, while he was walking, pulled up his cloak and started peeing. When Aesop saw him do this, he grabbed his cloak from behind, pulled him aside and said, "Sell me at once, or I'm running away right now." Xanthus said, "What's the matter?" And Aesop replied, "I cannot serve such a man." "Why?" said Xanthus. Aesop replied, "You are the master and are not afraid that anyone might detain you, and yet, though you have the authority, you don't grant indulgence to nature but pee while walking. When I then, as a slave, am sent hurrying on some errand, I'll have to shit while flying." Xanthus said, "This is why you're upset? I peed while walking in order to avoid three evils." Aesop said, "What are they?" Xanthus said, "While standing still, the sun would have burnt my head, the ground would have scorched my feet if I had stood still while peeing, and the acridness of the urine would have hurt my nostrils. These, then, were the three bad things I avoided when I peed while walking." "Walk on!" said Aesop, "you have convinced me."

29. Xanthus said, "Aesop, since my wife is fastidious and does not wish to be served by an ugly slave, wait in front of the gate until I go in to the mistress and build up your ridiculous image in some way, so that she doesn't see your decrepitude all of a sudden and flee, demanding back her dowry." Aesop said, "Go and do it quickly." Xanthus went in and said to his wife, "Mistress, no longer will you reproach me that I am served by your young slaves. Look, I, too, have bought you a slave, and you will see beauty such as you have never yet seen."

δὲ ante πόδας add. O | ἑστῶτος : om. O **12** ἄν post κατέκαυσεν suppl. Papath. **13** ἐκφεύγων O | Ὁ ... **14** λέγει : ὁ ἔσωπος λέγει περιπάτει O ‖ **29.1** ὅτε δὲ ἐπλησίασαν ἀμφότεροι πλησίον τοῦ πυλῶνος ante Ξάνθος add. O | ἔφη : λέγει O | ἐπεὶ : ἐπὶ O | ἐστὶ τὸ γύναιον inv. O | θέλων O **3** σου post κυρίαν add. O | γελίου O : γελοῖον corr. Papath. ex Perry ("malim γελοῖον" p. 149) | ἀπαγγελῶ O **4** φύγει O | Αἴσωπος ... **5** ποίει : om. O **5** αὑτοῦ post γυναῖκα add. O | φησι : om. O | κυρία : om. O | οὐκ ... **6** ὀνειδίσεις : οὐκέτι μωνειδήσης ἔφη O **6** ὑπὸ : ἀπὸ O | παιδαρισκαρίων : παιδισκαρίων corr. Perry, iter. Papath. fort. recte : φωνισκαρίων O **7** ἠγόρακα O | κάλλος : καλῶς O | οὐδέποτε O | ἐθεάσω O

30. Αἱ δὲ θεραπαινίδες ἀκούσασαι καὶ νομίσασαι ἀληθῆ εἶναι τὰ λεγόμενα ἤρξαντο πρὸς ἑαυτὰς μάχεσθαι καὶ λέγειν «ἐμοὶ ὁ δεσπότης ἄνδρα ἠγόρασεν.» Ἄλλη δέ φησι «τὰ κενά σου εἰς τὴν ὄψιν σοι. Ἐμοὶ γὰρ εἰς ὕπνους τοῦτον συνέθετο.» Ἄλλη δὲ ἔφη «ἐγὼ ἐν ὀνείροις ἐνυμφευόμην.» Τούτων δὴ διαμαχομένων ἡ γυνὴ τῷ Ξάνθῳ ἔφη «περὶ οὗ τοσαῦτα κατεβάλου ἐγκώμια, ποῦ ἐστι;» Ὁ δὲ ἔφη «μέχρι τοῦ πυλῶνος ἠκολούθησε, μὴ κληθεὶς δὲ εἰσελθεῖν ἔμεινεν ἔξω.» Ἡ δέ φησι «τὸν νεώνητόν τις καλεσάτω.» Μιᾶ γοῦν καπριῶσα τῶν ἄλλων μαχομένων «προδραμοῦμαι», φησί, «καὶ ἀρραβωνήσομαι αὐτόν.» Ἐξελθοῦσα δὲ πρὸ τοῦ πυλῶνος ἐβόα «ὁ νεώνητος ποῦ ἐστι, ὁ ἐμοὶ ἀγορασθείς;» Αἴσωπος ἔφη «ὧδέ εἰμι.» Ἡ δὲ κόρη θαμβηθεῖσα εἶπεν «σὺ εἶ;» Ὁ δέ, «ναί, ἐγώ.» Ἡ δέ φησι «ἀβάσκαντα, ποῦ σου ἡ κέρκος; Μὴ εἰσέλθῃς αἰφνιδίως καὶ φύγωσι πάντες.» Προλαβοῦσα δὲ ἐκείνη ταῖς λοιπαῖς ἔφη «ἐξελθοῦσαι ὄψεσθε πηλίκον κακόν, περὶ οὗ πᾶσαι διεμαχόμεθα.» Ἐξελθοῦσα δὲ ἄλλη καὶ ἰδοῦσα αὐτὸν εἶπεν «ψῶ! παταχθείη σου τὸ πρόσωπον. Δεῦρο εἴσελθε καὶ μὴ μοι κολλῶ.» Εἰσελθὼν δὲ ἄντικρυς τῆς δεσποίνης ἔστηκε.

31. Θεασαμένη δὲ αὐτὸν ἐκείνη ἀπεστράφη καί φησι πρὸς τὸν ἄνδρα «πόθεν μοι τὸ τέρας τοῦτο; Οὗτός ἐστιν ὃν ἐγκωμιάζεις; Ἔκβαλε αὐτὸν ἀπὸ τῆς ὄψεώς μου!» Ὁ Ξάνθος εἶπεν «ἀρκεῖ, κυρία. Μὴ σκῶπτέ μοι τὸν νεώνητον.» Ἡ γυνὴ ἔφη «μεμίσηκάς με, Ξάνθε. Ἑτέραν γῆμαι θέλων, αἰδούμενός μοι εἰπεῖν, ἵνα τῆς οἰκίας ὑποχωρήσω, ἤνεγκάς μοι τὸν κυνοκέφαλον τοῦτον ἐπίτηδες, ἵνα μὴ θέλουσα ὑπ' αὐτοῦ δουλευθῆναι φύγω. Δὸς οὖν τὴν προῖκά μου καὶ πορεύσομαι.» Ὁ δὲ Ξάνθος τῷ Αἰσώπῳ ἔφη «ἵνα <μὴ> εἰς τὴν ὁδὸν περιπατῶν οὐρήσω τοιαῦτά μοι ἔφης ῥήματα καὶ νῦν οὐδὲν λέγεις πρὸς αὐτήν;» Αἴσωπος εἶπε «ῥῖψον αὐτὴν εἰς τὸ σκότος.» Ὁ δέ, «σιώπα, κάθαρμα! Οὐκ οἶδας ὅτι θέλω αὐτὴν ὡς ἐμαυτόν;» Αἴσωπος· «ποθεῖς τὸ γύναιον;» Ὁ Ξάνθος, «ναί, δραπέτα.» Ὁ δὲ ῥίψας τὸν πόδα εἰς τὸ μέσον ἀνακέκραγε «Ξάνθος ὁ φιλόσοφος γυναικοκρατεῖται.

30.1 Αἱ : οἱ O | ἀληθής O 3 τὰ ... σοι : κενή σοι ἡ χαρά O 4 τοῦτον : τοῦτο O | δὴ : δὲ οὕτως O 5 περιεβάλου O 6 Ὁ ... ἔφη : om. M | εἰσελθὼν O 7 ἔξω ἔμεινεν inv. O | Ἡ δέ : ὁ δέ O | οὖν O 8 μαχομένων : om. O | προδιαδραμοῦσα O 9 ὁ ... ἐστι : ποῦ ὁ νεώνητος O 10 ὁ ante Αἴσωπος add. O 11 ἐγώ : om. O | ἀβάσκαντα : σε atramento rubro add. M^sl : σοι post ἀβάσκαντα add. O | Μὴ ... 12 πάντες : del. M et in marg. εἰ κέρκου χρῄζεις ἔχω, ἡ δέ add. M 12 ἐκείνη : ἔφη add. M^sl | ταῖς ... λοιπαῖς : τὰς λοιπὰς O | ἐξελθοῦσαι ... 13 διεμαχόμεθα : del. M : δεῦτε ἴδετε μέγιστον κακόν add. M^sl 14 παταχθείη : M^pc : παταχθήτω O | καὶ ... 15 κολλῶ :

30. The slave girls heard this and thought that what he said was true, so they began to quarrel among themselves and say, "The master has bought a husband for me." Another said, "Shit in your face; he was pledged to me in my sleep." And another said, "I was married to him in my dreams." As they were quarrelling, his wife said to Xanthus, "The one to whom you offered up such praises, where is he?" He replied, "He followed me up to the gate, but since he was not summoned to come in he remained outside." She said, "Let someone summon the new-bought slave." As the others were quarrelling, one girl, in high heat, said, "I'll run ahead and become engaged to him." She went out and hollered in front of the gate, "Where is the new-bought slave who was purchased for me?" Aesop said, "Here I am." The girl was astonished and said, "You're it?" and he said, "Yes, it's I." She said, "Bless you! Where is your tail? Don't enter suddenly so they don't all flee." She went ahead of him and said to the other girls, "Come out, and you will see how sorry a thing we were all quarrelling about." Another girl went out and when she saw him said, "Phew! Your face should be bashed in. Come here, but don't stick to me!" Aesop entered and stood directly in front of his mistress.

31. She observed him, then turned away and said to her husband, "Where have you found me this monster? This is the one you were eulogizing? Cast him out of my sight!" Xanthus said, "Enough, my lady. Do not mock the new-bought slave to me." His wife said, "You have grown to hate me, Xanthus, and want to marry another woman but are ashamed to tell me to leave the house, so you brought me this dog-headed thing on purpose, so that I wouldn't want to be served by him and so would flee. So give me my dowry, and I'll go." Xanthus said to Aesop, "You said those words to me so that I would not pee while walking on the road, and now you say nothing to her?" Aesop said, "Throw her out into the dark!" Xanthus said, "Silence, you trash! Don't you know that I love her like myself?" Aesop said, "You long for your wife?" And Xanthus said, "Yes, you damned slave." Aesop stamped his foot in their midst and cried out, "Xanthus the philosopher is under his wife's thumb!"

ἀκολύτως O 15 τῆς … ἕστηκε : ἔστη τῆς οἰκοδεσποίνης O ‖ **31.**2 ἐγκωμίαζες O 3 μοι: om. O 4 δὲ post ἑτέραν add. O | γῆμαι : γυνῆν O | μοι : με O 6 θέλω O | δουλευθῆναι : δουλεύ:- (sic) O | μοι post δὸς add. O 7 πορεύομαι O | τι post ἵνα add. O | ἵνα μὴ : corr. Westermann, iter. Perry 8 περιπατοῦντι καὶ οὐροῦντι O | τοιαῦτά : ταῦτα O 9 ὁ ante Αἴσωπος add. O 10 καὶ ὁ ante Αἴσωπος add. O 11 καὶ ante ὁ Ξ. add. O | δραπετᾶ O | 'Ο² … μέσον : ρίψας δὲ τὸν πόδα ὁ ἔσωπος εἰς τὸ μέσον O | ἀνέκραγεν O

32. Σὺ δέ, κυρία, ἐβούλου ἵνα ὁ ἀνήρ σου ὠνήσηταί σοι παῖδα νέον, εὔομματον, οὐλόκομον, λευκόν, ὀφείλοντα εἰς τὸ βαλανεῖον καὶ γυμνὴν βλέπειν σε καὶ εἰς τὸν κοιτῶνα κιρνᾶν καὶ τοὺς πόδας σου τρίβειν καὶ προσπαίξαντά σοι αἰσχῦναι τὸν φιλόσοφον. Ἀλλ' ὦ Εὐριπίδη, χρυσόν σου τὸ ἀψευδὲς στόμα ὅτε ἔλεγες

Πολλαὶ μὲν ὀργαὶ κυμάτων θαλασσίων,
δειναὶ δὲ ποταμῶν καὶ πυρὸς θερμοῦ πνοιαί,
δεινὸν δὲ πενία, δεινὰ δ' ἄλλα μυρία,
πλὴν οὐδὲν οὕτως ὡς γυνὴ ἐν ὑπερβολῇ κακῶν.

Σὺ δὲ φιλοσόφου γυνὴ οὖσα ὑπὸ καλῶν νεανιῶν δουλεύεσθαι θέλεις, ἵνα βινητιῶσα ὕβριν τῷ ἀνδρὶ ὑπενέγκῃς;» Ἡ δὲ ἀκούσασα ταῦτα ἔφη «πόθεν τοῦτο τὸ κακὸν ἤγρευσας; Ὅμως στωμύλος μοι ὁ σαπρὸς φαίνεται καὶ εὐτράπελος. Διαλλαγήσομαι αὐτῷ.» Ὁ Ξάνθος ἔφη· «Αἴσωπε, διήλλακταί σοι ἡ κυρία.» Ὁ δέ φησι «μέγα πρᾶγμα εἰ γύναιον πτῆξαν κατεπραΰνθη.»

33. missing

34. Ὁ Ξάνθος ἔφη «σιώπα τοῦ λοιποῦ. Ὠνησάμην σε εἰς δουλείαν, οὐ μὴν δὲ εἰς ἀντιλογίαν. Ἄρας οὖν ὠμόλινον ἀκολούθει μοι ὅπως ἀπὸ τῶν κήπων πριασώμεθα λάχανα.» Ὁ δὲ θεὶς ἐπὶ τὸν ὦμον τὸ ὠμόλινον ἠκολούθει τῷ Ξάνθῳ. Ἐλθόντων δὲ εἰς ἕνα κῆπον λέγει τῷ κηπουρῷ «δὸς ἡμῖν λάχανα.» Ὁ δὲ λαβὼν τὸ δρέπανον ἀπεθέριζεν αὐτῷ ἀσπαράγους, σεῦτλα, μαλάχας καὶ ἀρτύματα. Εὐτελὲς δὲ δεσμήσας φορτίον ἐπέδωκε τῷ Αἰσώπῳ. Ὁ δὲ Ξάνθος ἀνοίξας τὸ μαρσίππιον ἀπεδίδου τὸ κέρμα τῶν λαχάνων.

35. Ὁ δὲ κηπουρὸς ἔφη «ἔα, κύριε. Ἑνὸς γάρ σου λόγου χρείαν ποιοῦμαι ζητήματος ἕνεκεν.» Ὁ δέ φησιν «ὃ βούλει λέγε.» Καὶ ὁ κηπουρός· «καθηγητά, διὰ τί τὰ παρ' ἐμοῦ βαλλόμενα λάχανα εἰς τὴν γῆν σκαλιζόμενά τε καὶ ἀρδευόμενα βραδεῖαν ἔχει τὴν αὔξησιν, τὰ δὲ αὐτοματὶ ἀπὸ τῆς γῆς φυόμενα

32.1 μου post κυρία add. O | ὠνήσεται O 2 οὐλόκομον : ὁλόκαλον O | ὑπηρετεῖν post βαλανεῖον add. O 3 σε : atramento rubro M^sl : om. O | κιρᾶν O | τρίβειν : διατρίβειν M^ac (praepositio δια- deleta est atramento rubro) 4 Ἀλλ' : om. O 5 ὅτε : ὅτι M 6 Πολλαὶ ... 9 κακῶν : Eur. fr. 1059 Nauck, auctus habet Stobaeus IV 22, 136 7 θερμοῦ : corr. Perry, iter. Papath. : θερμὴ MO | πνοιαί : ex G corr. Perry, iter. Papath. : πνοιά M πνοιᾶ O 8 δ' : καὶ O 9 πλὴν : om. O 10 νεανίων O | δουλεύεσθαι ... θέλεις : δουλευθῆναι θέλης O 11 βινητιῶσα : corr. Perry, iter. Papath. : βυνιτιῶσα M : μηνητιῶσα O | ὑπενέγκῃς : προξενήσῃς O | ταῦτα ἀκούσασα inv. O 12 τὸ κακὸν τοῦτο inv. O | ἐπὶ πολὺ δὲ λέγοντος τοῦ Αἰσώπου στραφεὶς ἡ κυρία αὐτοῦ πρὸς

32. "You, mistress, wanted your husband to buy you a young slave, with pretty eyes, curly hair, light-skinned, doing duty at the bath, to see you naked and mingle in the bedroom and rub your feet, play with you and shame the philosopher. O Euripides, your truthful mouth was pure gold when you said,

Many the ragings of the sea's waves,
Terrible the blasts of rivers and hot fire,
Terrible is poverty and ten thousand other things,
But none so much as woman in abundance of evils.

You, though the wife of a philosopher, want to be served by handsome young men so that by screwing them you can bring dishonor upon your husband." When she heard this she said, "Where did you land this wretch? Nevertheless, the fellow seems to me to be eloquent and witty. I'll be reconciled with him." And Xanthus said, "Aesop, the lady is reconciled with you." Aesop replied, "It is a great event when a woman has been cowed and calmed down."

33. missing

34. Xanthus said, "Be quiet in the future. I bought you for servitude, certainly not for controversy. So pick up the sack and follow me so that we can buy some vegetables from the gardens." Aesop put the sack on his shoulder and followed Xanthus. When they arrived at a garden, he said to the gardener, "Give us vegetables." The gardener took a sickle and cut off for him asparagus, beets, mallow, and spices, then tied up the inexpensive produce and gave it to Aesop. Xanthus opened his purse and handed over a coin for the vegetables.

35. The gardener said, "Hold on, sir. May I make a request for a word from you concerning a puzzle?" Xanthus said, "Say what you wish." And the gardener said, "Professor, why do vegetables that I have set in the ground, hoed, and watered have a slow growth but those that spring from

---

τὸν ξάνθον ἔφη post ὅμως add. O | ὁ σαπρὸς : οὗτος add. M^sl 13 Διαλλαγήσομαι : διὰ ταῦτα in marg. atramento rubro add. M | Ὁ ... ἔφη : καὶ ὁ Ξ. τῷ ἐσώπῳ ἔφη O | Αἴσωπε : om. O 14 Ὁ ... φησι : σου ὁ δὲ φησὶ atramento rubro M^sl ‖ 34.1 Ὁ ... ἔφη : καὶ ὁ Ξάνθος πρὸς αὐτὸν O 2 ὁμόλινον vel ὁμάλινον O | τῶν κήπων : τοῦ κήπου m. recent. M 3 πριώμεθα O | θήσας O | τῶν ὤμων O | ὁμόλινον vel ὁμάλινον O 4 αὐτῶν post ἐλθόντων δὲ add. O 5 ἐθέριζεν O 6 λοιπὰ ante ἀρτύματα suppl. Papath. 7 μαρσίπιον M | ἐπεδίδου O ‖ 35.1 πρὸς τὸν Ξάνθον post ἔφη add. O | κύρι M 3 παρ' ἡμῖν O | λάχανα : om. O 4 αὐτομάτως O | ἐπὶ γῆς O

καὶ μηδαμῶς ἐπιμελούμενα τάχιον αὔξεται;» Ὁ δὲ ἀκούσας ἐμφιλόσοφον
ζήτημα καὶ μὴ εὑρὼν λῦσαι, «τῇ θείᾳ προνοίᾳ,» ἔφη, «πάντα διοικεῖται.»

36. Αἴσωπος δὲ ἀκούσας ἐγέλασεν. Καὶ ὁ Ξάνθος φησὶ πρὸς αὐτόν· «γελᾷς
ἢ καταγελᾷς;» Ὁ δὲ «καταγελῶ,» φησιν, «οὐ σοῦ, ἀλλὰ τοῦ διδάξαντός σε.
Τὰ γὰρ ὑπὸ θείας προνοίας διοικούμενα ὑπὸ σοφῶν διαλύονται. Ὑπόσχου οὖν,
κἀγὼ διαλύσω αὐτό.»

37. Ὁ Ξάνθος οὖν τῷ κηπουρῷ λέγει «κομψότατε, ἀπρεπές ἐστιν
ἐμὲ τὸν ἐν τοσούτοις ἀκροατηρίοις διαλεχθέντα νῦν ἐν κήποις αἰνίγματα
διαλύειν. Παῖς δὲ πολύπειρος ἀκολουθεῖ μοι· αὐτῷ προσανάθου καὶ διαλύσει
τὸ ζήτημα.» Ὁ κηπουρός φησι «οὗτος ὁ σαπρὸς γράμματα οἶδεν; Οὐαὶ τῇ
ἀτυχίᾳ! Εἰπέ», φησι, «εἰ ἐπίστασαι.» Αἴσωπος εἶπεν· «τοῦτο ζητεῖς ἀκοῦσαι,
διὰ ποίαν αἰτίαν τὰ φυτὰ εἰς τὴν γῆν βάλλεις καὶ ταῦτα ἐπιμελῶς ἐργάζῃ, τὰ
δὲ ἄγρια τάχιον ἀναβαίνει καὶ μᾶλλον τῶν ὑπὸ σοῦ βαλλομένων; Ἄκουε καὶ
πρόσεχε. Ὃν τρόπον γυνὴ πρὸς δεύτερον ἐρχομένη γάμον, τέκνα ἔχουσα ἐκ
προτέρου ἀνδρός, εὕροι δὲ καὶ τὸν ἄνδρα τέκνα ἔχοντα ἐκ προτέρας γυναικός,
γίνεται ὧν μὲν ἐπιφέρεται μήτηρ, ὧν δὲ εὑρίσκει μητρυιά. Τούτων δὲ ἡ
διαφορὰ πολλὴ γίνεται. Τὰ γὰρ ἐξ αὐτῆς γεννηθέντα φιλοστόργως τρέφει,
τὰ δὲ ἐξ ἀλλοτρίων ὠδίνων τεχθέντα μισεῖ ζήλῳ χρωμένη καὶ περικόπτουσα
μᾶλλον τὴν ἐκείνων τροφὴν τοῖς ἰδίοις δίδωσι τέκνοις. Τὰ γὰρ ἴδια ὡς φύσει
φιλεῖ, τὰ δὲ τοῦ ἀνδρὸς ὡς ξένα μισεῖ. Τὸν αὐτὸν οὖν τρόπον καὶ ἡ γῆ· τῶν
μὲν αὐτομάτως φυομένων ἐστὶ μήτηρ, τῶν δὲ παρὰ σοῦ βαλλομένων ἐστὶ
μητρυιὰ καὶ μᾶλλον τὰ ἴδια τρέφουσα θάλλειν ποιεῖ ἢ τὰ παρὰ σοῦ ὡς νόθα
φυτευθέντα.» Ἀκούσας δὲ ὁ κηπουρὸς λέγει «πολύ με τῆς λύπης ἐκούφισας.
Ἔχε τὰ λάχανα δωρεάν. Ἐὰν δέ τινος ἑτέρου χρείαν ἔχῃς, ὡς εἰς ἴδιον
παραγίνου κῆπον.»

38. deest

35.5 εἰς τὴν γῆν post ἐπιμελούμενα add. O | ἐμφιλόσοφον : τὸ τοιοῦτον O 6
λῦσαι : τὴν αὐτοῦ λύσιν O | ἔφη τῇ θείᾳ προνοίᾳ inv. O | διοικεῖται : οἰκεῖται O ‖
36.1 Καὶ … φησὶ : ὁ δὲ M 2 καγελᾷς O | Ὁ δὲ : om. O 4 διαλύσομαι O | αὐτό
: om. O ‖ **37.**1 Ὁ … οὖν : καὶ ὁ Ξάνθος O | λέγει : ἔφη O | ἀπρεπές : εὐπρεπές
O 2 ἐν … ἀκροατηρίοις : ἐν τοῖς ἀκροατηρίοις τοιούτοις O | κηπίοις O 3 διαλύειν
: διαλαλεῖν M | σου post διαλύσει add. O 4 φησι : πρὸς τὸν ἔσωπον O | οὗτος …
οἶδεν : οὗτος ὅσα πράγματα οἶδε O 5 Εἰπέ : om. O | Αἴσωπος … εἶπεν : καὶ ὁ ἔσωπος
πρὸς αὐτόν O 6 τὰ[1] : om. O | γῆν : om. O 7 καὶ[1] : om. O 8 γάμον ἐρχομένη inv. O
9 εὕρῃ O | ἐκ προτέρας γυναικὸς τέκνα ἔχοντα inv. O 10 μήτηρ … δὲ : absc. in M |

the ground on their own and are not tended at all will grow more quickly?" Xanthus heard the philosophical puzzle but was unable to solve it, so he said, "Everything is managed by divine providence."

36. Aesop heard this and laughed. Xanthus said to him, "Are you just laughing or laughing at me?" "I'm laughing," Aesop said, "not at you but at the one who taught you. For the things that are managed by divine providence are explained by the wise. Give your consent, then, and I will explain it."

37. So Xanthus said to the gardener, "My clever fellow, it is unbecoming for me, who have lectured in front of so many audiences, to chat about riddles in gardens. A highly experienced slave is accompanying me; pose your puzzle to him, and he will solve it." The gardener said, "This fellow knows his letters? What a misfortune! Tell me," he said," "if you know." Aesop said, "Is this what you seek to hear: What is the reason you set your plants in the earth and work them carefully, yet the wild ones grow faster and better than those that are planted by you? Listen and pay attention. You know the way when a woman enters into a second marriage but has children from her former husband, she may come upon a husband who also has children from a former wife: she is the mother of those she bore but the stepmother of those she comes upon. There is a great difference between the two, for she raises the ones who were born from her lovingly, but those who were brought forth out of the birth pangs of another she hates jealously, and she cuts off some of their food and gives it to her own children. For she loves her own because they're by nature, but she hates her husband's because they're foreign. In the same way the earth, too, is the mother of those that spring up on their own, but she is the stepmother of those that are sown by you, and she rather raises her own and makes them flourish than those that are planted by you and are bastards, as it were." When he heard this, the gardener said, "You have relieved me of considerable distress. Take the vegetables for free, and if you have need of anything else, come here as though to your own garden."

38. missing

εὑρίσκει μητρυιά : εὑρίσκεται μητρία O **11** γίνεται πολλή inv. O **12** τεχθέντα : om. O | καὶ περικόπτουσα : περικόπτουσα δὲ O **13** δῶσι O | ὡς : om. O **14** οὖν : om. O **15** ἐστὶ¹ ... **17** φυτευθέντα : γίνεται μητρία καὶ μᾶλλον τὰ ἴδια τρέφει οὖσα μήτηρ, θάλλειν ποιεῖ ἢ τὰ περὶ σοῦ φυτευθέντα ὡς νόθα O **16** μητρεία M **17** λέγει : ἔφη O **18** ἑτέρου : om. O | εἰς : om. O **19** παραγίνου : παραγί O | καὶ ἀνεχώρησαν οἴκαδε post κῆπον add. O

39. Ἐγένετο δὲ μεθ' ἡμέρας λουομένου τοῦ Ξάνθου εὑρεῖν φίλους καὶ φησι τῷ Αἰσώπῳ «πρόλαβε εἰς τὸν οἶκον καὶ βαλὼν φακὸν εἰς κάκκαβον ἕψησον ἡμῖν.» Δραμὼν δὲ ὁ Αἴσωπος καὶ εἰσελθὼν εἰς τὸ ταμεῖον, λαβὼν ἕνα κόκκον φακοῦ εἰς κάκκαβον βαλὼν ἕψει. Ὁ δὲ Ξάνθος σὺν τοῖς φίλοις λουσάμενος, «καταξιώσατέ», φησι, «εὐτελῶς ἀριστῆσαι· πρὸς φακὸν ἡμῖν ἐστιν. Οὐ δεῖ γὰρ τῇ ποικιλίᾳ τῶν ἐδεσμάτων τοὺς φίλους κρίνειν, ἀλλὰ τῇ προθυμίᾳ δοκιμάζειν.»

40. Καὶ ἀγαγὼν αὐτοὺς εἰς τὴν οἰκίαν φησὶν «Αἴσωπε, δὸς πιεῖν ἀπὸ βαλανείου.» Ὁ δὲ τὸν ξέστην λαβὼν καὶ εἰς τὸ βαλανεῖον δραμὼν πλήσας ἐκ τοῦ ἀπορρύματος καὶ κεράσας ἐπέδωκε τῷ Ξάνθῳ. Ὁ δὲ δυσωδίας ληφθεὶς φησι «ψῶ! Αἴσωπε, τί τοῦτο;» Ὁ δὲ «ἀπὸ βαλανείου» ἔφη. Ὁ δὲ Ξάνθος καὶ ἐν τούτῳ γυμνάζων αὐτοῦ τὸν νοῦν ἔφη «λεκάνην παράθες μοι.» Θεὶς δὲ κενὴν τὴν λεκάνην εἱστήκει. Ὁ Ξάνθος φησὶν «οὐ νίπτεις;» Αἴσωπος ἔφη «ἐντέταλκάς μοι ἵνα, ὅσα ἀκούω, ἐκεῖνα πράξω. Οὐκ εἶπας 'βάλε ὕδωρ εἰς τὴν λεκάνην καὶ νίψον μου τοὺς πόδας καὶ θὲς τὰ σανδάλια' καὶ ὅσα καθεξῆς.» Ὁ δὲ Ξάνθος τοῖς φιλοσόφοις ἔφη «μὴ γὰρ δοῦλον ἑαυτῷ ἠγόρασα, μᾶλλον δὲ καθηγητήν.»

41. Ἀνακλιθέντων δὲ τῶν φίλων ὁ Ξάνθος φησὶ «Αἴσωπε, ὁ φακὸς ἕψηται; Δὸς φαγώμεθα.» Ὁ δὲ ἀναλαβὼν κοχλιαρίῳ τὸν κόκκον τοῦ φακοῦ ἐπέδωκεν αὐτῷ. Λαβὼν δὲ ὁ Ξάνθος καὶ δοκῶν ὅτι πρὸς τὸ πειρᾶσαι τὴν ἕψησιν ἐπεδόθη, ἐκθλίψας ἔφη «καλῶς ἐψήθη. Κόμιζε καὶ φαγώμεθα.» Τοῦ δὲ βραδύνοντος ἔφη «ποῦ ὁ φακός;» «Ἔλαβες αὐτόν» φησιν. Ὁ Ξάνθος εἶπεν «ἕνα κόκκον ἔψησας;» Ὁ δὲ «ναί,» φησι· «φακὸν γὰρ εἶπας καὶ οὐ φακούς. Τὸ μὲν γὰρ ἑνικόν ἐστι, τὸ δὲ πληθυντικόν.» Ὁ Ξάνθος φησὶ «ἄνδρες σοφοί, οὗτός με ταχὺ εἰς μανίαν περιτρέψει.

42. Ἀλλ' ἵνα μὴ δόξω τοὺς φίλους ὑβρίζειν, ἀπελθὼν ὤνησαι χοίρου ἑνὸς πόδας τέσσαρας καὶ ἐκζέσας παράθες». Ὁ δὲ Αἴσωπος λαβὼν ἕψει. Ὁ Ξάνθος οὖν θέλων εὐλόγως δαμάσαι αὐτόν, τοῦ Αἰσώπου διά τινα χρείαν εἰς

39.1 τινάς post ἡμέρας add. O 2 εἰς τὸν κάκαβον O 3 ὁ : om. O | ταμιεῖον O 4 φακῶν M 5 σήμερον σὺν ἡμῖν post φησι add. O | πρὸς ... 6 ἐστιν : φακὸς γὰρ ἡμῶν ἐστιν ἡ τροφή O | ὑμῖν M 6 ἐδεσμάτων : βρωμάτων O | διακρίνειν O ‖ **40.**1 Καὶ ... αὐτοὺς : ἐπάρας οὖν αὐτοὺς, ἦκεν O | καὶ ante φησὶν add. O 2 βαλανίου O | Ὁ ... δραμὼν : δραμὼν δὲ ὁ ἔσωπος καὶ λαβὼν τὸν ξέστην O | πλήσας ... 3 ἀπορρύματος : πλήσας τε ἀπὸ τοῦ ἀπορρυήματος O 3 δυσωδία O 4 Αἴσωπε : om. O | τί τοῦτο : τι τοῦ τοῦτο (sic) O | λέγει post ὁ δὲ[1] add. O | ἔφη : om. O | Ὁ δὲ[2] : καὶ ὁ O 5 καὶ : om. O | γυμνάσας O | αὐτοῦ : αὐτῷ O | ἔφη : εἰσήχασεν καὶ φησί O | παράθες μοι λεκάνην inv. O 6 κενὴν ... λεκάνην : λεκάνην κενὴν O |

39. Some days later while Xanthus was bathing he met some friends and said to Aesop, "Go before us to the house and throw [some] lentil in a pot and boil it for us." Aesop ran and entered the storehouse, took a lentil seed, threw it in a pot, and boiled it. When Xanthus had bathed, along with his friends, he said, "Deign to dine frugally, for it is lentil for us. For one should not judge friends by the variety of their meats but rather assess them by their intentions."

40. Leading them to his house, he said, "Aesop, give us something to drink, coming from the bathhouse." Aesop took a jar, ran to the bathhouse, filled it with the spillover, stirred it, and offered it to Xanthus. He was seized by the foul smell and said, "Pew, Aesop, what is this?" Aesop said, "It's from the bathhouse." Xanthus, trying to exercise his mind even in this, said, "Set a basin here for me." Aesop set an empty basin and stood there. Xanthus said, "Won't you wash me?" Aesop said, "You ordered me to do just what I heard. You didn't say, 'Put water in the basin and wash my feet and put on my sandals' and so forth." Xanthus said to the philosophers, "I haven't bought a slave for myself but rather a teacher."

41. When his friends had reclined at the dinner table, Xanthus said, "Aesop, is the lentil boiled? Give us some to eat." Aesop took the lentil seed with a spoon and gave it to him. Xanthus took it, and, thinking that it had been given to him to test for the boiling, he squeezed it and said, "It's been well boiled. Bring us some, and let's eat." When Aesop delayed, he said, "Where's the lentil?" "You took it," said Aesop. Xanthus said, "You boiled one lentil?" "Yes," said Aesop; "You said 'lentil,' not 'lentils.' The one is singular, the other plural." Xanthus said, "O wise men, this fellow will soon drive me to insanity.

42. But so that I may not seem to insult my friends, go and buy me four feet of a single pig, boil them, and serve them to us." Aesop got them and boiled them. Xanthus wished to tame him in a plausible way, so when

Ὁ ... φησίν : καὶ ὁ Ξάνθος O | ὁ ante Αἴσωπος add. O **7** μοι : om. M | ἵνα : om. O | ἀκούσω O | καὶ ante πράξω add. O **8** λεκάνη O | νίψαι O **9** τοῖς φιλοσόφοις : om. O | ἑαυτῷ : om. O ‖ **41.1** Ἀνακλιθέντων ... φίλων : ἀνακληθέντες δὲ ἤτουν ποτὸν O | ὁ Ξ. : ὁ δὲ Ξ. O **2** φαγόμεθα O | λαβὼν O | τὸ κοχλιάριον O | φάκου O **3** καὶ : om. O **4** ἕψησιν : αὔξησιν O | ἐκθλίψας O | ἔψη O | καὶ : om. O | φαγόμεθα O **5** ἔφη : φησὶν ὁ Ξάνθος O | 'Ο ... εἶπεν : ὁ δὲ O **6** Ὁ δὲ : om. O | φακὸν ... εἶπας : φ. εἴρηκας M **8** περιτρέπει O ‖ **42,1** δόξῃ O | ὤνησαι : om. O **2** τέσσαρεις O | ζέσας O | ἕψει : corr. Perry, iter. Papath. : ἔψη O : ἔψησεν M **3** εὐλόγως ... αὐτόν : αὐτὸν εὐλόγως δαμάσαι inv. O | διά τινα : διάτινος O

τὸ ταμεῖον εἰσελθόντος, λαβὼν ἀπὸ τῆς χύτρας ἕνα πόδα ἔκρυψεν. Αἴσωπος δὲ ἐλθὼν καὶ εἰς τὴν χύτραν βλέψας, ὡς εἶδε τρεῖς μόνον πόδας, ἔγνω ὅτι ἐνέδρα αὐτῷ ἐγένετο. Κατελθὼν οὖν εἰς τὸ περίαυλον, μάχαιραν περιελών, τοῦ σιτευομένου χοίρου τὸν πόδα κόψας μαδίσας τε καὶ ἁλμίσας, εἰς τὴν χύτραν ἔρριψε καὶ συνέψει. Ὁ δὲ Ξάνθος ὑποπτεύσας μή πως ὁ Αἴσωπος τὸν λείποντα μὴ εὑρὼν πόδα δραπετεύσῃ, πάλιν αὐτὸν εἰς τὴν χύτραν ἔβαλε. Γίνονται οὖν πόδες πέντε. Οὐδεὶς δὲ αὐτῶν ᾔδει τὸ γεγονός.

43. Καὶ μετ' ὀλίγον, «Αἴσωπέ,» φησι, «εἰ τοὺς χοιρείους ἔψησας πόδας, δὸς φάγωμεν.» Ὁ οὖν Αἴσωπος κατακενοῖ τοὺς πόδας εἰς τὸν πίνακα καὶ ἰδού, πέντε. Ὁ δὲ Ξάνθος· «τί τοῦτο;» Αἴσωπος ὠχριάσας ἔφη «οἱ δύο χοῖροι πόσους πόδας ἔχουσιν;» Ὁ Ξάνθος ἔφη «ὀκτώ.» Αἴσωπος εἶπεν «εἰσὶν ὧδε πέντε καὶ ὁ χοῖρος κάτω τρίπους νέμεται.» Ὁ δὲ Ξάνθος τοῖς φίλοις ἔφη «οὐκ εἶπον ὅτι οὗτος ταχέως εἰς μανίαν με περιτρέπει;» Αἴσωπος ἔφη «δέσποτα, ἔδει σε μὴ ὁρίσαι μοι νόμον καὶ διηκόνησά σοι πρεπόντως. Τὰ γὰρ ἐκ περισσείας λεγόμενα κατὰ προσθήκην καὶ ὑφειλμὸν οὐ μέτριά εἰσιν ἁμαρτήματα.» Ὁ οὖν Ξάνθος μηδεμίαν ἀφορμὴν εὑρηκὼς τοῦ μαστιγῶσαι αὐτὸν ἡσύχασε.

44. Τῇ δὲ ἑξῆς εἰς τὸ ἀκροατήριον σὺν αὐτῷ παρεγένετο. Εἷς δὲ τῶν σχολαστικῶν δεῖπνον μέγα παρασκευάσας ἐκάλεσε τὸν Ξάνθον ἅμα τοῖς λοιποῖς σχολαστικοῖς. Ὁ οὖν Ξάνθος ἐν τῷ δείπνῳ λαβὼν μέρη πολλὰ ἐπέδωκε τῷ Αἰσώπῳ καί φησιν «ἄπαγε, δὸς τῇ εὐνοούσῃ.» Ὁ δὲ ἐν ἑαυτῷ ἔφη «νῦν καιρὸς τοῦ ἀνταμύνασθαί με τὴν κυρίαν μου ἀνθ' ὧν ἀγορασθέντα με ἔσκωπτεν. Ὄψεται τοίνυν τίς τῷ κυρίῳ εὐνοεῖ.»

45. Ἐλθὼν οὖν εἰς τὴν οἰκίαν ἐκάθισε καὶ προσκαλεσάμενος τὴν δέσποιναν παρέθηκε τὴν σπυρίδα ἔμπροσθεν αὐτῆς καὶ φησι «κυρία, μή τι τέτρωκται;» Ἡ δέ·«πάντα ὑγιῆ καὶ ἀσινῆ.» Αἴσωπος εἶπεν «ὁρᾷς ταῦτα πάντα; Ὁ δεσπότης πέπομφεν οὐ σοί, ἀλλὰ τῇ εὐνοούσῃ.» Ἡ δέ φησι «καὶ τίς αὐτῷ πλεῖον μου εὐνοεῖ;» Ὁ δὲ ἔφη «μεῖνον καὶ ὄψει.» Φωνήσας οὖν τὴν κύνα, «ἔρχου» φησι

Aesop went into the storehouse on some errand, he took one foot out of the pot and hid it. Aesop came back and looked at the pot, and when he saw only three feet, he realized that it was a trap for him. So he went down into the courtyard, pulled out a knife, and cut the foot off a pig that was being fattened. After singing the hairs off and salting it, he threw it into the pot and boiled it together with the rest. Xanthus, suspecting that Aesop might somehow discover the missing foot and run away, put it back in the pot. So the feet became five, but none of them realized what had happened.

43. After a little while, Xanthus said, "Aesop, if you have boiled the pig's feet, give them to us so we may eat." So Aesop emptied the feet into the platter, and lo, there were five! Xanthus said, "What is this?" Aesop grew pale and said, "How many feet do two pigs have?" Xanthus said, "Eight." Aesop said, "There are five here, and the pig down below spends its life on three legs." Xanthus said to his friends, "Didn't I say that this one will soon drive me to insanity?" Aesop said, "Master, you should not have set such a rule for me, and I would have served you properly. Things that are said superfluously by addition or subtraction are no small mistakes." So Xanthus, finding no motive for whipping him, kept his peace.

44. On the next day, Xanthus went to the lecture hall with Aesop. One of the students had prepared a great dinner and invited Xanthus along with the other students. So Xanthus, during the dinner, took many pieces and gave them to Aesop and said, "Go, give them to the female who is devoted to me." Aesop said to himself, "Now is the opportunity to avenge myself on my mistress for the way she mocked me when I was bought. She will see, then, just who is devoted to my master."

45. So he went to the house, sat down, and called to his mistress, and, placing the basket in front of her, he said, "My lady, has any been eaten?" She said, "It's all sound and untouched." Aesop said, "Do you see all this? My master has sent it not to you but to the female who is devoted to him." She said, "And who is more devoted to him than I?" He replied, "Wait, and you will see." So he called to the dog, "Come, Lycaena," he said, "and eat."

ὑφέλκων O   9 οὖν : δὲ O | οὐδὲ μίαν O | ἀφορμὴν εὑρηκὼς : εὑρηκὸς πρόφασιν O ‖ **44.**1 ἀκροτήριον O | σὺν αὐτῷ : om. O   3 οὖν : δὲ O | ἀνακληθείς post Ξάνθος add. O | πολλὰ : πόμα O | ἐπέδωκε : ἔδωκε O   4 ἄπαγε : ὔπαγε O | μοι post εὐνοούσῃ add. O   5 ἀνταμείνεσθαι O | με : om. O ‖ **45.**1 Ἐλθὼν οὖν : καὶ ἐλθὼν O | ἐκάθισε ... δέσποιναν : ἐκάλεσεν τὴν κυρίαν αὐτοῦ O   2 αὐτῆς : αὐτοῖς O | τέτρωκται : ἔφαγον O   3 ὑγιᾶ O | Αἴσωπος εἶπεν : καὶ ὁ ἔσωπος πρὸς αὐτήν O | ὁρᾷς ... πάντα : ἀλλὰ ταῦτα O   4 ἔπεμψεν O | εὐνούσῃ O | Ἡ δέ : καὶ ἡ γυνὴ τοῦ Ξάνθου O

«Λύκαινα καὶ φάγε.» Ἡ δὲ ποππύσασα προσέδραμεν αὐτῷ, καὶ ἔρριψε τῇ κυνὶ ἓν καθ' ἓν ὅλα τὰ μέρη λέγων «σοὶ εἶπεν ὁ δεσπότης δοθῆναι.» Μετὰ οὖν τὸ φαγεῖν τὴν κύνα ἀπῆλθεν Αἴσωπος πάλιν πρὸς τὸν δεσπότην.

46. Ὁ δὲ Ξάνθος λέγει αὐτῷ «δέδωκας τῇ εὐνοούσῃ τὰ μέρη;» Ὁ δέ φησι «πάντα λαβοῦσα ἐνώπιόν μου κατέφαγεν.» Ὁ Ξάνθος· «καὶ τί ἔλεγεν ἐσθίουσα;» Αἴσωπος εἶπεν «ἐμοὶ μὲν οὐδέν, τοῖς δὲ νεύμασιν ἐν ἑαυτῇ ηὔχετό σοι.» Ἡ δὲ γυνὴ τοῦ Ξάνθου περίλυπος γενομένη ἔλεγε «τὴν κύνα προκέκρικέ μου. Πῶς αὐτῷ εὐνοήσω; Οὐ μενῶ μετ' αὐτοῦ.» Καὶ εἰσελθοῦσα εἰς τὸν κοιτῶνα ἐπένθει.

47. Τοῦ δὲ πότου προκόπτοντος ζητήματα πρὸς ἀλλήλους ἐτίθεντο. Ἑνὸς δὲ εἰπόντος «πῶς ἔσται μεγάλη ταραχὴ ἐν ἀνθρώποις;» Αἴσωπος ἔφη ὄπισθεν ἑστὼς «ἐὰν οἱ νεκροὶ ἀνιστάμενοι τὰ ἴδια ἀπαιτήσωσι.» Γελάσαντες δὲ οἱ σχολαστικοὶ «νοήμων,» φασίν, «ὁ νεώνητος καὶ οὐκ ἄχαρις. Ἀλλὰ πάντα ὁ Ξάνθος ἐξάπινα διδάσκει αὐτόν, πλὴν πάντα καλῶς λέγει.»

48. Ἄλλος ἔφη «διὰ τί τὸ μὲν πρόβατον ἑλκόμενον εἰς θυσίαν οὐ βοᾷ, ὁ δὲ χοῖρος μεγάλα κράζει;» Αἴσωπος πάλιν ἑστὼς ἔφη «τὸ μὲν πρόβατον συνήθως ἀμελγόμενον καὶ κειρόμενον ἑλκόμενον ἀκολουθεῖ, σκελιζόμενον δὲ καὶ τὸν σίδηρον βλέπον οὐδὲν ὑποπτεύει· δοκεῖ γὰρ τὸ τοῦ πόκου βάρος ἀποτίθεσθαι καὶ τὴν τοῦ γάλακτος ἄμελξιν. Ὁ δὲ χοῖρος μήτε γάλα εὔχρηστον ἔχων μήτε τρίχας, εἰδὼς ὅτι πρὸς χρῆσιν τῶν κρεῶν τὸ αἷμα αὐτοῦ τις κενῶσαι θέλει, κέκραγε, μὴ ἔχων τι ἕτερον προσδοῦναι.» Οἱ δὲ σχολαστικοὶ θαυμάσαντες ἐπῄνεσαν αὐτόν. Καὶ οὕτως ἀνέλυσαν ἐκ τοῦ δείπνου.

49. Ὁ δὲ Ξάνθος εἰσελθὼν πρὸς τὴν γυναῖκα αὐτοῦ ἐν τῷ κοιτῶνι ἐκολάκευεν αὐτήν. Ἡ δὲ αὐτὸν ἀπεστρέφετο καί φησι «μὴ θίγῃς μου· δός μοι τὴν προῖκά μου· οὐ μένω μετὰ σοῦ. Ἀπελθὼν τὴν κύνα κολάκευε, ᾗτινι τὰ μέρη πέπομφας.» Ὁ Ξάνθος ἐν ἑαυτῷ· «τί ποτέ μοι πάλιν ὁ Αἴσωπος ἤρτυσε;» Καί φησι «κυρία μου, ἐγὼ πέπωκα καὶ σὺ μεθύεις; Τίνι ἔστειλα τὰ

45.6 ποππύσασα : ex mss. MSW corr. Perry, iter. Papath. : ποπτύσασα M (ποππύσασα legit Papath.) : προσπτύσασα O | ἐπέρριψεν O   7 Μετὰ ... 8 δεσπότην : πάλιν ἐπορεύθη πρὸς τὸν δεσπότην αὐτοῦ O ‖ **46.1** αὐτῷ : om. O | τῇ εὐνοούσῃ : om. O 2 φησι : ἔφη O | κατέφαγεν ἐνώπιόν μου inv. O | καὶ ὁ Ξάνθος O | καὶ : om. O 3 Αἴσωπος εἶπεν : ὁ δὲ O 5 μου : μοι O | οὖν post πῶς add. O | μένω O | κατελθοῦσα O ‖ **47.1** Τοῦ ... πότου : τοῦ δεσπότου O   2 Αἴσωπος ... 3 ἑστὼς : ἔσωπος ὄπισθεν ἑστὼς ἔφη O   3 δὲ : οὖν O   4 νοήμον O | φασίν : ἔφησαν O | ἀχαρὴς O 5 λέγει : ἔφη M ‖ **48.1** μὲν : om. M | τὸ post πρόβατον add. M | ἑλκόμενον ... θυσίαν :

The dog smacked its lips and ran to him, and one by one he threw all the pieces to the dog and said, "My master said that they were to be given to you." So after the dog had eaten, Aesop went back to his master.

46. Xanthus said to him, "Did you give the pieces to the female who is devoted to me?" Aesop said, "She took them all right in front of me and gulped them down." Xanthus said, "And what did she say while she was eating?" Aesop said, "To me, nothing, but by her nods she was praying for you inwardly." Xanthus's wife was very hurt and said, "He has preferred the dog to me. How shall I be devoted to him? I will not stay with him." And she went into the bedroom and lamented.

47. As the drinking advanced they began posing puzzles to one another, and one of them said, "How will the greatest disturbance among human beings occur?" Aesop, standing behind him, said, "If the dead rise up and demand back their own." The students laughed and said, "The new-bought slave is intelligent and not unpleasant. Xanthus teaches him everything on the spur of the moment, but he replies very well."

48. Another said, "Why does a sheep, when it is led to the sacrifice, not cry out, whereas a pig squeals mightily?" Aesop, again standing behind, said, "The sheep is used to being milked and shorn, so it follows when you drag it, and when it is made to kneel and sees the knife, it suspects nothing, for it thinks it's just for removing the weight of its fleece and milking. But the pig has neither milk nor wool that's useful, and so, knowing that someone wants to drain its blood so as to make use of its meat, it squeals, since it has nothing else to give." The students were impressed and praised him. And so they departed from the dinner.

49. Xanthus went to his wife in the bedroom and began to sweet-talk her. But she turned him away and said, "Don't touch me. Give me my dowry; I'm not staying with you. Go and sweet-talk the dog you sent the pieces to." Xanthus said to himself, "What on earth has Aesop prepared for me this time?" And he said, "My lady, I've done the drinking, and you're

---

εἰς θυσίαν ἐρχόμενον M 2 μεγάλα : om. O | πάλιν ἑστὼς : om. O | συνήθως : πρὸς τὸ σύνηθες M 3 καὶ ante ἑλκόμενον add. M | δὲ : om. O | τὸν ... 4 σίδηρον : τὴν μάχεραν O 4 βλέπων O 5 τὴν : om. O | ἔχων : corr. Perry, iter. Papath. : ἔχον MO 6 τρίχας : ἔριον O | πρὸς χρῆσιν : πρὸς χρείαν M 7 κέκραγε : om. O | προσδοῦναι : δράσε βοᾷ ἐξόχως O 7–8 ἐθαύμασαν καὶ ἐπῄνεσαν M 8 ἐκ : om. M ‖ **49**.1 εἰσελθὼν : κατελθὼν O 2 καί φησι : λέγουσα O | θίγεις O 3 οὐ : οὐκέτι O | ᾗτινι : ἥν O | ᾗτινι ... 4 μέρη : absc. in M 4 Ὁ ... ἑαυτῷ· : ὁ δὲ πρὸς αὐτήν O | ὁ² : om. O 5 κυρία ... πέπωκα : μὴ θίγῃς μου·δός μοι M | σὺ ... ἔστειλα : absc. M

μέρη; Οὐχὶ σοί;» Ἡ δὲ ἔφη «οὐκ ἐμοί, ἀλλὰ τῇ κυνί.» Ξάνθος εἶπεν «Αἴσωπόν μοί τις καλεσάτω.»

50. Ἐλθόντος δὲ αὐτοῦ λέγει «τίνι ἔδωκας τὰ μέρη;» Ὁ δὲ ἔφη «τῇ εὐνοούσῃ.» Ὁ Ξάνθος φησίν «οὐδὲν ἔλαβε.» Καὶ ἡ γυνὴ ἐφώνησεν «οὐδὲν εἴληφα ἐγώ.» Αἴσωπος ἔφη «τίνι εἶπας δοθῆναι τὰ μέρη;» Ὁ Ξάνθος εἶπε «τῇ εὐνοούσῃ.» Ὁ Αἴσωπος· «μὴ οὖν αὕτη σου εὐνοεῖ;» Ὁ δέ· «ἀλλὰ τίς, δραπέτα;» Αἴσωπος φωνήσας τὴν κύνα φησίν «αὕτη σου μᾶλλον εὐνοεῖ· γυνὴ δὲ κἂν λέγῃ εὐνοεῖν, οὐκ εὐνοεῖ. Εἰ γὰρ ἐπ' ἐλάχιστον λυπηθῇ, ὑβρίζει, ἀντιλέγει, ἀναχωρεῖ. Τὴν δὲ κύνα δεῖρον, δίωξον, καὶ οὐ μὴ ὑποχωρήσει, ἀλλ' εὐθὺς ἐπιλαθομένη πάλιν τὴν κέρκον τῷ δεσπότῃ σείει. Ἔδει σε δὲ εἰπεῖν 'τῇ γυναικί μου ταῦτα ἀπόφερε' καὶ μὴ 'τῇ εὐνοούσῃ'.» Ὁ Ξάνθος τῇ γυναικὶ εἶπε «βλέπεις, κυρία, ὅτι οὐκ ἐμὸν τὸ αἴτιον, ἀλλὰ τοῦ ἐπενέγκαντος; Μακροθύμησον οὖν καὶ εὑρήσω πρόφασιν δι' ἧς αὐτὸν μαστιγώσω.»

50a. Ἡ δὲ «ἀπὸ τοῦ νῦν οὐ συνοικήσω μετὰ σοῦ» ἔτι φήσασα, ἐξελθοῦσα δὲ λαθραίως ἐπορεύθη πρὸς τοὺς ἑαυτῆς γονεῖς. Ὁ δὲ Αἴσωπος ἔφη τῷ κυρίῳ αὐτοῦ· «δέσποτα, οὐκ εἶπόν σοι ὅτι ἡ κύων σοι εὐνοεῖ καὶ οὐχ ἡ κυρία μου;» Ἡμερῶν δὲ διελθουσῶν καὶ ταύτης ἀδιαλλάκτου μενούσης ἔπεμψεν ὁ Ξάνθος παρακαλῶν αὐτὴν ὅπως εἰς αὐτὸν ὑποστρέψῃ. Ἡ δὲ οὐκ ἐπείθετο. Ἐν πολλῇ οὖν ἀθυμίᾳ ὑπάρχων ὁ Ξάνθος διὰ τὴν τῆς γυναικὸς στέρησιν ἤσχαλλεν ἔτι δὲ καὶ ἠδημόνει. Ὁ δὲ Αἴσωπος προσελθὼν λέγει αὐτῷ «μὴ λυποῦ, ὦ δέσποτα, περὶ τούτου· ἐγὼ γὰρ αὔριον ποιήσω αὐτὴν ὅπως μόνη ἀνακάμψῃ πρὸς σὲ μηδενὸς ζητήσαντος.» Καὶ αἰτήσας νομίσματα καὶ λαβὼν ἐξῄει εἰς τὴν ἀγοράν, καὶ ὠνησάμενος ὄρνιθάς τε καὶ χῆνας καὶ ἕτερα ἄττα ἀπῄει βαστάζων αὐτά, διερχόμενος κατὰ τὸν τόπον ἐν ᾧ ἡ κυρία αὐτοῦ ἦν, προσποιούμενος δῆθεν μὴ γινώσκειν ὅτι ἐκεῖσε <ὑπάρχει> ἡ τοῦ Ξάνθου γυνή. Εὑρὼν δέ τινα <τῶν> οἰκετῶν τῶν ἐκείνης ἔφη αὐτῷ «ἆρά γε, ἀδελφέ, μὴ ἔχωσιν ἐν τῷδε τῷ οἴκῳ ἢ χῆνας ἢ ἕτερόν τι τῶν πρεπόντων εἰς γάμους;» Ὁ δέ· «καὶ τί τούτων χρείαν ἔχεις;» Καὶ ὁ Αἴσωπος· «Ξάνθος ὁ φιλόσοφος

49.6 Ἡ ... ἐμοί : οὐκ ἐμοί ἔφη O ‖ 50.1 ἐλθόντι δὲ αὐτῷ M | δέδωκας O | ἔφη : om. O 2 ἔλαβες O | ἐφώνησεν : φησίν O 3 Αἴσωπος ... 4 εὐνοούσῃ : om. O 4 καὶ ante ὁ Αἴσωπος add. O | αὕτη : αὐτῇ O | σου : σοι O | Ὁ δέ : om. M | ἀλλὰ : καὶ O 5 τὴν κύνα φωνήσας inv. O | σου : σοι O 6 λέγει O | εὐνοεῖ O | ἐπ' ἐλαχίστω O 7 δῆρον M | ὑποχωρήσῃ M 8 ἐπιλαθομένη : ὑπελαχομένη O | σίει O | δὲ : οὖν O 9 πρόσφερε O | Ὁ ... 10 εἶπε : καὶ ὁ Ξάνθος πρὸς τὴν γυναῖκα φησί O

the one who's intoxicated? To whom did I send the pieces? Wasn't it to you?" And she said, "Not to me but to the dog." Xanthus said, "Let someone summon Aesop to me."

50. When Aesop arrived, Xanthus said to him, "To whom did you give the pieces?" And he said, "To the female who is devoted to you." Xanthus said, "She got nothing." And his wife declared, "I for one got nothing." Aesop said, "To whom did you say that the pieces were to be given?" Xanthus said, "to the female who is devoted to me." And Aesop, "And isn't she devoted to you?" Xanthus, "Who, then, you damned slave?" Aesop called to the dog and said, "She is more devoted to you; even if your wife says she is devoted, she is not devoted. For if she is in the least bit distressed, she insults you, she contradicts you, she leaves you. But beat the dog, torment it, and it won't shun you but will immediately forget and again wave its tail for its master. You should have said, 'Bring these things to my wife' and not 'to the one who is devoted to me.'" Xanthus said to his wife, "You see, my lady, that the fault is not mine but of the one who brought the food. So bear up, and I will find some excuse to beat him."

50a. She still said, "From now on I will not live with you," and she left and secretly went to her parents. Aesop said to his lord, "Master, didn't I tell you that the dog is devoted to you and not my mistress?" As the days went by and she remained unreconciled, Xanthus sent to beseech her to return to him, but she would not be persuaded. Xanthus was in a deep depression on account of the absence of his wife and was continually upset and troubled. Aesop came up and said to him, "Don't be distressed, master, about this. Tomorrow I'll make her return to you by herself, with no one seeking her out." And he asked for some coins, and taking them he went to the marketplace and bought chickens and geese and some other things and went off carrying them. He passed by the place where his mistress was, pretending to be sure that he did not know that Xanthus's wife was there. He met up with one of her slaves and said to him, "Brother, might they have in this house geese or something else that is suitable for a wedding?" And he said, "What need do you have of those things?" And Aesop said, "Tomorrow, Xanthus the philosopher is going to be married." The slave

---

10 ἐνέγκαντός O ‖ **50a.1** : cap. hoc deest in OLo et G, praebet M cum SBP **7** ἔτι δὲ : suppl. Papath. : δὲ evan. in M | ἠδιμόνει M **9** ἀνακάμψει M **10** ἐξίει M | ἕτερα ἄττα : scripsit Papath. : ἕτεραττα M **11** κατὰ : evan. in M **12** ὑπάρχει : ex mss. BPWV corr. Perry, iter. Papath. **13** τῶν¹ : ex mss.BPSA suppl. Perry, iter. Papath. **14** τί ... **15** χρείαν : evan. in M

τῇ αὔριον μέλλει γυναικὶ συζευχθῆναι.» Ὁ δὲ δρομαίως ἀναβὰς ἀνήγγειλε ταῦτα τῇ τοῦ Ξάνθου γυναικί. Ἡ δὲ ἀκούσασα ἀπῄει μετὰ πολλῆς σπουδῆς πρὸς τὸν Ξάνθον καὶ κατεβόα αὐτοῦ λέγουσα «ὦ Ξάνθε, ἐμοῦ ἐν τοῖς ζῶσιν ὑπαρχούσης ἑτέρᾳ γυναικὶ ἁρμοσθῆναι οὐ δύνασαι.»

51. Μεθ' ἡμέρας δὲ ὀλίγας προσκαλεσάμενος ὁ Ξάνθος σχολαστικοὺς εἰς ἄριστον τῷ Αἰσώπῳ ἔφη «ἀπελθὼν ὀψώνησον εἴ τι καλόν, εἴ τι τερπνόν.» Αἴσωπος ἀπιὼν πρὸς ἑαυτὸν ἔλεγεν «ἐγὼ αὐτῷ δείξω μὴ μωρὰ διατάσσεσθαι.» Φθάσας δὲ εἰς τὸ μάκελλον πάντων τῶν τεθυμένων χοίρων ἠγόρασε τὰς γλώσσας καὶ ἐλθὼν ἐσκεύασεν. Ἀνακλιθέντων τῶν φίλων σὺν τῷ Ξάνθῳ μετὰ τὸ πιεῖν «Αἴσωπε, δὸς ἡμῖν φαγεῖν», ὁ Ξάνθος εἶπεν. Ὁ δὲ παρέθηκεν ἑκάστῳ γλῶσσαν ἐκζεστὴν σὺν ὀξογάρῳ. Οἱ δὲ σχολαστικοὶ τὸν Ξάνθον ἐπῄνεσαν λέγοντες «ὦ καθηγητά, τὸ ἄριστόν σου φιλοσοφίας μεστόν. Εὐθέως γὰρ γλώττας ἐπέδωκας, δι' ὧν πᾶσα φιλολογία εἰσπέμπεται, καὶ τὸ κρεῖττον ἐξ ὕδατος· πᾶσα γὰρ γλῶσσα ἐν ὑγρῷ καθέστηκεν.» Ἔφαγον οὖν ἡδέως.

52. Μετὰ δὲ τὸ πιεῖν ὁ Ξάνθος φησὶν «Αἴσωπε, δὸς ἡμῖν τι φαγεῖν.» Ὁ δὲ παρέθηκεν ἑκάστῳ γλῶσσαν ὀπτὴν δι' ἁλὸς καὶ πεπέρεως. Οἱ σχολαστικοὶ «οὐᾶ, καθηγητά,» πάλιν εἶπον, «οἰκείως καὶ μεγάλως γλῶσσα ὀπτή· πᾶσα γὰρ γλῶσσα πυρὶ ἠκόνηται, καὶ τὸ κρεῖττον δι' ἁλοπεπέρεως. Τὸ γὰρ ἁλυκὸν τῷ δριμεῖ συγκέκραται καὶ τὸ δάκνον ἐπιδέξεται.» Πάλιν ἔφαγον ἡδέως. Καὶ μετ' ὀλίγον ὁ Ξάνθος «Αἴσωπε, δὸς ἡμῖν φαγεῖν τι.» Ὁ δὲ ἑκάστῳ δέδωκεν γλῶσσαν ἀρτυτήν. Οἱ σχολαστικοὶ πρὸς ἀλλήλους ἔλεγον «ἡμεῖς τὰς γλώσσας ἠλγήσαμεν, γλώσσας τρώγοντες. Οὐκ ἔχομεν ἕτερόν τι φαγεῖν;» Πάλιν Αἴσωπος ἑκάστῳ γλῶσσαν ζωμευτὴν παρέθηκε. Οἱ δὲ σχολαστικοὶ ἀγανακτήσαντες «ἕως πότε γλώσσας; Ψῶ, τὸ ἄριστον τοῦτο!» ἔλεγον. Θυμωθεὶς οὖν ὁ Ξάνθος ἔφη «Αἴσωπε, οὐκ ἔχεις τι ἕτερον;» Ὁ δὲ εἶπεν «οὔ.»

50a.16 ἀνήγγειλε ... 17 Ξάνθου : evan. in M   17 πολλῆς ... 18 καὶ : absc. in M : ex ms. S corr. Perry, iter. Papath. **18–19** -ῶσιν ὑπαρχούσης absc. in M ‖ **51.1** : Περὶ τοῦ ἀρίστου (titul. cap.) in lin. atramento rubro add. M | καλέσας O | τινὰς post σχολαστικοὺς add. O **2** ἀπελθὼν : ἄπελθε καὶ O | ὀψόνισον M | εἴ² ... τερπνόν : καὶ χρηστόν O **3** ἀπιὼν ... ἑαυτόν : πρὸς ἀπιὼν ἑαυτῷ O | αὐτῷ : αὐτὸν O **4** εἰς τὸν O | προτεθημένων O **5** ἀνακληθέντων δὲ O | μετὰ τοῦ Ξάνθου M **6** φησί post Αἴσωπε add. O | ὁ ... εἶπεν : om. O **7** ἐκζεστὴν ... ὀξογάρῳ : ὀπτὴν καὶ ὀξύγαρον O | ἐπῄνεσαν τὸν Ξάνθον inv. O **8** καὶ ante τὸ ἄριστόν σου add. O **9** ἐπέδωκας : ἐπὶ δέδωκας O | δι' ὧν : δι' ἧς O | φιλολογία : φιλοσοφία O | εἰσπέμπεται : ἐκπέμπεται O | γὰρ post κρεῖττον add. O **10** γὰρ : om. O | οὖν : om. O ‖ **52.1** Μετὰ ... πιεῖν : καὶ πιόντες O **2** Οἱ ... 3 εἶπον : οὐᾶ καθηγητά, εἶπον οἱ σχολαστικοὶ O **3** γλῶσσαν

left at a run and reported this to Xanthus's wife, and when she heard it she went with great haste to Xanthus and screamed at him and said, "Xanthus, while I am among the living you cannot betroth yourself to another wife."

51. After a few days Xanthus summoned some students to lunch and said to Aesop, "Go and buy food, whatever is fine and enjoyable." Aesop went off saying to himself, "I'll show him not to order stupid things." He went to the butcher shop and bought the tongues of all the slaughtered pigs, then returned and prepared them. When Xanthus and his friends reclined at the table, after drinking, Xanthus said, "Give us something to eat." Aesop served each one a boiled tongue with a vinegar fish sauce. The students praised Xanthus and said, "Professor, your lunch is stuffed with philosophy, for first off you have given us tongues, by which the whole of philology is emitted, and best of all, cooked with water. For every tongue is set in liquid." And so they ate happily.

52. After the drinking, Xanthus said, "Aesop, give us something to eat." He served each a tongue roasted with salt and pepper. The students said, "Wow, Professor," said the students once more, "roasted tongue, very appropriately, since every tongue is sharpened by fire, and best of all, with salt and pepper, for the saltiness harmonizes with the tartness and the spiciness when they are united." And again they ate happily. And after a short while Xanthus said, "Aesop, give us something to eat." He gave each a spiced tongue, and the students said to one another, "Our tongues are sick of eating tongues. Don't we have anything else to eat?" Again, Aesop served each a tongue soup. The students grew irritated and said, "How long will it be tongues? Phew, what a lunch!" So Xanthus became angry and said, "Aesop, don't you have anything else?" And he replied, "No."

ὀπτήν O **4** γάρ¹ : om. O | εἰκόνηται O | ἁλυκὸν : ex G corr. Perry, iter. Papath. : ἁλυκτὸν M : ἑλικτὸν O **5** δρυμὺ O | συγκέκραται : ex G corr. Perry, iter. Papath. : συγκρᾶται O : συγκροτεῖ M | τῷ δάκνοντι M | ἐπιδέξεται : ex λ corr. Perry : ἐπιδέξηται O : ἐπειδὰν ἐνωθεῖ M | Πάλιν : εἶτα O | ἡδέως : om. O **6** Αἴσωπε : post φαγεῖν trans. O | τι : om. O | δέδωκεν ... 7 ἀρτυτήν : γλῶσσαν ἔθηκεν ἀρτιτὴν O **7** δὲ : om. M | ἔλεγον πρὸς ἀλλήλους inv. O **7–8** ἡμῶν post τὰς γλώσσας add. O **8** τι ἕτερον inv. O **9** οὖν ὁ ante Αἴσωπος add. O | γλῶσσαν ... παρέθηκε : γλῶσσαν παρέθηκεν ζευμευτὴν O | δὲ : om. M **10** ἀγανακτοῦντες ἔλεγον O | ἐσθίωμεν post γλώσσας add. O **11** οὖν : δὲ O | ἔφη : φησίν O | τι ἕτερον : ἄλλο τίποτε O | Ὁ δὲ : καὶ O ǁ

53. Καὶ ὁ Ξάνθος φησὶν «οὐκ εἶπόν σοι, κατάρατε, εἴ τι καλὸν καὶ χρηστόν, ὤνησαι;» Ὁ δέ φησι «χάριν ἔχω ὅτι ἀνδρῶν φιλοσόφων παρόντων μέμφῃ μοι. Εἶπας εἴ τι καλὸν καὶ χρηστόν. Καὶ τί μεῖζον ἐν βίῳ γλώσσης; Διὰ γλώττης πᾶσα φιλοσοφία καὶ παιδεία συνέστηκε. Δι' αὐτῆς δόσεις, δι' αὐτῆς λήψεις,
5 ἀσπασμοί, ἀγορασίαι, δόξαι, μοῦσαι, γάμοι, πόλεις ἀνορθοῦνται καὶ πάλιν 5 καταβάλλονται· γλῶσσα ἄνδρα ταπεινοῖ καὶ πάλιν ὑψοῖ. Διὰ γλώσσης πᾶς ὁ βίος συνέστηκεν. Οὐδὲν οὖν αὐτῆς ἐστι κρεῖττον.» Οἱ σχολαστικοὶ «καλῶς λέγει», ἔφησαν, «οὐδὲν κρεῖττον γλώσσης. Σὺ ἥμαρτες, καθηγητά.» Ὕβριν δὲ τοῦτο λογισάμενοι ἀνέστησαν ἀπὸ τοῦ δείπνου, ὁλονυκτὶ δυσφορήσαντες.

10 54. Τῇ δὲ ἑξῆς ἡμέρᾳ μεμφθεὶς ὑπὸ τῶν φίλων ὁ Ξάνθος ἔφη «οὐ γέγονε κατὰ τὴν ἐμὴν θέλησιν, ἀλλὰ κατὰ τὴν τοῦ ἀχρείου δούλου. Σήμερον δὲ ἀνταλλάξω τὸν δεῖπνον. Ἐνώπιον δὲ ὑμῶν διαλεχθήσομαι αὐτῷ.» Καὶ φησιν «Αἴσωπε, ἀπελθὼν ἀγόρασον εἴ τι σαπρόν, εἴ τι χεῖρον, ἐπεὶ πρὸς δεῖπνον καλῶ τοὺς σχολαστικούς.» Αἴσωπος δὲ μηδὲν ταραχθεὶς ἀπῆλθεν εἰς 5
15 τὸ μάκελλον καὶ πάλιν γλώσσας ἐπαγοράσας ἐποίησεν ὡσαύτως. Ἐλθόντες οὖν οἱ σχολαστικοὶ ἀνεκλίθησαν καὶ φησιν ὁ Ξάνθος «Αἴσωπε, δὸς ἡμῖν τι φαγεῖν.» Παρέθηκεν οὖν ὁ Αἴσωπος ἑκάστῳ γλῶσσαν ἐξ ὕδατος καὶ ὄξους. Οἱ δὲ πρὸς ἑαυτοὺς ἔλεγον «χοίρειαι πάλιν γλῶσσαι! Πάντως θέλων ἀπὸ τῆς χθὲς διαρρυέντα τὸν στόμαχον τῷ ὄξει ἀνακτήσασθαι, τοῦτο Ξάνθος πεποίηκεν.» 10
20 Εἶτα πάλιν τοῦ Ξάνθου φωνήσαντος Αἴσωπος γλώσσας αὖθις παρέθηκε. Οἱ δὲ σχολαστικοὶ ἐταράχθησαν.

55. Ὁ Ξάνθος· «τί τοῦτο, Αἴσωπε; Μή τί σοι εἶπον 'εἴ τι καλόν, εἴ τι χρηστόν'; Μᾶλλον οὐκ εἶπόν σοι 'εἴ τι σαπρόν, εἴ τι χεῖρον';» Ὁ δὲ ἔφη «καὶ τί ἐστι χεῖρον γλώσσης; Διὰ γὰρ γλώσσης ἔχθραι, διαβολαί, μέμψεις, ἔριδες,

---

53.1 φησὶν : om. O 2 ὤνησαι : om. O | Ὁ δέ φησι : καὶ τι μεῖζον ὁ ἔσωπος, γλώττης, ὅμως O | φιλολόγων O 3 Εἶπας ... χρηστόν : om. O | καλὸν : atramento nigro M^{sl} | Καὶ ... γλώσσης : τι βέλτιστον γλώττης ἐν τῷ βίῳ O | γλώσσης O 4 Δι' αὐτῆς : διὰ γλώσσης O | Δι' ... 6 ὑψοῖ : post κρεῖττον trans. O | δόσις O : evan. in M | δι' αὐτῆς : om. O | λῆψις O 5 μοῦσαι : om. O | γάμοι : evan. in M : δι' αὐτῆς ψαλμῳδίαι post γάμοι add. O | ἀνορθούμεναι O | πάλιν : πόλεις M 7 συνέστηκεν : ἐν τάξει γίνεται O | οὖν ... κρεῖττον : evan. in M | Οἱ σχολαστικοὶ : ἀκούσαντες δὲ οἱ σχολαστικοὶ ἔλεγον O | καλῶς ... 8 ἔφησαν : τὰ πάντα διατάσσεται καλῶς O 8 γλώσσης : evan. in M 9 ἀνέστησαν : evan. in M | ἀνέστησαν ... δείπνου : κατέλυσαν τοῦ ἀρίστου O | τοῦ δεί- lit. evan. in M ‖ **54.**1 δὲ ἑξῆς : evan. in M | μεμφθεὶς ... ἔφη : ὑπὸ τῶν φιλοσόφων ὁ Ξάνθος μεμφθεῖς, ἔφη πρὸς αὐτούς O 3 ἀνταλλάξομαι O | τὸ δεῖπνον O |

53. And Xanthus said, "Didn't I tell you, you abominable thing, to buy whatever was fine and good?" Aesop said, "I am grateful that you are blaming me when men who are philosophers are present. You said whatever is fine and good. And what is better in life than the tongue? It is by the tongue that all philosophy and education have been established. It is by virtue of the tongue that there are givings and takings, greetings, purchases, opinions, songs, weddings; thanks to it cities are restored and are overturned again. The tongue humbles a man and in turn elevates him. It is by virtue of the tongue that all life has its basis. So nothing is better than it." "He speaks well," the students said, "nothing is better than the tongue. It's you who you were wrong, Professor." But they considered this to be an insult and left the dinner and were indisposed the entire night.

54. On the next day Xanthus was faulted by his friends, and he said, "It was not done by my wish but by that of my useless slave. But today I will change the dinner. I will discuss it with him in your presence." And he said, "Aesop, go and buy food, whatever is rotten, whatever is the worst, as I am inviting the students to dinner." Aesop, not in the least perturbed, went to the butcher shop and again bought tongues and prepared them in the same way. The students came and reclined for dinner, and Xanthus said, "Aesop, give us something to eat." So Aesop served each a tongue cooked with water and vinegar. They said among themselves, "Pig tongue again! Surely Xanthus did this out of a desire to soothe our stomachs with vinegar, after yesterday's diarrhea." Then, when Xanthus called to him again, Aesop once more served tongues, and the students were upset.

55. Xanthus said, "What is this, Aesop? Did I say to you 'whatever is fine and good'? Or did I rather say to you 'whatever is rotten, whatever is worst'?" Aesop said, "And what is worse than a tongue? For thanks to

---

Ἐνώπιον δὲ : καὶ ἐνώπιον O 4 ἐπεὶ δοκεῖ σοι τὰ εὔχρηστα λαλεῖν καγὼ σοι τα ἐναντία διαπράξομαι add. post Αἴσωπε O | εἰ² τι χεῖρον : om. O 5 Αἴσωπος δὲ : ὁ δὲ ἔσωπος O | εἰς : πρὸς O 6 ἐπαγοράσας : ἠγόρασεν O | ἐποίησεν ὡσαύτως : καὶ ὥς ἔναγχος ἔδρασεν O 7 κατεκλήθησαν O | καί ... 8 φαγεῖν : μετὰ δὲ τὸ πιεῖν O 8 Παρέθηκεν ... γλῶσσαν : ἑκάστῳ γλῶσσα παρέθηκεν O 9 ἑαυτοὺς : om. O 10 διαρρυέντα : διαρρίας ἤγουν O | τῷ ὀξεῖ O | τοῦτο ... πεποίηκεν : ταῦτα προσήνεγκεν O 11 Εἶτα ... παρέθηκε : καὶ μετ' ὀλίγον πάλιν ἀνέκειντο γλῶσσαι O || 55.1 Ὁ Ξάνθος : καὶ ὁ Ξάνθος φησὶ O | ἔσωπε, τι τοῦτο inv. O | Μή ... 2 χεῖρον' : οὐκ εἶπόν σοι εἴ τι σαθρὸν εἴ τι χεῖρον O 2 ἔφη : φησὶ O | καὶ : om. O 3 γλώττης O | διὰ γὰρ ταύτης πολλοὶ ἀπόλλωντο καὶ εἰς πενίαν ἐσχάτην κατήντησαν ante διὰ γὰρ γλώσσης add. O | γὰρ : om. O | γλώττης O | ἔριδες : om. O

φθόνοι, ζηλοτυπίαι, ἀφανισμοὶ πόλεων. Καὶ τί ἔτι λέγω; Οὐδέν πω χεῖρόν ἐστι γλώττης.» Τίς δὲ τῶν ἀνακειμένων τῷ Ξάνθῳ ἔφη «τούτῳ ἐὰν πρόσσχῃς, εἰς μανίαν σε περιτρέψει· οἷα γὰρ ἡ μορφή, τοιάδε καὶ ἡ ψυχή.» Αἴσωπος ἔφη «σύ μοι δοκεῖς κακεντρεχέστερος εἶναι παροξύνων δεσπότην κατ' οἰκέτου. Ὡς περίεργος εἶ τὰ ἀλλότρια μεριμνῶν!»

56. Ὁ οὖν Ξάνθος ζητῶν ἀφορμὴν τοῦ μαστιγῶσαι τὸν Αἴσωπον λέγει «δραπέτα, ἐπεὶ περίεργον εἶπας τὸν φίλον, δεῖξόν μοι ἄνθρωπον ἀπερίεργον.» Ὁ δέ φησι «δέσποτα, εἰσὶ πολλοὶ τὰ οἰκεῖα τρώγοντες καὶ πίνοντες καὶ τὰ ἴδια μεριμνῶντες, ἔνιοι δὲ τῶν ἀνθρώπων τῶν ἰδίων οὐ μνημονεύοντες τὰ ἀλλότρια περιεργάζονται.» Ξάνθος εἶπεν «ἕτερον δεῖπνον ἑτοιμάσω. Σὺ δὲ πορευθεὶς κάλει μοι ἄνθρωπον ἀπερίεργον, ἵνα ὃ ἐὰν ἴδῃ ἢ ἀκούσῃ μὴ περιεργάσηται.»

57. Ὁ δὲ Αἴσωπος ἐξελθὼν ἐζήτει ἄνθρωπον ἀπερίεργον καὶ ἐλθὼν εἰς τὴν ἀγορὰν εὗρε γινομένην μάχην καὶ ὄχλον πολὺν ἑστῶτα, ἕνα δὲ παρ' ἓν μέρος καθεζόμενον καὶ ἀναγινώσκοντα. Καί φησιν Αἴσωπος καθ' ἑαυτόν «τοῦτον καλέσω. Ἀπερίεργος φαίνεται καὶ μενῶ ἄπληγος.» Ἀπελθὼν οὖν πρὸς αὐτόν, φησὶ «κομψότατε, Ξάνθος ὁ φιλόσοφος μαθών σου τὴν πραότητα ἐπὶ δεῖπνόν σε καλεῖ.» Ὁ δέ φησιν «ἐλεύσομαι· εὑρήσεις δέ με πρὸ τοῦ πυλῶνος.» Ἐλθὼν οὖν ὁ Αἴσωπος ηὐτρέπισε τὸ δεῖπνον. Ὁ δὲ Ξάνθος φησὶν «ποῦ ὁ ἀπερίεργος ἄνθρωπος;» Ὁ δέ· «πρὸ τοῦ πυλῶνος ἕστηκε.» Τῇ δὲ τακτῇ ὥρᾳ εἰσήγαγεν αὐτὸν καὶ κατεκλίθη μετὰ τῶν φίλων.

58. Ὁ Ξάνθος εἶπε δοθῆναι πρῶτον τῷ ξένῳ οἰνόμελι. Ὁ δέ φησιν «οὐχί, κύριε. Σὺ πρῶτον πίε, εἶτα ἡ γυνή σου, ἔπειτα ἡμεῖς οἱ φίλοι σου.» Ὁ δὲ Ξάνθος νεύει τῷ Αἰσώπῳ «ἔχω ἅπαξ. Καὶ πῶς ἐφαίνετο ἀπερίεργος;» Εἶτα ἰχθύων

55.4 καὶ πόλεων ἀφανισμοί O | Καὶ ... 5 γλώττης : om. O 5 Τίς : εἶς O | τῷ Ξάνθῳ : om. O | καθηγητά post ἔφη add. O | τούτῳ : τοῦτο O | πρόσσχῃς : ex λ Perry : μὴ (suppl. ex B) πρόσσχῃς Papath. : προσχῇς M : προσέχει O 6 Αἴσωπον δείξας ante εἰς μανίαν add. M | σε : om. O | περιτρέπει O | ἔφη : εἶπεν O 7 μοι : om. O | κακεντριχέστερος O | κατ' : μετὰ O 8 εἶ : καὶ O ‖ 56.1 οὖν : δὲ O | τὸν ... Αἴσωπον : αὐτὸν O | αὐτῷ post λέγει add. O 2 δραπετά O | πάντως πᾶς ἄνθρωπος περίεργος, εἰς πᾶσαν τέχνην καὶ δουλίαν καὶ ὃ ἐὰν εἴδει περιεργάζεται post φίλον add. O | σὺ post δεῖξον μοι add. O 3 Ὁ ... φησι : καὶ ὁ ἔσωπος O | μου post δέσποτα add. O | οἳ post πολλοὶ add. O | καὶ² ... ἴδια : οὐ M 4 μεριμνῶσιν M | ἀνθρώπων : ὀθνείων O | τῶν² ... μνημονεύοντες : om. O | καὶ ante τὰ ἀλλότρια add. O

it there are enmities, slanders, censures, conflicts, envies, jealousies, and destruction of cities. What more can I say? There is nothing worse than the tongue." One of the students who was reclining said to Xanthus, "If you pay attention to this one," and he pointed to Aesop, "he will drive you to insanity, for like his shape, so, too, is his soul." Aesop said, "You seem to me more evil-minded, to be inciting a master against a slave. What a meddler you are, concerning yourself with other people's affairs!"

56. So Xanthus, seeking a pretext for whipping Aesop, said, "You damned slave, since you said that my friend is a meddler, show me a person who is a nonmeddler." Aesop said, "Master, there are many people who eat and drink their own things and do not meddle, but some people do not mind their own things but meddle in other people's." Xanthus said, "I will prepare another dinner. You go and invite for me a person who is a nonmeddler, so he won't meddle whatever he sees or hears."

57. Aesop, accordingly, went out and looked for a person who was a nonmeddler and, when he arrived at the marketplace, he came upon a quarrel and a large crowd standing round, but one man was sitting to one side and reading. And Aesop said to himself, "I'll invite this one. He seems to be a nonmeddler, and I'll remain without a beating." So he went up to him and said, "My clever fellow, Xanthus the philosopher learned of your gentleness and invites you to dinner." The other said, "I'll come. You will find me in front of the gate." So Aesop went and got the dinner ready. Xanthus said, "Where is the person who is a nonmeddler?" Aesop replied, "He was standing in front of the gate." At the set time he led him in and seated him next to Xanthus's friends.

58. Xanthus said that mead should be given first to the stranger to drink. He said, "No, sir. You drink first, then your wife, then we your friends." Xanthus said to Aesop, "That's one. And how did he measure up

---

5 περιεργάζονται : περιεργαζόμενοι O | ὁ δὲ ante Ξάνθος add. O 6 ἐὰν : evan. in M (spatium est) ‖ 57.1 δὲ : τοίνυν M 2 γινομένην : μινομένην O | ἑστῶτα : ἐστ- evan. in M : συνεστῶτα ex W corr. Perry, iter. Papath. | παρ' ἕν : παρὰ ἕν O 3 αὐτὸν ante καθεζόμενον add. O | Καί ... ἑαυτόν : ἔσωπος φησί καθευατόν O 4 μένω O | οὖν : om. O 5 κοψώτατε O | ἐπὶ : πρὸς O 6 σε : om. O | μὴ περιεργασάμενος διὰ ποίαν αἰτίαν κέκληκε ante ἐλθών add. O 7 ὁ¹ : om. M | ἔσωπε post φησὶν add. O 8 εἱστήκει M 9 σὺν τοῖς ὑποδήμασι καὶ τῷ πηλῷ ὁ δὲ Ξάνθος τις ἐστιν οὗτος. ἔσωπος φησί. ἄνθρωπος ἀπερίεργος post φίλων add. O ‖ 58.1 Ὁ Ξάνθος : ὁ δὲ Ξ. O | εἶπε : ἔταξεν O | πρῶτον ... οἰνόμελι : τῷ ξένω πρῶτον οἰνόμελη O | πιεῖν post οἰνόμελι add. M | οὐχί : οὐ O 2 εἶτα : om. O | σου² : om. O | Ὁ δὲ : om. M 3 νεύει : λέγει M | ἀπερίεργος : ἀπερί O : περίεργος corr. Perry, iter. Papath.

λοπὰς παρετέθη. Ὁ Ξάνθος ἐπαφορμιζόμενος ἔφη «τοσαῦτά μου ἀρτύματα δεδωκότος κατεφρονήθη ἡ μαγειρία. Οὔτε γὰρ ἀρώματα οὔτε ἔλαιον οὔτε ὁ ζωμὸς σύγχυλος. Τυφθήτω ὁ μάγειρος.» Ὁ ξένος φησὶ «παῦσαι, δέσποτα! Οὐδὲν αἴτιον, πάντα καλά.» Ὁ Ξάνθος πάλιν νεύει τῷ Αἰσώπῳ «ἰδοὺ, δύο.»
5 Εἶτα εἰσφέρεται πλακοῦς πολυσήσαμος. Ὁ Ξάνθος γευσάμενος λέγει «κάλει τὸν ἀρτοκόπον. Διὰ τί ὁ πλακοῦς οὔτε μέλι οὔτε σταφίδας ἔχει;» Ὁ ξένος πάλιν λέγει «δέσποτα, καὶ ὁ πλακοῦς καλὸς καὶ οὐδὲν τῷ δείπνῳ λείπει. Μὴ εἰκῇ τύψῃς τοὺς δούλους.» Ὁ Ξάνθος νεύει τῷ Αἰσώπῳ «ἴδε, τρίτον.» Ὁ δέ, «ἀνέχου,» φησί. Ἀναστάντων δὲ αὐτῶν ἀπὸ τοῦ δείπνου κρεμᾶται ὁ Αἴσωπος
10 καὶ τύπτεται. Ὁ Ξάνθος αὐτῷ φησι «καὶ ταῦτα μὲν ἔχεις. Εἰ δὲ μὴ καλέσῃς μοι ἄνθρωπον ἀπερίεργον, πεδήσας διαρρήξω σε.»

59. Τῇ δὲ ἐπαύριον ἔξω τῆς πόλεως ἀπελθὼν ἐζήτει εὑρεῖν ἄνθρωπον ἀπερίεργον. Πολλοὺς οὖν βλέπων παροδίτας εἶδέ τινα τῇ μὲν θέᾳ ἄγροικον, τοῖς δὲ ἤθεσι πολιτικὸν ὄντα, ὀνάριον ἐλαύνοντα μεστὸν ξύλων καὶ τῆς
15 λεωφόρου ὁδοῦ ἐκνενευκότα καὶ πρὸς τὴν τῶν πολλῶν ἀπάντησιν, ἱστάμενον καὶ πρὸς τὸ ὀνάριον λαλοῦντα. Ὁ δὲ ἐπηκολούθει αὐτῷ, τοῦτον ἀπερίεργον στοχασάμενος. Ὁ δὲ χωρικὸς τῷ ὀναρίῳ φησὶ «περιπάτει, ὅπως ταχέως φθάσωμεν εἰς τὴν πόλιν καὶ πραθῶσι τὰ ξυλάρια ἀσσαρίων δώδεκα. Καὶ ἕξεις σὺ δύο εἰς χόρτον καὶ κριθήν, κἀγὼ δύο εἰς ἐμαυτόν, τὰ δὲ ὀκτὼ τηρήσωμεν
20 εἰς ἑτέρας τύχας, μή τις ἡμῶν ἀσθενήσῃ ἢ καὶ αἰφνιδίως χειμὼν γένηται.»

60. Ὁ Αἴσωπος λέγει ἐν ἑαυτῷ «τί ταῦτα; Τῷ ὀναρίῳ διαλέγεται; Ὡς μᾶλλον ἀπερίεργός ἐστιν. Ἀσπάσομαι αὐτόν.» Καὶ ἀσπασάμενος «χαῖρε», φησίν. Ὁ δὲ ἀντησπάσατο αὐτὸν «χαῖρε» εἰπών. Αἴσωπος ἔφη «πόσου τὰ ξυλάρια;» Ὁ χωρικὸς ἔφη «δώδεκα ἀσσαρίων.» Αἴσωπος λέγει «Ξάνθον οἶδας
25 τὸν φιλόσοφον;» Ὁ δέ φησιν «οὔ, τέκνον.» Αἴσωπος λέγει «διὰ τί;» Ὁ ξένος

58.4 Ὁ Ξάνθος : ὁ δὲ Ξ. O | μου : μοι O 5 μου post κατεφρονήθη add. O 6 σύγχυλος : ex Wl corr. Perry, iter. Papath. : σύγχειλος M : σύχολος O | παῦσαι : ἐὰν O 7 ἰδοὺ : ἰδὲ O 8 πολυσισάμους O 9 μελίου O | ʽΟ ... 10 λέγει : καὶ λέγει O 10 πάλιν : om. O | λέγει : ἔφη O 11 Ὁ Ξάνθος : om. O | πάλιν ante νεύει add. O 12 ἀνέχου : ἀπέχω O | αὐτῶν : om. O 14 μοι : με M | πεδήσας ... σε : om. O ‖ 59.1 Τῇ ... 2 ἀπερίεργον : om. O 2 Πολλοὺς ... παροδίτας : πολλοὺς οὕς βλέπεις παροδίτας καὶ τοὺς ἄλλους ἐκλεξόν μοι παρὰ πάντων ἀπερίεργον. ὁ δὲ ἔσωπος τοὺς πάντας περιέργως βλέπων O | εἶδέ : οἶδε O | ἄγροικον : ex Wl Perry, iter. Papath. : ἄγρικον O : ἄγριον M 3 ὄντα : om. M | ἐλαύνοντα : ἐπικαθήμενον ὑπῆρχεν δὲ O | καὶ ... 4 ἐκνενευκότα :

as a nonmeddler?" Then a platter of fish was served, and Xanthus, taking the opportunity, said, "Although I had given him so many condiments, my cooking has been disgraced, for there are no spices or olive oil, and the sauce is not thickened. Let the cook be beaten." The stranger said, "Stop, master! There is no fault; everything is fine." Xanthus nodded to Aesop again and said, "See, that's two!" Then a sesame cake was brought in. Xanthus tasted it and said, "Summon the baker. Why does this cake have no honey or raisins?" Again the stranger said, "Master, the cake, too, is excellent and nothing is wanting in the dinner. Don't beat the slaves needlessly." Xanthus nodded to Aesop and said, "See, that's three!" Aesop said, "Wait!" but they got up from the table and Aesop was strung up and beaten. Xanthus said to him, "You're getting this, but if you don't invite me a person who is a nonmeddler, I will bind you and break you to pieces."

59. On the next day Aesop went out of the town and looked to find a person who was a nonmeddler. So he looked at many passers-by and saw one who was uncultivated in appearance but civilized in his manners, driving an ass loaded with wood, who was turning off the highway and away from encounters with many people, and who was standing still and talking to the ass. Aesop followed him, guessing that he was a nonmeddler. The rustic fellow said to the ass, "Walk on, so that we may arrive quickly to the town and the wood may be sold at twelve cents. And you will have two cents for greens and barley, and I two for myself, and we'll save eight for other occasions, in case either of us should get sick or a storm should suddenly arise."

60. Aesop said to himself, "What is this? He converses with the ass? So he is rather a nonmeddler. I'll greet him." And greeting him, he said, "Cheers!" The other greeted him in turn and said, "Cheers." Aesop said, "How much are you selling the wood for?" And the rustic said, "Twelve cents." Aesop said, "Do you know Xanthus the philosopher?" And he

---

καὶ τῇ λεωφόρῳ ὁδῷ ἐνευκότα O   4 καὶ … ἀπάντησιν : καὶ πρὸς τὴν (corr. : τοὺς M) τῶν πολλῶν ἀπάντησιν : καὶ τῇ τῶν πολλῶν ἀπαντήσει O | ἱστάμενον : ὑπεσταλμένον ex G corr. Perry, iter. Papath.   5 πρός : παρά O | ἔσωπος post ὁ δὲ add. O | ἠκολούθη O | τοῦτον : om. O   6 χωρικὸς : χωρητικὸς O   8 κρίθην O   9 μή … ἀσθενήσῃ : μή τις ἀσθένεια περιδράμει O | ἢ : om. O | γένηται χειμών inv. O ‖ 60.1 Ὁ … ἑαυτῷ : Αἴσωπος δὲ ἐν ἑαυτῷ λογιζόμενος M   2 Ἀσπάσομαι αὐτόν : om. O   3 φησίν : λέγει αὐτῷ O | αὐτὸν … εἰπών : om. O | ἔφη : φησί O   4 πωλεῖς post ξυλάρια add. M | Ὁ … ἔφη : om. O | λέγει : ἔφη O   5 φησιν : om. O | τέκνον : om. O | Αἴσωπος … τί : διατί φησι O | Ὁ² … 6 ἔφη : καὶ ὁ ξένος O

ἔφη «ἐγὼ ἄγροικός εἰμι. Οὐδένα ἐπίσταμαι.» Ὁ δὲ Αἴσωπος «ἐκείνου δοῦλός εἰμι.» Ὁ ξένος ἔφη «τί; Ἠρώτησά σε πότερον δοῦλος εἶ ἢ ἐλεύθερος; Ἐμοὶ τί διαφέρει;» Αἴσωπος ἔφη «ἀγαθά σοι γένοιτο! Ἀκολούθει μοι κἀγώ σοι δώσω τὸ ἀργύριον μετὰ καὶ τοῦ ἀρίστου.»

61. Ἀγαγὼν δὲ αὐτὸν εἰς τὸν οἶκον καθεῖλε τὰ ξυλάρια δεδωκὼς τὸ τίμημα καί φησι «ὁ δεσπότης μου ἐρωτᾷ παρ' αὐτῷ ἀριστῆσαι.» Ὁ δὲ ἄγροικος οὐ περιεργασάμενος διὰ ποίαν αἰτίαν καλεῖται, εἰσελθὼν σὺν τῷ πηλῷ καὶ τοῖς ὑποδήμασιν οὕτως ἀνέπεσεν. Ὁ Ξάνθος ἔφη «τίς οὗτος;» Αἴσωπος ἔφη «ἀπερίεργος ἄνθρωπος.» Ἰδὼν δὲ αὐτὸν ἐκεῖνος ἄγροικον ὄντα λέγει τῇ γυναικὶ «κυρία, ὑποκρίθητί μοι ἵνα δαμάσω τὸν Αἴσωπον. Καὶ ἀναστᾶσα, βαλοῦσα ὕδωρ εἰς τὴν λεκάνην πρόσφερε τῷ ξένῳ ὡς νίπτουσα αὐτοῦ τοὺς πόδας. Ἴσως εὐλαβηθεὶς φανῇ περίεργος καὶ δαρήσεται ὁ Αἴσωπος.» Ἡ δὲ θέλουσα τὸν Αἴσωπον τυφθῆναι ὑπεκρίθη καὶ λαβοῦσα λέντιον προσέφερε τῷ ξένῳ τὴν λεκάνην. Ὁ δὲ θεασάμενος καὶ γνοὺς ὅτι ἐστὶν ἡ οἰκοδέσποινα, φησὶ πρὸς ἑαυτόν, «πάντως τιμῆσαί με θέλει. Εἰ δὲ ἤθελέ μου τοὺς πόδας ὑπὸ δούλου νιφθῆναι, εἶχεν ἂν ἐπιτάξαι.» Καὶ προτείνας τοὺς πόδας ἔφη «νίψον, κυρία.» Καὶ νιψάμενος ἀνέπεσεν.

62. Ὁ Ξάνθος φησὶ «δοθήτω τῷ ξένῳ πρῶτον οἰνόμελι.» Ὁ ξένος πρὸς ἑαυτόν· «αὐτοὺς μὲν ἔδει πρῶτον πιεῖν. Ἐπεὶ δὲ αὐτοῖς οὕτως δοκεῖ, οὐ περιεργάσομαι.» Καὶ λαβὼν ἔπιεν. Ἀριστούντων δὲ αὐτῶν παρετέθη ἰχθύς. Ὁ Ξάνθος τῷ ξένῳ λέγει «φάγε.» Ὁ δὲ ὡς δελφὶς ἤσθιε τοὺς ἰχθύας. Ὁ Ξάνθος ἐπαφορμιζόμενος λέγει τῷ μαγείρῳ «διὰ τί κακῶς ἤρτυσας; Ἐκδυθεὶς δαρήτω.» Ὁ ἄγροικος ἐν ἑαυτῷ· «καλῶς ἔψηται καὶ οὐδὲν λείπει. Εἰ δὲ διὰ προφάσεως θέλει δεῖραι τὸν δοῦλον, τί πρὸς ἐμέ;» Δαρέντος δὲ τοῦ δούλου καὶ

60.6 Ὁ δὲ Αἴσωπος : ὁ ἔσωπος ἔφη O **7** Ὁ ξένος ἔφη : καὶ ὁ ξένος πρὸς αὐτόν O | σε : om. O | πρότερον O | κἂν τε ante δοῦλος add. O | εἶ ἢ : κἂν τε O **8** ἔσωπος φησί post γένοιτο O ‖ **61.1** Ἀγαγὼν … οἶκον : ἀγομένων δὲ αὐτῶν εἰς τὴν οἰκίαν O **2** παρ' αὐτῷ : ἐπ' αὐτῷ M **4** Ὁ … ἔφη : ὁ δὲ ξάνθος O | Αἴσωπος ἔφη : καὶ ὁ ἔσωπος O **5** ἄνθρωπος ἀπερίεργος inv. O | αὐτὸν ἐκεῖνος : αὐτὸς ἐκεῖνον O **6** δαμάσω : τυπτήσω O **7** βαλοῦσα : βάλε O | καὶ ante πρόσφερε add. O | πρόσφερε … ξένῳ : om. M | ὡς νίπτουσα : ὡς νίπτειν μέλλεις O **8** εὐλαβηθῇ O | καὶ … Αἴσωπος : καὶ ὁ ἔσωπος δαρήσεται O **9** καὶ λαβοῦσα : absc. in M **10** καὶ … ὅτι : absc. in M | τοῦ οἴκου post οἰκοδέσποινα add. O **11** πρὸς ἑαυτόν om. M | καὶ διὰ τοῦτο

answered, "No, my son." Aesop said, "Why?" The stranger said, "I'm a country fellow; I don't know anyone." Aesop said, "I am his slave." The stranger said, "Why? Did I ask you whether you were a slave or free? What do I care?" Aesop said, "May good things befall you! Follow me and I'll give you the money along with lunch."

61. He led him to the house, unloaded the wood, and gave him the money, and he said, "My master asks you to have lunch with him." The country fellow did not wonder about the reason why he was invited but entered with his muddy sandals and reclined, just like that. Xanthus said, "Who is this?" and Aesop said, "A nonmeddlesome man." Seeing that he was a rustic fellow, Xanthus said to his wife, "My lady, pretend for me so that I can punish Aesop. Get up and pour some water in the basin, and bring it to the stranger as though you are going to wash his feet. Perhaps out of discretion he will be shown to be meddlesome and Aesop will be beaten." And she, eager to have Aesop beaten, took up the pretense, grabbed a towel and brought the basin to the stranger. When he saw her and realized that she was the mistress of the house, he said to himself, "Assuredly he wants to honor me. If he'd wanted my feet to be washed by a slave, he would have ordered it." He extended his feet and said, "Wash, my lady," and when he'd been washed, he reclined.

62. Xanthus said, "Let mead be given first to the stranger." The stranger said to himself, "They should have drunk first, but since this seems best to them, I will not meddle," and he took it and drank. As they were dining, fish was served. Xanthus said to the stranger, "Eat." He ate the fish like a dolphin. Xanthus, finding an opportunity, said to the cook, "Why have you seasoned it so badly? Let him be stripped and beaten." The country fellow said to himself, "He boiled it excellently, and nothing was missing. But if he wants to beat his slave on some pretext, what's it to me?" As the slave was beaten and the stranger kept silent, Xanthus brooded. After a bit the cake

---

αὐτοχείρως νίπτει μου τοὺς πόδας post θέλει add. O 12 ἔφη : φησί O ‖ 62.1 δὲ ante Ξάνθος add. O | πρῶτον τῷ ξένῳ inv. O | 'O² ... 2 ἑαυτόν : καὶ ὁ ξένος πρὸς αὐτὸν ὑποψηθηρίζων ἔλεγεν O 2 αὐτοῖς οὕτως : οὕτως αὐτοὺς O 3 Ἀριστούντων codd. : ἀριστώντων corr. Perry, iter. Papath. | παρετέθη ἰχθύς : ἰχθύων λοπὰς παρετέθη O 4 'O¹ ... λέγει : καὶ ὁ Ξάνθος τῷ ξένῳ φησί O | δέλφις O | 'O³ ... 5 μαγείρῳ : ὁ δὲ ξάνθος ἐπαφορμισάμενος τῷ μαγείρῳ λέγει O 5 τοὺς ἰχθύας post ἤρτυσας add. O | Ἐκδυθείς ... 6 δαρήτω : καὶ φησὶ πρὸς τοὺς ἐστῶτας ἐκδύσατε καὶ τύψατε αὐτὸν σφοδρῶς O 6 πάλιν post ἄγροικος add. O | ἡσύχως ἔλεγεν post ἐν ἑαυτῷ add. O | ἔψεται O | αὐτοῖς post οὐδὲν add. O 7 δῆραι M : τύψαι O | δὲ : οὖν O

τοῦ ξένου σιωπῶντος, ὁ Ξάνθος ἠδολέσχει. Καὶ μετὰ μικρὸν ἠνέχθη πλακοῦς. Ὁ ξένος μηδέπω ἰδὼν ἤρξατο ψωμοὺς ποιεῖν ὡς πλίνθους καὶ ἐσθίειν.

63. Ἰδὼν δὲ αὐτὸν ὁ Ξάνθος ἡδέως τρώγοντα ἀνέκραγεν τὸν ἀρτοκόπον καί φησι «διὰ τί, κατάρατε, ὁ πλακοῦς οὔτε μέλι οὔτε πέπερι ἔχει, ἀλλὰ καὶ ὤξισεν;» Ὁ δὲ ἔφη «εἰ ὠμὸς ὁ πλακοῦς, ἐμὲ δεῖρον. Εἰ δὲ οὐκ ἤρτυται καλῶς, οὐκ ἐγὼ αἴτιος ἀλλ' ἡ κυρία βραδύνασα δοῦναι τὴν ἄρτυσιν.» Ὁ Ξάνθος ἔφη «ἐὰν παρὰ τὴν τῆς γυναικὸς ἀμέλειαν γέγονε, ζῶσαν αὐτὴν κατακαύσω.» Τῇ δὲ γυναικὶ ἔφη «συνυποκρίθητί μοι.» Καί φησιν «Αἴσωπε, ἄγαγέ μοι κληματίδας καὶ ἄψον εἰς τὸ μέσον, ὡς τὸ δοκεῖν καυθῆναι τὴν κυρίαν σου.» Διεβλέπετο δὲ τὸν ἄγροικον εἰ ἀναπηδήσας διακωλύσει αὐτὸν τοῦτο πρᾶξαι.

64. Ὁ δὲ ἄγροικος πρὸς ἑαυτὸν ἔλεγεν «αἰτίου μὴ ὄντος τί οὗτος θυμοῦται;» Καί φησι πρὸς αὐτὸν «οἰκοδέσποτα, εἰ τοῦτο κέκρικας, μικρὸν μεῖνον ἕως κἀγὼ ἀπελθὼν ἐνέγκω μου τὴν γυναῖκα ἀπὸ τοῦ ἀγροῦ. Καὶ τὰς δύο ὁμοῦ κατάκαυσον.» Ὁ δὲ Ξάνθος ἀκούσας καὶ θαυμάσας τὸ ἔμψυχον τοῦ ἀγροίκου, πρὸς τὸν Αἴσωπον ἔφη «ἴδε, ἀληθῶς ἄνθρωπος ἀπερίεργος. Νενίκηκας· ἀρκεῖ· τὸ λοιπὸν πιστῶς καὶ εὐνοϊκῶς δούλευσόν μοι ἵνα τύχῃς παρ'ἐμοῦ ἐλευθερίας.» Ὁ δὲ ἔφη «οὐκέτι μοι μέμψῃ, δέσποτα.»

65. Τῇ δὲ ἐπαύριον λέγει ὁ Ξάνθος τῷ Αἰσώπῳ «τῇ τακτῇ ὥρᾳ ἄπελθε εἰς τὸ βαλανεῖον καὶ βλέψον ἐὰν οὐ πολυοχλῇ ἵνα λούσωμαι.» Πορευομένου δὲ τοῦ Αἰσώπου ὑπήντησεν αὐτῷ ὁ στρατηγὸς καὶ γνωρίσας ὅτι τοῦ Ξάνθου ἐστί, λέγει αὐτῷ «ποῦ πορεύει;» Ὁ δὲ Αἴσωπός φησι «οὐκ οἶδα.» Δόξας δὲ ὁ στρατηγὸς ὅτι καταγελᾷ αὐτοῦ, ἐκέλευσεν βληθῆναι αὐτὸν εἰς τὴν φυλακήν. Αἴσωπος δὲ ἀπαγόμενος ἔφη «ὁρᾷς ὅτι καλῶς σοι ἀπεκρίθην; Μὴ προσδοκῶν γὰρ ὑπηντηκέναι σοι, εἰς φυλακὴν ἄπειμι.» Ἐκπλαγεὶς δὲ ὁ στρατηγός εἰς τὸ εὐαπολόγητον αὐτοῦ, παρῆκεν αὐτόν.

62.8 Καὶ : om. O 9 καὶ ante ὁ ξένος add. O | μήποτε O | τοιοῦτον post ἰδὼν add. O | ποιεῖν ψωμοὺς inv. O ‖ 63.1 τρώγον O | ἀνέκραξε τῷ ἀρτοκόπῳ M 2 καί φησι : om. M | οὔτε[1] ... ἔχει : οὔτε μελίου σταπίδας ἔχει, οὔτε πέπεριν O 3 ὄξυσεν O | ἔφη : λέγει O | εἰ ὠμὸς : εἰ ὁμῶς ἐστὶν O | ἐμὲ : om. O | δῆρον M | οὐχ ἤρτυται M : οὐκ ἤρτησται O 4 αἴτιος : ἄξιος O | ἡ ante βραδύνασα add. M | ἀρτυσίαν M 5 τις post ἐὰν add. O | τοῦτο post ἀμέλειαν add. O 6 Τῇ ... ἔφη : καὶ φησὶ πρὸς τὴν γυναῖκα, σὺ κυρία O | ὑποκρίθητί μοι O | εἴσω ἔσωπος τυπτηθῇ post μοι (prim.) add. O | Αἴσωπε : ἑνὶ τῶν οἰκετῶν O | μοι[2] : om. M 7 ὡς τὸ : ὥστε O | τὴν ... σου : τὴν κυρία μου leg. Papath. : om. O 8 κολύσαι O | μὴ ante πρᾶξαι add. M ‖ 64.1 πρὸς ... ἔλεγεν : ἔλεγεν καθεαυτόν O | αἰτίας μὴ οὔσης O | τί οὗτος : ἵνα τί οὕτως O 2 θυμοῦται : θαμβεῖται M | γενέσθαι εἰ τοῦτο ἢ νητρεκῶς (sic)

was brought. The stranger, having never seen one before, began to make chunks like bricks and to eat them.

63. When Xanthus saw him happily gobbling it down he cried out to the baker, "Why, you abomination, does the cake have no honey or pepper but tastes sour?" The baker said, "If the cake is underdone, beat me. If it has not been seasoned well, it is not I who am responsible but the mistress, who was slow in giving me the spices." Xanthus said, "If it happened because of my wife's neglect, I will burn her alive." To his wife he said, "Play along with me." And he said, "Aesop, bring brushwood and light it in the midst, so that it looks like your mistress is to be burnt." He stared at the country fellow to see if he would jump up and prevent him from doing this.

64. The rustic said to himself, "Since there is no cause, why is this fellow angry?" And he said to him, "Master of the house, if you have decided this, wait a little until I to go and bring my wife from the field, and then burn the two of them together." When Xanthus heard this and was amazed at the spirit of the rustic, he said to Aesop, "Look, this person is truly a nonmeddler. You have won. Enough! In the future, serve me faithfully and devotedly so that you may gain your freedom from me." And Aesop said, "Don't find fault with me any longer, master."

65. On the following day Xanthus said to Aesop, "At the assigned hour go to the bathhouse and see if it is not crowded, so I can wash." As Aesop was going along, he came across the governor, who recognized that he was Xanthus's, and said to him, "Where are you going?" Aesop said, "I don't know." Thinking that he was laughing at him, the governor ordered that he be thrown into prison. As Aesop was being led away, he said, "Do you see how well I answered you? For I didn't expect to run into you, and I am going to prison." The governor was astonished at his clever defense and released him.

---

post κέκρικας add. O 2–3 μεῖνον μικρὸν inv. O 3 μου τὴν γυναῖκα : τὴν γυναῖκα μου M | Καὶ ... 4 κατάκαυσον : ὅπως ἂν ὁμοῦ κατακαύσῃς τὰς δύο O 4 Ὁ ... 5 ἀγροίκου : ἀκούσας δὲ ταῦτα ὁ Ξάνθος καὶ θαυμάσας τοῦ ἀνδρὸς τὸ μεγαλόψυχον O 5 πρὸς ... ἔφη : ἔφη πρὸς τὸν ἔσωπον O 6 πείσας με post νενίκηκας add. O | οὖν post ἀρκεῖ add. O | τὸ λοιπὸν : λοιπὸν ἀπὸ τοῦ νῦν O | ἵνα : ὅπως O 7 μοι μέμψῃ : -έμψῃ evan. in M : μέψῃ με O ‖ 65.1 δὲ : οὖν O | τῷ Αἰσώπῳ : πρὸς τὸν ἔσωπον O | ὥρᾳ : absc. in M 2 εἰς ... καὶ : om. O | βλέψον : βλέπε O | ἐὰν ... πολυοχλῇ : πολυοχλῆται corr. Papath. : ἐὰν οὐ πολλοὶ ὄχλοι εἰσέρχονται ἐν τῷ βαλανίῳ O | ἵνα : ὅπως O | λούσωμαι : absc. in M : λούσομαι O 4 αὐτῷ : om. O | Αἴσωπός : om. O 7 ὑπηντηκέναι : ὑπηντηκώς ex L corr. Perry, iter. Papath. : ὑπηντικός O 7–8 ἐπὶ τῷ εὐαπολογήτῳ M 8 ἀφῆκεν O

66. Ὁ δὲ Αἴσωπος παραγενόμενος εἰς τὸ βαλανεῖον εἶδε πλῆθος λαοῦ καὶ πρὸς τὸ μέσον τῆς εἰσόδου κείμενον εἰκῇ λίθον, ἐν ᾧ ἕκαστος τῶν εἰσερχομένων προσκόπτων κατηρᾶτο τὸν τεθεικότα. Εἷς δέ τις μεταθεὶς αὐτὸν εἰσῆλθε λούσασθαι. Ὁ δὲ Αἴσωπος ἐλθὼν εἰς τὸν οἶκον λέγει τῷ κυρίῳ «εἰ κελεύεις, δέσποτα, λούσασθαι ἕνα ἄνθρωπον εἶδον ἐν τῷ βαλανείῳ.» Ὁ Ξάνθος λέγει «καλὸν τὸ εὐρυχώρως λούσασθαι. Ἆρον τὰ πρὸς βαλανεῖον καὶ ὕπαγε.» Εἰσελθὼν δὲ ὁ Ξάνθος καὶ ἰδὼν πλῆθος τῶν λουομένων λέγει «Αἴσωπε, οὐκ εἶπας 'ἕνα μόνον ἄνθρωπον εἶδον';» Ὁ δέ, «καὶ μάλα,» φησίν· «εἶδον γὰρ τὸν λίθον τοῦτον πρὸ τῆς εἰσόδου κείμενον πρὸς ὃν εἰσιόντες πάντες προσέκοπτον. Εἷς δὲ μὴ προσκόψας, ἄρας μετέθηκε πρὸς τὸ μηδένα προσκόπτειν. Ἐκεῖνον κρίνας παρὰ τοὺς λοιποὺς ἄνθρωπον εἶναι, ἐδήλωσά σοι τὴν ἀλήθειαν.» Ὁ Ξάνθος εἶπεν «οὐδὲν παρὰ τῷ Αἰσώπῳ ἀργὸν πρὸς ἀπολογίαν.»

67. Λουσάμενος δὲ παρεγένετο ἐπὶ τὸν δεῖπνον. Μετὰ δὲ τὸ δειπνῆσαι τῆς γαστρὸς νυξάσης ἐξῆλθε πρὸς ὑποχώρησιν. Τοῦ δὲ Αἰσώπου παρεστῶτος καὶ ξέστην ὕδατος ἐπιφερομένου λέγει ὁ Ξάνθος «δύνασαί μοι εἰπεῖν διὰ τί ἔθος τοῖς ἀνθρώποις, ὅταν καθεζώμεθα εἰς τὰ ἀναγκαῖα, πυκνῶς τὰ ἑαυτῶν βλέπομεν ἀφοδεύματα;» Αἴσωπος ἔφη «κατὰ τοὺς παλαιοὺς σοφός τις διὰ σπατάλην πολὺν χρόνον ἐκαθέζετο εἰς τὰ ἀναγκαῖα, μέχρις οὗ καθεζόμενος τὰς ἰδίας ἔχεσε φρένας. Ἀπ' ἐκείνου οὖν οἱ ἄνθρωποι φοβούμενοι, διαβλέπουσι τὰ ἴδια ἀφοδεύματα μὴ καὶ αὐτοὶ τὰς ἰδίας χέσωσι φρένας. Ἀλλὰ σύ, δέσποτα, μηδὲν ἀγωνιάσῃς. Οὐ γὰρ ἔχεις φρένας.»

68. Τῇ δὲ ἐπαύριον τοῦ Ξάνθου ἐπὶ πότον μετὰ φίλων ἀνακλιθέντος καὶ τοῦ πότου ἐπικρατοῦντος, ἐγένετο προβλήματα ἱκανά. Τοῦ δὲ Ξάνθου ἀρξαμένου συνταράττεσθαι, ἐπιγνοὺς ὁ Αἴσωπος ὅτι μάχην μεγάλην μέλλει ποιεῖν, λέγει «δέσποτα, Διόνυσος <εὑρὼν> τὸ οἰνικὸν πόμα †τρεῖς κράσεις τῷ ἀνθρώπῳ διὰ πόματος χρήσασθαι εἶπεν†· τὴν μὲν πρώτην ἡδονῆς εἶναι,

66. Aesop arrived at the bathhouse and saw a multitude of people and a stone lying at random at the middle of the entrance, and everyone who was entering and stumbled against it cursed the one who had put it there. One of these moved it and entered to wash. Aesop went into his house and said to his master, "If you are asking to wash, master, I saw only one man in the bathhouse." Xanthus said, "It's great to wash when it's roomy. Grab the bathing gear, and let's go. Entering the bathhouse and seeing a multitude of people washing, Xanthus said, "Aesop, didn't you say, 'I saw only one man'?" "Indeed," said Aesop, "for I saw this stone lying in front of the entrance, and everyone who was going in stumbled against it. But one didn't stumble against it but picked it up and moved it so that no one would stumble against it. I judged him to be a man in comparison with the rest and told you the truth." Xanthus said, "Aesop is never slow to come up with a defense."

67. Having washed, Xanthus went to dinner. After dining, at the urging of his belly, he went out to relieve himself. Aesop was standing by bringing a pitcher of water, and Xanthus said, "Can you tell me why people have this habit, that whenever we sit down in the toilet, we frequently look at our excrement?" Aesop said, "According to the ancients, some sage out of self-indulgence used to sit too long at the toilet, until by sitting there he shat out his own brains. From then on, in fact, people have been afraid and look at their own excrement so that they, too, don't shit out their brains. But don't you worry, my master, for you don't have any brains."

68. On the next day, Xanthus was reclining with some friends at drink, and when the drink overpowered them, problems enough arose. Xanthus began to be upset, and Aesop, realizing that he was about to cause a great quarrel, said, "Master, Dionysus who discovered the drink of wine said that people should use three mixings when they drink wine: the first for plea-

---

καθεζόμεθα O 5 ἀποβλεπόμεν O | σοφοὺς post παλαιοὺς add. O 6 σπατάλης O | ἐκάθητο M | οὗ : οὖν O | καθεζόμενος : ἐπιλαθόμενος corr. Papath. ex G 7 Ἀπ' : ἐπ' O | οὖν : γοῦν M | διαβλέπουσι ... 8 ἴδια : τὰ οἰκεῖα διαβλέπονται M 9 μηδὲν : μὴ O ‖ 68.1 ἐπαύριον : ἑξῆς O | πότου O | μετὰ ... ἀνακλιθέντος : κληθέντος μετὰ φίλου O 2 ἐπικρατοῦντες O | ἐγένετο : ἐνένοντο (sic) O 3 συντάσσεσθαι O | μεγάλην μάχην inv. O | μέλλει... 4 ποιεῖν : ποιεῖ O 4 εὑρὼν : post Διόνυσος ex G suppl. Perry, iter. Papath. | κεράσας post κράσεις ex G suppl. Papath. 5 τῷ ἀνθρώπῳ : evan. in M | πῶς δεῖ post ἀνθρώπῳ ex G suppl. Papath. | καὶ εὐφροσύνης post ἡδονῆς add. O | εἶναι : om. O

τὴν δὲ δευτέραν εὐφροσύνης, τὴν δὲ τρίτην ὕβρεως. Διό, δέσποτα, πιόντες καὶ εὐφρανθέντες, παραχωρήσατε [...] ἐν οἷς δεδώκατε ἀπόδειξιν.» Ὁ δὲ Ξάνθος μεθύων φησὶ «σιώπα, σύμβουλε Ἅιδου.» Αἴσωπος εἶπεν «ἔκδεξαι καὶ εἰς Ἅιδου καταβαίνεις.»

69. Τὶς δὲ τῶν σχολαστικῶν ἰδὼν τὸν Ξάνθον περιφερόμενον λέγει «καθηγητά, εἰ πάντα δυνατὰ ἀνθρώπῳ;» Ὁ Ξάνθος ἔφη «πανοῦργον τὸ ζῷον καὶ δυνατὸν ἐν πᾶσι τὰ ὑπὲρ λόγον πράττειν.» Ὁ δὲ σχολαστικὸς εἶπεν «δύναται ἄνθρωπος τὴν θάλασσαν ἐκπιεῖν;» Καὶ ὁ Ξάνθος «ναί,» φησι, «κἀγὼ αὐτὸς δύναμαι τὴν θάλασσαν ἐκπιεῖν.» Καὶ ὁ σχολαστικὸς «ἐὰν δὲ μὴ ἐκπίῃς, τί;» Ὁ δὲ Ξάνθος νενικημένος ὑπὸ τοῦ οἴνου, ἔφη «τίθημι τὰς συνθήκας ὑπὲρ παντὸς τοῦ βίου μου.» Καὶ ἐπὶ τούτοις προσβαλόντες τοὺς δακτυλίους ἐκύρωσαν τὰς συνθήκας.

70. Πρωΐας δὲ γενομένης ἀναστὰς ὁ Ξάνθος καὶ τὴν ὄψιν νιπτόμενος, οὐκ ἰδὼν τὸν δακτύλιον ἐζήτει. Καί φησιν «Αἴσωπε, τί μου γέγονεν ὁ δακτύλιος;» Αἴσωπος ἔφη «οὐκ οἶδα, ἀλλὰ τοῦτο γινώσκω ὅτι ξένος ἐγένου τοῦ βίου σου.» Ὁ δὲ Ξάνθος· «τί λέγεις;» Αἴσωπος ἔφη «παρὰ τῷ χθὲς πότῳ συνθήκας ἔθου τὴν θάλασσαν ἐκπιεῖν ὑπὲρ ὅλου τοῦ βίου σου καὶ τὸν δακτύλιον προεβάλου.» Ὁ Ξάνθος εἶπε «καὶ πῶς ἐγὼ δύναμαι τὴν θάλασσαν ἐκπιεῖν; Ἀλλὰ δέομαί σου, εἰ δυνατὸν ᾖ διὰ τῆς ἐνούσης σοι ἐμπειρίας, βοήθησόν μοι ἵνα διὰ προφάσεως νικήσω ἢ λύσω τὰς συνθήκας.» Αἴσωπος ἔφη «νικῆσαι μὲν οὐ δυνατόν, λυθῆναι δὲ ποιήσω.» Ὁ Ξάνθος «δός μοι γνώμην», φησί, «ποίῳ λόγῳ.»

71. Αἴσωπος ἔφη «ὅταν ἔλθῃ ὁ συνθηκοφύλαξ ἅμα τῷ ἀντιδίκῳ σου λέγοντες 'τὴν θάλασσαν ἔχεις ἐκπιεῖν', μὴ ἀρνοῦ, ἀλλὰ ἅπερ παρ' οἴνῳ συνέθου, ταῦτα καὶ νήφων λέγε. Καὶ κέλευσον στρώματα παρὰ τὸν αἰγιαλὸν καὶ τράπεζαν τεθῆναι καὶ παῖδας πιγκέρνας παραστῆναι. Ὅταν δὲ ἴδῃς ὅτι τὰ πάντα ἤδη πεπλήρωται, τοῦ ὄχλου πρὸς τὴν θέαν παντὸς συνδραμόντος,

sure, the second for good cheer, and the third for abuse. Therefore, master, when you have drunk and have reached the state of good cheer, leave off [...] in which you have given proofs." Xanthus, now drunk, said, "Silence, you counselor of hell." Aesop said, "Just wait, and you're going down to hell."

69. One of the students, seeing that Xanthus was giddy, said, "Professor, is everything possible for a human being?" Xanthus said, "This creature is cunning and can certainly do anything, even beyond reason." The student said, "Can a human being drink up the sea?" "Yes," said Xanthus. "In fact, I myself can drink up the sea." And the student said, "And if you can't drink it up?" Xanthus, overcome by the wine, said, "I make you a bet for my entire livelihood." Upon this, they held out their rings in ratification of their pledges.

70. In the morning Xanthus woke up and, washing his face, didn't see his ring. He started looking for it and said, "Aesop, what happened to my ring?" Aesop said, "I don't know, but I do know this, that you have alienated yourself from your livelihood." Xanthus said, "What do you mean?" Aesop said, "Yesterday, at the drinking, you made a bet for your entire livelihood that you would drink up the sea, and you held out your ring on it." Xanthus said, "And how can I drink up the sea? But I beg you, if it is possible in your own experience, help me so that I can win by some pretext or else nullify the bet." Aesop said, "It is not possible to win, but I will have the bet nullified." "Give me your advice," said Xanthus, "by what argument."

71. Aesop said, "When the guarantor of the bet arrives together with your opponent and they say, 'You have to drink up the sea,' do not deny it but repeat now that you are sober what you agreed to when you were drunk. And order matresses and a table to be placed by the beach and cup-bearing slaves to stand by. When you see that everything has been fully

---

add. O 4 Ὁ δὲ Ξάνθος : καὶ ὁ Ξάνθος O | Αἴσωπος ἔφη : καὶ ὁ ἔσωπος πρὸς αὐτόν O 6 προσεβάλου O | Ὁ ... εἶπε : ὁ δὲ O | ἐγὼ : om. O 7 σοι post δυνατὸν add. O | ἦ : εἶ O | σοι : μοι O | ἐμπειρίας ... 8 συνθήκας : ἐπὶ τὰς συνθήκας O 9 καὶ ante ὁ Ξάνθος add. O | φησί : om. O ‖ 71.1 Αἴσωπος ἔφη : om. O 2 ἔχεις : om. O | σὺ ante μὴ add. O | ἀλλὰ : ἀλλ' O | παρ' οἴνῳ : scripsi : παροιν. M (παροινῳ leg. Perry et Papath.) : παροῖνον O : παροινῶν corr. Perry, iter. Papath. 3 παρέθου O | παρὰ : πρὸς O 4 πιγκέρνας : ex W corr. Perry, iter. Papath. : πιγκερνίους M : κέρνας O | παρασταθῆναι O 5 τὰ : om. O | ἤδη : om. O | πεπλήρωνται O | τοῦ ὄχλου ... συνδραμόντος : καὶ τὸν ὄχλον συνδραμόντα O

ἀναπεσὼν κέλευσον πλησθῆναι σκάφην ἀπὸ τῆς θαλάσσης καὶ εἰπὲ δημοσίᾳ πρὸς τὸν συνθηκοφύλακα 'πῶς τεθείκαμεν τὰς συνθήκας;' καὶ ἐρεῖ σοι 'ἵνα τὴν θάλασσαν ἐκπίῃς.' Εἰπὲ οὖν 'μή τι πλέον;' ἐρεῖ, 'οὔ.' Καὶ τοῦτο μαρτυράμενος λέγε· 'ἄνδρες πολῖται, πολλοί εἰσι ποταμοὶ χείμαρροι καὶ
5 ἀέναοι οἵτινες τῇ θαλάσσῃ ἐπιχέονται. Συνεθέμην οὖν μόνην τὴν θάλασσαν 10 ἐκπιεῖν, οὐχὶ καὶ τοὺς ἐπιρρέοντας ποταμούς. Ἄπελθε οὖν καὶ ἐπίστρεψον τὰ ἐπεισερχόμενα ὕδατα, κἀγὼ τὴν θάλασσαν ἐκπίω.' Καὶ οὕτως τὸ ἀδύνατον τῷ ἀδυνάτῳ λυθήσεται.»

72. Ὁ δὲ Ξάνθος ἐπιγνοὺς περιχαρὴς γέγονεν. Ὁ δὲ τὴν συνθήκην θεὶς
10 ἅμα τοῖς ἐντιμοτέροις τῆς πόλεως ἐξεδέχετο, προελθόντος δὲ τοῦ Ξάνθου ἐζήτει ἐκβιβασθῆναι τὴν συνθήκην. Αἴσωπος εἶπε «σὺ μὲν δίδου τὸ σὸν βίον τῷ δεσπότῃ μου. Αὐτῷ γὰρ ἤδη ἡμίκενος γέγονεν ἡ θάλασσα.» Ὁ σχολαστικός ἔφη «ἐμὸς εἶ, Αἴσωπε, οὐκέτι Ξάνθου.» Ὁ δὲ Ξάνθος ἐκέλευσε 5 κλίνην πρὸς τῷ αἰγιαλῷ στρωθῆναι καὶ τράπεζαν τεθῆναι, τὸ δὲ πλῆθος τῆς
15 πόλεως συνέδραμον ἰδεῖν. Τοῦ δὲ Ξάνθου ἀναπεσόντος, δραμὼν Αἴσωπος καὶ σκύφον λαβὼν καὶ πλήσας ἐκ τῆς θαλάσσης ἐπέδωκε τῷ Ξάνθῳ.

73. Ὁ δὲ λαβὼν λέγει τῷ συνθηκοφύλακι «εἰπὲ δημοσίᾳ πῶς ἐθήκαμεν τὰς συνθήκας.» Ὁ δὲ λέγει «ἵνα τὴν θάλασσαν ἐκπίῃς.» Ὁ Ξάνθος· «μή τι ἕτερον;» Ὁ δὲ «οὔ.» Ὁ Ξάνθος ἔφη «ἄνδρες πολῖται, πολλοὶ ποταμοὶ ὕδωρ
20 εἰσάγουσιν ἐν τῇ θαλάσσῃ. Ἀποκλεισάτω γοῦν ὁ ἀντίδικός μου τὰ τούτων στόματα κἀγὼ ἰσχύσω μόνην ἐκπιεῖν τὴν θάλασσαν.» Ἀνέκραξαν δὲ ἅπαντες 5 εὐφημοῦντες τὸν Ξάνθον. Ὁ δὲ σχολαστικὸς πεσὼν πρὸς τοὺς πόδας τοῦ Ξάνθου λέγει «μέγας εἶ, καθηγητά, νενίκηκάς με. Παρακαλῶ λυθῆναι τὰς συνθήκας.»

25 74. Ἐλθόντος δὲ αὐτοῦ εἰς τὴν οἰκίαν, προσελθὼν αὐτῷ ὁ Αἴσωπος λέγει «ὁ πάντα σου τὸν βίον σώσας ἄξιός εἰμι τυχεῖν ἐλευθερίας.» Ὁ δὲ Ξάνθος

71.6 σκάφου Ο | ἐκ τῆς θαλάττης Ο | πρὸς τὸν λαόν, ἐξόχως δὲ post δημοσίᾳ add. Ο 7 συνοφύλακα Ο | συνθήκας : συν Ο 8 ἐκπιεῖς Ο | αὐτῷ post οὖν add. Ο | κἀκεῖνος ante ἐρεῖ add. Ο 9 μαρτυράμενος : -υρά- evan. in M | λέγε : φῆσον M | καὶ : evan. in M 10 ταῦτα ante ἀέναοι add. Ο | τὴν : evan. in M 10–11 ἐκπιεῖν τὴν θάλασσαν inv. Ο 11 οὐχὶ : οὐ μὴν δὲ Ο | οὖν : λοιπὸν Ο | καὶ ἐπίστρεψον : καὶ ἐπί- evan. in M 12 Καὶ οὕτως : evan. in M ∥ 72.1 γέγονεν : ἐγένετο Ο | θεὶς : om. Ο 2 ἅμα τῷ ἐντιμοτέρῳ Ο | ἐξεδέχετο : ἐκδεχόμενος πρὸ τοῦ πυλῶνος Ο | προελθόντος ... Ξάνθου : ἐξελθόντι δὲ τῷ Ξάνθῳ Ο 3 ὁ σχολαστικός post ἐζήτει add. Ο | ἐκβιβασθῆναι : ἐκπερωθῆναι Ο | Αἴσωπος εἶπε : ἔσωπος δὲ πρὸς αὐτὸν ἀπεκρήθη Ο 4 ἡμίκενος γέγονεν : κενοῦται Ο 4–5 καὶ ante ὁ σχολ. add. Ο 5 ἔφη : om. Ο |

arranged and a whole crowd has gathered to watch, recline and order a bowl to be filled from the sea and declare publicly to the guarantor, 'What were the terms of the bet?' And he will answer you, 'That you would drink up the sea.' So say, 'Nothing more?' and he will answer, "No." And calling them as witnesses, say, 'Gentlemen and citizens, there are many torrential and ever-flowing rivers that run into the sea. But I agreed to drink up only the sea and not also the rivers that flow into it. So go and turn back the waters that are entering it, and I will drink up the sea.' And in this way the impossible will be nullified by the impossible."

72. Xanthus understood and became very cheerful. The one who had made the bet, together with the most distinguished men of the town, was waiting for him. When Xanthus came forward, the student sought to have the bet carried out. Aesop said, "Give your livelihood to my master, since the sea is already half empty for his sake." The student said, "You are mine, Aesop, no longer Xanthus's." Xanthus ordered a couch to be made up by the beach and a table to be set, and a multitude from the city gathered to see. When Xanthus had reclined, Aesop ran and took a cup and filled it from the sea and gave it to his master.

73. Xanthus took it and said to the guarantor, "Declare publicly: What were the terms of our bet?" And he said, "That you would drink the sea." And Xanthus said, "Nothing else?" "No," he said. Xanthus said, "Gentlemen and citizens, many rivers bring water into the sea. Let my opponent, then, close off the mouths of these, and I will succeed in drinking up the sea alone." Everyone shouted, applauding Xanthus. The student fell at the feet of Xanthus and said, "You are great, Professor, and have defeated me. I beg you to nullify the bet."

74. When Xanthus returned to his house, Aesop came up to him and said, "Since I have saved your entire livelihood, I deserve to gain my freedom." Xanthus arrogantly chased him away and said, "What? Couldn't I

οὐκέτι ... Ξάνθου : καὶ πάντα τὰ ἐν τῷ οἴκῳ τοῦ κυρίου σου O 6 πρὸς ... στρωθῆναι : στρωθῆναι ἐν τῷ αἰγιαλῷ O 7 συνέδραμεν O | τοῦ ἰδεῖν O | ὁ ante Αἴσωπος add. O | καὶ : om. O 8 πληρώσας O | τῷ Ξάνθῳ : τῷ κυρίῳ αὐτοῦ M ‖ 73.1 τεθήκαμεν O : τεθείκαμεν ex W corr. Perry, iter. Papath. 2 ἐκπίῃς : ex W corr. Perry, iter. Papath. : ἐκπίεις O : πίῃς M | ἔφη post Ξάνθος add. O 3 Ὁ δὲ : om. M | φησιν post οὔ add. M | Ὁ ... ἔφη : καὶ ὁ Ξ. O 3–4 ἐν τῇ θαλάσσῃ ὕδωρ εἰσάγουσι inv. O 4 οὖν O 5 ἰσχύσω : νικήσω O | ἐκπιεῖν : ἐκπιῶ O 6 τὸν : evan. in M | πρὸς : παρὰ O | τοῦ ... 7 Ξάνθου : αὐτοῦ O ‖ 74.1 ὁ : om. M 2 ἄξιός εἰμι : ἀξιώσεις μοι O

ὑβρίσας ἐξεδίωξεν αὐτὸν λέγων «τί; Ἐγὼ τοῦτο οὐκ ἐνεθυμούμην;» Αἴσωπος δὲ ἀχαριστηθεὶς ἐλυπήθη καί φησι «μεῖνον με. Ἐγώ σε ἀνταμυνοῦμαι.»

75. Ἐν μιᾷ οὖν τῶν ἡμερῶν μονωθείς, ἐκδυσάμενος καὶ τὰς χεῖρας ἑαυτοῦ κροτῶν καὶ τινάσσων, ἤρξατο ποιεῖν τὸ ποιμενικὸν καὶ ἄτακτον σχῆμα. Ἡ δὲ τοῦ Ξάνθου γυνή, ἐκ τοῦ οἴκου αἴφνης καταλαβοῦσα, φησὶν «Αἴσωπε, τί τοῦτο;» Ὁ δὲ λέγει «κυρία, εὐεργετοῦμαι καὶ τὴν γαστέρα ὠφελεῖ.» Θεασαμένη δὲ ἐκείνη τὸ μῆκος καὶ τὸ πάχος τῆς αἰδοῦς αὐτοῦ ἑάλω, καὶ ἐπιλαθομένη τῆς ἀμορφίας αὐτοῦ εἰς ἔρωτα ἐτρώθη. Φωνήσασα δὲ αὐτὸν κατ' ἰδίαν φησί «νῦν μοι, ἐὰν τὰ ἀρεστὰ ποιήσῃς μὴ ἀντιπίπτων, ἔσῃ εὐφραινόμενος πλεῖον τοῦ κυρίου σου.» Ὁ δὲ πρὸς αὐτήν· «οἶδας ὅτι ⟨ἐὰν⟩ ὁ δεσπότης μου τοῦτο μάθῃ, οὐ μικρὸν ἐπάξιον λυγρὸν ἀνταμείψει;» Ἡ δὲ γελάσασα ἔφη «ἐάν μοι δεκάκις συνέλθῃς, στολήν σοι ἱματίων χαρίσομαι.» Ὁ δέ φησιν «ὄμοσόν μοι.» Ἐκείνη δὲ καπριῶσα ὤμοσεν αὐτῷ. Ὁ δὲ Αἴσωπος πιστεύσας, θέλων δὲ καὶ τῷ δεσπότῃ ἀνταμύνασθαι, ἐπετέλει τὸ πάθος ἕως ἐννέα καί φησι «κυρία, ἄλλο οὐ δύναμαι.» Ἡ δὲ πεῖραν λαβοῦσα λέγει «εἰ μὴ τὰ δέκα πληρώσῃς, οὐδὲν λαμβάνεις.» Πολλὰ οὖν κοπιάσας τὸ δέκατον εἰς τὸ μηρὸν ἐτέλεσεν καί φησι «δός μοι τὰ ἱμάτια, ἐπεὶ ἐγκαλῶ κατὰ σοῦ τῷ δεσπότῃ.» Ἔφη δὲ ἡ γυνὴ «ἐγὼ εἰς τὸν ἐμόν σε ἐμισθωσάμην ἀγρὸν σκάπτειν. Σὺ δὲ ὑπερβὰς τὸ μεσότοιχον εἰς τὰ τοῦ γείτονος ἔσκαψας. Ἀπόδος οὖν καὶ λάβε τὴν στολήν.»

76. Ὁ δὲ Αἴσωπος ἐλθόντι τῷ Ξάνθῳ προσῆλθε καί φησι «κριθῆναι ⟨με⟩ μετὰ τῆς κυρίας μου ἐπὶ σοί.» Ὁ δὲ ἀκούσας, «τί;» φησι. Καὶ ὁ Αἴσωπος· «δέσποτα, ἡ κυρία μετ' ἐμοῦ πορευομένη εἶδε κοκκυμηλέαν κατάκαρπον. Θεασαμένη κλάδον ἕνα πλήρη ἐπιθυμήσασα λέγει 'ἐὰν δυνήσῃ ἕναν λίθον βαλεῖν μοι δέκα κοκκύμηλα, παρέχω σοι στολὴν ἱματίων.' Βαλὼν οὖν ἐγὼ εὐστόχως ἑνὶ λίθῳ, ἤνεγκα αὐτῇ δέκα. Ἓν δὲ ἐξ αὐτῶν ἔλαχεν εἰς κόπρον ἐμπεσεῖν καὶ νῦν οὐ θέλει μοι τὴν στολὴν δοῦναι.» Ἐρίσασα δὲ ἐκείνη λέγει τῷ ἀνδρὶ «ὁμολογῶ εἰληφέναι τὰ ἐννέα, τὸ δὲ εἰς τὴν κόπρον οὐ λογίζομαι. Βαλέτω οὖν πάλιν καὶ ἐκτιναξάτω μοι τὸ ἓν κοκκύμηλον καὶ λαμβανέτω τὰ ἱμάτια.» Αἴσωπος ἔφη «οὐκέτι μου ὁ καρπὸς εὐτονεῖ.» Ἔκρινεν οὖν Ξάνθος

74.3 ἐδίωξεν O   4 μεῖνον με : om. O | ἀνταμείνομαι O 75.1 : cap. 75–76 desunt in M (praeb. in O, Lo)   5 ὠφελεῖ : corr. Perry, iter. Papath. : οφέλει O | αἰδοῦς : corr. Perry, iter. Papath. : αἰδῶ O   8 ἐὰν : suppl. Perry, iter. Papath.   9 ἀνταμείψει : corr. Perry, iter. Papath. : ἀνταμείψοι O   10 χαρίσομαι : corr. Perry, iter. Papath. : χαρήσομαι O   12 ἀνταμύνασθαι : corr. Perry, iter. Papath. : ἀνταμείνασθαι O   14 πληρώσῃς : πληρώσεις corr. Perry | λαμβάνεις : corr. Perry, iter. Papath. : λαμβάνης O   15 τὸ : τὸν μηρὸν corr. Perry, iter. Papath.   ‖ 76.1 με : suppl. Perry, iter. Papath.   3 εἶδε :

think of it myself?" Aesop was hurt by this ingratitude and said, "You wait; I will get back at you."

75. One day when he was alone, Aesop stripped and clapped and shook his hands and started the well-known vulgar and disorderly movement. Xanthus's wife, coming suddenly out of the house, caught him in the act and said, "Aesop, what's this?" He said, "Mistress, I'm treating myself well, and it does good for my belly." When she saw the size and thickness of his private part, she was overcome, and forgetting his ugliness she was pierced by passion. She summoned him and said in private, "Now, if you do what is pleasing to me and do not resist, you will be much happier than my lord." He said to her, "You know that, if my master learns of this, I will pay for it with no small misery, and well deserved." She laughed and said, "If you make love to me ten times, I will give you a robe made of cloth." He said, "Swear it to me." She, in heat, swore to him, and Aesop, believing her and wishing to pay back his master, fulfilled her passion up to nine times and said, "Mistress, I cannot do it again." She put him to the test and said, "If you don't fulfill ten, you get nothing." So, after great effort he finished the tenth one on her thigh and said, "Give me the clothing, otherwise I will report you to the master." The wife said, "I hired you to dig in my field, but you crossed over the wall and dug the neighbor's. So pay me back and then take the robe."

76. Aesop approached Xanthus when he came in and said, "It is up to you to judge me along with my mistress." When Xanthus heard this, he said, "What?" And Aesop said, "Master, my mistress was traveling with me and saw a plum tree that was in fruit. When she noticed one branch that was full, she desired it and said, 'If you can knock down ten plums for me with one stone, I will give you a robe of cloth.' So I knocked them down with one well-aimed stone and brought her ten. But one of them chanced to fall in manure, and now she doesn't want to give me the robe." She challenged him and said to her husband, "I agree that I received nine, but I don't count the one in the manure. So let him throw again and shake down that one plum for me and then he can take the clothes." Aesop said, "My wrist is no longer able." Xanthus judged that the robe be given to Aesop

---

corr. Perry, iter. Papath. : οἶδε O   **4** ἑνὶ λίθῳ corr. Perry, iter. Papath.   **5** δέκα κοκκύμηλα : corr. Perry, iter. Papath. : δέκοκύμυλα O   **7** Ἐρίσασα : corr. Papath. : ἐρήσασα O : ἀκούσασα ex Lo "audiens" corr. Perry   **9** Βαλέτω : corr. Papath. : βαλλέτω O | κοκκύμηλον : corr. Perry, iter. Papath. : κοκκόμηλον O   **10** εὐτονεῖ : εὐγονεῖ legit Perry

δοθῆναι τῷ Αἰσώπῳ τὴν στολὴν καί φησι πρὸς αὐτὸν «Αἴσωπε, πορευσώμεθα ἕως τῆς ἀγορᾶς ὅτι νωχελεύω. Ἅμα δὲ ἐκτινάξεις μοι τὰ κοκκύμηλα ὅπως καὶ τῇ κυρίᾳ ἐνέγκωμεν.» Ἡ δὲ εἶπεν «μὴ θέλῃς, κῦρι, ἵνα σοι βάλῃ ἐξ αὐτῶν. Ἐγὼ δέ, ὡς ἐκέλευσας, δώσω τὰ ἱμάτια.»

77. Ὁ Ξάνθος λέγει τῷ Αἰσώπῳ «δεδῶναι ἑστῶσαί εἰσι· ἔξελθε οὖν πρὸ τοῦ πυλῶνος καὶ ἐὰν ἴδῃς δικόρωνον ἀνάγγειλόν μοι, ὅτι καλὸν τὸ σημεῖον, εἰ δὲ μονοκόρωνον, κακὴ ἡ οἰωνοσκοπία.» Ἐξελθὼν δὲ ὁ Αἴσωπος καὶ ἰδὼν κατὰ τύχην δικόρωνον πρὸ τοῦ πυλῶνος, εἰσῆλθε καὶ ἀνήγγειλε τῷ Ξάνθῳ καὶ προσελθὼν παρῄνει. Ἐν δὲ τῷ ἐξέρχεσθαι αὐτὸν ἡ μία ἀνέπτη. Τὴν δὲ μίαν ἰδὼν ἔφη «οὐκ εἶπάς μοι, κατάρατε, ὅτι δικόρωνον εἱστήκει πρὸ τοῦ πυλῶνος;» Αἴσωπος ἔφη «ναί, ἀλλ' ἡ μία ἔπτη.» Ὁ δὲ Ξάνθος φησὶ «ἔθος σοι τοῦ χλευάζειν με.» Καὶ ἐκέλευσεν αὐτὸν γυμνωθέντα τύπτεσθαι. Τυπτομένου δὲ αὐτοῦ ἐλθών τις ἐπὶ δεῖπνον ἐκάλει τὸν Ξάνθον. Ὁ δὲ Αἴσωπος ἔφη «οἴμοι, ὁ τάλας, ἐγὼ ἰδὼν τὸ δικόρωνον ἐμαστιγώθην, σὺ δὲ μονοκόρωνον ἰδὼν ἐπὶ τρυφὴν πορεύῃ. Οὐκοῦν μάτην ὀρνεοσκοπία;» Ὁ δὲ Ξάνθος θαυμάσας αὐτοῦ τὸν λόγον «μηκέτι,» φησί, «τυπτέσθω.»

77a. Μεθ' ἡμέρας δέ τινας προσκαλεσάμενος αὐτὸν ἔφη «ποίησον ἡμῖν ἄριστον καλόν. Σχολαστικοὺς γὰρ κέκληκα.» Ὁ δὲ Αἴσωπος τὰ πρὸς ὑπηρεσίαν εὐτρεπίσας, καὶ τῆς κυρίας αὐτοῦ ἐπὶ τῆς κλίνης ἀνακειμένης, ἔφη πρὸς αὐτὴν ὁ Αἴσωπος «πρόσεχε, ὦ κυρία μου, τῇ τραπέζῃ, μή πως ἡ κύων ἐλθοῦσα καταφάγῃ τι τῶν ἐδεσμάτων.» Ἡ δὲ ἔφη πρὸς αὐτὸν «ἄπελθε περὶ τούτου μηδὲν φροντίζων· ἐμοῦ γὰρ καὶ ὁ κῶλος ὀφθαλμοὺς ἔχει.» Τοῦ δὲ Αἰσώπου εἰς ἑτέρας ἀσχολουμένου δουλείας, ὑποστρέψαντος δὲ αὖθις ἐπὶ τὴν τράπεζαν, εὗρε τὴν κυρίαν αὐτοῦ κοιμωμένην καὶ τὰ ὄπισθεν ἐπὶ τὴν τράπεζαν ἔχουσα. Φοβηθεὶς μή πως ἡ κύων ἀνελθοῦσα ἀχρειώσῃ τὴν τράπεζαν, ἀνεμνήσθη εἰπούσης τῆς κυρίας ὅτι «ὁ κῶλός μου ὀφθαλμοὺς ἔχει», καὶ ἀνακομβώσας τοὺς αὐτῆς χιτῶνας καὶ τὰ ὄπισθεν ἐπιγυμνώσας εἴασεν αὐτὴν οὕτως κεῖσθαι καὶ τηρεῖν τὴν τράπεζαν. Τοῦ δὲ Ξάνθου σὺν τοῖς

76.12 νωχελεύω : scripsi : νωχλεύω corr. Perry : νοχλεύω O : νωχελεύομαι corr. Papath. fort. recte 13 μὴ … αὐτῶν : del. Perry | θέλῃς : corr. Papath. : θέλῃ O | βάλῃ : corr. Papath. : βάλλει O ‖ 77.1 δὲ post ὁ add. M | λέγει … Αἰσώπῳ : τῷ ἐσώπῳ λέγει O | δεδῶναι … εἰσι : scripsi : δεδόνιστος εἰμί O : οἰωνιστής εἰμι corr. Perry, iter. Papath. | οὖν : om. M 2 ἀπάγγειλόν O 3 ἀνάγγειλόν μοι ὅτι post μονοκόρωνον add. M | κακὴ ἡ : om. O | οἰωνοσκοπία : ὀρνεοσκοπία M | ὁ : om. M | καὶ ἰδὼν : ἴδε O 4 εἰσῆλθε … ἀνήγγειλε : καὶ εἰσελθὼν ἀπείγγειλε O 5 καὶ … παρῄνει : om. O |

and said to him, "Aesop, let's go to the market because I'm feeling sluggish. At the same time, you can shake some plums down for me so that I can bring them to the mistress." But she said, "Don't request, my lord, that he knock some of those down for you, and I will give him the clothes, as you ordered."

77. Xanthus said to Aesop, "There are crows outside. Go out in front of the gate, and if you see a pair of crows, report it to me, since it is a good sign. But if it is a single crow, report it to me because that augury is bad." Aesop went out and seeing, as it chanced, a pair of crows in front of the gate, he went in and reported it to Xanthus, and, approaching, he congratulated him. When Xanthus went out one of them had flown away. Seeing only one, he said, "Didn't you tell me, you abomination, that a pair of crows was in front of the gate?" Aesop said, "Yes, but one flew away." Xanthus said, "It is your habit to mock me," and he ordered that he be stripped and beaten. While he was being beaten, someone came and invited Xanthus to dinner. Aesop said, "Woe is me, poor wretch, I saw a pair of crows, and I am being punished, you saw one crow and look!, you're going for a meal. So isn't augury useless?" Xanthus was impressed by his reasoning and said, "Let him stop being beaten."

77a. Some days later, Xanthus summoned him and said, "Prepare me a fine lunch. I have invited students." Aesop got everything ready for serving and said to his mistress, who was reclining on a couch, "Pay attention, my mistress, to the table, so that the dog doesn't come and eat some of the meats." She said to him, "Go and don't worry about this, for even my behind has eyes." Aesop went off to busy himself with some other errand, and when he returned to the table he found his mistress sleeping with her rear end toward the table. Fearing that the dog might somehow climb up and ruin the table, he recalled that his mistress had said "My behind has eyes," and so, rolling up her tunic, he exposed her rear end and left her lying there to keep watch over the table. When Xanthus arrived with his

---

αὐτὸν : τὸν Ξάνθον O | ἀνέπτη : ἀνεπετάσθη M (αὐτῶν ... επετάσθη leg. Papath. : ... επετάσθη leg. Perry) 7 Αἴσωπος ἔφη : ὁ δὲ O | ἔπτη : evan. in M | Ὁ ... φησὶ : καὶ ὁ Ξάνθος ἔφη O 8 ἐκέλευσεν οὖν M | γυμνωθέντα : ... .-έντα lit. evan. in M 9 ἐπὶ μέγα δεῖπνον O | ἐκάλει : evan. in M 10 τὸ : om. O | ἰδοὺ post ἰδὼν add. M 11 τρυφὴν : τροφὴν M | πορεύει O | οἰωνοσκοπία καὶ ὀρνοσκοπία O 12 τύπτεσθαι O ‖ 77a.1 : cap. 77a et 77b solum in M tradita sunt; desunt in OLo (G)

σχολαστικοῖς ἐλθόντος ἀνῆλθον ἐπὶ τὸ ἄριστον. Ἰδόντες οὖν τὴν τοῦ Ξάνθου γυναῖκα γεγυμνωμένην καὶ ὑπνώττουσαν, αἰσχυνθέντες ἀπεστράφησαν τὰς ὄψεις αὐτῶν. Ὁ δὲ Ξάνθος λέγει τῷ Αἰσώπῳ «τί τοῦτο, ὦ κατάρατε;» Ὁ δέ φησι «δέσποτα, ἐμοῦ τὰ πρὸς θεραπείαν ὑμετέραν ἑτοιμάζοντος καὶ εἰπόντος
5 τῇ κυρίᾳ μου προσέχειν τῇ τραπέζῃ, μή πως ἀνελθοῦσα ἡ κύων καταφάγῃ τι, αὕτη ἔφησε πρός με 'ἄπελθε καὶ περὶ τούτου μηδὲν φρόντιζε· ἐμοῦ γὰρ καὶ ὁ κῶλος ὀφθαλμοὺς ἔχει.' Ἄρτι δέ, ὡς ὁρᾷς, ὑπνοῖ, κύριέ μου· ἐγὼ δὲ ἐγύμνωσα αὐτὴν ὅπως οἱ τοῦ κώλου ὀφθαλμοὶ ὁρῶσι τὴν τράπεζαν.» Καὶ ὁ Ξάνθος «πλειστάκις με, ὦ δραπέτα, ἠχρείωσας. Τούτου δὲ ἀχρειότερον
10 οὔπω εἰργάσω, αἰσχύνας οὐ μόνον ἐμὲ ἀλλὰ καὶ τὴν κυρίαν σου. Ἀλλὰ διὰ τοὺς κεκλημένους οὐκ ὀργισθήσομαι. Εὑρήσω γὰρ ὥραν ὅτε μαστιγώσω σε σφοδρῶς καὶ ἀπολέσω.»

77b. Μετὰ ταῦτα δὲ ῥήτορας καὶ φιλοσόφους τοῦ Ξάνθου καλέσαντος ἔφη ὁ Ξάνθος τῷ Αἰσώπῳ «πρὸ τοῦ πυλῶνος σταθεὶς μὴ ἐάσῃς τινὰ τῶν
15 ἰδιωτῶν ἀνδρῶν εἰσελθεῖν ἐν τῷ οἴκῳ μου, ἀλλ' ἢ μόνον σοφούς.» Τῇ δὲ ὥρᾳ τοῦ ἀρίστου κλείσας ὁ Αἴσωπος τοὺς τοῦ οἴκου πυλῶνας ἐκαθέζετο ἔσωθεν. Ἐλθόντος δέ τινος τῶν κεκλημένων καὶ κρούσαντος τὸν πυλῶνα ἔσωθεν ὁ Αἴσωπος λέγει «τί σείει ὁ κύων;» Ὁ δὲ ἡγησάμενος ὅτι κύνα αὐτὸν ἀπεκάλεσεν, ὀργισθεὶς ἀνεχώρησεν. Οὕτως οὖν πολλοὺς <ἀπολεγουμένου>
20 ἀνεχώρουν ἅπαντες, ὕβριν τὸν λόγον νομίζοντες εἶναι. Εἷς δὲ ἐλθὼν καὶ εἰς τὸν πυλῶνα κρούσας, τοῦ δὲ Αἰσώπου φήσαντος «τί σείει ὁ κύων;» «τὴν κέρκον,» φησί. Καὶ ὁ Αἴσωπος τοῦτον ἀκούσας καλῶς ἀπολογησάμενον, ἀνοίξας εἰσήγαγεν αὐτόν. Ἐπελθὼν δὲ πρὸς τὸν κύριον αὐτοῦ ἔφη «δέσποτα, ἕτερος φιλόσοφος οὐκ ἦλθε τοῦ συνεστιαθῆναί σοι, εἰ μὴ μόνος οὗτος.» Ὁ δὲ
25 Ξάνθος ἐλυπήθη πάνυ προσδοκῶν ὅτι παρελογίσαντο αὐτόν. Τῇ οὖν ἐπαύριον ἐλθόντων ἐν τῇ διατριβῇ, λέγουσι τῷ Ξάνθῳ «καθηγητά, ὡς ἔοικεν ἐπιθυμῶν τοῦ ἐξουθενῆσαι ἡμᾶς καὶ αἰδούμενος, ἔστησας τὸν σαπρὸν Αἴσωπον τοῦ ἐξουθενῆσαι καὶ ὑβρίσαι ἡμᾶς καὶ κύνας ἀποκαλέσαι.» Καὶ ὁ Ξάνθος· «ὅραμα τοῦτο ἢ ἀληθές;» Καὶ οἱ σχολαστικοί· «εἰ οὐ κοιμώμεθα, ἀληθές ἐστι.» Καὶ
30 ὁ Ξάνθος· «Αἴσωπόν μοί τις καλεσάτω.» Τοῦ δὲ ἐλθόντος ἔφη ὁ Ξάνθος «λέγε μοι, κάθαρμα, διὰ τί τοὺς ἐμοὺς φίλους καὶ φοιτητάς, ἀντὶ τοῦ μετὰ πάσης τιμῆς εἰσαγαγεῖν σε αὐτοὺς ἐν τῷ οἴκῳ μου τοῦ συνευφρανθῆναί μοι, ἐξουθένησας καὶ ὕβρισας καὶ ἀτίμως ἀπέστρεψας;» Καὶ ὁ Αἴσωπος· «δέσποτα, οὐ σύ μοι εἴρηκας 'μὴ ἐάσῃς τινὰ τῶν ἀνοήτων ἀνδρῶν εἰσελθεῖν ἐν τῷ οἴκῳ
35 μου, εἰ μὴ ῥήτορας καὶ φιλοσόφους;» Καὶ ὁ Ξάνθος, «ναί,» φησι, «καὶ τί,

---

77a.15 ὦ : evan. in M ‖ **77b.5** εἰς ante τὸν suppl. Papath. 7 ἀπολεγουμένου : suppl. Papath. (in M ἀπολογουμένου leg. Papath.) : amissis octo fere litteris antecedenti-

students, they went in for lunch. When they saw Xanthus's wife naked and dozing, they turned their eyes away in shame. Xanthus said to Aesop, "What is this, you abomination?" Aesop said, "Master, while I was preparing things for your comfort, I told the mistress to pay attention to the table so that the dog might not come up and eat something, and she said to me, 'Go and don't worry about this, for even my behind has eyes.' Right now, as you see, she is dozing, my master. I bared her so that the eyes in her behind might watch the table." Xanthus said, "Very often, you damned slave, you have offended me, but you have never yet done anything more offensive than this, putting to shame not only me but your mistress as well. But because of these invited guests I will not be angry, but I will find a time when I'll punish you severely and destroy you."

77b. After this, Xanthus invited some orators and philosophers and said to Aesop, "Stand in front of the gate, and don't let any of the ordinary men enter my house, but only the sages." At the hour of the lunch, Aesop locked the gates of the house and sat within. When one of those who had been invited came and knocked on the gate, Aesop said from inside, "What does a dog shake?" Thinking that Aesop was calling him a dog, he got angry and left. And so, Aesop spoke to many in this way, and they all left, thinking that his words were an insult. Then one came and knocked at the gate, and Aesop said, "What does the dog shake?" and he answered, "Its tail." And Aesop, when he heard this one respond correctly, opened up and led him in. When he went in he said to his master, "Master, no other philosopher came to join you at the feast, but only this one." Xanthus was very hurt, believing that they thought ill of him. On the next day, when they came in for the lecture, the students said to Xanthus, "Professor, it seems that you wished to make little of us and were ashamed, since you set that ugly Aesop to make little of us and insult us and call us dogs." And Xanthus said, "Is this a dream or true?" And the students said, "If we are not sleeping, it is true." And Xanthus said, "Let someone summon Aesop to me." When Aesop entered, Xanthus said, "Tell me, you trash, why did you make little of my friends and students and insult them and turn them away dishonorably, instead of leading them with all honor into my house to rejoice with me?" And Aesop said, "Master, didn't you tell me, 'Don't let any unintelligent men enter my house but only orators and philosophers?'" "Yes,"

---

bus in M : ἀπολογουμένου ex BLV suppl. Perry **9** τί σείει : ex SBλW corr. Perry, iter. Papath. : τίς εἶ M

μορμολύκειον; Οὐκ εἰσὶν οὗτοι τῶν φιλοσόφων;» Καὶ ὁ Αἴσωπος· «οὐχί, ἀλλὰ καὶ πάνυ ἰδιῶται τυγχάνουσι. Τῷ γὰρ πυλῶνι τῷ σῷ προσκεκρουκότων, ἐγὼ δὲ ἱστάμενος ἔσωθεν, ἠρώτων αὐτοὺς 'τί σείει ὁ κύων;'. Καὶ οὐδεὶς ἐξ αὐτῶν ἐπέγνω τὸ ῥῆμα τοῦτο, καὶ τῷ ἀνοήτους αὐτοὺς εἶναι οὐκ εἰσήγαγον αὐτούς, εἰ μὴ τοῦτον μόνον τὸν σαφῶς ἀνταποκριθέντα μοι, τὸν τῷ κυρίῳ μου συνεστιαθέντα.» Οὕτως τοῦ Αἰσώπου ἀπολογηθέντος ἔφησαν ἅπαντες ὀρθῶς αὐτὸν λέγειν.

78. Μεθ' ἡμέρας δέ τινας ὁ Ξάνθος ἅμα τῷ Αἰσώπῳ ἐπὶ τὰ μνήματα παρεγένετο καὶ τὰ ἐν ταῖς λάρναξιν ἐπιτάφια ἀναγινώσκων ἐτέρπετο. Ὁ δὲ Αἴσωπος ἰδὼν ἐφ' ἑνὶ λάρνακι ἀσύμφωνα στοιχεῖα κεχαραγμένα, α', β', δ', ο', ε', θ', χ', ἐπιδείξας τῷ Ξάνθῳ φησὶ «τί ἐστιν ἄρα ταῦτα;» Ὁ δὲ ἐπιμελῶς καταμαθὼν καὶ πολλὰ στρεβλωθεὶς οὐχ εὗρε τὴν τούτων λύσιν καί φησιν «Αἴσωπε, ἠπόρησα. Σὺ δὲ τὸ ζήτημα διασάφησον.» Ὁ δὲ πρὸς αὐτόν· «δέσποτα, ἐὰν διὰ ταύτης τῆς στήλης θησαυρὸν χρυσίου δώσω σοι, τί μοι χαρίζεις;» Ὁ Ξάνθος ἀκούσας λέγει «θάρσει, Αἴσωπε. Λήψει τὴν ἐλευθερίαν καὶ τὸ ἥμισυ τοῦ χρυσίου.»

79. Ὁ δὲ Αἴσωπος ἀκούσας καὶ λαβὼν ὄστρακον, ἀνεπόδισεν ἀπὸ τῆς στήλης βήματα τέσσαρα καὶ ὀρύξας τὸν θησαυρὸν ἀνελάβετο καὶ τῷ δεσπότῃ προσήνεγκε. Καί φησι «δέσποτα, δός μοι τὴν ἐπαγγελίαν.» Ὁ δὲ Ξάνθος «οὐ δώσω,» φησί, «ἐὰν μή μοι φράσῃς ποίᾳ ἐπινοίᾳ εὗρες τὸν θησαυρόν. Τὸ γὰρ μαθεῖν πολὺ τοῦ εὑρέματος τιμιώτερον.» Αἴσωπος ἔφη «δέσποτα, ὁ τὸν θησαυρὸν καταθέμενος ὡς φιλόσοφος τὰ ἑπτὰ ἐχάραξε στοιχεῖα, ἃ λέγουσι οὕτως· α' ἀποβάς, β' βήματα, δ' τέσσαρα, ο' ὀρύξας, ε' εὑρήσεις, θ' θησαυρόν, χ' χρυσίου.» Ξάνθος λέγει «ἐπείπερ τοιοῦτος εἶ πανοῦργος καὶ συνετός, οὐ τεύξῃ τῆς ἐλευθερίας.» Ὁ δὲ πρὸς αὐτόν· «δέσποτα, παραγγέλλω τὸ χρυσίον δοθῆναι βασιλεῖ τῶν Βυζαντίων, Διονυσίῳ.» «Πόθεν οἶδας;» φησίν. Αἴσωπος ἔφη «ἐκ τῶν γραμμάτων ἐπέγνων, ὡς λέγει· α', ἀπόδος, β', βασιλεῖ, δ' Διονυσίῳ, ο' ὃν εὗρες, ε' ἐνθάδε, θ' θησαυρόν, χ' χρυσίου.»

77b.24 μορμολύκειον : μορμολύκιον Perry : μορμολυκεῖον Papath. 25 προσκεκρουκότων : ex S corr. Papath. : προσκεκρόντων M : προσκεκρουκότες ex BPW corr. Perry 28 σαφῶς : σοφῶς ex BP corr. Papath. fort. recte ‖ 78.1 τινας : om. M 2 παρεγένοντο O | τὰ ... ἐπιτάφια : ἐπὶ τοὺς τύμβους ὁρῶν τὰ γράμματα O | ἐτέρπετο : εὐφραίνετο O 3 σύμφωνα O | ἔχοντα οὕτως post κεχαραγμένα add. O 4 ὁ ἔσωπος καὶ post Ξάνθῳ add. O | ἐστιν : om. O 5 στρεβλωθεὶς : στρεθείς O 7 σοι post ἐὰν add. O | σοι post θησαυρὸν trans. O 8 χαρίζει O | τὴν : om. O ‖ 79.1 Αἴσωπος : om. O | καὶ ... ὄστρακον : ὄστρακον λαβὼν O | ἀνεπόδισεν : ἀναπηδήσας M 2 τέσσαρα : δ' O |

said Xanthus, and what about it, you troll? Aren't these philosophers?" And Aesop said, "No, they happen to be very ordinary people, for when they knocked at your gate, I was standing inside and I asked them, 'What does a dog shake?' and no one of them recognized this line, and because they were unintelligent I didn't lead them in, except for this one who answered me clearly, the one who joined my master's feast." When Aesop had made his defense, they all said that he had spoken correctly.

78. Some days later Xanthus went with Aesop to the graveyard and was enjoying reading the epitaphs on the urns. Aesop saw some incongruous letters inscribed on one urn—G', S', D', E', F', T', G'—and he pointed them out to Xanthus and said, "What are these, then?" Although Xanthus studied them carefully and strained much, he could not find the solution and said, "Aesop, I'm at a loss. Explain the puzzle to me." Aesop said to him, "Master, if I give you a treasure of gold, thanks to this stela, what will you grant me?" Xanthus heard and said, "Courage, Aesop: you will receive your freedom and half of the gold."

79. Upon hearing this, Aesop took a potsherd, jumped back four steps from the stela, dug down, unearthed the treasure, and bore it to his master, and said, "Master, give me what you promised." "I will not give it to you," said Xanthus, "unless you tell me by what reasoning you found the treasure, for learning something is far more valuable than the discovery itself." Aesop said, "Master, the one who buried the treasure inscribed the seven letters like a philosopher, and they read as follows: G' "go back," S' "steps," Δ' "four," E' "excavate," F' "you will find," T' "a treasure," G' "of gold." Xanthus said, "Since you're so wily and clever, you will not gain your freedom." Aesop said to him, "Master, I order you to give the gold to Dionysius, king of the Byzantians." "How do you know this?" said Xanthus. Aesop said, "I found it out from the letters, which read: G' "Give back," S' "soon," D' "to King Dionysius," E' "everything," F' "you find here, T' "of the treasure," G' "of gold."

ὀρύξας : ῥύξας O | ἔλαβε O **3** Ὁ δὲ Ξάνθος : om. O **4** ἐὰν ... 5 μαθεῖν : om. O **5** ἀλλὰ ante πολὺ add. O | εὑρήματος O | τιμιώτερος O | Αἴσωπος ἔφη : ὁ δὲ λέγει O **6** ἐχάραξε στοιχεῖα : γράμματα κατασκάψας ἐχάραξεν O | ἃ ... 7 οὕτως : οἷον τὸ ἄλφα λέγει O **7** τὸ ante lit. β, δ, ο, ε, θ, χ add. O | ῥύξας O **8** χρυσίον O | ὁ Ξάνθος O | ἐπεὶ O **9** τεύξει O | παραγγέλω O **10** ἀποδοθῆναι O | τῷ ante βασιλεῖ add. O | βιζαντίῳ O | Αἴσωπος ... 11 ἔφη : om. O **11** γραμμάτων : πραγμάτων O | φησὶν post ἐπέγνων add. O | λέγουσιν M **12** ἐνταῦθα M

80. Ὁ δὲ Ξάνθος ἀκούσας τοῦ βασιλέως εἶναι τὸ χρυσίον λέγει «λαβὼν τὸ ἥμισυ τοῦ εὑρέματος ἡσύχαζε.» Αἴσωπος ἔφη «οὐ σύ μοι χαρίζῃ, ἀλλ' ὁ τὸ χρυσίον καταθέμενος. Ἄκουε γάρ» φησι. «Α' ἀνελόμενοι, β' βαδίσαντες, δ' διελέσθαι, ο' ὃν εὕρετε, ε' ἐνθάδε, θ' θησαυρόν, χ' χρυσίου.» Ὁ δὲ Ξάνθος «δεῦρό» φησι, «εἰς τὴν οἰκίαν ἵνα καὶ τὸ χρυσίον διελώμεθα καὶ τὴν ἐλευθερίαν λάβῃς.» Ἐλθόντων δὲ αὐτῶν, φοβούμενος ὁ Ξάνθος τὴν γλῶσσαν αὐτοῦ ἐκέλευσε αὐτὸν εἰς φυλακὴν βληθῆναι. Ὁ δέ φησιν «ἔχε τὸ χρυσίον καὶ δός μοι τὴν ἐλευθερίαν.» Ξάνθος εἶπεν «γενναίως εἶπας, ἵνα ἐλευθερίας τυχὼν ἰσχυρότερόν μου κατηγορήσῃς.» Ὁ δὲ Αἴσωπος εἶπεν «ἄκων ἔχεις τοῦτο εἰς ἐμὲ πρᾶξαι.»

81. Κατὰ δὲ τὸν καιρὸν ἐκεῖνον συνέβη τι σημεῖον ἐν τῇ Σάμῳ γενέσθαι. Πανδήμου γὰρ ἀγομένου καὶ τῶν θυμελικῶν παιζομένων ἄφνω ἀετὸς καταπτὰς καὶ τὸν δημόσιον ἁρπάσας δακτύλιον, ἔρριψεν αὐτὸν εἰς δούλου κόλπον. Οἱ δὲ Σάμιοι θροηθέντες ἐν πολλῷ γεγόνασιν ἀγῶνι περὶ τοῦ σημείου. Ἐκκλησίαν οὖν συναθροίσαντες ἤρξαντο δέεσθαι τοῦ Ξάνθου ὡς πρωτοπολίτου καὶ φιλοσόφου ὅπως διαλύσῃ αὐτοῖς τὸ σημεῖον.

82. Ὁ δὲ Ξάνθος διαπορῶν καὶ αἰτήσας διωρίαν εἰς τὸν ἴδιον ἦλθεν οἶκον.

83–85. Ἐν πολλῇ δὲ γενόμενος ἀθυμίᾳ ἔμελλεν ἑαυτὸν διαχειρίσασθαι, μὴ δυνάμενος τὸ σημεῖον λῦσαι. Ὁ δὲ Αἴσωπος διαγνούς, ἤδη σοφὸς καὶ φιλοδέσποτος ὤν, προσελθὼν τῷ Ξάνθῳ ἔφη «δέσποτα, τί σύννους εἶ καὶ οὕτω δυσθυμεῖς ὥστε κινδυνεύειν; Ἐμοὶ τοῦτο προσανάθου καὶ μὴ δυσθύμει. Ἕωθεν οὖν προσελθὼν εἰπὲ τοῖς Σαμίοις 'οὐκ εἰμὶ ἐγὼ σημειολύτης οὐδὲ ὀρνεοσκόπος. Οἰκέτην δὲ ἔχω πολύπειρον καὶ αὐτὸς ὑμῖν τὸ σημεῖον διαλύσει.' Καὶ εἰ μὲν ἐπιτύχω, σὺ ἕξεις τὴν δόξαν. Εἰ δὲ ἀποτύχω, ὑπὲρ δόξης δεσπότου ἐγὼ ὑβρισθήσομαι.»

86. Πεισθεὶς οὖν ὁ Ξάνθος τῷ Αἰσώπῳ ἕωθεν προθύμως ὑπήντησεν εἰς τὸ θέατρον καὶ στὰς ἐν τῷ μέσῳ, ἔφη τοὺς λόγους οὓς ὑπέδειξεν αὐτῷ ὁ Αἴσωπος. Οἱ δὲ παρεκάλουν ἐλθεῖν τὸν οἰκέτην αὐτοῦ.

80.1 τὸ χρυσίον εἶναι inv. M 2 εὑρέματος : χρυσίου M | καὶ ὁ ante Αἴσωπος add. O | οὐ : οὐχὶ O | μοι : μὴ O | χαρίζει O 3 ἀνελόντες M 4 διελέσθαι : -ελέσθαι evan. in M | εὕρατε O 5 φησι : ἔφη post οἰκίαν O | εἰς τὸν οἶκον M 6 δὲ post φοβούμενος add. O 7 αὐτὸν : τὸν Αἴσωπον M | ἐμβληθῆναι εἰς τὴν φυλακὴν O | Ὁ δέ : καὶ ὁ O 8 μου post ἐλευθερίαν add. O | Ξάνθος εἶπεν : Καὶ ὁ Ξάνθος O 9 ἰσχυροτέρως κατηγορίσῃς μου O | Ὁ … εἶπεν : ἔσωπος ἔφη O 10 εἰς ἐμὲ τοῦτο inv. O ‖ 81.1 ἐν : om. O 2 Πανδήμου γὰρ ἀγομένου codd. : πανδήμου γὰρ ἑορτῆς ἀγομένης ex SBPΛW corr. Perry, iter. Papath. | πεζόμενων O 3 καὶ : om. O | αὐτὸν : om. O 4 θρηλληθέντες O 5 πρώτου πολίτου M 6 διαλύσει O | αὐτοῖς : αὐτῶν O ‖ 82.1 καὶ : om. O | διορίαν O |

80. When Xanthus heard that the gold belonged to the king, he said, "Take half of the find and be still." Aesop said, "It isn't you who are granting it to me but the one who buried the gold. For listen," he said, G "Get it," S "and step along," D "and divide," E "everything," F "you find here, T "of the treasure," G "of gold." Xanthus said, "Let's go to the house so that we may divide the gold and you can have your freedom." But when they arrived, Xanthus, fearing Aesop's tongue, ordered him to be thrown into prison. Aesop said, "Keep the gold, and give me my freedom." Xanthus said, "What a great idea! Once you have gained your freedom, you can accuse me all the more forcefully." Aesop said, "You will have to do this for me, even if unwillingly."

81. At that time there happened to occur an omen in Samos. While the whole population was gathered and a show was going on, suddenly an eagle flew down, seized the official's ring, and dropped it into the lap of a slave. The Samians were frightened and very worried about the omen. So they convoked an assembly and began to ask Xanthus, inasmuch as he was the leading citizen and a philosopher, to explain the omen to them.

82. Xanthus was at a loss, so he asked for time and went to his house.

83–85. Xanthus was very despondent and was on the point of killing himself, since he couldn't interpret the omen. But Aesop, who was by now wise and loved his master, understood it, and he approached Xanthus and said, "Master, why are you gloomy and so despairing as to be in dire peril? Lay this one on me, and don't despair. In the morning, then, go and say to the Samians, 'I am not an omen interpreter or a bird augur. But I have a very experienced slave, and he is the one who will solve the omen for you.' And if I succeed, you will have the glory, but if I fail, I'll be vilified for the sake of my master's reputation."

86. Xanthus heeded Aesop, and in the morning he went eagerly into the theater, and, standing in the middle of the stage, he uttered the words that Aesop had told him to. The others demanded that his slave appear.

οἶκον ἦλθε inv. O ‖ **83–85**.1 διαχειρίσαι O 2 μὴ : διὰ τὸ μὴ O ǀ σημεῖον : ση ... leg. in M Perry et Papath., sed ego non lego nunc : ζήτημα O ǀ ἤδη σοφὸς : ἠδύσοφος corr. Papath. 3 καὶ ἀκούσας περὶ τοῦ γενομένου σημείου post ὧν add. O ǀ προσελθών : evan. in M (π ... leg. Perry et Papath.) : προσῆλθε O ǀ ἔφη : καὶ φησὶ O 4 δυσφημεῖς O ǀ ὥστε κινδυνεύειν : ὥστε κινδυ- evan. in M : ὥστε κινδυνεύειν σε O ǀ τοῦτο : om. O ǀ δυσθύμει : ἀπαναίνου O 5 οὖν : om. O ǀ προσελθών : προσελθὼν εἰ- lit. evan. in M 6 καὶ : om M ǀ αὐτὸς : οὗτος O ǀ διαλύσῃ O 7 ἐὰν O ǀ ἔχεις M ‖ **86**.2 ἔφη : ἐφώνησεν O ǀ ὑπέδειξεν : εἶπεν M 3 ἐλθεῖν ... αὐτοῦ : συνιδεῖν τὸν Αἴσωπον M

87. Ἐλθόντος δὲ αὐτοῦ εἰς τὸ μέσον, κατανοήσαντες οἱ Σάμιοι τὴν τούτου μορφὴν ἐμπαίζοντες αὐτῷ ἔλεγον «αὕτη ἡ ὄψις σημειολύτου; ἐκ τοῦ σαπροῦ τούτου τί ἀγαθὸν ἀκουσόμεθα;» Καὶ ἤρξαντο γελᾶν. Ὁ δὲ Αἴσωπος ἐφ' ὑψηλοῦ στὰς καὶ τὰς χεῖρας τῷ ὄχλῳ κατασείσας ᾔτησεν ἡσυχίαν. Σιγῆς δὲ γενομένης ἔφη.

88. «Ἄνδρες Σάμιοι, τί μου σκώπτετε τὴν θέαν; Οὐκ εἰς τὴν ὄψιν ἀποβλέπειν δεῖ, ἀλλ' εἰς τὴν διάνοιαν. Πολλάκις γὰρ κακίστῃ μορφῇ ἡ φύσις ἔδωκε νοῦν σώφρονα. Οὐδὲ εἰς τὴν ἀρετὴν τῶν κεραμίων κατανοεῖν δεῖ, ἀλλ' εἰς τὴν ἔνδοθεν τοῦ οἴνου γεῦσιν.» Ταῦτα ἀκούσαντες οἱ ὄχλοι διεπόππυζον εἰς ἀλλήλους καὶ ἔλεγον «Αἴσωπε, δυνάμενος λέγειν τῇ πόλει, λέγε.» Ὁ δὲ γνοὺς ἑαυτὸν ἐπαινούμενον μετὰ παρρησίας ἔφη

88a. «Ἄνδρες Σάμιοι, εὐκαταφρονήτους ἡ ἀμορφία εἴωθε ποιεῖν τοὺς νοῦν ἔχοντας σώφρονα καὶ ὄντας εὐγενεῖς τὸ λαλεῖν. Καὶ γὰρ ἐν ἀκάνθαις φύονται κάλλιστα ῥόδα.» Οἱ δὲ ὄχλοι πεισθέντες αὐτοῦ τῇ πιθανολογίᾳ εἶπον «θάρσει, Αἴσωπε, καὶ εὐψύχει λέγων. Καλῶς λέγεις.» Ὁ δὲ Αἴσωπος σιγὴν αἰτήσας εἶπεν

89. «Ἄνδρες Σάμιοι καὶ τίμιοί μου, ἐπεὶ ἡ Τύχη φιλόκαλος οὖσα ἀγῶνα δόξης τέθεικε δεσπότῃ τε καὶ δούλῳ, καὶ ὁ μὲν δοῦλος, ἐὰν ἀμείνων τοῦ δεσπότου φανῇ ται, τὰς διὰ μαστίγων λήψεται ὕβρεις. Ἐὰν οὖν μοι δι' ἐλευθερίας τὴν παρρησίαν χαρίσησθε, μετὰ πάσης ἀδείας κἀγὼ φράσω τὰ ζητούμενα.»

90. Οἱ δὲ ὄχλοι πανπληθεὶ ἔκραζον «Ξάνθε, ἐλευθέρωσον Αἴσωπον, ἐπάκουσον Σαμίοις, χάρισαι τῇ πόλει τὴν ἐλευθερίαν.» Ὁ δὲ «οὐκ ἐλευθερῶ δοῦλον ὀλίγον μοι ἐξυπηρετήσαντα χρόνον.» Ὁ δὲ πρύτανις ἔφη «ἐὰν μὴ τῷ πλήθει ὑπακούσῃς, ποιήσω αὐτὸν ἀπελεύθερον τῆς Ἥρας καὶ ἔσται σοὶ ὁμότιμος.» Οἱ δὲ φίλοι συμβουλεύοντες τῷ Ξάνθῳ ἔλεγον «ἐλευθέρωσον αὐτὸν σύ. Ἐὰν γὰρ τῆς Ἥρας ἀπελεύθερος γένηται, ἐλευθερικὰ κατέχει

87.1 Ἐλθόντος ... μέσον : ἐλθόντων δὲ αὐτῶν τοῦ τε Ξάνθου καὶ τοῦ ἐσώπου καὶ στὰς ἐν τῷ μέσῳ ὁ ἔσωπος κατεγέλουν ἐμπέζοντες O | οἱ σάμιοι κατανοήσαντες inv. O 2 ἐμπαίζοντες ... ἔλεγον : οἳ καὶ ἔλεγον O | οὐκ ἔστιν post σημειολύτου add. O 3 ἀκουσώμεθα O 3–4 ἐφ' ὑψηλοτέρου O 4 καὶ τὴν χεῖρα O ‖ 88.3 Οὐδὲ εἰς : οὐδ' εἰς in M leg. Perry et Papath. : οὐδεὶς O | κατανοεῖν : σκάπτειν O 4 ἀποκειμένην post ἔνδοθεν add. M | διεπόππυζον : διεπόππυζον O, - πτυζον R (unde initium cap. R) 5 Αἴσωπε : om. M | ἦν δὲ (γὰρ R) ὁ ὄχλος πολὺς ἀθροισθεὶς ἐν τῷ τόπῳ post λέγε add. OR 6 ἐν τῷ τόπῳ post ἑαυτὸν add. O ‖ 88a.1 ἀκούσατέ μου post Σάμιοι (ἀκούσητέ μου post εὐκαταφρονήτους leg. Perry et Papath.) add. M | εὐκαταφρονήτους ἡ ἀμabsc. in M | εἴωθε ... 2 ἔχοντας : τὸν νοῦν εἴωθε δρᾶν ἔχοντας O 2 σώφρονας MO | τὸ : τοῦ OR | λαλεῖν : absc. in M | ἀκάνθῳ O 3 φύεται R : φυέντα O | αὐτοῦ : absc.

87. When Aesop had stood in the middle, the Samians seeing his ugly form made fun of him and said, "Is this the look of an omen interpreter? What good thing could we ever hear from this fellow?" And they began to laugh. Aesop stood on the platform and waved his hands at the crowd and demanded silence. When there was silence, he said,

88. "Men of Samos, why are you mocking my looks? One shouldn't look at one's external appearance but rather at one's mind, because nature often bestows a wise mind on the worst shape. One shouldn't examine the quality of the ceramic pots but the taste of the wine that is inside." When they heard this, the crowd shushed each other and said, "Since you can speak to the city, speak!" Aesop realized that he was being approved, and so he spoke freely.

88a. "Honorable citizens of Samos, hear me! Ugliness usually makes those who have a wise mind and are gracious talkers easy to despise; indeed, amid thorns there grow the most beautiful roses." The crowd was persuaded by his plausible analogy and said, "Courage, Aesop, take heart and speak. You're speaking excellently." Aesop asked for silence and said,

89. "Citizens of Samos, since Fortune, which likes excellence, has set up this contest in reputation between a master and slave, if the slave appears better than the master, he will receive injuries through beatings. But if you grant me candor by giving me my freedom, I will show you what you are looking for with utter fearlessness."

90. The crowd cried out unanimously, "Xanthus, free Aesop, listen to the Samians, grant his freedom to the city." Xanthus said, "I will not free a slave who has served me only a short while." The head official said, "If you don't obey the people, I will make him a freedman of Hera, and he will be your peer." His friends counseled Xanthus and said, "Free him yourself, for if he becomes a freedman of Hera, he will have all the rights of a free man."

---

in M | πειθανολογίᾳ OR 4 λέγεις : λέγε (λ evan.) M 5 εἶπεν : ἔφη R ‖ 89.1 Σάμιοι ... μου : πολῖται M | οὖσα : absc. in M 2 τε : om. OR | ἀμείνω OR 2-3 φανῇ τοῦ δεσπότου OR 3 τὰς : om. M | οὖν : δὲ M 4 τὴν : absc. in M | παρουσίαν OR | χαρίσησθαι O ‖ 90.1 πανπληθεὶ : παν- evan. in M : πανπληθῇ OR | Ξάνθε : om. OR 2 ὑπάκουσον OR | χάρισαι MON (unde initium cap. N) : χάρισον R | Ὁ δὲ : ὁ δὲ Ξάνθος O : ὁ δὲ Ξάνθος ἔφη N : om. R | οὐκ ... 3 δοῦλον : οὐκ ἐλευθερῶ ἔφη OR : οὐκ ἐλεύθερον ποιήσω τὸν Αἴσωπον N 3 γὰρ post ὀλίγον add. N | ὑπηρετήσαντα OR | Ὁ δὲ : ἡ δὲ O 4 ἐλεύθερον OR | Ἥρας : ἱερᾶς RN | σοὶ : σου N 5 συμβουλεύονται N : συμβουλεύσαντες M | καὶ ἔλεγον N 6 Ἐὰν : εἰ R : ἡ O | Ἐὰν ... 7 δίκαια : om. N | Ἥρας : ἱερᾶς R | τις ante ἀπελεύθερος add. OR | γένηται : absc. in M : γίνεται O | ἐλευθερικὰ : ἐλευθελοκαλεῖ O | κατέχειν O

δίκαια.» Ἀναγκασθεὶς οὖν ὁ Ξάνθος ἔδωκε τὴν ἐλευθερίαν. Καὶ ὁ κῆρυξ ἐβόα «Ξάνθος Δεξικράτους Σαμίοις Αἴσωπον ἐλευθεροῖ.»

91. Τούτου δὲ γενομένου ἐλθὼν εἰς τὸ μέσον ὁ Αἴσωπος καὶ σιγὴν αἰτήσας ἔφη «ἄνδρες εὐσεβεῖς, ἐπεὶ ὁ ἀετός ἐστι τῶν ὀρνέων κύριος, ὡς βασιλεὺς
5 τῶν ἀνθρώπων, τὸν δὲ ἀπὸ τῶν νόμων στρατηγικὸν δακτύλιον ἁρπάσας ἔβαλεν εἰς δούλου κόλπον, τίς τῶν νυνὶ βασιλέων θέλει ὑμῶν τὴν ἐλευθερίαν καταδουλῶσαι καὶ τοὺς νόμους ἀκυρῶσαι.» 5

92. Ταῦτα ἐν τῷ θεάτρῳ παρὰ τοῦ Αἰσώπου ἀκούσαντες οἱ ὄχλοι περίλυποι γεγόνασιν. Καὶ ὄντων συνηθροισμένων ἰδοὺ γραμματοφόρος ἐν χλανίδι
10 διαλεύκῳ ζητῶν τοὺς ἄρχοντας Σαμίων. Μαθὼν δὲ ἐκκλησίαν γίνεσθαι παρῆν εἰς τὸ θέατρον καὶ δέδωκε τοῖς ἐξάρχοις τὰ γράμματα. Λύσαντες δὲ εὗρον οὕτως· «Βασιλεὺς Λυδῶν Σαμίων ἄρχουσι, βουλῇ καὶ δήμῳ χαίρειν. 5 Κελεύω ὑμᾶς ἀπὸ τοῦ νῦν φόρους μοι παρέχειν καὶ τέλη χορηγεῖν. Ἐὰν δὲ μὴ πεισθῆτε, ὅσον ἡ ἐμὴ ἰσχύει βασιλεία τοσοῦτον ὑμᾶς βλάψω.»

15 **93.** Ἐβουλεύσαντο οὖν ἅπαντες ὑπήκοοι τῷ βασιλεῖ γενέσθαι. Συνεῖδον οὖν καὶ τὸν Αἴσωπον ἐρωτῆσαι τί δεῖ ποιεῖν. Ὁ δὲ Αἴσωπος ἔφη «τῶν ἀρχόντων ὑμῶν πεισθέντων φόρους τῷ βασιλεῖ χορηγεῖν, γνώμην μὲν οὐ δώσω, λόγον δὲ ἐρῶ ὑμῖν καὶ τὸ συμφέρον γνῶτε.

94. Ἡ Τύχη δύο ἔδειξεν ὁδοὺς ἐν τῷ βίῳ, μίαν μὲν ἐλευθερίας, ἧς ἡ ἀρχὴ
20 τραχεῖα καὶ δύσβατος, τὸ δὲ τέλος ὁμαλὸν καὶ ἴσον, ἑτέραν δὲ δουλείας, ἧς ἡ ἀρχὴ πεδινή, τὸ δὲ τέλος σκληρὸν καὶ ἐπικίνδυνον.»

95. Ταῦτα ἀκούσαντες οἱ Σάμιοι καὶ τὸ συμφέρον γνόντες, ἀνεφώνησαν «ἐλεύθεροι ὄντες δοῦλοι οὐ γενόμεθα» καὶ σκληρῶς τὸν ἀποκρισιάριον ἀπεπέμψαντο. Ὁ δὲ διωχθεὶς ἀπήγγειλεν Κροίσῳ τῷ βασιλεῖ ἅπαντα τὰ
25 γενόμενα. Ὁ δὲ Κροῖσος ἀκούσας ἐταράχθη καὶ ἐβουλεύσατο πρὸς ὑπόδειγμα

90.7 δέδωκε OR 8 ὁ ante Ξάνθος add. R | Ξάνθος ... ἐλευθεροῖ : ἔξελφε· δοκεῖ σοι σαμίων αἴσοπε ἐλευθεροῖ N | Δεξηκράτους R | ἐλευθεροῖ : ἐλευθερο- evan. in M : ἐλευθέρωσον R ‖ **91.**1 Τούτου δὲ : καὶ τούτου O : τούτου N | τὸ : om. RN | ὁ : om. N 2 ἔφη : absc. in M | ἐπειδὴ OR | ὁ : om. O | ἐστι ... κύριος : τῶν ὀρνέων ἐστὶ κύριος ON : ἐστὶ κύριος τῶν ὀρνέων R | ὁ post ὡς add. OR 3 τῶν ἀνθρώπων : absc. in M | τὸν : τῶν OR : τὸ M | ἀπὸ τῶν νόμων : ἁπάντων νόμων OR : ἅπαντα νόμον N 3-4 ἁρπάσαι καὶ βαλεῖν M 4 ἔβαλλεν N | νυνὶ : νῦν N : om. OR | τὴν ante ὑμῶν trans. OR 5 καταδουλώσασθαι M ‖ **92.**1 ἀκούσαντες οἱ ὄχλοι παρὰ τοῦ ἐσώπου OR | οἱ ὄχλοι : om. M 2 αὐτῶν post ὄντων add. N | ὄντων συνηθροισμένων : om. M | γραμματηφόρος R | ἐν ... 3 διαλεύκῳ : ἐν χλανί διαλεύκω O : ἑλληνίδι διαλέκτω N

And so Xanthus was forced to give Aesop his freedom. And the herald cried out, "Xanthus son of Dexicrates frees Aesop for the Samians."

91. After this happened, Aesop proceeded to the middle, asked for silence, and said, "O pious gentlemen, since the eagle is lord of the birds, as a king is over men, the fact that it snatched the governor's official ring and dropped it in the lap of a slave means that some current king wants your freedom reduced to slavery and your laws to be annulled."

92. When the crowd heard this in the theater, they were exceedingly distressed. And when they had gathered, lo! a letter-carrier appeared in a bright white mantle asking for the archons of the Samians. When he learned that an assembly was in session, he went to the theater and gave the letter to the leaders. When they opened it, what they found was as follows: "The king of the Lydians greets the Samian archons, council, and people. I order you from now on to provide tribute and to pay taxes. If you do not obey, I will punish you to the full extent of my kingdom's power."

93. So they all resolved to become subjects of the king, but they judged that they should also ask Aesop what they should do. Aesop said, "Since your archons have been persuaded to pay tribute to the king, I will not give my opinion, but I will tell you a story, and you decide what is in your best interest."

94. "Fortune has revealed two paths for our lives: one is that of freedom, the beginning of which is rough and hard to walk on, but the end is level and even, while the other is that of slavery, and its beginning is flat, but its end is harsh and dangerous."

95. When they heard this and decided what was best for them, the Samians cried out, "We are free and will not become slaves," and they sent the emissary back harshly. Driven off, the emissary reported to Croesus all that had happened. When Croesus heard this, he was upset and decided to

---

3 γίνεσθαι : om. OR   4 παρήει O : παρείη R | ἐξάρχουσι ON   5 οὕτω O | κρείσσος post Λυδῶν add. R | Σαμίοις M | βουλῇ ... δήμῳ : om. N   6 ἡμᾶς O | φόρον ON | τέλει OR : τέλος M | εἰ O   7 τοσοῦτον : om. M | ἡμᾶς O | ὑμᾶς βλάψω : τιμωρήσομαι ὑμᾶς M ‖ **93.**1 γίνεσθαι M   2 οὖν : δὲ M   3 μὲν : ὑμῖν RN : om. O   4 δὲ : δ' O | ὑμῖν : om. M | δὲ (ὑμᾶς leg. Papath.) post συμφέρον add. M ‖ **94.**1 Ἡ Τύχη : ἔτυχε N | ἔδειξεν : ἔλεξεν M : om. N ὁδοὺς : δοὺς N | ἐν : om. M   3 πεδηνή N: δεινή OR | τὸ δὲ τέλος : τὸ τέλος δὲ N | σκληρὸν : ὁμαλὸν N ‖ **95.**1 γνῶντες ORN | ἀνεφώνησαν : om. N   2 οὐ γενόμεθα : οὖν γενόμεθα N : ante –μεθα lit. evan. in M   3 -ήγγειλεν evan. in M   3-4 πάντα τὰ γινόμενα ON   4 ἀκούσας : om. OR | ἐταράχθη : -άχθη evan. in M | πρὸς : om. O

τῶν ἄλλων τὴν Σάμον κατασκάψαι. Ὁ δὲ ἀποκρισιάριος ἔφη τῷ βασιλεῖ «οὐ
δύνασαι Σαμίους ὑποτάξαι τοῦ Αἰσώπου αὐτοῖς γνώμας διδόντος. Δύνασαι
οὖν δόλῳ πέμψαι πρεσβευτὰς καὶ αἰτῆσαι παρ' αὐτῶν τὸν Αἴσωπον ἔκδοτον,
ὑποσχόμενος ἀντ' αὐτοῦ χάριτας δοῦναι καὶ φόρους μὴ λαβεῖν, καὶ ἴσως τότε
δυνήσῃ ἐγκρατὴς αὐτῶν γενέσθαι.»

96. Ὁ δὲ Κροῖσος ἀρεσθεὶς τῷ σκοπῷ ἕνα τῶν ἀρχόντων αὐτοῦ ἔστειλεν
εἰς τὴν Σάμον. Ὁ δὲ παραγενόμενος καὶ ἐκκλησίαν συναγαγὼν ἔπεισε τοὺς
Σαμίους ἔκδοτον δοῦναι τὸν Αἴσωπον. Ὁ δὲ Αἴσωπος εἰς μέσον ἐλθὼν ἔφη
«ἄνδρες Σάμιοι, κἀμοὶ πόθος ἐστὶ παρὰ τοὺς πόδας τοῦ βασιλέως γενέσθαι.
Θέλω δὲ ὑμῖν λόγον εἰπεῖν.

97. Καθ' ὃν καιρὸν ἦν ὁμόφωνα τὰ ζῷα, πόλεμον ἔσχον οἱ λύκοι μετὰ
τῶν προβάτων. Οἱ οὖν λύκοι κατεδυνάστευον τὰ πρόβατα. Τῶν δὲ κυνῶν
συμμαχησάντων τοῖς προβάτοις ἀπεσόβησαν τοὺς λύκους. Οἱ δὲ λύκοι ἕνα
πρέσβυν στείλαντες πρὸς τὰ πρόβατα εἶπον 'ἐὰν θέλετε μετὰ εἰρήνης ζῆν
καὶ πολέμου ὑποψίαν μὴ ἔχειν, ἔκδοτε ἡμῖν τοὺς κύνας.' Τὰ δὲ πρόβατα
μωρὰ ὄντα ἐπείσθησαν τοῖς λύκοις καὶ παρέδωκαν τοὺς κύνας. Οἱ δὲ λύκοι
διασπαράξαντες τοὺς κύνας εὐκαίρως διέφθειραν τὰ πρόβατα. Ὁ μῦθος οὖν
ἔδειξε μὴ εἰκῇ τοὺς εὐχρήστους προδιδόναι.»

98. Οἱ δὲ Σάμιοι ταῦτα νοήσαντες ἠβουλήθησαν κατασχεῖν τὸν Αἴσωπον.
Ὁ δὲ οὐκ ἠνέσχετο μεῖναι, ἀλλὰ μετὰ τοῦ πρεσβευτοῦ συμπλεύσας ἀφίκετο
πρὸς τὸν βασιλέα Κροῖσον, καὶ εἰσελθὼν ἔστη ἐνώπιον αὐτοῦ. Ὁ δὲ βασιλεὺς
ἰδὼν τὸν Αἴσωπον ἠγανάκτησε λέγων «ἴδε τίς ἐκώλυσέ με τοσοῦτον ὑποτάξαι
λαόν.» Αἴσωπος ἔφη «μέγιστε βασιλεῦ, οὐ βίᾳ οὐδὲ ἀνάγκῃ ἑλκόμενος ἥκω
πρὸς σέ, ἀλλ' αὐτοβούλως πάρειμι. Ὅμοια δὲ πάσχετε οἱ ἐξ ἀκοῆς ὀργιζόμενοι
τοῖς αἰφνιδίως τραυματιζομένοις καὶ ἀνακράζουσι. Καὶ τὰ μὲν τραύματα

95.5 τῷ βασιλεῖ ἔφη inv. M **6** Σαμίοις ON | διδόντος R : διδόναι N **7** γοῦν M | πέμψαι : παραπέμψαι N : om. O | πρεσβευτὰς : πρεσβύτας ORN fort. recte | αἰτῆσαι O | τὸν : om. O | ἔσωπον ἔκδοτων O : ἔκδοτ.. τὸν Αἴσωπον N **8** τότε : τοῦτο OR : τούτου N **9** δυνήσῃ : δρῶντες O : ποιήσαντες R | ἐγκρατεῖς R | γενέσθαι : ὑπάρξεις OR ‖ **96.**1 ἀρεστὴς O | αὐτοῦ post σκοπῷ add. N | αὐτοῦ : om. M **4** πόθος : πόθεν N | ἐστὶν RN | παραγενέσθαι OR **5** οἱ δὲ, λέγε, καὶ ὁ ἔσωπος post εἰπεῖν add. OR : οἱ δὲ λέγε add. N ‖ **97.**1 ὁμόφρονα N **2** τὰ πρόβατα O : τῶν προβάτων (post τῶν lit. evan.) M : om. RN **3** τοῖς προβάτοις : τῶν προβάτων O | κατεσόβησαν N **4** πρέσβιν M : πρέσβην O : πρεσβύτην N | ἐὰν θέλετε : Εἰ θέλετε O : absc. in M : ἐὰν θέλητε ex SBP corr. Papath. | μετ' ORN **5** ἔκδοτε N | ἡμῖν : ὑμῖν O : absc. in M **6** τοῖς : om. O **7** τοὺς κύνας διασπαράξαντες inv. OR | διέφθειραν : διασπαράξαντες O | καὶ ante τὰ πρόβατα add. R | Ὁ μῦθος : ὁμοίως M **8** ἔδειξεν ORN | μὴ : μοι N | οἰκῇ N | εὐχρίστους R : εὐχρήστους πράττοντας N : εὐχαρίστους O | προδιδοῦναι O ‖

raze Samos to the ground as an example to others. The emissary said to the king, "You cannot subjugate the Samians as long as Aesop is advising them. But you can send ambassadors deceitfully and demand of them that Aesop be surrendered, promising to show gratitude to them in exchange and not to take tribute, and then you can perhaps gain power over them."

96. Croesus was pleased by the plan and sent one of his leading men to Samos. The man went, convened the assembly, and persuaded the Samians to surrender Aesop. Aesop placed himself in the middle and said, "Samian gentlemen, I, too, have a desire to go and lie at the feet of the king, but I wish to tell you a story."

97. "Once upon a time, when the animals spoke the same language, the wolves started a war with the sheep. So the wolves oppressed the sheep, but the dogs allied themselves with the sheep and frightened off the wolves. The wolves sent an ambassador to the sheep and said, 'If you wish to live in peace and not be apprehensive about war, surrender the dogs to us.' The sheep, being stupid, obeyed the wolves and handed over the dogs. The wolves tore the dogs to pieces and duly destroyed the sheep. So, what the fable shows is not to betray casually those who are useful to you."

98. The Samians then understood this and were willing to keep Aesop. But he did not suffer to remain but sailed along with the ambassador and came to the king, Croesus, and he went and stood before him. When the king saw Aesop, he was displeased and said, "Look at who prevented me from subjugating so numerous a people." Aesop said, "Greatest king, I have come to you, not dragged by force or necessity, but I am here of my own free will. You who get angry on the basis of rumor experience something similar to those who are wounded suddenly and cry out. Wounds are

---

98.1 δὲ : οὖν M | νοήσαντες : ἀκούσαντες O | ἐβουλήθησαν RN | τὸν : om. OR 2 ἔσωπος post Ὁ δὲ add. O | ἠνέσχετο : ἠνοίξατο N : ἠθέλησεν OR | μεῖναι : om. R | πρεσβευτοῦ : πρεσβύτου ORN fort. recte | συμπλέξας N 3 πολλὰ δὲ παρακαλέσαντες αὐτὸν οἱ σάμμιοι τὸ μὴ εἰπεῖν τί κατ' αὐτῶν τὸν βασιλέα ἀλλὰ μᾶλλον πρεσβεύειν ὑπὲρ αὐτῶν post Κροῖσον add. N | καὶ εἰσελθὼν : εἰσελθὼν δὲ ὁ αἴσωπος N : καὶ ἐλθὼν M | αὐτοῦ : τοῦ βασιλέως N 4 τὸν Αἴσωπον : αὐτὸν N | ἠγανάκτησεν OR : ἠγανάκτει N | ἐκώλυσέν μοι O | τοσούτων N : τοιοῦτον OR | μὴ ante ὑποτάξαι add. R : μοι O 5 ὁ δὲ ante Αἴσωπος add. M | οὐδὲ : οὐδ' M | τινὶ post ἀνάγκῃ add. M | ἑλκόμενος ἥκω : ἑλκόμενος εἰσῆλθον R : εἰσῆλθον πρός σε ἑλκόμενος O | ἥκω : ἥκ- evan. in M 6 αὐτόβουλος O | ὁμοῖα O : ὁμοῖον N | δὲ : om. O | οἱ ... ὀργιζόμενοι : ἡ ἐξ ἀκοῆς ἐργαζομένη N 7 αἴφνη O | ἀνακράζουσι : ἀναγκάζουσι M | Καὶ : ὥστε O | τραύματα : hic desinit N

ἐπιστήμῃ ἰατρῶν ὑγιάζεται, τὴν δὲ σὴν ὀργὴν ὁ ἐμὸς θεραπεύσει λόγος. Ἐὰν γὰρ ἐγὼ αὐτοθελῶς ἐλθὼν πρὸς σὲ παρὰ τοῖς ποσί σου ἀποθάνω, καταγράψω σου τὴν βασιλείαν εἰς ἐλάττωσιν γενέσθαι. Τοὺς γὰρ φίλους σου ἐναντίας σοι ἀναγκάσεις γνώμας συμβουλεύειν. Ἐὰν γὰρ οἱ τὰ ὀρθὰ συμβουλεύοντες κακῶς παρὰ σοὶ κρίνωνται, πάντοτε τὰ ἐναντία σοι ἐροῦσιν. Οἱ δὲ ταχὺ ἐμπιστεύοντες λόγοις ὥσπερ τὰ κενὰ τῶν ἀγγείων τοῖς ὠταρίοις εὐβάστακτοι εὑρίσκονται.

99. Ἄκουσον δέ,» φησι· «ἄνθρωπός τις πένης ἀκρίδας θηρεύων ἤγρευσε τὴν εὔλαλον τερετίστριαν τέττιγα καὶ ἤθελεν ἀποκτεῖναι. Ἡ δὲ πρὸς αὐτὸν εἶπε 'μή με μάτην ἀποκτείνῃς. Οὐ στάχυν ἀδικήσω οὔτ' ἀκρέμονας βλάψω. Συνθέσει δὲ πτερῶν καὶ ποδῶν ἁρμονίᾳ χρηστὰ φθέγγομαι ὁδοιποροῦντας τέρπουσα. Φωνῆς δὲ πλείω παρ' ἐμοὶ οὐδὲν εὑρήσεις.' Καὶ ταῦτα ἀκούσας ἀφῆκεν αὐτήν. Κἀγώ, βασιλεῦ, δέομαί σου τῶν ποδῶν, μὴ εἰκῇ με ἀποκτείνῃς. Οὔτε γὰρ δυνατός εἰμί τινα ἀδικῆσαι. Ἐν εὐτελείᾳ δὲ σώματος χρηστὰ φθέγγομαι βίους μερόπων ὠφελῶν.»

100. Ὁ δὲ βασιλεὺς θαυμάσας ἅμα δὲ καὶ συμπαθήσας αὐτῷ ἔφη «Αἴσωπε, ἐγώ σοι τὸ ζῆν οὐ δίδωμι, ἀλλ' ἡ μοῖρα. Ὃ δὲ θέλεις αἴτησαί μοι καὶ λήψει.» Αἴσωπος ἔφη «δέομαί σου, δέσποτα, διαλλάγηθι Σαμίοις.» Εἰπόντος δὲ τοῦ βασιλέως «κατήλλαγμαι» προσπεσὼν Αἴσωπος ηὐχαρίστησε. Συγγράψας οὖν τοὺς ἰδίους μύθους, τοὺς μέχρι νῦν ἀναγινωσκομένους, κατέλιπε τῷ βασιλεῖ. Καὶ λαβὼν παρ' αὐτοῦ γράμματα πρὸς τοὺς Σαμίους ὡς ἕνεκεν Αἰσώπου καταλλαχθῆναι αὐτοῖς τὸν βασιλέα πολλά τε δῶρα εἰληφώς, πλεύσας ἦλθεν εἰς τὴν Σάμον. Ὡς οὖν εἶδον αὐτὸν οἱ Σάμιοι, στέμματα καὶ χορείαν ἤγειραν εἰς τὴν πόλιν. Ὁ δὲ ἐκκλησίαν ἐπιστησάμενος ἀνέγνω αὐτοῖς τὰ τοῦ βασιλέως γράμματα, δείξας αὐτοῖς ἀνταμοιβὴν τῆς παρ' αὐτῶν γενομένης εἰς αὐτὸν ἐλευθερίας. Οἱ δὲ Σάμιοι εὐεργετηθέντες τιμὰς καὶ τέμενος αὐτῷ ἐψηφίσαντο, καλέσαντες τὸν τόπον ἐκεῖνον Αἰσώπειον.

98.8 ὑγιάζετε M : ὑγιάζονται OR | ὁ : om. OR | θεραπεύσῃ OR | Ἐὰν ... 14 εὑρίσκονται : om. OR 10 Τοὺς ... σου : ex W corr. Perry, iter. Papath. : τοῖς γὰρ φίλοις σου M 12 παρὰ : absc. in M 13 λόγοις : ex W corr. Perry, iter. Papath. : absc. in M | τοῖς ὠταρίοις : ex W suppl. Perry, iter. Papath. : om. M | εὐβάστακτοι : M^sl : εὐβάστακτα M ‖ 99.1 Ἄκουσον ... φησι : ἄκουε φησί R : om. O | ἄνθρωπος τις πέ- absc. in M | τις : om. R | ἤγρευσεν OR 2 καὶ ante τὴν add. OR | τερετιστρίαν corr. Perry, iter. Papath. : τερεντίστριαν R | -κτεῖναι absc. in M 3 με : post ἀποκτείνῃς trans. OR | οὔτ' ἀκρέμονας : ex L corr. Perry, iter. Papath. : οὔτ' ἀκρέμονα R: οὐ τοὺς κραίμονας O : ante -κραίμονας lit. evan. in M 4 Συνθέσει : σὺν δύο OR | πτερῶν : πτεροῖς R : πτεροῖς ἀμφοῖν O | καὶ : om. O | ὁδοιποροῦντας : ὁδο- evan. in M : ὁδοιπόρους O 5 πλεῖον R : ποίῳ O | οὐδὲν : οὐ μὴ O | Καὶ : ὁ δὲ OR 6 τῶν ποδῶν : om. O | εἰκῇ : μάτην OR | με : post ἀποκτείνῃς trans. R : om. O 7 Οὔτε : absc. in M | σώματος δὲ inv. R |

healed by the expertise of doctors, while my stories will treat your anger. For if I have come willingly to you and die at your feet, I will set it down that your kingdom is headed for defeat, since you will force your friends to give you advice that is contrary to your interests. For if those who give correct advice are judged negatively by you, they will invariably tell you things that are the contrary. Those who quickly trust words are revealed to be like empty jugs that are easy to lift by their handles."

99. "Listen," he said. "A poor man was hunting grasshoppers and caught a sweet-sounding chirping cicada and wished to kill it. The cicada said to him, 'Do not kill me needlessly. I will not injure your wheat or harm your trees. By the combination of my wings and feet I make useful sounds that delight travelers by their harmony. You will get nothing more from me than my voice.' And when he heard this, he released it. I, too, king, at your feet I beg you, do not kill me needlessly, for I am not able to injure anyone. In the shabbiness of my body, I make useful sounds that help the lives of mortals."

100. The king was impressed and at the same time sympathized with him and said, "Aesop, it is not I but fate who is granting you your life. Ask of me what you wish, and you will receive it." Aesop said, "I beg you, master, to be reconciled with the Samians." The king said, "I am reconciled," and Aesop kneeled before him and thanked him. He wrote down his fables, which are read until today, and bequeathed them to the king. After he had secured from him a letter for the Samians saying how, for the sake of Aesop, he was reconciled with them and received many gifts from him, Aesop sailed to Samos. And so, as the Samians saw him, they held a celebration, with dances and garlands, in the city. Aesop called an assembly and read to them the king's letter, indicating the recompense for the freedom they had granted him. The Samians, in return for his services, decreed honors and a sanctuary for Aesop and called that place the Aesopeum.

χρηστὰ : τινα OR **8** ὀφελῶ OR ‖ **100.1** βασιλεὺς : om. O | ἤδη post θαυμάσας add. OR | δὲ² : om. OR **2** δίδωμι : δύναμαι O | μοῖρα : Τύχη O | Ὁ δὲ : absc. in M | αἴτησε M | μοι : codd. : με corr. Perry, iter. Papath. **3** δέομαί ... δέσποτα : δέομαι, δέσποτα M : δέσποτά μου O **4** ὁ ante Αἴσωπος add. R | ηὐχαρίστησεν O | Συγγράψας οὖν : συγγράψας O : γράψας οὖν R **5** κατέλιπε ... **6** Σαμίους : om. OR **7** καταλλαχθῆναι : scripsi : κατηλλάχθη ex L corr. Perry, iter. Papath. : κα ... χθαι M : κατηλλάχθαι R : κατήλλαχθαι O | τὸν ... δῶρα : πολλά τε δῶρα τοῦ βασιλέως M : <παρὰ> τοῦ βασιλέως corr. Papath. | εἴληφε O | καὶ ante πλεύσας add. M **8** εἰς τὴν Σά- absc. in M | Ὡς ... Σάμιοι : om. OR | χορίαν O **9** Ὁ ... ἐπιστησάμενος : ὁ δὲ σιγήν αἰτήσας OR | αὐτοῖς : om. O **10** γράμματα : absc. in M | τῆς : τοῖς O | γενομένοις O : δεδομένης R **11** παρ' (δι' R) αὐτοῦ post εὐεργετηθέντες add. OR **12** Αἰσώπειον : Αἰσώπου OR

Life of Aesop the Philosopher

101. Μετὰ δὲ ταῦτα ἐπορεύετο τὴν οἰκουμένην καὶ ἐν τοῖς ἀκροατηρίοις διελέγετο. Παραγενομένου δὲ αὐτοῦ ἐν Βαβυλῶνι καὶ τὴν αὐτοῦ ἐπιδειξαμένου σοφίαν μέγας ἐγένετο παρὰ Λυκούρῳ τῷ βασιλεῖ.

102. Ἐν ἐκείνοις γὰρ τοῖς καιροῖς οἱ βασιλεῖς πρὸς ἀλλήλους εἰρηνεύοντες καὶ τερπόμενοι προβλήματα φιλοσοφικὰ διὰ γραμμάτων ἔστελλον πρὸς ἀλλήλους καὶ οἱ μὴ διαλυσάμενοι φόρους παρεῖχον τοῖς προτιθεμένοις. Ὁ δὲ Αἴσωπος τὰ στελλόμενα τῷ Λυκούρῳ προβλήματα ἐπιλυόμενος, εὐδοκιμεῖν ἐποίει τὸν βασιλέα. Αὐτὸς δὲ διὰ τοῦ Λυκούρου προβλήματα τοῖς βασιλεῦσιν ἔπεμπε καὶ μὴ δυνάμενοι λῦσαι φόρους παρεῖχον τῷ Λυκούρῳ. Καὶ οὕτως ἡ τῶν Βαβυλωνίων προέκοπτε βασιλεία.

103. Ὁ δὲ Αἴσωπος ἄτεκνος ὑπάρχων ἰδιοποιήσατο παῖδα εὐγενῆ ὀνόματι Αἶνον καὶ τῷ βασιλεῖ προσήνεγκεν ὡς οἰκεῖον τέκνον, προπαιδείαν καὶ πᾶσαν διδάξας σοφίαν. Ὁ δὲ Αἶνος γαμετῶν μιᾷ τῶν τοῦ βασιλέως παλλακῶν συνεπλάκη. Γνοὺς δὲ ὁ Αἴσωπος πικρὸν αὐτῷ ἠπείλησε θάνατον.

104. Ὁ δὲ Αἶνος φόβῳ συσχεθεὶς ψευδέσι λόγοις ὑποβάλλει τὸν Αἴσωπον πρὸς τὸν βασιλέα. Γράψας γὰρ πλαστὴν ἐπιστολήν, ὡς ἐκ τοῦ Αἰσώπου πρὸς τοὺς ἀντιδίκους Λυκούρου ὡς ἐκείνοις βοηθοῦντος, καὶ σφραγίσας τῷ τοῦ Αἰσώπου δακτυλίῳ, ὑπέδειξε τῷ Λυκούρῳ. Ὁ δὲ βασιλεὺς πεισθεὶς τῇ σφραγῖδι καὶ ὀργισθεὶς τῷ Αἰσώπῳ, ἐκέλευσε τῷ Ἑρμίππῳ τοῦτον ὡς προδότην ἀποκτεῖναι. Ὁ δὲ Ἕρμιππος φίλος ὢν τοῦ Αἰσώπου ἔθετο αὐτὸν ἐν τάφῳ μηδενὸς εἰδότος καὶ ἔτρεφεν αὐτὸν ἐν τῷ κρυπτῷ. Ὁ δὲ Αἶνος τὴν τοῦ Αἰσώπου διοίκησιν παρέλαβεν.

105. Μετὰ δὲ χρόνον τινὰ ἀκούσας Νεκτεναβὼ τὸν Αἴσωπον τεθνηκέναι, ἔστειλεν ἐξ Αἰγύπτου πρὸς τὸν Λυκοῦρον δι' ἐπιστολῆς ζητήματα

101.1 εἰς ante τὴν add. OR | ἀκροτηρίοις OR 2 παραγενόμενον δὲ αὐτὸν O | αὐτοῦ correxi : αὐτοῦ M : ἑαυτοῦ OR | ἐπιδειξάμενος OR 3 ἐθαυμαστώθη καὶ post σοφίαν add. R | μέγας ... βασιλεῖ : μέγα τὸ τούτου ὄνομα ἦν καὶ παρὰ Λυκούρῳ τῷ βασιλεῖ μέγας ἐγένετο M | Λυκούργῳ OR ‖ **102.**2 φιλοσοφίας OR | διὰ γραμμάτων : om. R | ἐστέλοντο O 3 καὶ ... διαλυσάμενοι : καὶ μή τι (καὶ εἰ μὴ R) διελύσαντο (διεγροίσσοντο R) OR | τοῖς προτεθημένοις O : τοὺς προτεθημένους R | Ὁ ... 5 βασιλέα : om. OR 5 Αὐτὸς ... Λυκούρου : Ὁ δὲ βασιλεὺς Λυκοῦργος διὰ τοῦ αἰσώπου OR | προβλήματα ... 6 ἔπεμπε : τοῖς βασιλεῦσι προβλήματα πέμπων OR **6** δυναμένοις OR | φόρους : om. O | τῷ βασιλεῖ Λυκούργῳ OR 7 προέκοπτε βασιλεία : βασιλεία καὶ (ἡ add. R) ἀρχὴ προέκοπτε διὰ τοῦ λογιωτάτου καὶ πανσόφου (διὰ τοῦ πανσόφου καὶ εὐλογιωτάτου R) Αἰσώπου OR ‖ **103.**1 ὑπάρχων : ὢν OR | ἰδιοποιήσατο : ἰδιωποιήσ ... M : ἰδιοποιησάμενος O | εὐγενῆ τινὰ παῖδα O

101. After this Aesop traveled around the world and spoke in front of large audiences. He went to Babylon, where he gave a display of his wisdom, and he became great at the side of the king Lycurus.

102. In those times the kings were at peace with one another, and, for their pleasure, they used to send by letter philosophical problems to each other, and those who could not solve them paid tribute to those who posed them. Aesop solved the problems sent to Lycurus and caused the king to be highly esteemed. On the other hand, he sent problems via Lycurus to the kings, and those who were unable to solve them paid tribute to Lycurus. And thus the kingdom of the Babylonians prospered.

103. Aesop had no children, and so he adopted a noble child by the name of Aenus and presented him to the king as his own child, having taught him the elementary curriculum and the whole of wisdom. Aenus conceived a passion for one of the king's concubines and slept with her. When Aesop found out, he threatened him with a horrid death.

104. Aenus was seized with fear and maligned Aesop to the king. For he wrote a forged letter, as if from Aesop to the opponents of Lycurus, as though he were assisting them, and he sealed it with Aesop's ring and showed it to Lycurus. The king was convinced by the seal and grew angry at Aesop and ordered Hermippus to kill him as a traitor. Hermippus, however, was a friend of Aesop's, and so, without anyone knowing, he put him in a tomb and fed him in secret. Aenus inherited Aesop's property.

105. After a time, Nectenabo heard that Aesop was dead and sent to Lycurus from Egypt by letter some problem puzzles that went like this:

---

2 προσήνεγγε O | τέκνον : absc. in M | προπαίδειαν M : πρὸς παιδείαν O : πρὸς παιδείαν πᾶσαν R | καὶ² ... 3 σοφίαν : καὶ φιλοσοφίαν O : καὶ διδασκαλίαν φιλοσοφίας R 3 γαμητιῶν : om. OR | μιᾷ : absc. in M | μιᾷ ... παλλακῶν : μιᾷ τοῦ βασιλέως παλακῇ OR 4 ὁ : om. M | ὑπήλησεν R ‖ 104.1 Ὁ δὲ Αἶνος : ὁ δ' αἶνος R | ψευδέσι λόγοις : λόγους OR | τὸν Αἴσωπον : αὐτῷ OR 2 τὸν : om. O | ἐπιστολήν : om. O 3 Λυκούργου OR | βοηθοῦντα OR 4 τοῦ : om. OR | ἐσώπω O | Λυκούργω OR 4–5 πεισθεὶς τὴν σφραγίδα R : τὴν σφραγίδα θεασάμενος O 5 τῷ ἐπάρχω ἑρμίππω R : τῷ ἑρμίππω ἐπάρχω O | τοῦτον : ἵνα OR 6 τὸν Αἴσωπον post προδότην add. OR | ἀποκτείνῃ R | δὲ : δ' OR | ἔθετο : ἔκρυψεν OR | ζῶντα post αὐτὸν add. R 7 τινὶ post τάφῳ add. O : τινὸς R | μηδὲν R | ἔτρφεν O | δὲ : δ' OR | τὴν ... 8 παρέλαβεν : ἀπέλαβεν τὴν τοῦ ἐσώπου διοίκησιν καὶ δουλείαν OR ‖ 105.1 τινὰ hic desinit O | ὁ βασιλεὺς αἰγύπτου ante Νεκτεναβὼ add. R | τεθνάναι R 2 λυκοῦργον R

προβλημάτων ἔχοντα οὕτως· «Νεκτεναβὼ βασιλεὺς Αἰγυπτίων Λυκούργῳ βασιλεῖ Βαβυλωνίων χαίρειν. Ἐπειδὴ θέλω οἰκοδομῆσαι πύργον μήτε γῆς μήτ' οὐρανοῦ ἁπτόμενον, πέμψον μοι τοὺς οἰκοδομήσοντας τὸν πύργον καὶ τὸν ἀποκριθησόμενόν μοι ὅσα ἂν ἐπερωτήσω αὐτόν. Καὶ λάβε ἀπ' ἐμοῦ ὑπὲρ ὅλης τῆς ὑπ' ἐμὲ ἀρχῆς φόρους ἐτῶν δέκα. Εἰ δ' ἀπορεῖς, πέμψον μοι ὑπὲρ πάσης τῆς ὑπὸ σὲ γῆς φόρους ἐτῶν δέκα.»

106. Ταῦτα ἀκούσας Λυκοῦρος περίλυπος ἐγένετο ἐπὶ τῇ τοιαύτῃ ἀποτομίᾳ Νεκτεναβῶ καὶ συγκαλέσας ὅλους τοὺς φίλους ἔφη «εἰ δύνασθε τοῦ πύργου λῦσαι τὸ ζήτημα;» Πάντων δὲ ἀπορούντων καθίσας εἰς τὸ ἔδαφος ἐθρήνει τὸν Αἴσωπον λέγων ὅτι «τὸν κίονα τῆς βασιλείας μου ἀπώλεσα.»

107. Ὁ δὲ Ἕρμιππος λυπούμενον ἰδὼν τὸν βασιλέα διὰ τὸν Αἴσωπον, θέλων τὸ αὑτοῦ ἁμάρτημα εὔκαιρον δεῖξαι, προσελθὼν τῷ βασιλεῖ εἶπε «δέσποτα βασιλεῦ, μὴ οὕτω κατάλυπος γίνου· ἣν γὰρ ἀπόφασιν δέδωκας κατὰ Αἰσώπου οὐκ ἐποίησα, εἰδὼς ὅτι μετάμελον εἶχεν. Αἴσωπος ζῇ, ἀλλὰ διὰ τὸν βασιλικὸν νόμον ζῶντα αὐτὸν εἰς τάφον ἔβαλον τρέφων αὐτὸν ἄρτῳ καὶ ὕδατι.» Ὁ δὲ βασιλεὺς ἐξ ἀνελπίστων χαρᾶς μεγάλης πλησθείς, ἀναστὰς ἀπὸ τῆς γῆς ἠσπάσατο τὸν Ἕρμιππον καί φησιν «εἴθε ἠδυνάμην τὴν σήμερον ἡμέραν αἰωνίαν ποιῆσαι, ἐὰν ἀληθεύῃ ὅτι Αἴσωπος ζῇ. Ἐκεῖνον γὰρ τηρήσας τὴν ἐμὴν ἐφύλαξας βασιλείαν.» Καὶ κελεύει αὐτὸν κληθῆναι. Παραγενομένου δὲ τοῦ Αἰσώπου ἐν ῥύπῳ καὶ κόμῃ δυσώδει διὰ τὴν χρονίαν συνοχήν, ἀποστραφεὶς ὁ βασιλεὺς ἐδάκρυσε καὶ ἐκέλευσεν αὐτὸν λουσάμενον ἀλλάξαι.

108. Ὁ δὲ Αἴσωπος εἰς ἑαυτὸν καταστὰς ἠσπάσατο τὸν βασιλέα καὶ ἀπελογήσατο ὑπὲρ ὧν κατηγόρησεν αὐτοῦ ὁ Αἶνος ὁ παρ' αὐτοῦ υἱοποιηθείς. Τοῦ δὲ βασιλέως μέλλοντος ἀνελεῖν τὸν Αἶνον, ὡς εἰς πατέρα ἀσεβήσαντα, ᾐτήσατο αὐτὸν Αἴσωπος, εἰπὼν «τεθνεῶτα αὐτὸν ὄψει. Εἰς ἑαυτὸν γὰρ

105.3 βασιλεὺς Αἰγυπτίων Νεκτεναβῶ inv. R | λυκούργω R 4 Ἐπειδὴ θέλω : βούλομαι γὰρ R 5 πέμψον : ἀπόστειλον οὖν R | οἰκοδομήσοντας τὸν πύργον : οἰκοδομοῦντας R 6 ἀποκριθησόμενον : ἀπο- evan. in M : ἀποκρίναντα R | Καὶ ... 7 δέκα : om. R | ἐμοῦ ὑπὲρ absc. in M 7 Εἰ ... 8 δέκα : om. M ‖ **106.**1 λυκοῦργος R | ἠγονία τε καὶ ἐδυσφόρει post περίλ. ἐγένετο add. R | γέγονεν R | τοιαύτῃ : om. R 2 ἀποτολμία R | τοῦ ante Νεκτεναβῶ add. M | ὅλους τοὺς φίλους : πάντας R | εἰ : om. R 3 λῦσαι τοῦ πύργου inv. R | ἀπορησάντων R 4 λέγων ὅτι : καὶ στενάξας ἐκ βάθους τῆς καρδίας ἔλεγεν R | τὸν² ... ἀπώλεσα : ποία ἡμαρμένη με ἐξώγρισεν ἀπωλέσαι τὸν αἴσωπον R ‖ **107.**1 Ὁ ... βασιλέα : Γνοὺς δὲ ὁ ἔπαρχος ἕρμιππος ὅτι περίλυπος ἦν λυκοῦργος R 2 αὐτοῦ correxi : αὑτοῦ R : αὐτοῦ absc. in M : ἑαυτοῦ ex WL corr. Perry, iter. Papath. 3 δέσποτα βασιλεῦ : βασιλ- evan. in M : δέσποτα βασιλεῦ om. R | μὴ ... γίνου : ἵνα τί περίλυπος εἶ καὶ ἵνα τί συνταράττει· ὁ δὲ βασιλεὺς ἔφη· οἴμοι ἕρμιππε τῶν συμβάντων ἀπώλεσα τὸν εὔλαλον αἴσωπον. Τότε

"Nectenabo king of the Egyptians to Lycurus king of the Babylonians, greetings. Since I wish to build a tower that touches neither the earth nor the sky, send me some men who will build the tower and someone who will answer me everything that I ask him. And receive from me on behalf of my entire kingdom a tribute for ten years. But if you are at a loss, send me on behalf of all your land tribute for ten years."

106. When he heard this, Lycurus was very distressed at such curtness from Nectenabo and called together all his friends and said, "Can you solve the puzzle of the tower?" Since all were at a loss, he sat on the floor and lamented over Aesop, saying that "I have lost the pillar of my kingdom."

107. When Hermippus saw that the king was distressed on account of Aesop, wishing to show that his error was opportune he approached the king and said, "Master, king, do not be so upset: I did not carry out the order that you gave concerning Aesop, because I knew that it would bring regret. Aesop is alive, but on account of the royal decree I threw him in a tomb and fed him with bread and water." The king was suffused with great joy by this unexpected news, and rising from the ground he embraced Hermippus and said, "If only I were able make this day last a lifetime, if it is true that Aesop is alive. By saving him you have defended my kingdom." And he ordered Aesop to be summoned. When Aesop appeared, filthy and with foul hair because of his long imprisonment, the king turned away and wept and ordered that he be washed and changed.

108. Aesop, when he had recovered, greeted the king, and he defended himself against the accusations lodged by his adopted son Aenus. When the king was on the point of killing Aenus, on the grounds that he had acted impiously toward his father, Aesop appealed to him, saying, "You will

---

ἕρμιππος ἔφη. Καὶ οὕτως πράττε ὦ βασιλεῦ R | ἦν : τὴν R | ἦν post ἀπόφασιν add. R   4 κατὰ Αἰσώπου : τῷ αἰσώπῳ R | ἐγὼ ante οὐκ add. R | ἐποίησα : absc. in M | μεταμεληθῆναι ἔχεις R : μετάμελον ἔχεις ex W corr. Perry, iter. Papath.   5 ζῶντα αὐ- absc. in M | τρέφων αὐτόν : καὶ ἔτρεφον R   6 ἀνελπίστου R | μεγάλης : om. R   8 ἀληθεύεις R | Αἴσωπος : om. R   9 ἐφύλαξας : ἐτήρησας R   10 ἐν ... δυσώδει : καὶ πολλῇ τῇ κόνι δυσειδοὺς ὄντως R | δυσώδει : δυσειδεῖ Perry, Papath. | χρονίαν : absc. in M   11 συνοχήν : κάθηρξιν R | ἀποστραφεὶς : ἐπιστραφεὶς οὖν πρὸς αὐτὸν R | αὐτὸν λους ... ἀλλάξαι M : λούσασθαι αὐτὸν καὶ ἀλλάξαι R ‖ 108.1 εἰς ... καταστὰς : om. R | καὶ ... 2 ἀπελο- absc. in M   2 ὧν : οὗ R | αὐτοῦ[1] : om. R | ἰδιοποιηθείς R   3 -οῦ βασι- evan. in M | Τοῦ ... Αἴνον : ὁ δὲ βασιλεὺς μέλλων αὐτὸν ἀναιρεῖν R   4 αὐτὸν Αἴ- evan. in M | Αἴσωπος ... 6 ἔφη : αἴσωπος συνεπάθησεν αὐτῷ. Καὶ ὁ βασιλεὺς ἔφη τῷ αἰσώπῳ R

τῆς αἰσχύνης ὑπὸ τῆς συνειδήσεως ἔχει τὸν θάνατον.» Ἐκείνῳ γοῦν τὸ ζῆν
συγχωρήσας τῷ Αἰσώπῳ ἔφη «λαβὼν τὴν ἐπιστολὴν τοῦ βασιλέως Αἰγυπτίων
ἀνάγνωθι.» Ἐπιγνοὺς δὲ ὁ Αἴσωπος τὸ ζήτημα, μειδιάσας ἔφη «ἀντίγραψον
αὐτῷ· 'ἐὰν ὁ χειμὼν παρέλθῃ, πέμψω σοι τοὺς τὸν πύργον οἰκοδομήσοντας καὶ
τὸν ἀποκριθησόμενόν σοι'.» Γράψας οὖν ταῦτα ἀπέστειλε τοὺς πρέσβεις τῶν
Αἰγυπτίων, τῷ δὲ Αἰσώπῳ πάντα τὰ αὐτοῦ ἀποδοὺς τὴν ἐξ ἀρχῆς διοίκησιν
τῶν πραγμάτων ἐχαρίσατο, δοὺς αὐτῷ καὶ τὸν Αἶνον ἔκδοτον. Ὁ δὲ λαβὼν
ἐνουθέτησεν αὐτὸν λέγων·

109. «Ἐπάκουσον τῶν ἐμῶν λόγων, τέκνον, καὶ φύλαξον ἐν τῇ καρδίᾳ
σου κἂν μέχρι τοῦ νῦν οὐ δικαίας μοι χάριτας ἀνταπέδωκας. Πάντες δὲ ἐσμὲν
εἰς τὸ νουθετεῖν σοφοί, αὐτοὶ δ' ἁμαρτάνοντες οὐ γινώσκομεν. Ἄνθρωπος
ὢν μέμνησο τῆς κοινῆς τύχης· αἱ ταύτης γὰρ δόσεις οὐκ εἰσὶ ἔμμονοι. Πρὸ
πάντων σέβου τὸ θεῖον, βασιλέα δὲ τίμα. Ἄνθρωπος ὢν ἀνθρώπινα φρόνει·
ἄγει γὰρ τὸ θεῖον τοὺς κακοὺς πρὸς τὴν δίκην. Ἄδικον τὸ λυπεῖν ἑκουσίως
τοὺς φίλους. Τὰ δὲ συμβαίνοντα ἀνδρὶ γενναίως δεῖ φέρειν. Τοῖς ἐχθροῖς σου
δεινὸν ἑαυτὸν κατασκεύαζε, ἵνα μὴ καταφρονήσωσί σου, τοῖς δὲ φίλοις πρᾶον
καὶ μεταδοτικὸν ἵνα εὐνοϊκώτεροί σου γένωνται. Τοὺς ἐχθρούς σου εὔχου
ἀρρωστεῖν καὶ πένεσθαι, ἵνα ἀδυνατῶσι βλάπτειν σε, τοὺς δὲ φίλους κατὰ
πάντα εὐτυχεῖν θέλε. Τῇ συγκοίτῳ σου χρηστὰ ὁμίλει, ὅπως ἄλλου ἀνδρὸς μὴ
ζητήσῃ πεῖραν λαβεῖν· κοῦφον γὰρ τὸ γυναικεῖον γένος καὶ κολακευόμενον
ἐλάττω φρονεῖ καὶ κακά. Πάντα δεινὸν ἄνδρα φεῦγε, ἐπιστάμενος αὐτοῦ
ἰσχυρότερον ἀνταγωνιστὴν μὴ εἶναι. Ἀνὴρ πονηρὸς δυστυχεῖ κἂν εὐτυχῇ.
Ὀξυτέραν τοῦ λέγειν κτῆσαι τὴν ἀκοήν, τῆς δὲ γλώττης ἐγκρατὴς γίνου. Ἐν
οἴνῳ μὴ βαττολόγει σοφίαν ἐπιδεικνύμενος· ἀκαίρως γὰρ κατασοφιζόμενος
καταγελασθήσῃ. Τοῖς εὖ πράττουσι μὴ φθόνει, ἀλλὰ σύγχαιρε. Φθονῶν
γὰρ ἑαυτὸν βλάψεις. Τῶν οἰκετῶν σου ἐπιμελοῦ ἐπὶ ἀφθονίᾳ, ἵνα μὴ μόνον
ὡς κύριον ἀλλὰ καὶ ὡς εὐεργέτην ἐντρέπωνται. Θυμοῦ κράτει. Ἀεὶ γὰρ ὁ
θυμὸς αἴτιός ἐστι τοῦ βλάπτειν. Τὸ φρονεῖν ἀεὶ αἴτιόν ἐστι τοῦ πλουτεῖν.

108.5 συνειδήσεως : συνει- evan. in M 6 τῶν ante Αἰγυπτίων add. R 7 ἔφη : φησί R
8 οἰκοδομοῦντας R 9 ἀπολογούμενον R | εἰς τὰς σὰς ἐπερωτήσεις post σοι add. R |
Γράψας : absc. in M | ἀπέστειλε : ἀπέλυσε R | πρέσβυς R 10 παραδοὺς R 11 αὐτῷ
ante ἐχαρίσατο trans. R 12 ἐνουθέτει R | αὐτὸν : om. R | πρόσχες post λέγων add.
R ‖ **109.**1 ἄκουσον τοὺς ἐμοὺς τέκνον λόγους R | ἐμῶν : absc. in M 2 κἂν : om. M
| νῦν : ζῆν M | δικαίας : διττὰς R | μοι χάρι- absc. in M | ἀντέδωκας R | δὲ : γὰρ R
| ἐσμὲν : εἰσὶ R 3 ἀεὶ post δ' add. R | οὐ γινώσκομεν : καλὸν ἴδιον οὐκ ἐπίσταται R |
Ἄνθρωπος ... 5 φρόνει : ἄνθρωπον ὄντα δεῖ φρονεῖν τὰ ἀνθρώπινα R 4 μεμνημένος R
| δόσεις οὐκ εἰ- absc. in M | ἔμμονοι : βέβαιοι R 5 δὲ : om. R 6 ἄγει ... 7 φέρειν :

see that he is dead. For he has brought upon himself the death of shame, on account of his conscience." So the king ceded Aenus's life to Aesop and said, "Take the letter of the king of the Egyptians and read it." Aesop understood the puzzle, and he smiled and said, "Write back to him, 'When winter has passed, I will send you men who will build the tower and someone who will answer you.'" So the king wrote this and sent away the Egyptian ambassadors, and he gave Aesop back everything that was his and granted him his original control of his affairs, delivering Aenus into his hands as well. Aesop received Aenus and advised him, saying,

109. "Listen to my words, my son, and guard them in your heart even if up to now you have not returned due gratitude to me. We are all wise at giving advice, but we do not know when we ourselves are erring. Since you are a human being, remember our common fate: its gifts are not permanent. First of all, be pious toward the divine and honor the king. Since you are a human being, think human thoughts, for the gods bring evil people to justice. It is unjust to cause pain to friends voluntarily. One must bear the things that befall a man nobly. Make yourself frightening to your enemies, so that they will not despise you, but gentle and generous to your friends, so that they may be more devoted to you. Pray that your enemies may be sick and poor so that they are unable to harm you, but desire that your friends prosper in all things. Treat your wife well so that she will not seek to have experience of another man, for the female gender is vain, and when it is flattered it thinks petty and evil thoughts. Avoid a shrewd man, knowing that there is no stronger opponent than he. A wicked man is unfortunate even when he is fortunate. Keep your hearing sharper than your speech, and be master of your tongue. When you drink, do not become garrulous and show off your wisdom, for by being clever at the wrong time you will be laughed at. Do not envy those who are faring well, but rejoice with them, since by envying them you will harm yourself. Care for your slaves unstintingly, so that they will regard you not only as a master but as a benefactor. Master your anger, for anger is ever cause to do harm, whereas being

---

om. R **6–7** ἑκουσίως τοὺς φ- absc. in M **7** συμβαίνοντα : corr. Perry, iter. Papath. : συμφέροντα M **8** μὴ ante δεινὸν add. R | κατασκεύαζε : παρασκευάζειν R **9** μεταδοτικὸν ἵνα : om. R | εὐνοηκότερον γίνονται R | Τοὺς ... 11 θέλε : om. R **11** συγκοίτῳ R **12** ζοῦφον R | γυναικεῖον : τῶν γυναικῶν R **13** ἐλάττω ... κακά : κακὰ φρονεῖ R | κακά : κακίω corr. Papath. | Πάντα : πᾶν M | Πάντα ... 14 εὐτυχῇ : om. R **15** ὀξυτέροις R | κτῆσαι : χρῆ σε R | ἐγκρατεῖς R | γενοῦ R **16** βατολογήσει R | σοφιζόμενος R **18** γὰρ : τοῖς φίλοις R | ἐπὶ ἀφθονίᾳ : om. R **19** ἐντρέπουνται R | Θυμοῦ ... 20 βλάπτειν : om. R **20** Ἀεὶ δὲ τὸ φρονεῖν R

Παρηκμακὼς μανθάνειν μὴ ἐπαισχύνου τὰ κρείττονα· βέλτιον ὀψιμαθῆ καλεῖσθαι ἢ ἀμαθῆ. Τῇ γυναικί σου μηδέποτε ἀπόρρητα φθέγγου· ἀεὶ γὰρ ὁπλίζεται πῶς σου κυριεύσει.

110. Τὸν καθημερινὸν ζήτει προσλαμβάνειν ἄρτον καὶ εἰς τὴν αὔριον [μὴ] ἀποθησαύριζε. Βέλτιον γάρ ἐστι τελευτῶντα ἐχθροῖς καταλιπεῖν ἢ ζῶντα τῶν φίλων ἐπιδέεσθαι. Εὐπροσήγορος ἔσο τοῖς συναντῶσί σοι, εἰδὼς ὅτι καὶ τῷ κυνὶ ἡ κέρκος ἄρτον προσπορίζεται. Αἰσχρὸν ἀτυχοῦντα ἐπιγελᾶν. Ἀεὶ θέλε χρήσιμα προσμανθάνειν καὶ φρόνιμα ἐπιτάσσειν. Πάντα γὰρ καιρῷ ἰδίῳ χάριν ἔχει. Πάντα γὰρ θάλλει καὶ πάλιν μαραίνεται. Καιρὸς γὰρ παρέχει καὶ πάλιν ἀφαιρεῖται. Λαβών τι ταχὺ ἀπόδος προθύμως, ἵνα πάλιν λάβῃς. Δυνάμενος ἀγαθοποιεῖν μὴ ἀπαναίνου. Ψίθυρον καὶ διάβολον ἄνδρα πρότερον ἐρωτῶντα ἔκβαλε θυρῶν· ὡσαύτως γὰρ τὰ ὑπὸ σοῦ λεγόμενα ἢ πραττόμενα ἑτέροις ἀναθήσεται. Πρᾶσσε τὰ μὴ λυποῦντά σε· ἐπὶ δὲ τοῖς συμβαίνουσι μὴ λυποῦ, ἀλλ' ὑπόφερε. Πονηρὰ μὴ βουλεύου μηδὲ τρόπους κακοὺς μιμοῦ. Ξένον ξένιζε καὶ προτίμα, μήποτε καὶ σὺ ξένος γένῃ. Ὁ λόγος ἰατρός ἐστι τῶν κατὰ ψυχὴν πόνων. Μακάριος ὃς ἔτυχε γνησίου φίλου. Μακάριος ὃς χάριτας καλὰς ἐκτιννύειν οἶδεν. Οὐδεὶς γὰρ κακῶς πράσσοντι γίνεται καλὸς φίλος. Πάντα δὲ τὰ καλυπτόμενα ὁ χρόνος εἰς φῶς ἄγει.» Ταῦτα εἰπὼν τῷ νεανίᾳ ὁ Αἴσωπος ἐχωρίσθη. Ὁ δὲ Αἶνος διὰ λόγων μαστιγωθεὶς καὶ ὑπὸ τῆς συνειδήσεως τρυχόμενος ἐπὶ τῷ ἠδικηκέναι Αἴσωπον, ἀποκρημνισάμενος μετήλλαξε τὸν βίον.

111. Μετὰ δὲ ταῦτα συγκαλέσας Αἴσωπος πάντας τοὺς ἰχνευτὰς ἐκέλευσε συλληφθῆναι ἀετῶν πρωτείων νεοσσοὺς τέσσαρας. Συλληφθέντων δὲ αὐτῶν ἀφείλετο τὰ ἔσχατα πτερά, οὕτως τε αὐτοὺς διδάξας τρέφεσθαι καὶ μανθάνειν παῖδας διὰ θυλακίων βαστάζειν. Γενόμενοι δὲ τέλειοι οἱ ἀετοὶ καὶ τοὺς παῖδας ἤδη βαστάζοντες ἀνίπταντο εἰς ὕψος δεδεμένοι καλῶς. Ὑπήκοοι δὲ τοῖς παισὶν ἐγίνοντο πρὸς τὸ ἐκείνων βούλημα φερόμενοι· ὅταν γὰρ ἤθελον

109.21 Παρηκμακὼς ... 23 κυριεύσει : om. R 23 ὁπλίζεται : μηχανωμένη post ὁπλίζεται ex G P.Oxy.3720 et Vind. 128 suppl. Papath. | κυριεύσῃ ex P.Oxy. 3720 corr. Papath. ‖ 110.1 Τὸν ... 2 ἀποθησαύριζε : Τῷ καθημερινῷ ζήτει ⟨τι⟩ προσλαμβάνειν ἄρτῳ καὶ εἰς τὴν αὔριον [μὴ] ἀποθησαύριζε Papath. : om. R 2 τελευτῶν R | τοὺς ἐχθροὺς R 3 ζῶν R | Εὐπροσήγορος ... 4 ἐπιγελᾶν : om. R 4 ἀτυχοῦντι ex SBP corr. Papath. 5 μανθάνειν R 6 πάλιν : πάντα R | Καὶ μαραίνεται πάλιν post μαραίνεται add. R | Καιρὸς γὰρ : Καὶ ὁ κόρος R 8 ἀπαναίνου :

prudent is ever cause to be rich. Do not be ashamed of learning something better when you are past your prime: it is better to be called a late learner than unlearned. Never utter secrets to your wife, for she is ever prepared to dominate you."

110. "Seek to acquire your daily bread and store it up for tomorrow, for it is better to die and leave it to your enemies than to live and be indebted to your friends. Be amiable to those who meet you, knowing that the dog's tail, too, provides it with bread. It is shameful to laugh at one who is unfortunate. Wish always to learn more things that are useful and to give as commands things that are sensible. Everything has grace at its own right moment, and everything blooms and wilts again, for the moment provides and takes away again. If you receive something promptly, repay it eagerly, so that you may receive things again. When you can do good, do not refuse. When a man who is a mudslinger and a slanderer asks you questions, sooner cast him out of your door, for in this way what you do and say will be made known to others. Do things that do not cause you pain, but do not be pained by things that just happen, but rather endure them. Do not plan wicked things or imitate evil ways. Be hospitable and generous to guests, for someday you may be a guest yourself. Reason is a physician for the ills of the soul. Blessed is he who has found a genuine friend, and blessed he who knows how to repay fine favors, because a man who is not generous will never acquire a good friend. Time brings all things hidden to light." Having said these things to the youth, Aesop departed. Aenus, having been punished verbally and tortured by the consciousness of having wronged Aesop, threw himself from a cliff and ended his life.

111. After this, Aesop summoned all the hunters and ordered them to collect four nestlings of high-quality eagles. When they were collected, he removed their outer feathers, and instructed that they should be reared and taught to carry boys in small sacks. When the eagles reached their full age and were by then used to carrying the boys, they were tied well and began to fly up to heights. They became obedient to the boys, moving according

---

μετανόει R 9 ἔκβαλλε R 10 πρᾶσαι R | σε : om. R | συμβαίνουσι : συνέβουσί σοι R 11 κακῶν R | μιμήσει R 13 ὅς¹ : ὅστις R 14 ἐκτείνειν R : ἐκτίνειν ex W corr. Perry, iter. Papath. 15 καταληπτόμενα R 16 τὸν νεανίαν R | ὁ¹ : om. R 17 τῷ : τὸ R | ἑαυτὸν post ἀποκρημνισάμενος add. R ‖ 111.1 συγκαλεσάμενος R | πάντας : om. M 2 τέσσαρους R 3 ἀφείλατο R | διδάξας : om. M : ἐκέλευσε ex G suppl. Perry, iter. Papath. 4 παῖδας : om. R | διὰ ... βαστάζειν : δια θηλάκων παίδων βαστάζεσθαι R | οἱ : om. R 5 καλῶς : κάλως Westermann iter. Perry et Papath. fort. recte 6 ἐγένοντο R | ὥστε ante πρὸς add. R | φερόμενοι : ἐφέροντο R | ὅταν : Ὅτε R

οἱ παῖδες ἀνίπταντο εἰς ἀέρα ἄνω, ὅτε δὲ πάλιν ἠβούλοντο κατήεσαν εἰς τὴν γῆν. Τῆς δὲ χειμερινῆς παρελθούσης τροπῆς πάντα εὐτρεπίσας Αἴσωπος τὰ πρὸς ὁδοιπορίαν, συνταξάμενος τῷ Λυκούργῳ ἀπέπλευσεν εἰς τὴν Αἴγυπτον σὺν τοῖς παισὶ καὶ τοῖς ἀετοῖς μετὰ καὶ ἑτέρας παρασκευῆς πολλῆς πρὸς κατάπληξιν τῶν Αἰγυπτίων.

112. Ἰδόντες δὲ οἱ Αἰγύπτιοι τὸν Αἴσωπον μυσαρὸν ὄντα τῇ θέᾳ ἔδοξαν παίγνιον εἶναι, μὴ εἰδότες ὅτι ἐν σαπροῖς σκεύεσι βάλσαμον πολυτελὲς ἢ οἶνος κάλλιστος ἐγκατοικίζεται. Ἀκούσας δὲ Νεκτεναβὼ Αἴσωπον παραγεγονέναι, μετακαλεσάμενος τοὺς φίλους εἶπεν «ἐνεδρεύθην μεμαθηκὼς Αἴσωπον τεθνάναι.» Τῇ δὲ ἐπαύριον κελεύει πάντας αὐτοῦ τοὺς ἄρχοντας λευκὰς στολὰς περιβαλέσθαι, αὐτὸς δὲ περιεβάλετο στολὴν ἱερὰν καὶ κίδαριν καὶ διάδημα κατὰ τὴν κεφαλὴν ἔχον κέρατα διὰ λίθων. Προκαθίσας δὲ ἐπὶ θρόνου ὑψηλοῦ κελεύει τὸν Αἴσωπον εἰσελθεῖν.

113. Εἰσελθὼν δὲ καὶ τὴν παρασκευὴν θεασάμενος, προσκυνήσας ἔστη. Ὁ δὲ Νεκτεναβὼ πρὸς αὐτὸν ἔφη «τίνι ἴκελον βλέπεις με καὶ τοὺς περὶ ἐμέ;» Αἴσωπος ἔφη «σὲ μὲν τὴν σεληνιακὴν διχομηνίαν ἔχοντα, τοὺς δὲ περὶ σὲ τοῖς ἄστροις· ὥσπερ γὰρ ἡ σελήνη διαφέρει τῶν λοιπῶν ἄστρων, οὕτω καὶ σὺ τῇ κερατοειδεῖ μορφῇ σελήνης τρόπον ἔχεις, οἱ δὲ ἄρχοντές σου τοῖς περὶ ἐκείνην ἄστροις.» Ταῦτα ἀκούσας Νεκτεναβὼ καὶ θαυμάσας ἔδωκεν αὐτῷ δῶρα.

114. Τῇ δὲ ἐχομένῃ ἡμέρᾳ ἐνδυσάμενος Νεκτεναβὼ πορφύραν ἐμφανὴ ἔστη σὺν τοῖς περὶ αὐτὸν ἔχων ἄνθεα πολλά. Καὶ ἐκέλευσε τὸν Αἴσωπον εἰσελθεῖν. Εἰσελθόντος δὲ ἐπηρώτησε λέγων «τίνι ἴκελόν με βλέπεις καὶ τοὺς περὶ ἐμέ;» Ὁ δὲ ἔφη «σὲ μὲν ἡλίῳ τῷ τῆς ἐαρινῆς ὥρας, τοὺς δὲ περὶ σὲ τοῖς ἐκ τῆς γῆς καρποῖς· ὡς γὰρ βασιλεὺς πορφυρίζουσαν ἔχεις τὴν ἀπὸ τῆς ὁράσεως τέρψιν καὶ τοὺς καρποὺς εὐανθεῖς ἀναλαμβάνεις.» Ὁ δὲ βασιλεὺς θαυμάσας αὐτοῦ τὸ νοερὸν δῶρα ἐπέδωκε.

115. Τῇ δὲ ἐχομένῃ ἡμέρᾳ στολὴν λευκὴν καὶ καθαρὰν ἐνδυσάμενος καὶ τοῖς φίλοις κόκκινα περιθείς, ἐλθόντος τοῦ Αἰσώπου ὡσαύτως ἐπύθετο

111.7 τὸν post εἰς suppl. Perry, iter. Papath. | φερόμενοι post ἀέρα add. M | οἱ ἀετοί post ἄνω add. R | ἐβούλοντο R | κατίεσαν R 8 τροπῆς : ῥοπῆς R 9 καὶ ante συνταξάμενος add. R | Λυκούργῳ R 10 σὺν τοῖς ἀετοῖς καὶ τοῖς παισίν inv. R | μετὰ : om. R | κατασκευῆς R ‖ 112.2 μὴ εἰδότες : καὶ οὐκ εἴδησαν R | βάλσαμος πολυτελὴς R 3 Νεκτεναβῶ R | παραγενόμενον R 4 εἶπεν : ἔφη R 5 ἐκέλευσεν R 6 περιβαλέσθαι R | περιεβάλετο R 7 κατὰ τῆς κεφαλῆς R | ἔχων R | διάλιθα R 8 ἐκέλευσεν R ‖ 113.1 ἔστη ... 3 Αἴσωπος : om. R 3 τὴν ... ἔχοντα : τῇ σελήνῃ

to their will. When the boys wished they went flying up into the sky, and when the boys so desired they dropped down again to the earth. When the winter solstice had passed, Aesop prepared everything for the voyage and, arranging it with Lycurus, sailed to Egypt with the boys and the eagles and much other equipment to astonish the Egyptians.

112. When the Egyptians saw Aesop, loathsome in appearance, they thought it was a joke, not realizing that expensive balsam or the finest wine is stored in lousy vessels. When Nectenabo heard that Aesop had arrived, he summoned his friends and said, "I was drawn into a trap when I was informed that Aesop was dead." On the next day he ordered all his leading men to put on white robes, and he himself donned a priestly robe and on his head a tiara and diadem that had horns set with gems. Sitting in state on a high throne, he ordered Aesop to enter.

113. Aesop entered, and, when he saw how they were decked out, he prostrated himself. Nectenabo said to him, "What do I and those around me look like to you?" Aesop said, "You are wearing the full moon, and those around you are like stars, for just as the moon differs from the other stars, so, too, you have the guise of the moon with its horned shape, and your leading men are like the stars around it." When he heard this, Nectenabo was impressed and gave Aesop gifts.

114. On the following day Nectenabo put on a bright purple garment and stood with his men around him, holding many flowers, and he ordered Aesop to enter. Aesop entered, and Nectenabo asked again, saying, "What do I and those around me look like?" Aesop said, "You are like the sun in the spring season, and those around you are like the fruits of the earth, for as king you delight the eyes with your purple raiment, and you gather to yourself the fruits in flower." The king was impressed at his intelligence and gave him additional gifts.

115. On the following day Nectenabo donned a pure white robe and robed his friends in scarlet, and when Aesop came he inquired similarly,

---

τῇ διχομηνίαν ἐχούσῃ (vel ἀγούσῃ) corr. Papath. | διχομηναίαν R | ὁρῶ ante ἔχοντα add. R | ἰκέλους post σὲ² suppl. Papath. 4 ἀστέρων R 5 κερατοειδῆ R | ἴκελοί εἰσι post σου suppl. Papath. 6 καὶ θαυμάσας : ἐθαύμασε καὶ R ‖ 114.1 ἐχομένη : ἐπιούσῃ R 2 αὐτὸν : αὐτοῦ R | ἄνθεα : ἔνθεα R 3 Εἰσελθὼν M | βλέπεις ἐμὲ R 4 ἔφη : φησί R | σὲ¹ : σὺ R | τοὺς : οἱ R 5 τῶν ἐκ τῆς γῆς καρπῶν R | τῆς² : τὴν R 6 τέρψιν : an ὄψιν scribendum Papath. | εὐανθῶς R | πάλιν post βασιλεὺς add. R 7 ἀπέδωκεν R ‖ 115.1 Τῇ ... ἡμέρᾳ : ἐπὶ τὴν αὔριον δὲ R 2 ἐπυνθάνετο R

«τίνι ἴκελον νομίζεις με εἶναι;» Αἴσωπος ἔφη «σὲ μὲν τῷ ἡλίῳ, τοὺς δὲ σοὺς ταῖς ἀκτῖσιν· ὥσπερ γὰρ ὁ ἥλιος λαμπρὸς καὶ διαυγὴς ὑπάρχει, οὕτω καὶ σὺ λαμπρὸς καὶ καθαρὸς εἶ ὡς ὁ ἡλιακὸς κύκλος, οὗτοι δὲ διάπυροι ὡς τοῦ ἡλίου αἱ ἀκτῖνες.» Ὁ δὲ Νεκτεναβὼ ἔφη «ὥστε κατὰ τὴν ἐμὴν βασιλείαν οὐδὲν εἶναι Λυκοῦρον.» Ὁ δὲ Αἴσωπος μειδιάσας ἔφη «μὴ εὐχερῶς ἐκεῖνον πρόφερε· πρὸς γὰρ τὸ ἴδιον ἔθνος ἐπιδεικνυμένη ἡλίου καὶ σελήνης αὐγὴ φαίνει ἡ ὑμῶν βασιλεία. Ἐὰν δὲ Λυκοῦρος ὀργισθῇ, ταύτης τὴν λαμπρότητα ἀφανῆ ποιήσει. Πάντων γὰρ τῇ ὑπεροχῇ διαφέρει.»

116. Καταπλαγεὶς δὲ τὴν εὐστοχίαν τῶν λόγων αὐτοῦ ὁ Νεκτεναβώ, μετ' ὀλίγον ἔφη «ἤνεγκας τοὺς οἰκοδομήσοντας τὸν πύργον;» Αἴσωπος ἔφη «ἕτοιμοί εἰσιν, ἐὰν τὸν τόπον δείξῃς.» Ὁ δὲ βασιλεὺς ἔξω τῆς πόλεως εἰς τὸ πεδίον σὺν τῷ Αἰσώπῳ ἀφίκετο καὶ μέτρα ποιησάμενος ἔδωκεν. Ὁ δὲ Αἴσωπος στήσας κατὰ γωνίαν τοῦ δειχθέντος τόπου τοὺς ἀετούς, τοὺς δὲ παῖδας διὰ τῶν ἡμιτελῶν θυλάκων τοῖς ποσὶν ἀναρτήσας καὶ μύστρας αὐτοῖς ἐπιδούς, ἑκάστῳ ἀναπτῆναι ἐκέλευσεν. Οἱ δὲ εἰς ὕψος γενόμενοι ἐφώνουν «δότε ἡμῖν πηλόν, δότε πλίνθους, δότε ξύλα καὶ ὅσα πρὸς οἰκοδομὴν χρειώδη κομίσατε.» Ὁ δὲ Νεκτεναβὼ θεασάμενος τοὺς παῖδας ὑπὸ ἀετῶν εἰς ὕψος φερομένους ἔφη «πόθεν ἐμοὶ πτηνοὶ ἄνθρωποι;» Αἴσωπός φησιν «ἀλλὰ Λυκοῦρος ἔχει. Σὺ δὲ θέλεις, ἄνθρωπος ὤν, ἴσα θεῷ ἐρίζειν βασιλεῖ;» Ὁ δὲ Νεκτεναβὼ ἔφη «Αἴσωπε, ἥττημαι. Ὃ δὲ ἐρωτῶ σε ἀποκρίθητί μοι.»

117. Καί φησι «μετεπεμψάμην ἵππους ἀπὸ τῆς Ἑλλάδος καὶ τοῖς ἐνθάδε συνέμιξα ἵπποις. Αἱ οὖν θήλειαι, ὅταν ἀκούσωσι τῶν ἐν Βαβυλῶνι ἵππων χρεμετιζόντων, ἐκτιτρώσκουσιν.» Αἴσωπος ἔφη «αὔριόν σοι περὶ τούτου ἀποκριθήσομαι.» Ἐλθὼν δὲ εἰς τὴν οἰκίαν, ἐκέλευσε τοῖς ἰδίοις αἴλουρον συλλαβέσθαι. Συλλαβόντες δὲ ἕνα παμμεγέθη, ἤρξαντο δημοσίᾳ μαστίζειν. Οἱ δὲ Αἰγύπτιοι θεασάμενοι καὶ δεινοπαθοῦντες συνέδραμον εἰς τὴν οἰκίαν τοῦ Αἰσώπου ἀπαιτοῦντες τὸν αἴλουρον. Ὁ δὲ οὐ προσεποιεῖτο. Ἐλθόντες δὲ προσεφώνησαν τῷ βασιλεῖ. Ὁ δὲ ἀγανακτήσας μετεπέμψατο τὸν Αἴσωπον.

115.3 τίνι ... εἶναι : om. R | σὲ : σὺ R | τοὺς δὲ σοὺς : οἱ δὲ περὶ σὲ R 4 ὥσπερ : ἑσπέρας R | λαμπρὸς καὶ : om. R | οὕτως R 5 ὡς² : om. R | αἱ ante τοῦ ἡλίου ex BP suppl. Papath. 6 ὥστε : ὡς R | μηδὲν R 7 λυκοῦργος R | εὐχέρως R | προσφέρου R 8 γὰρ : δὲ R | ἐπιδεικνυμένου M | αὐγὴ : αὐγῆς R 9 λυκοῦργος R | ταύτης : ταῦτα R ‖ 116.1 τὴν ... Νεκτεναβώ : Νεκτεναβὼ τὴν εὐστοχίαν τῶν λόγων αὐτοῦ R 2 μοι post ἤνεγκας add. R | τοὺς οἰκοδομοῦντας R 3–4 σὺν τῷ Αἰσώπῳ εἰς τὸ πεδίον inv. R 4 δέδωκεν R 5 γωνίας ex B corr. Papath. | δοθέντος R 6 ἡμιτελῶν : del. Perry : an ἡμιφανῶν scribendum interog. Papath. | θυλάκων M | ἀπαρτήσας R |

"What do you think I am like?" Aesop said, "You are like the sun, and your familiars are like the rays, for just as the sun is bright and radiant, so, too, are you bright and pure like the solar orb, and these are fiery like the rays of the sun." Nectenabo said, "Thus in comparison with my kingdom, Lycurus is nothing." Aesop smiled and said, "Do not disparage him so lightly, for your kingdom seems like the manifest ray of the sun and moon to your own people, but if Lycurus grows angry, he will extinguish your brilliance, for he stands out among all men."

116. Nectenabo was astounded by Aesop's shrewdness, and after a short while he said, "Have you brought men to build the tower?" Aesop said, "They are ready, if you show me the place." The king went with Aesop to a plain outside the city, and he calculated and gave him the dimensions. Aesop placed the eagles at each corner of the designated place, attached the boys to the eagles by placing them in the half-open bags, gave them trowels, and ordered each one to fly. When they were high up they called out, "Give us mud, give us bricks, give us wood, and bring us whatever is necessary for building." When Nectenabo saw the boys carried on high by the eagles, he said, "Where on earth have these flying humans come from?" Aesop said, "But Lycurus has them. Do you, though you are human, wish to compete with a godlike king on an equal basis?" Nectenabo said, "Aesop, I am beaten. But answer me what I ask you."

117. And he said, "I sent for some horses from Greece and mated them with local horses. The mares, when they hear the horses in Babylon neighing, miscarry." Aesop said, "Tomorrow I will answer you concerning this." He went to his house and ordered his men to catch a cat. They caught a very large one and began to beat it publicly. When the Egyptians saw this, they were terribly upset and gathered outside Aesop's house demanding the cat. Aesop would not hand it over, so they went and called upon the king. He grew angry and sent for Aesop. When Aesop arrived, Nectenabo said, "You

---

μύστρας : an μύστρα scribendum interrog. Papath. 7 ἑκάστῳ : om. R | ἐκέλευσεν ἀναπτῆναι inv. R | γενόμενοι : πετώμενοι R | ἡμῖν : om. R 8 χρειώδη : χρὴ ὧδε R 9 τῶν ante ἀετῶν add. R 10 πόθεν : πόθ᾽ R | φησιν : ἔφη R | λυκοῦργος R 11 Σὺ δὲ ἄνθρωπος ὤν, θέλεις inv. R | ἴσα θεῷ ἐρίζειν : ἐρίζειν ἰσοθέῳ R | ἔφη : πρὸς αὐτόν R 12 ἐρωτῶ σε : ἐρωτήσω R | ἀποκρίνου μοι R ‖ 117.1 μετεπεμψώμην R 2 γοῦν M 3 Αἴσωπος ἔφη : Καὶ ὁ αἴσωπος R 4 Ἐλθὼν δὲ : Καὶ ἐλθὼν R | παισὶ post ἰδίοις add. R 4–5 συλλαβέσθαι αἴλουρον inv. R 5 αὐτοὶ post δὲ add. R | παμμεγέθη R | ἤρξατο M 7 τοῦ : om. R | ἀπαιτοῦντες : ζητοῦντες M 8 μεταπέμπεται R

Ἐλθόντος δὲ αὐτοῦ ἔφη «κακῶς πέπραχας, ὦ παῖ. Θεοῦ γὰρ Βουβάστεως
τοῦτο εἴδωλόν ἐστιν, ὃ μάλιστα σέβονται οἱ Αἰγύπτιοι.»

118. Αἴσωπος ἔφη «Λυκοῦρος ὁ βασιλεὺς ὑπ' αὐτοῦ ἠδικήθη. Ἐν τῇ
νυκτὶ γὰρ ταύτῃ ὁ αἴλουρος οὗτος ὃν εἶχεν ἀλεκτρυόνα γενναῖον καὶ μάχιμον,
ἔτι δὲ καὶ τὰς ὥρας αὐτῷ σημαίνοντα, ἀπέκτεινεν.» Ὁ δὲ Νεκτεναβὼ ἔφη
«οὐκ αἰσχύνῃ ψευδόμενος; Πῶς γὰρ ἐν μιᾷ νυκτὶ αἴλουρος ἀπ' Αἰγύπτου εἰς
Βαβυλῶνα ἐπορεύθη;» Ὁ δὲ μειδιάσας ἔφη «πῶς οὖν ἐν Βαβυλῶνι τῶν ἵππων
χρεμετιζόντων ἐνθάδε αἱ θήλειαι ἀκούσασαι ἐκτιτρώσκουσιν;» Ἀκούσας δὲ ὁ
βασιλεὺς ἐμακάρισεν αὐτοῦ τὴν φρόνησιν.

119. Τῇ δὲ ἐχομένῃ ἡμέρᾳ μετεπέμψατο ἀπὸ Ἡλιουπόλεως ἄνδρας
σοφοὺς ἐπισταμένους τὰ φυσικὰ ἐπερωτήματα, καὶ διαλεχθεὶς αὐτοῖς περὶ
Αἰσώπου ἅμα αὐτῷ ἐκάλεσεν ἐπὶ δεῖπνον. Ἀνακλιθέντων δὲ αὐτῶν, τις τῶν
Ἡλιοπολιτῶν πρὸς τὸν Αἴσωπον ἔφη «ἀπεστάλημεν παρὰ θεοῦ πρὸς σὲ
λόγους εἰπεῖν, ὅπως αὐτοὺς διαλύσῃς.» Ὁ δὲ «ψεύδῃ,» φησί. «Θεὸς γὰρ παρὰ
ἀνθρώπου οὐδὲν βούλεται μαθεῖν, ἐτάζειν δὲ οἶδεν ἑκάστου τὸν νοῦν καὶ τὸν
τρόπον. Ὑμεῖς δὲ καὶ ἑαυτῶν κατηγορεῖτε καὶ τοῦ θεοῦ ὑμῶν. Πλὴν εἴπατε
ὃ θέλετε.»

120. Ὁ δέ φησιν «ἔστιν ναὸς καὶ στῦλος ἐν τῷ ναῷ πόλεις ἔχων δώδεκα,
ἑκάστη δὲ πόλις ἐστεγασμένη τριάκοντα δοκοῖς. Ταύτας περιτρέχουσι δύο
γυναῖκες.» Αἴσωπος ἔφη «τοῦτο τὸ πρόβλημα καὶ οἱ παρ' ἡμῖν παῖδες
διαλύσουσιν. Ὁ ναὸς οὖν ἐστιν ἡ οἰκουμένη διὰ τὸ περιέχειν ἅπαντα, ὁ δὲ
ἐπὶ τῷ ναῷ στῦλος ὁ ἐνιαυτός ἐστι, αἱ δὲ ἐπὶ τούτῳ δώδεκα πόλεις οἱ δώδεκα
μῆνές εἰσιν, οἱ δὲ λ' δοκοὶ αἱ λ' εἰσὶ ἡμέραι τοῦ μηνός. Αἱ δὲ περιερχόμεναι
δύο γυναῖκες ἡ ἡμέρα ἐστὶ καὶ ἡ νύξ, ἄλλη παρ' ἄλλην πορευόμεναι τὸν
καθημερινὸν μερόπων εὐθύνουσι βίον.» Καὶ ταῦτα εἰπὼν ἐπέλυσεν αὐτοῦ τὸ
ζήτημα.

121. Τῇ δὲ ἑξῆς συναγαγὼν ὁ Νεκτεναβὼ πάντας τοὺς φίλους αὐτοῦ,
φησὶ πρὸς αὐτούς «διὰ τὸν Αἴσωπον τοῦτον μέλλομεν φόρους τελεῖν Λυκούρῳ,

---

117.9 ὦ παῖ : εἰς τὸν αἴλουρον R | Θεοῦ : θέας R | Βουβάστεως : Perry ex S,
iter. Papath. : βουβάστερος M : βουλῆς τεῶς R **10** σεύουσιν R | οἱ : om. R ‖
118.1 Λυκοῦργος R | Ἐν ... 3 ἀπέκτεινεν : Πῶς φησί. ὁ δέ· ἀλεκτριόνα εἶχε γενναῖον
καὶ μάχημον ἔτι δὲ καὶ τὰς ὥρας αὐτῷ σημαίνοντα, καὶ ὁ αἴλουρος οὗτος ἐν ταύτῃ τῇ
νυκτὶ ἀπέκτεινεν R **3** Ὁ ... ἔφη : Καὶ ὁ βασιλεὺς R **4** αἴλουρος : ὁ αἴλουρος οὗτος
R | ἀπ' : ἀπὸ R **5** οὖν : om. R | ἐκ Βαβυλῶνος M **6** αἱ θηλίαι ἐνθάδε inv. R ‖
119.1 ἐχομένῃ : ἐπιούσῃ R **3** αὐτῷ : αὐτοῖς M | ἀνακληθέντων R **4** Ἡλιοπολιτῶν
: ἡλίου πολιτῶν R : Ἡλιουπολιτῶν Perry et Papath. | τοῦ ante θεοῦ add. R **5** ψεύδῃ
φησί : absc. in M **6** ἀνθρώπου : ἀνθρώποις R | δὲ : om. R **7** καί[1] : ἐστέ R |
κατηγορεῖτε : κατηγορηταί R | ἡμῶν R ‖ **120.1** Ὁ δέ φησιν : ἀπεκρίθη R | ἐπὶ τὸν

have behaved badly, boy, for this is an image of the goddess Boubastis, which the Egyptians most revere."

118. Aesop said, "King Lycurus was wronged by it, for during this night this cat killed a rooster that was noble and warlike and that was, furthermore, announcing the hours to him." Nectenabo said, "Are you not ashamed to lie? How did a cat travel in one night from Egypt to Babylon?" Aesop smiled and said, "How, then, do the mares hear the horses that are neighing in Babylon and miscarry?" When the king heard this, he congratulated him on his wisdom.

119. On the following day Nectenabo sent for some wise men from Heliopolis who knew natural science questions, and, after conversing with them about Aesop, he summoned him to join them for dinner. When they had reclined, one of the Heliopolitans said to Aesop, "We have been sent by the god to you to tell you to solve some riddles." "You are lying," said Aesop, "for a god desires to learn nothing from a human being but knows how to test the mind and character of everyone. In this way, you cast blame on both yourselves and your god. But say what you wish."

120. He said, "There is a temple and a column in the temple that has twelve cities, and each city is roofed over with thirty beams. Two women run around them." Aesop said, "Among us, even children will solve this problem. The temple, then, is the inhabited world, since it surrounds everything, and the column in the temple is the year, the twelve cities on this are the twelve months, the thirty beams are the thirty days of the month. The two women who run around it are the day and the night, each following the other and governing the daily life of mortals." And with these words he solved the man's puzzle.

121. On the next day Nectenabo gathered all his friends and said to them, "Because of this Aesop we are going to pay tribute to Lycurus, king of

---

ναὸν R | πόλεις ἔχων : πό- absc. in M : ἔχων πόλεις inv. R **2** Ταύτας : ex BPWV corr. Perry, iter. Papath. : ταύταις R | ταύτας περι- absc. in M **3** οἱ ... παῖδες : absc. in M | ὑμῖν R **4** διαλύσωσιν R | περιέχειν ἅπαντα : absc. in M **5** -ώδεκα πόλεις absc. in M **6** εἰσὶ μῆνες inv. R | οἱ : αἱ R | αἱ τοῦ μηνὸς τριάντα εἰσὶν ἡμέραι R | τοῦ μηνός : absc. in M | αἱ δὲ περι- absc. in M **7** πορευόμεναι : absc. in M **8** εὐθύνουσαι R | ἐπέλυσεν : absc. in M | αὐτοῦ : αὐτῶν R **9** καὶ ἄλλα πλείω τούτων ἐπερωτώμενος παρ' αὐτῶν, ἐπέλυε προβλήματα πείθων αὐτοὺς κατὰ πάντα post ζήτημα add. R ‖ **121.1** -άντας τοὺς φίλους absc. in M **2** φησὶ πρὸς αὐτοὺς : λέγει R | τελεῖν Λυκούρῳ : absc. in M | Λυκούργῳ R

τῷ βασιλεῖ τῶν Βαβυλωνίων.» Εἷς δὲ τῶν φίλων αὐτοῦ εἶπε «ἐπερωτήσωμεν αὐτῷ προβλήματα καὶ φράσει ἡμῖν ὃ οὔτε ἠκούσαμεν οὔτε εἴδομεν καὶ ὃ ἐὰν εἴπῃ, ἐροῦμεν 'τοῦτο ἡμεῖς ἠκούσαμεν καὶ εἴδομεν'". Ἀρεσθεὶς ὁ Νεκτεναβὼ εἶπεν «Αἴσωπε, φράσον ἡμῖν τι ὃ οὔτε εἴδομεν οὔτε ἠκούσαμεν.» Ὁ δέ φησιν
5 «ἔνδοτέ μοι ἡμέρας τρεῖς καὶ ἀποκριθήσομαι.»

122. Πανοῦργος δὲ ὢν τυποῦται συγγραφὴν δανείου τοιαύτην, δεδανεισμένον τὸν Νεκτεναβὼ παρὰ Λυκούργῳ τάλαντα χίλια προσθεὶς καὶ χρόνον τὸν παρεληλυθότα. Μετὰ δὲ τὰς τρεῖς ἡμέρας ἦλθεν ὁ Αἴσωπος καὶ εὗρεν τὸν Νεκτεναβὼ μετὰ τῶν φίλων αὐτοῦ ἐκδεχόμενον. Εἰσελθὼν δὲ δέδωκε τὸν
10 χάρτην. Οἱ δὲ πρὸ τοῦ τὴν δύναμιν διαγνῶναι ἔφασαν τοῦτο ἐπίστασθαι. Ὁ δὲ Αἴσωπος ἔφη «χάριν ἔχω, ἐπεὶ ἡ γὰρ προθεσμία τῆς ἀποδόσεως παρῆλθεν.» Ἀναγνοὺς δὲ ὁ Νεκτεναβὼ εἶπεν «ἐμοῦ Λυκούργῳ μηδὲν χρεωστοῦντος ὑμεῖς μαρτυρεῖτε;» Οἱ δὲ εἶπον «οὔτε εἴδομεν οὔτε ἠκούσαμεν.» Αἴσωπος εἶπεν «εἰ ταῦτα οὕτως δοκεῖ, λέλυται τὸ ζήτημα.»

15 123. Ὁ δὲ Νεκτεναβὼ ἔφη «μακάριος Λυκοῦρος ἔχων τοιαύτην φιλοσοφίαν ἐν τῇ βασιλείᾳ αὐτοῦ.» Δοὺς δὲ αὐτῷ φόρους ἐτῶν δέκα ἀπέπεμψεν. Ὁ δὲ Αἴσωπος παραγενόμενος εἰς Βαβυλῶνα διηγήσατο πάντα Λυκούργῳ τῷ βασιλεῖ τὰ ἐν Αἰγύπτῳ πραχθέντα, ἀποδοὺς καὶ τὰ χρήματα. Ὁ δὲ Λυκοῦρος ἐκέλευσεν ἀνδριάντα χρυσοῦν ἀνατεθῆναι τῷ Αἰσώπῳ.

20 124. Μετ' ὀλίγον δὲ χρόνον τῷ βασιλεῖ συνταξάμενος, ἐβουλεύσατο εἰς τὴν Ἑλλάδα ἀποπλεῦσαι, ὀμόσας αὐτῷ ὑποστρέψαι πάλιν εἰς Βαβυλῶνα κἀκεῖ τὸν λοιπὸν βιῶσαι χρόνον. Περιερχόμενος οὖν τὰς πόλεις τῆς Ἑλλάδος καὶ τὴν ἑαυτοῦ ἐπιδεικνύμενος σοφίαν, παρεγένετο καὶ ἐν Δελφοῖς. Οἱ δὲ ὄχλοι ἡδέως μὲν αὐτοῦ ἠκροῶντο, οὐδὲν δὲ αὐτὸν ἐτίμησαν.

25 125. Προσκρούσας δὲ πρὸς αὐτοὺς ἔφη «ὅμοιοί ἐστε ξύλῳ ἐν θαλάσσῃ φερομένῳ. Ἐκεῖνο γὰρ θεωροῦντες ἐκ πολλοῦ διαστήματος ὑπὸ τῶν κυμάτων φερόμενον, δοκοῦμέν τινος χρυσίου ἄξιον εἶναι, ἐπειδὰν δὲ αὐτῷ ἐγγυτάτω

121.3 τῷ : om. R | εἶπε : -πε evan. in M : ἔφη R 4 αὐτῷ : αὐτὸν corr. Papath. | δ¹ : ἃ R | ἠκούσαμεν οὔτε : absc. in M | ἴδομεν R | καὶ² ... 5 εἴδομεν : om. R 5 καὶ εἴδομεν : absc. in M | οὖν post Ἀρεσθεὶς add. R 6 εἶπεν Αἴσωπε : προσεκαλέσατο τὸν αἴσωπον καὶ φησί R | τι : om. R | ὃ : absc. in M | οὔτε¹ ... ἠκούσαμεν : οὔτε ἠκούσαμεν οὔτε ἴδομεν inv. R | φησιν : om. R 7 ἡμέρας : absc. in M ‖
122.1 ἐτυπώσατο R | συγγραφὴν : absc. in M | δανίου M : δανείως R | τοιαύτην : ταύτῃ M | δεδανεισμένον ... 2 Νεκτεναβὼ : τῷ Νεκτεναβὼ δεδανεισμένῳ R 2 Λυκούργῳ R | -υκούρῳ τάλαντα absc. in M | καὶ : om. R 3 δὲ ... ὁ : absc. in M | εὑρὼν M 4 αὐτοῦ ... δὲ : absc. in M | ἐπέδωκε R 4–5 τὸ χαρτίον R 5 γνῶναι R | ἔφασαν τοῦτο : absc. in M | Ὁ ... 6 ἔφη : Καὶ ὁ αἴσωπος πρὸς αὐτοὺς R 6 ἐπεὶ : om. R | ἡ γὰρ προθεσμία : absc. in M 7 ὁ : om. R | εἶπεν ... Λυκούργῳ : absc. in M | ἐμοὶ μηδὲν Λυκούργῳ χρεωστοῦντι R 8 οὔτε¹ ... οὔτε² : absc. in M | Οὔτε

the Babylonians." One of his friends said, "Let us ask him some problems, and he will tell us something we have never heard or seen, and whatever he says, we will say, 'we have heard and seen this.'" Nectenabo was pleased and said, "Aesop, tell us something we have neither seen nor heard." And Aesop said, "Give me three days, and I will answer."

122. Being full of guile, Aesop drew up the following kind of contract of loan, that Nectenabo had borrowed from Lycurus a thousand talents, adding as well the time that had passed. After the three days, Aesop went and found Nectenabo with his friends, waiting for him. He entered and gave him the document. They, even before they knew its contents, said that they knew it. Aesop said, "I am grateful, since the due date of the payment has arrived." Nectenabo read it and said, "Do you all bear witness that I owe nothing to Lycurus?" And they replied, "We neither have seen nor heard this." Aesop said, "If you think so, then the question is resolved."

123. Nectenabo said, "Lycurus is blessed to have such philosophy in his kingdom." He gave Aesop tribute for ten years and sent him off. Aesop arrived in Babylon and related to King Lycurus all that had happened in Egypt and gave him the money. Lycurus ordered a gold statue to be dedicated to Aesop.

124. After a short while, Aesop decided to sail to Greece and made an arrangement with the king, swearing to him to return to Babylon afterward and to live there for the rest of his life. So he went round the cities of Greece and demonstrated his wisdom, and he arrived at Delphi. The crowd heard him with pleasure, but they did not honor him at all.

125. He took offense with them and said, "You are like a piece of wood drifting in the sea. When we see it from a great distance, borne by the waves, we think it is worth its weight in gold, but when we come nearer, we see that

---

ἠκούσαμεν οὔτε ἴδομεν R | εἶπεν : ἔφη R **9** οὐκοῦν ante εἰ ταῦτα add. M | δοκεῖ λέλυται τὸ ζή- absc. in M ‖ **123.1** Ὁ δὲ Νεκτεναβὼ : ὁ δὲ βασιλεὺς R | Λυκοῦργος R | -κοῦρος ἔχων τοιαύτην absc. in M **2** φόρους αὐτῷ inv. R | φόρους ἐτῶν δέκα : absc. in M **3** -ὶς Βαβυλ. διηγήσα- absc. in M | Λυκούρῳ ... **4** βασιλεῖ : om. R **4** καὶ τὰ χρήματα : absc. in M | λυκοῦργος R **5** ἀνατεθῆναι τῷ : ἀνατεθῆναι τοῦ R : ἀνε ... ῷ M : ἀνε<γεῖραι?> Perry, Papath. | Αἰσώπῳ : αἰσώπου R | καὶ ἐτίμησε μεγάλως εὐφημοῦντα αὐτόν post Αἰσώπῳ add. R ‖ **124.1** συνταξάμενος τῷ βασιλεῖ inv. R **2** πλεῦσαι R | πάλιν : om. R **3** περιερχομένου R : absc. in M **4** ἐπιδεικνυμένου R | ἐθαυμαστώθη. Καὶ μετὰ ταῦτα post σοφίαν add. R | καὶ² : om. R **5** ἠκροῶντο οὐδὲν : absc. in M | ἐτίμων R ‖ **125.1** πρὸς αὐτοὺς : αὐτοῖς R | ὅμοιοί ἐστε : absc. in M **2** ἐκ πολλοῦ δια- absc. in M | τῶν : om. R **3** τινος ... εἶναι : R : τινος ἄ ... M | αὐτῷ : ἐν R

προσέλθωμεν, ἐλάχιστον ὁρῶμεν. Ἔτι δὲ κἀγὼ πόρρωθεν ὑπάρχων τῆς ὑμῶν
πόλεως κατεπλησσόμην ὑμᾶς ὡς μεγάλους. Ἐλθὼν δὲ πρὸς ὑμᾶς, ὦ Δελφοί,
εὗρον ὑμᾶς ταπεινοτέρους τῶν ἄλλων ἀνθρώπων. Πεπλάνημαι οὖν καλὴν
ἔχων ὑπὲρ ὑμῶν διάνοιαν. Οὐδὲν ἀνάξιον ποιεῖτε τῶν προγόνων ὑμῶν.»

126. Ταῦτα ἀκούσαντες οἱ Δελφοὶ ἔφησαν «τίνες γάρ εἰσιν οἱ πρόγονοι
ἡμῶν;» «Ἀπόδουλοι,» ὁ δέ. «Εἰ ἀγνοεῖτε, μάθετε,» φησί. «Νόμος ἦν παρὰ τοῖς
Ἕλλησιν, ἐὰν πόλις καταβάληται, τῶν λαφύρων τὸ δέκατον μέρος πέμπειν
ἀπό τε βοῶν, προβάτων, αἰγῶν, καὶ τῶν λοιπῶν κτηνῶν, ἀπὸ χρημάτων,
ἀπὸ σωμάτων, ἀνδρῶν τε καὶ γυναικῶν. Ἐκ τούτων οὖν ὑμεῖς γεννηθέντες
ἀνελεύθεροί ἐστε· ἐκεῖθεν γεννηθέντες τῶν Ἑλλήνων δοῦλοι καθίστασθε.»
Ταῦτα εἰπὼν ὁ Αἴσωπος περὶ ἐκδημίαν ἐγένετο.

127. Οἱ δὲ Δελφοὶ λογισάμενοι ὅτι καὶ εἰς ἑτέρας πόλεις ἀπελθὼν
Αἴσωπος χεῖρον αὐτοὺς κακολογήσει, ἐβουλεύσαντο δόλῳ αὐτὸν ἀνελεῖν καὶ
ὡς ἱερόσυλον αὐτὸν καταδικάσαι. Παρατηρησάμενοι οὖν τὸν δοῦλον αὐτοῦ
πρὸ τῆς πύλης τῆς πόλεως σκεύη φέροντα, ἔκρυψαν εἰς τὰ στρώματα αὐτοῦ
ἣν ἔλαβον φιάλην χρυσῆν ἐκ τοῦ ἱεροῦ τοῦ Ἀπόλλωνος. Ὁ δὲ Αἴσωπος ἀγνοῶν
τὰ συνεσκευασμένα αὐτῷ ὤδευσεν εἰς τὴν Φωκίδα.

128. Οἱ δὲ Δελφοὶ δραμόντες ἐκράτησαν αὐτὸν καὶ εἰσήγαγον εἰς τὴν
πόλιν. Διαπορουμένου δὲ τοῦ Αἰσώπου «τί τοῦτο;» ἔφησαν, «ἃ ἔκλεψας ἐκ
τοῦ ἱεροῦ καὶ ἡμεῖς διαβεβαιούμεθα.» Τοῦ δὲ ἀπολέσθαι λέγοντος ἐὰν κατα-
γνωσθῇ τοῦτο, ἐκτινάξαντες ἐκεῖνοι τὸ στρῶμα εὗρον τὴν χρυσῆν φιάλην
τοῦ Ἀπόλλωνος ἐπεδείκνυόν τε πᾶσι τοῖς ἐν τῇ πόλει μετὰ θορύβου καὶ ταρα-
χῆς περιβομβίζοντες αὐτόν. Ὁ δὲ Αἴσωπος αἰσθόμενος τὴν ἐπιβουλὴν πολλὰ
ἐδέετο ἀπολυθῆναι. Οἱ δὲ ἐνέκλεισαν αὐτὸν εἰς φυλακήν. Ὁ δὲ Αἴσωπος οὐχ
εὑρίσκων μηχανὴν τῆς πονηρᾶς τύχης, ὡς θνητὸς ὢν οὐ δυνήσεται τὸ μέλλον
ἐκφυγεῖν, ἐπένθει.

125.4 προσέλθμεν R | ἔτι δὲ κἀγὼ π- absc. in M 5 κατεπλησσώμην R | ὡς μεγάλους : absc. in M | Δέλφιοι R 6 ταπεινωτέρους R | τῶν ἄλλων ἀνθρώπ- absc. in M | οὖν : om. R 7 Οὐδὲν ἀνάξιον ex L corr. Perry, iter. Papath. (ex G) : Οὐδὲν ἄξιον R : absc. in M | τοῖς προύχουσιν ὑμῶν καὶ τοῖς προγόνοις post ὑμῶν add. R ‖
126.1 Ταῦτα ... 2 ἡμῶν : om. R | Δέλφιοι ἔφη- absc. in M 2 σύνδουλοι R | Εἰ ... μάθετε : absc. in M | φησί : om. R 3 πόλις καταβαλῆται M : πόλεις καταβάλλοντε R : πόλεις καταβάλωνται ex W corr. Perry, iter. Papath. | τῶν λαφ- absc. in M | δωδέκατον M 4 αἰγῶν καὶ τῶν : absc. in M 5 καὶ ... Ἐκ : absc. in M 6 ἐλεύθεροι R | οὐχὶ post ἐστε add. R | γεννηθέντες : absc. in M | καθεστήκατε R 7 ὁ αἴσωπος περὶ ἐκ- absc. in M ‖ **127.**1 Δέλφιοι R | καὶ : ἐὰν R | εἰς ἑτέρας πόλεις ἀπέλθῃ R 2 ὁ ante Αἴσωπος add. R | ἐβουλεύσαντο δό- absc. in M 3 αὐτὸν : om. R |

it is trifling. I, too, when I was far from your city was amazed at you, thinking that you were great, but when I came to you, citizens of Delphi, I found you were lowlier than other people. So I was misled, having a high opinion of you, but you are doing nothing unworthy of your ancestors."

126. When the Delphians heard this, they said, "Who are our ancestors?" "Freedmen," said he. "If you don't know, learn," he said. "It was a custom among the Greeks, if a city were captured, to send the tenth part of the spoils of cattle, sheep, goats, and other animals, as well as of money and slaves, both men and women. So since you were descended from these, you are not free; with such a descent, you have become slaves of the Greeks." Having said this, Aesop prepared to depart.

127. The Delphians figured that, when he went to other cities, too, Aesop would speak ill of them, so they decided to kill him by treachery and condemn him as a temple robber. And so, keeping a lookout for his slave who was carrying his baggage in front of the city gates, they hid in his bedding a golden bowl that they had taken from the temple of Apollo. Aesop, not knowing what had been contrived against him, traveled on to Phocis.

128. The men of Delphi ran and arrested him and led him into the city. Aesop was at a loss and said, "What is this?" They said, "We are ready to testify about the things that you stole from the temple." When he said that he was prepared to die if such a thing were proved, they shook out the bedding and discovered the gold bowl of Apollo and showed it to everyone in the city, buzzing around him with tumult and confusion. Aesop perceived the plot and kept begging them to release him, but they locked him up in prison. Aesop, unable to devise a stratagem against his ill fortune and since, as a mortal, he would not be able to escape what was coming, began to mourn.

-δικάσαι πα- absc. in M | ὑπήντησαν post αὐτοῦ add. R 4 τῆς² ... σκεύη : absc. in M | Καὶ ἀπέκλεισαν αὐτόν· τὰ δὲ σκεύη post φέροντα add. R | αὐτοῦ : om. R 5 ἦν ... Ἀπόλλωνος : μετὰ καὶ τῆς φυάλης τοῦ ἀπόλωνος, πρὸς τὸ ποιῆσαι σκευὴν κατὰ τοῦ αἰσώπου ὡς ἄτε χρυσὴν R | φιάλην ... ἱεροῦ : absc. in M 6 τὰ συνεσκευασμέ- absc. in M ‖ **128.1** Δέλφιοι R | -μόντες ἐκράτη- absc. in M 2 τοῦ αἰσώπου τί τοῦ- absc. in M | ἔφασαν M | ἃ : σὺ R 3 καὶ : om. R | -ούμεθα absc. in M | Τοῦ δὲ εἰπόντος R 4 εἰς ἐμὲ ἀποθανῶ post τοῦτο add. R | τοῦτο ἐκτινάξαντες : absc. in M | ἐκεῖνοι : οἱ τὴν σκευωρίαν ποιήσαντες R | τὸ στρῶμα : τὰ σκεύη R 5 ἐπεδείκνυόν τε : ἐπιδεικνύντες R 6 περιβομβίζοντες : περιμείζοντες R 7 ἐνέκλεισαν αὐτόν : -σαν αὐτόν absc. in M | τὴν ante φυλακήν add. R | Αἴσωπος : om. R 8 εὑρὼν R | -ηρᾶς τύχης absc. in M | οὐ : καὶ πῶς R : del. Perry, iter. Papath.

129. Φίλος δὲ αὐτοῦ τις, Δημᾶς ὀνόματι, παρακαλέσας τοὺς φύλακας, εἰσῆλθε πρὸς αὐτὸν καὶ ἰδὼν αὐτὸν κλαίοντα, ἔλεγεν αὐτῷ «τί πενθεῖς οὕτω;» Ὁ δὲ Αἴσωπος λόγον αὐτῷ εἶπεν· «γυνὴ προσφάτως τὸν ἄνδρα θάψασα καθ' ἡμέραν πρὸς τὸ μνῆμα αὐτοῦ ἔκλαιεν. Ἀροτριῶν δέ τις σύνεγγυς 5 ἐπεθύμησεν μετ' αὐτῆς συγγενέσθαι. Καταλιπὼν οὖν τοὺς βόας καὶ ἐλθὼν ἔκλαιεν μετ' αὐτῆς. Ἡ δὲ ἐπύθετο αὐτοῦ 'διατί καὶ αὐτὸς κλαίεις;' Ὁ δὲ εἶπεν 'κἀγὼ οὖν καλὴν γυναῖκα κατώρυξα· ὅταν οὖν κλαύσω τῆς λύπης κουφίζομαι.' Ἡ δὲ ἔφη 'κἀγὼ τὸ αὐτὸ πάσχω.' Κἀκεῖνός φησιν 'εἰ τοίνυν ταῖς αὐταῖς περιεπέσαμεν λύπαις, τί οὐκ ἐπισυγγινόμεθα ἑαυτοῖς; Ἐγὼ μὲν γὰρ 10 ἀγαπήσω σὲ ὡς ἐκείνην, σὺ δὲ ἐμὲ ὡς τὸν ἄνδρα σου.' Ταῦτα λέγων ἔπεισε τὴν γυναῖκα καὶ συγγενόμενος ἐνέπαιξεν αὐτήν. Ἐλθὼν δέ τις καὶ λύσας τοὺς βόας ἀπήλασεν. Ὁ δὲ ἐλθὼν καὶ μηδὲν εὑρὼν ἤρξατο θρηνεῖν καὶ κόπτεσθαι ὀδυρόμενος. Ἡ δὲ γυνὴ εὑροῦσα αὐτὸν ὀλοφυρόμενόν φησι 'πάλιν κλαίεις;' Ὁ δέ· 'ἄρτι ἐν ἀκριβείᾳ τῷ ὄντι κλαίω.' Καὶ ἐκεῖνος μὲν οὕτως. Σὺ δὲ βλέπων 15 τὴν ἔχουσάν με ἐξ ἐνέδρας τύχην, διατί ὀδύρομαι ἐρωτᾷς;»

130. Ὁ δὲ ἐπ' αὐτῷ λυπούμενος ἔφη «τί γάρ σοι ἔδοξεν ὑβρίζειν τοὺς Δελφοὺς καὶ μάλιστα ἐν τῇ ἰδίᾳ πατρίδι;» Ὁ δὲ Αἴσωπος πάλιν αὐτῷ ἕτερον λόγον εἶπεν.

131. «Γυνή τις εἶχεν θυγατέρα παρθένον μωράν. Πάντοτε οὖν ηὔχετο 20 τὴν θυγατέρα νοῦν ἔχειν. Εὐχομένης δὲ αὐτῆς παρρησίᾳ ἡ παρθένος ἤκουσε καὶ τὸν λόγον κατέσχε. Μεθ' ἡμέραν δὲ σὺν τῇ μητρὶ εἰς ἀγρὸν ἐξελθοῦσα καὶ τῆς προαυλίου προκύψασα θύρας, εἶδεν ὄνον θήλειαν ὑπὸ ἀνθρώπου βιαζομένην. Καὶ προσελθοῦσα τῷ ἀνθρώπῳ εἶπεν 'τί ποιεῖς;' Ὁ δέ φησι 'νοῦν αὐτῇ ἐντίθημι.' Ἀναμνησθεῖσα δὲ ἡ μωρὰ ὅτι καθ' ἑκάστην ἡ μήτηρ αὐτῆς 25 νοῦν αὐτῇ ἔχειν ηὔχετο, παρεκάλει λέγουσα 'ἔνθες, ἄνθρωπε, κἀμοὶ νοῦν. Καὶ γὰρ ἡ μήτηρ μου πολλά σοι πρὸς τοῦτο εὐχαριστήσει.' Ὁ δὲ ὑπακούσας,

129. A friend of his, Demas by name, having begged the guards, went in, saw him crying, and said to him, "Why do you mourn so?" Aesop told him a story: "A woman had recently buried her husband and wept daily at his tomb. A man who was plowing nearby desired to sleep with her, so he left his oxen behind and went and cried along with her. She asked him, 'Why are you, too, crying?' He replied, 'I, too, in fact, have buried an excellent wife; whenever I cry, I am relieved of the grief.' She said, 'I, too, experience the same thing.' And he said, 'Since, then, we have met with the same grief, why don't we join with each other? For I will love you as I did her, and you will love me as you did your husband.' With these words, he persuaded the woman, slept with her, and deceived her. But someone came and untied the oxen and drove them away. When he returned and found nothing, he began to lament and moan and beat himself. When the woman found him wailing, she said, 'Are you crying again?' He said, 'Now I am really and truly crying.' That's how things were with him, and you, seeing the ill fortune into which I have been entrapped, ask why I am lamenting?"

130. His friend said to him in his distress, "But why did you get it into your head to insult the people of Delphi, and above all in their own country?" And Aesop again told him another story.

131. "A certain woman had a virgin daughter who was stupid, so she continually prayed that her daughter would acquire sense. When she was praying openly, the virgin girl heard her and kept her words in mind. The next day she went out into the field with her mother, and, leaning over the gate of the cattle pen, she saw a female ass being violated by a man. She approached the man and said, 'What are you doing?' He replied, 'I am inserting sense in her.' The stupid girl remembered that her mother prayed every day that she would acquire sense, and so she asked him, 'Insert sense in me, too, sir, for my mother will indeed thank you greatly for this.' When

---

bsc. in M 2 Δελφοὺς : Δελφίους R ‖ ἡ τοιαύτη σου σοφία εἰς τὸ ἀτιμάζειν πολίτας κατήντησεν post Δελφοὺς add. R : ex RWB(P) cum dubit. (om. MLS, nescio an recte) suppl. Perry, iter. Papath. ‖ αὐτῶν ex G et P. Golenischeff post ἰδίᾳ suppl. Papath. | μάλιστα : τοὺς R | μάλιστα ... ἰδίᾳ : -ιστα ἐν τῇ ἰδίᾳ absc. in M | ὄντας post πατρίδι add. R | αὐτῷ πάλιν inv. R ‖ 131.1 Γυνή : absc. in M | θυγάτριον M | Πάντοτε οὖν : Καὶ πάντοτε R 2 τὴν θυγατέρα : absc. in M 3 τὸν λόγον : ex LS corr. Perry, iter. Papath. : τῶν λόγων R : -κουσε καὶ τὸν λόγον absc. in M | Μεθ' ἡμέρας δὲ τινὰς R | εἰς ἀγρὸν σὺν τῇ μητρὶ inv. R | ἐλθοῦσα R 4 καὶ τῆς προαυλίου : absc. in M | προαυλείου scr. Papath. | θηλίαν R 5 -μένην καὶ προσελ- absc. in M 6 -θημι absc. in M 7 ἔχειν αὐτῇ inv. R | ἐπίθες R 8 πολλά σοι : absc. in M | ἐν τούτῳ πολλά σοι R

καταλιπὼν τὴν ὄνον διεπαρθενεύσατο αὐτήν. Ἡ δὲ ἀναβᾶσα πρὸς τὴν μητέρα εἶπεν 'ἰδού, μῆτερ, κατὰ τὴν εὐχήν σου νοῦν ἔλαβον.' Ἡ δὲ μήτηρ αὐτῆς φησιν 'εἰσήκουσάν μου τῶν εὐχῶν οἱ θεοί;' Ἡ μωρὰ ἔφη 'ναί, μῆτερ.' 'Καὶ πῶς,' φησι, 'οἶδας, τέκνον;' Ἡ δὲ εἶπεν 'ὁ τοῦτόν μοι ἐνθεὶς μακρὸν πυρρὸν νευρῶδες ἔσω ἔξω ἐντρέχον ἐνέβαλέ μοι κἀγὼ ἐτερπόμην.' Ἡ δὲ μήτηρ ἀκούσασα ἔφη 'ὦ τέκνον, ἀπώλεσας καὶ ὃν πρότερον εἶχες νοῦν.'"

132. Ὁ δὲ φίλος πρὸς αὐτὸν ἔφη «σὲ οἱ Δελφοὶ ἀνέκαμψαν ψηφισάμενοι ὡς βλάσφημον καὶ ἀλαζόνα καὶ ἱερόσυλον ἀπὸ κρημνοῦ βληθῆναι ἵνα μηδὲ ταφῆς τύχῃς.» Ταῦτα αὐτοῦ ἐν τῇ φυλακῇ τῷ Αἰσώπῳ λαλοῦντος, ἐλθόντες οἱ Δελφοὶ καὶ ἐκβαλόντες τὸν Αἴσωπον ἐκ τῆς φυλακῆς εἷλκον μετὰ βίας ἐπὶ τῷ κρημνίσαι αὐτόν. Ὁ δὲ Αἴσωπος παρεκάλει αὐτοὺς ἀκοῦσαι αὐτοῦ. Ἐπιτρεψάντων δὲ αὐτῶν ἔφη.

133. «Ὅτε ἦν ὁμόφωνα τὰ ζῷα, μῦς βατράχῳ φιλιωθεὶς ἐκάλεσεν αὐτὸν εἰς δεῖπνον καὶ ἀπήγαγεν αὐτὸν εἰς ταμεῖον πλουσίου, ὅπου ἦν ἄρτος, τυρός, μέλι, ἰσχάδες καὶ ὅσα ἀγαθά, καί φησιν 'ἔσθιε ἐξ ὧν βούλει.' Ὁ δὲ βάτραχός φησιν 'ἐλθὲ οὖν καὶ σὺ πρὸς ἐμὲ καὶ πλήσθητι τῶν ἀγαθῶν μου. Ἀλλ' ἵνα μὴ ὄκνος σοι γένηται, προσαρτήσω τὸν πόδα σου τῷ ποδί μου.' Δήσας οὖν τὸν πόδα τοῦ μυὸς ὁ βάτραχος τῷ ἑαυτοῦ ποδί, ἥλατο εἰς τὴν λίμνην ἕλκων καὶ τὸν μῦν δέσμιον. Ὁ δὲ πνιγόμενος ἔλεγεν 'ἐγὼ μὲν ὑπὸ σοῦ νεκρωθήσομαι, ἐκδικηθήσομαι δὲ ὑπὸ ζῶντος.' Κόραξ δὲ θεασάμενος τὸν μῦν πλέοντα καταπτὰς ἥρπασεν. Ἐφέλκεται οὖν σὺν αὐτῷ καὶ ὁ βάτραχος καὶ οὕτως ἀμφοτέρους διεσπάραξεν. Οὕτως οὖν καὶ αὐτὸς ἐγὼ ἀβούλως παρ' ὑμῶν ἀποθανὼν νόμῳ ἐκδικηθήσομαι. Βαβυλὼν δὲ καὶ ἡ Ἑλλὰς ὅλη τὸν ἐμὸν ἐκδικήσωσι θάνατον.»

131.9 καταλιπὼν τὴν ὄνον : κατέλιπε τὴν ὄνον καὶ R | ὄνον : absc. in M | διεπαρθένευσεν R 10 εἶπεν : ἔφη R | ἰδού μῆτερ : absc. in M 11 εἰσήκουσάν μου : absc. in M | τῶν εὐχῶν οἱ θεοί : οἱ θεοὶ τῆς εὐχῆς R | Ἡ μωρὰ ἔφη : ἡ δὲ R 12 οἶδας τέκνον : absc. in M | Ἡ : Ὁ R τοῦτο R | ἐνθεὶς : ἐντιθεῖς ἦν R | παχὺ post μακρὸν add. R | πυρρὸν : corr. Perry, iter. Papath. : πυρὸν R : πυρον M 13 νευρῶ- absc. in M | ἔξω καὶ ἔσω M | ἐντρέχον : corr. Perry, iter. Papath. : ἐντρέχων R : ἐντρέχοντα M | ἡ δὲ μήτη- absc. in M | αὐτῆς post μήτηρ add. R 14 πρότερον : πρῶτον R ‖ 132.1 ὁ δὲ φ- absc. in M | πρὸς αὐτόν : πρὸς τὸν αἴσωπον R | Δέλφιοι R | ἀνέκαμψαν ψηφισάμενοι : ἐψηφήσαντο R 2 ὡς βλ- absc. in M | βληθῆναι : ριφῆναι R | μηδὲ : μὴ R 3 τοῦ αἰσώπου R | ἐλθόντες : συνῆλθον R 4 Δέλφιοι R | ἐκβαλόντες : ἐξέβαλον R | ἐκ : ἀπὸ R | εἷλκον : εἱλκ- absc. in M : ἕλκοντες R 5 ἐπὶ τὸ R | αὐτόν : om. M | Αἴσωπος :

he heard this, he abandoned the ass and deflowered the girl. She went back to her mother and said, 'Look, mother, I have acquired sense, according to your prayer.' Her mother said, 'Have the gods heard my prayers?' The stupid girl said, 'Yes, mother.' 'And how do you know this, child?' said the mother. The girl said, 'The man who gave it to me inserted in me this big, reddish, sinewy thing, moving in and out, and I felt pleasure.' The mother heard this and said, 'O child, you have also lost what sense you had before.'"

132. Aesop's friend said to him, "The men of Delphi have returned and decreed that you should be thrown from a cliff as a blasphemer and a boaster and a temple robber so that you may not even have a burial." After he said these things to Aesop in the prison, the men of Delphi came and took him out of the prison and dragged him by force to the place where he should be cast down. Aesop entreated them to listen to him. When they turned to him, he said,

133. "Back when the animals spoke the same language, a mouse, as it happens, who had made friends with a frog invited him to dinner and led him to a rich man's storehouse, where there was bread, cheese, honey, dried figs, and many goodies, and said, 'Eat whatever you wish.' The frog said, 'You, too, should come, then, and fill yourself on my goodies at my place. But so that you don't feel alarm, I will tie your foot to my foot.' So, when the frog had tied the mouse's foot to his own foot, he jumped into the lake, dragging along the captive mouse. As the mouse was drowning, it said, 'I'll be murdered by you, but I'll be avenged by one who is alive.' A crow that saw the mouse floating flew down and seized it; the frog, too, was dragged along with it, and so it ripped them both to pieces. So, too, I, who am dying foolishly at your hands, will be avenged by the law. Babylon and the whole of Greece will avenge my death."

---

om. R | ἐπὶ τὸ ante ἀκοῦσαι add. R ‖ **133.1** ὁμόφωνα : ... φρονα M | γοῦν post μῦς add. M | αὐτὸν : om. R **2** τυρός : τύροι R | τυρός, μ- absc. in M **3** βάτραχε post ἔσθιε add. R | Ὁ δὲ βάτραχός : absc. in M **4** φησιν : λέγει R | οὖν : νῦν R | πρός με post τῶν ἀγαθῶν μου trans. M | Ἀλλ' ... μὴ : absc. in M **5** ἃς ante προσαρτήσω add. R | προσαρτίσω R | τὸν¹ ... μου : τὸν πόδα μου τῷ ποδί σου R | μου. Δήσας : absc. in M **6** ὁ βάτραχος : om. R | εἰς τὴν λίμνην ἔλ- absc. in M | καὶ ... **7** μῦν : τὸν μυῖα R **7** μῦς post δὲ add. R | μὲν ὑπὸ σοῦ νεκρω- absc. in M **7–8** ἐκδικηθήσωμαι R **8** Κόραξ : Γούπης R | θεασάμενος τὸν : absc. in M | τὸν μυῖα R **9** ἐφέλκετο R | καὶ¹ ... βάτραχος : absc. in M **10** ἐγὼ ἀβούλως : absc. in M | νόμῳ : an λοιμῷ scribendum? Papath. **11** καὶ ἡ Αἴγυπτος post Βαβυλῶν δὲ add. R | καὶ ... ὅλη : absc. in M | ἐκδικήσουσι Papath. : ἐκδικήσειε M (-ε M^sl)

134. Τοῦτο ἀκούσαντες οἱ Δελφοὶ οὐκ ἐφείσαντο αὐτοῦ, ἀλλ᾽ ἤγαγον ἐπὶ τὸν κρημνόν. Τοῦ δὲ Αἰσώπου δραμόντος καὶ ἐπὶ τὸ ἱερὸν τοῦ Ἀπόλλωνος καταφυγόντος, οὐκ ἠλέησαν αὐτόν, ἀλλ᾽ ἤγαγον αὐτὸν μετ᾽ ὀργῆς. Ἀπαγόμενος δὲ Αἴσωπος ἔφη «ἀκούσατέ μου, Δελφοί.

135. Λαγωὸς ὑπὸ ἀετοῦ διωκόμενος κατέφυγεν πρὸς κοίτην κανθάρου, δεόμενος σωθῆναι. Ὁ δὲ κάνθαρος ἱκέτευε τὸν ἀετὸν μὴ ἀνελεῖν τὸν ἱκέτην, καὶ ἐξώρκιζεν αὐτὸν κατὰ τοῦ μεγάλου Διὸς μὴ καταφρονῆσαι αὐτοῦ τῆς σμικρότητος. Ὀργισθεὶς δὲ ὁ ἀετὸς καὶ ταῖς πτέρυξι ῥαπίσας τὸν κάνθαρον καὶ ἁρπάσας τὸν λαγωὸν κατέφαγεν.

136. Ὁ δὲ κάνθαρος λυπηθεὶς συνεπετάσθη τῷ ἀετῷ καὶ παρατηρησάμενος αὐτοῦ τὴν νοσσιὰν διέφθειρε τὰ ᾠά. Ὁ δὲ ἀετὸς ἐδεινοπάθησεν ἐπὶ τῇ φθορᾷ τῶν ἰδίων ᾠῶν καὶ ἐζήτει τὸν τοῦτο τολμήσαντα. Τοῦ δὲ καιροῦ πάλιν ἐλθόντος εἰς ὑψηλότερον ὁ ἀετὸς ᾠοποίησε τόπον. Ὁ δὲ κάνθαρος τὰ αὐτὰ διαπραξάμενος, διέφθειρεν πάλιν τὰ ᾠά. Ἐλθὼν δὲ ὁ ἀετὸς καὶ τὸ συμβὰν εὑρηκὼς ἐθρήνει λέγων «ἐκ θεῶν μοι εἶναι τὸν χόλον ἵνα τὸ τῶν ἀετῶν σπανισθῇ γένος.»

137. Τοῦ δὲ καιροῦ πάλιν ἀνοίξαντος δυσφορῶν ὁ ἀετὸς οὐκέτι εἰς τὴν νοσσιὰν ἔθηκε τὰ ᾠά, ἀλλ᾽ ἀναβὰς ἐπὶ τὰ γόνατα τοῦ Διὸς καὶ ἱκετεύσας ἔφη «δεύτερον ἤδη ἠρήμωμαι, τὸ δὲ τρίτον σοὶ τὰ ᾠὰ παρατίθημι ἵνα αὐτὰ διατηρήσῃς.» Καὶ ἔθηκεν αὐτὰ ἐπὶ τοῖς τοῦ Διὸς γόνασιν. Ὁ δὲ κάνθαρος ἐπιγνοὺς κατέπασεν ἑαυτὸν πλῆθος κόπρου, ἀναβάς τε πρὸς τὸν Δία καὶ περινοστῶν διετινάξατο τὴν κόπρον ἐπὶ τὸ τοῦ Διὸς πρόσωπον. Ὁ δὲ ἀναπηδήσας καὶ ἐπιλαθόμενος ὅτι ἐν τοῖς κόλποις εἶχε τὰ τοῦ ἀετοῦ ᾠά, ῥίψας αὐτὰ κατήρραξε.

138. Γνοὺς δὲ ὁ Ζεὺς τὴν ἀδικίαν καὶ παρασπόνδησιν τοῦ κανθάρου ᾔσθετο τὴν ἐξ αὐτοῦ πρὸς τὸν ἀετὸν βλάβην. Καὶ δὴ παραγενομένου αὐτοῦ ἔφη «δικαίως ἀπώλεσας τὰ τέκνα σου. Κάνθαρός ἐστιν ὁ ἀδικήσας σε. Ὁ δὲ

134.1 Τοῦτο : Ταῦτα R | οἱ Δ. οὐκ ἐφ- absc. in M | Δέλφιοι R | ἤγαγον : ἥλκον R 2 Τοῦ ... 3 ὀργῆς : ὁ δὲ αἴσωπος ἀποδράσας ἐξ αὐτῶν, προσέδραμεν ἐπὶ τὸ ἱερὸν τοῦ ἀπόλλωνος, ἀλλ᾽ οὐδὲ οὕτως κατηλέησαν αὐτόν R | δραμόντος καὶ : absc. in M 3 αὐτόν ... αὐτόν : absc. in M 4 Αἴσωπος : om. R | ἔφη : λέγει πρὸς αὐτοὺς μετ᾽ ὀδύνης R | ἀκούσατέ μου Δελφοί : ἠκούσατέ μου Δέλφιοι R : -σατέ μου Δελ- absc. in M | τόνδε τὸν λόγον post Δελφοί add. R ‖ 135.1 ὑπ᾽ ἀετοῦ R | εἰς κανθάρου κοίτην R 2 διασωθῆναι R | οἰκέτην MR 3 ἐξόρκιζεν R | μὴ : om. R 4 μικρότητος R | καὶ ταῖς : absc. in M : καὶ τοῖς R 5 καὶ ἁρπάσας : ἥρπασεν R | καὶ post λαγωὸν add. R ‖ 136.1 ὁ δὲ κάν- absc. in M 2 αὐτοῦ τὴν νοσσιὰν : τὴν νοσσιὰν ἑαυ ... R | νοσσιὰν :

134. When they heard this, the men of Delphi did not spare him but led him to the cliff. Although Aesop ran and took refuge in the temple of Apollo, they did not pity him but led him away in anger. As he was being led away, Aesop said, "Listen to me, men of Delphi.

135. "A hare was being chased by an eagle and fled to the nest of a dung beetle and begged it to save him. The dung beetle beseeched the eagle not to kill the suppliant and begged him, invoking the name of great Zeus, not to disregard him because of his small size. The eagle grew angry, beating the dung beetle with its wings; it snatched the hare and ate it.

136. "The dung beetle was distressed and flew after the eagle; it watched its nest carefully and destroyed the eggs. The eagle complained loudly about the destruction of its eggs and searched for the one who had dared to do this. When the season returned, the eagle laid its eggs in a higher place. The dung beetle did the same thing, again destroying the eggs. When the eagle came and found what had happened, it lamented and said, 'There is some wrath of the gods against me so that the race of eagles may be wiped out.'

137. "When the season came again, the eagle, now highly vexed, no longer placed its eggs in a nest but climbed on the knees of Zeus and beseeched him as a suppliant saying, 'Twice now I am bereft of offspring, and the third time I am placing my eggs with you so that you may watch over them.' And he placed them upon the knees of Zeus. When the dung beetle realized this, he spattered a large quantity of dung over himself and went up to Zeus, and as he went round he shook the dung on Zeus's face. Zeus jumped up and, forgetting that he had the eagle's eggs in his lap, he threw them off and broke them.

138. "When Zeus learned the injustice and breaking of faith that had been committed against the dung beetle, he understood why it had harmed the eagle. When the eagle arrived, Zeus said, 'You have justly lost your

---

absc. in M | αὐτοῦ post διέφθειρε add. R | ἐδεινοπάθη R | διαφθορᾶ R 3 τῶν ἰδίων : absc. in M | ποιῆσαι post τολμήσαντα add. R 4 -ηλότερον absc. in M | ᾠὰ ἐποίησε M 5 πάλιν τὰ ᾠὰ διέφθειρεν inv. R 6 εὑρηκὼς : θεασάμενος R 6–7 ἵνα τὸ γένος τῶν ἀετῶν σπανισθῇ inv. R ‖ 137.1 Τοῦ δὲ : absc. in M 1–2 εἰς τὰς νοσιὰς R 2 ἔθηκε : absc. in M | καὶ : om. R 3 -τερον absc. in M | μοι post ἵνα add. R 4 διατηρήσῃς : δια- absc. in M | κάνθαρος : -νθαρος absc. in M 5 πλῆθος : εἰς πλῆθος R 6 -νοστῶν absc. in M | διετίναξε R 7 ἐν τῷ κόλπῳ αὐτοῦ R 8 αὐτὰ : absc. in M | κατήρραξε : κατέαξεν R ‖ 138.1 παραπόνησιν R | -άρου ... 2 ᾔσθετο absc. in M 3 ἔφη δικαίως : absc. in M | ὁ σὲ ἀδικήσας inv. R | Ὀ ... 4 κάνθαρος : absc. in M

κάνθαρος ἔφη «οὐκ ἐμὲ αὐτὸς ἐξουθένησεν ὁ ἀετός, ἀλλὰ καὶ εἰς σὲ ἠσέβησεν. Ὀρκισθεὶς γὰρ οὐκ ἐπέπειστο, ἀλλὰ τὸν ἱκέτην ἀπέκτεινεν. Οὐ παύσομαι δὲ εἰ μὴ τελείως αὐτὸν ἀνταμύνομαι.»

139. Ὁ δὲ Ζεὺς μὴ θέλων τὸ τῶν ἀετῶν γένος σπανισθῆναι, συνεβούλευσε τῷ κανθάρῳ διαλλαγῆναι. Τοῦ δὲ μὴ βουλομένου μετέβαλεν ὁ Ζεὺς τὸν τοκετὸν τῶν ἀετῶν, ὁπόταν μὴ φαίνηται κάνθαρος μήτε βλάπτειν δύναιτο. Καὶ ὑμεῖς, ἄνδρες Δελφοί, μὴ ἀτιμάσητε τὸν θεὸν τοῦτον, διότι τὸ ἱερὸν αὐτοῦ τοῦτο μικρὸν ὑπάρχει. Ἐνθυμήθητε δὲ τὸ τοῦ κανθάρου καὶ αἰδέσθητε τὸν Ἀπόλλωνα διὰ τὸ ἐμὲ εἰς αὐτὸν καταφυγεῖν.»

140. Οἱ δὲ τοῖς ὑπ' αὐτοῦ λεγομένοις μὴ πεισθέντες ἀπήγαγον αὐτὸν ἐπὶ τὸν κρημνὸν καὶ ἔστησαν αὐτὸν ἐπὶ τοῦ ἄκρου. Ὁ δὲ Αἴσωπος βλέπων τὸν ἑαυτοῦ μόρον εἶπεν «ἄνδρες ἀτίθασοι, ἐπεὶ παντοίως ὑμᾶς οὐ πείθω, ἀκούσατέ μου τόνδε τὸν λόγον. Γεωργός τις γηράσας ἐπ' ἀγρῷ καὶ μηδέποτε εἰς πόλιν εἰσελθὼν παρεκάλει τοὺς ἰδίους τὴν πόλιν θεάσασθαι. Οἱ δὲ οἰκεῖοι αὐτοῦ ἔζευξαν ἅμαξαν καὶ ὀνάρια εἰπόντες αὐτῷ 'ἔλαυνε μόνον καὶ αὐτά σε ἐν ἔθει ὄντα καταστήσουσι εἰς τὴν πόλιν.' Χειμῶνος δὲ γενομένου σκοτοειδοῦς κατὰ τὴν ὁδὸν τὰ ὀνάρια πλανηθέντα εἰσῆλθον εἴς τινα τόπον ἀπόκρημνον. Ὁ δὲ τὸν ἴδιον θεασάμενος κίνδυνον ἔφη 'ὦ Ζεῦ, τί σε ἠδίκησα ὅτι οὕτως ἀπόλλυμαι, καὶ ταῦτα οὐχ ὑπὸ ἵππων ἐντίμων οὔτε ὑπὸ ἡμιόνων γενναίων, ἀλλ' ὑπὸ ὀναρίων ἐλαχίστων·' Κἀγὼ δὲ ὡσαύτως δυσφορῶ, ὅτι οὐχ ὑπὸ ἐντίμων ἢ ἐλλογίμων ἀνδρῶν ἀπόλλυμαι, ἀλλ' ὑπὸ κακίστων καὶ ἀχρείων δούλων.»

141. Μέλλων δὲ ἀπὸ τοῦ κρημνοῦ ὑπ' αὐτῶν ἐκκυλίεσθαι ἕτερον ἔφη λόγον. «Ἀνήρ τις ἐρασθεὶς τῆς ἰδίας θυγατρὸς καὶ εἰς ἔρωτα τρωθείς, ἔπεμψεν εἰς τὸν ἀγρὸν τὴν γυναῖκα αὐτοῦ, τὴν δὲ θυγατέρα ἐκράτησε καὶ ἐβιάσατο. Ἡ δὲ ἔλεγε 'πάτερ, ἀνόσια πράττεις· εἴθε μᾶλλον ἑκατὸν ἀνδράσι με παρασχεῖν ἢ σοί.' Τοῦτο κἀγὼ πρὸς ὑμᾶς, ὦ Δελφοί. Προῃρούμην Σικελίαν ὅλην κακοπαθῶν κυκλεῦσαι ἢ ἐνθάδε παραλόγως ὑφ' ὑμῶν ἀποθανεῖν.

138.4 αὐτὸς ... ἀετός : μόνον ἠδίκησεν R | εἰς σὲ ἠσέβησεν : absc. in M 5 Ὀρκισθεὶς : ὀρκι- evan. in R | οὐ πέπεισθαι R | ἀλλὰ : absc. in M | οἰκέτην MR | -κτεινεν οὐ παύσομαι absc. in M 6 ἀνταμείνομαι R ‖ 139.1 θέλων τὸ τῶν : absc. in M | σπανίσαι M | συνεβούλευε R 2 - λλαγῆναι τοῦ δὲ absc. in M | ὑπακοῦσαι καὶ τοῦ ἀετοῦ λέγοντος μὴ παρακοῦσαι ἀπὸ τὴν σήμερον τὴν γῆν ὁρκίζοντος post μὴ βουλομένου add. R | τὸν ... 3 ἀετῶν : τόπον τῶν ἀετῶν τοκετόν R 3 ὁπόταν μὴ : absc. in M : ex L suppl. Perry, iter. Papath : ὅπ' ὅτε R | φαίνεται R | μὴ τί βλάψαι δύναται R 4 διὸ ante καὶ add. R | Καὶ ... ἄνδρες : -αὶ ὑμεῖς ἄ- absc. in M | Δέλφιοι R | τοῦτον : ἀπέναντι καὶ R | διότι : om. R | διότι ... 5 αὐτοῦ : absc. in M : suppl. Perry, iter. Papath. 5 ὑπάρχει : τυγχάνῃ R | δὲ : οὖν R | καὶ αἰδέσθητε : absc. in M ‖ 140.1 αὐτὸν : om. R 3 μόρον :

young. The dung beetle is the one who wronged you.' The dung beetle said, 'The eagle not only made nothing of me but was also impious toward you. For having sworn he did not keep faith but killed the suppliant. I will not stop unless I pay him back completely.'"

139. "Since Zeus did not wish to wipe out the race of eagles, he advised the dung beetle to be reconciled. When it did not wish to, Zeus changed the birthing of eagles to when the dung beetle did not appear and could not do harm. You, too, men of Delphi, do not dishonor this god because this temple of his is small. Consider the story of the dung beetle and respect Apollo, since I took refuge with him."

140. They were not persuaded by his words and led him to the cliff and placed him at the edge. Aesop saw his own fate and said, "Savage men, since I cannot in any way persuade you, listen to this story of mine. A certain farmer who had grown old in the country had never gone to the city, so he asked his relatives to let him see the city. His relations yoked a carriage and asses and said to him, 'Just drive, and the asses, since they are accustomed, will take you into the city.' A dark storm arose along the route, and the asses got lost and entered a certain precipitous spot. When he perceived his danger, the farmer said, 'O Zeus, what wrong did I do to you that I am killed in this way, and this not by honorable horses or noble mules but by the lowliest asses?' I, too, am vexed in the same way that I am killed not by honorable or reputable men but by the worst and most useless slaves."

141. As he was about to be rolled off the cliff by them, he related another story: "A certain man fell in love with his own daughter, and, wounded by passion, he sent his wife into the country and overpowered and violated his daughter. She said, 'Father, you are doing something unholy; I would rather be given to a hundred men than to you.' I, too, say this to you, O men of Delphi: I would prefer to suffer circling all of Sicily than to die here unreasonably at your hands."

θάνατον R **4** καὶ ante τόνδε add. R | τις : om. R | ἀγροῦ R | μηδέπω R **5** οἴκιοι R **6** αὐτῷ : om. R | ἐν ... **7** ὄντα : om. R **7** καταστήσει R **8** καὶ post ὁδὸν add. R | ἦλθον R **9** ὦ : om. R **10** οὔτε ... **11** ἐλαχίστων' : ἢ ἐκλογήμων ἀνδρῶν R **11** Κἀγὼ ... ὅτι : ἐπίσης δὲ κἀγὼ R | ἐντίμων ... **12** ἐλλογίμων : ἐνδόξων R **12** ἀπόλλυμαι : post ἀχρείων δούλων trans. R | ἀλλ' ... δούλων : ἀλλ' ὑπὸ κακίστων δούλων καὶ ἀχρείων R ‖ **141.1** ὑπ' αὐτῶν : om. R | ἐκκυλίεσθαι : ἀπολύεσθαι R | αἴσωπος post ἕτερον add. R **2** ἰδίας : desinit R | ἀπέπεμψεν in marg. R **3** τὸν : om. R | γυναῖκα : desinit in marg. R **5** Προη- absc. in M **6** ὑφ' ὑμῶν : ὑφ' ὑμ- absc. in M : ὑφ' ὑμῶν ex WL corr. Perry : παρ' ὑμῶν ex BP corr. Papath.

142. Καταρῶμαι οὖν ὑμῶν τὴν πατρίδα καὶ θεοὺς μαρτύρομαι, οἳ ἐπακούσουσί μου ἀπολλυμένου καὶ ἔκδικοι γένωνται.» Οἱ δὲ ὠθήσαντες ἔρριψαν αὐτὸν κατὰ τοῦ κρημνοῦ, καὶ οὕτως ἀπέθανε. Λοιμῷ οὖν καὶ συνοχῇ ἰσχυρᾷ κατασχεθέντες οἱ Δελφοί, χρησμὸν ἔλαβον ἐξιλεώσασθαι τὸν τοῦ Αἰσώπου μόρον. Ἐτύπτοντο γὰρ ὑπὸ τῆς συνειδήσεως δολοφονήσαντες τὸν Αἴσωπον. Ναοποιήσαντες οὖν ἔστησαν αὐτῷ στήλην. Μετὰ δὲ ταῦτα ἀκούσαντες οἱ τῆς Ἑλλάδος ἔξαρχοι καὶ οἱ λοιποὶ διδάσκαλοι τὸ εἰς τὸν Αἴσωπον πραχθέν, παραγενόμενοι ἐν Δελφοῖς καὶ ἐκκλησίαν ποιησάμενοι ἐξεδίκησαν τὸν τοῦ Αἰσώπου μόρον.

142.1 μαρτύρομαι ... 2 ἐπακούσουσί : -ρομαι, οἳ ἐπ- absc. in M **2** - σαντες ... 3 ἔρριψαν absc. in M **3** συνοχῇ ... 4 ἰσχυρ- absc. in M **4** τὸν τοῦ ... 5 Αἰσώπ- absc. in M **5** -φονήσαντες absc. in M **6** Μετὰ δὲ ταῦτα : absc. in M **7** τὸ εἰς τὸν : absc. in M

142. "So I curse your country, and I call the gods in witness, who will hear me as I die and be my avengers." The Delphians gave him a push and threw him off the cliff, and in this way he died. And so while the Delphians were afflicted by an unremitting and violent plague, they received an oracle to propitiate the death of Aesop, for they were stricken by conscience for having slain Aesop treacherously. So they built a temple and set up a stela in his honor. Afterward, when the leaders of Greece and the other teachers heard what had been done to Aesop, they went to Delphi and formed an assembly and avenged the death of Aesop.

COMMENTARY

Chapter 1

1.1. Βιωφελέστατος. This is the reading of MS M, much better than that of MS O βιοφιλέστατος. The first derives from the adjective βιωφελής ("useful in life"; see LSJ and *DGE*, s.v.). The second is due to the phonetic confusion (1) between long /o/ and short /o/, which is frequently observed in papyri and inscriptions "in the Koine by the beginning of the Roman period" (Gignac 1976, 277), and (2) between /i/ and /e/ before a liquid, which is also attested in the papyri of that period (250 CE). The reading βιοφιλέστατος could derive from an adjective *βιοφιλής (< βίος + φιλῶ, "life lover"), which is, however, not attested (either in lexica or in the TLG). The reading βιοφιλέστατος instead of βιωφελέστατος also occurs in MS G (22r.3).[1]

1.3. Κοντοτράχηλος. The word seems to be of a late date. The first attestation comes from the Life and specifically from the recensions MORN and BPThSA; it subsequently appears in Byzantine literature (see *LBG*, s.v.). It is interesting that MS O has, instead of κοντοτράχηλος, the reading κοντοδείρης (possibly a synonym), which is attested only in the text of MS O.

Chapter 2

2.9. Λιμανθείς. The reading λιμανθείς is a correction by Perry, whereas Papathomopoulos suggests λιμπισθείς. MS O offers the reading λιπανθείς, while in MS M the passage is not readable. In the recension BPThSA there is no textual correspondence. Furthermore, MSS LFV have λυμπιασθείς and MS W λιχνευσάμενος. Perry's correction seems to be closer to the read-

---

[1]. See on this Stamoulakis 2016, 91.

ing of MS O, as the letters μ and π are often interchanged in codices; the lemma λιμαίνω is found in LSJ (with the sense "suffer from famine") but does not seem to be attested in the middle or passive voice. The suggested form λιμπισθείς presumably comes from the verb λιμβίζομαι,[2] which is quite late and closer to the reading of MSS LFV.

2.16–17. Εἴ τι ἀπόληται. The form ἀπόληται is a correction by Perry, accepted also by Papathomopoulos. Since the form ἀπολῆται of MS M does not exist, and since MS O has the phrase ὅτι ἀπόλυται, it seems reasonable to accept Perry's correction, which is paleographically closer to the reading of M, and to attribute the reading of MS O to the common interchange between η and υ.

Chapter 3

3.20. The reading of MS O τὸν δόλον δρᾶν instead of τοῦτο λανθάνει ποιῶν seems to be an interpolation by the scribe of MS O, who is inclined to make such changes in his text (see, e.g., chs. 2, 24, 32, 37, 87).

Chapter 4

4.1. ζευκτῷ. The word is not at all readable in MS M, while MS O gives the reading ζευτω (not ζευγω, as Perry suggested).[3] The reading ζευκτῷ of MSS LV is quite close to ζευτω, since the simplification of the cluster /kt/ to /t/ is a rather common mistake in Greek codices. It is interesting to see that the false reading by Perry appears as a *hapax* in TLG and that *LBG* creates the form ὁ ζεῦγος in this sense ("Gespann").

Chapter 5

5.1. τὰς χεῖρας. The appearance of the dual τὼ χεῖρε in MS M, not attested in any other manuscript of the versions of the *Life*, is strange. Perhaps it is an effort by a scribe (Libadenos?) to adjust the text to the prayer that is quoted.

---

2. See *LBG*, s.v. "λιμβίζω." See also Stephanus, s.v. "λιμβίζομαι."
3. Perry expresses his doubts in the apparatus criticus: "ζευγω (vel ζευτω) καθήσας O" (1952, 136).

Chapter 6

6.2. ἐτράπη. This is the reading of MS O, shared by most codices of the Westermanniana version. Only MS M gives the reading ἐτράπετο. The use of middle/passive voice instead of the active is common from the Hellenistic period onward,[4] but its presence in this case seems to be restricted to only one manuscript or to a related branch of the textual tradition.

Chapter 7

7.1. Τύχη. Τύχη is the reading of M (and of most manuscripts of the Westermanniana version). MS O (along with MSS P and W) has the word Φιλοξενία instead of Tyche. In the archetype of the Life, the relevant word was probably Isis.[5]

Chapter 9

9.3. ῥάβδῳ κατέξαινεν. This is the reading of MS O and almost all others manuscripts of the Westermanniana (see Perry 1952, 137) except for MS M, which has τύπτει ῥάβδῳ here. The reading of M seems to be a verbatim quotation of Prov 10:13 from the Septuagint: ὃς ἐκ χειλέων προφέρει σοφίαν, ῥάβδῳ τύπτει ἄνδρα ἀκάρδιον.

9.6. τοῦτο ἦν τῷ οἰκονόμῳ ὄνομα. This parenthetical sentence, which looks like an interpolation, is attested only in M, while a variant (τοῦτο γὰρ ἦν ὄνομα αὐτῷ [τῷ οἰκονόμῳ S]) is attested in MSS SB as well. In these two manuscripts, it is placed correctly after Zenas and only in M after ἀκούσας. It could have been transposed in the same way in the MORN redaction, as Papathomopoulos suggested, but there is no need to add the particle γάρ, as both editors, Perry and Papathomopoulos, proposed.

9.8. Προκαταλάβομαι. Both manuscripts (MO) transmit an indicative present. It need not be corrected to a subjunctive (see Perry), as it can be interpreted as a future-referring present (Goodwin 1893, §32; Tronci 2020).

---

4. See Karla 2001, 106, with bibliography.
5. On this issue, see Perry 1936, 12 n. 11; La Penna 1962, 268–70; Jedrkiewicz 1989, 88–89; Holzberg 1992a, 45 n. 59; Pervo 1998, 92 n. 68; Robertson 2003, 249; Jedrkiewicz 2009, 176 n. 23.

9.8–9. ἐπεὶ τοῦ δεσπότου ἐλθόντος κατηγορήσας μεταστήσει με τῆς οἰκονομίας. The syntax here is peculiar, since the subject of the main clause verb is the same as that of the *genitivus absolutus* (δεσπότου ἐλθόντος) and the participle in the nominative has Αἴσωπος as its subject. The phenomenon is probably related to the changes in participle usage attested in Koine.[6]

Chapter 10

Chapter 10 is more detailed in version G, and the dialogue between Zenas and his master is more vivid there, with allusions to Old Comedy. The corresponding episode in the MORN recension seems to be an abridgement, which could account for a number of textual problems.[7]

10.6. καὶ ὁ δεσπότης. This reading is given by MS O, while it is absent from MS M. It needs to be kept, as it signals the change of speaker. The same happens a few lines later (10.10), where the phrase ὁ δεσπότης should be added from version G, as Perry had already suggested.

10.7–9. «οἱ θεοὶ χολωθέντες ἀνθρώπῳ πρὸς ὀλίγον <χρόνον ἀφείλαντο τὴν φωνὴν αὐτοῦ, νῦν δὲ> πάλιν διαλλαγέντες ἐχαρίσαντο.» The text, as transmitted by both manuscripts,[8] makes no sense. It must be "healed" on the basis of version G, since the corresponding passage does not occur at all in BPThSA. It does not seem necessary to introduce here the whole phrase from G, as Perry did in the edition of the Westermanniana (<ὁ δεσπότης· "διὰ τί; εἰ>), because, as mentioned above, the episode in MORN is quite abridged and does not present the vivid dialogue of version G. Since not all the rhetorical questions of G are preserved, the phrase διὰ τί; may be omitted. In the same way, it is not necessary to add the hypothetical conjunction εἰ.

---

6. See, e.g., Horrocks 2010, 94. The same phenomenon can also be observed in recension BPThSA (Karla 2001, 124). For the phenomenon in classical times, see Kühner, Blass, and Gerth 1904, 2.§494; in the New Testament, see Blass and Debrunner 1990, §423.3.

7. The defective passages are omitted in the BPThSA recension. See Karla 2001, 133–34.

8. M: οἱ χολωθέντες ἀνθρώπῳ πρὸς ὀλίγον πάλιν διαλλαγέντες ἐχαρίσαντο; O: οἱ θεοὶ σχολασθέντες ἐν ἀνθρώπῳ πρὸς ὀλίγον πάλιν διαλλαγέντες ἐχαρίσαντο.

Chapter 11

11.2. πρᾶξον. It is difficult to choose between the two forms of the imperative: O's πρᾶξον (aorist) and M's πρᾶσσε (present). The reading πρᾶξον is presented by two more manuscripts (WB), whereas πρᾶσσε is attested only in MS M. Neverthelesss, because the preceding imperatives (πώλησον, χάρισον, ἀπόλυσον) are in the aorist, this last form must be in the aorist, too.

Chapter 14

14.3. Εἰ μὴ φωνὴν εἶχεν, εἰρήκει τις. MS M has the form εἰρήκει (third-person singular, plusquamperfect), MS O εἴρηκα (first-person singular, perfect). It is not necessary to correct to εἰρήκειν ἄν on the basis of G, as Perry (and Papathonopoulos) suggested or to εἰρήκοι (as proposed by Westermann), since "the addition of ἄν to the apodosis is no longer obligatory" (Blass and Debrunner 1990, §360). Consequently, we can adopt here the reading of MS M.

Chapter 15

15.2. Ὅ τι προσεκαλέσω με. Both manuscripts (MO) give the reading ὅτι. Perry corrected ὅ τι to τί (as in G), and Papathomopoulos suggested <τί> ὅτι. However, this use of ὅ τι is confirmed by the text of New Testament, where "ὅ τι is used more frequently ... to introduce a direct question with the meaning 'why'" (Blass and Debrunner 1990, §300.2, with several examples; see also Jannaris 1897, §2044).

15.3. παρατήρημα. The reading παρατήρημα is found in both manuscripts (MO). Perry deleted it as a gloss, while Papathomopoulos corrected to περίτριμμα. In LSJ (s.v.) the word has the meaning "observation" or "condition to be observed,"[9] which is not appropriate here, since a derisory sense is needed. The only example that I could find with this meaning is in *Spanos*, a Byzantine text of the twelfth century in colloquial Greek (rec. D, vv. 49–50: καὶ τῶν ἀνθρώπων τὸ παρατήρημα), where many such words are used to characterize the protagonist negatively.

---

9. The sense proposed in *LBG* ("einzuhaltende Vorschrift") is also inappropriate.

15.6. σωματεμπορείῳ. The word is only attested in the Life, as a search in the TLG shows (see also LSJSup, s.v. "σωματεμπόριον"). Papathomopoulos writes also σωματεμπορείῳ as attested in MS M.

15.7. Ἀγόρασόν με καὶ κατάστησόν με παιδαγωγόν. In MS M the verb κατάστησον is without an object, although all other manuscripts (O, Lo "compara me et fac me") of this recension have it. In all manuscripts the verb κατάστησον invariably appears with an object (με in λP) or a prepositional construction (W: ἐπ' αὐτῶν; B: ἐπ' αὐτοῖς). Consequently, the object με should be introduced here.

15.8. ἀντὶ μορμολυκίου φοβέριστρον. All manuscripts of the Westermanniana except MS O have the word φοβέριστρον. Lo transmits "et ero illis in figura lupi, et mittam in eis timorem" and so confirms the existence of φοβέριστρον in the MORN recension. Perry deleted it in his edition of Westermanniana. Μορμολυκίου is attested by both manuscripts (MO), whereas Papathomopoulos corrected to μορμολυκείου. Both forms are attested in lexica (LSJ, LSJ Sup, *LBG*, s.v.).

Chapter 16

16.4. κατὰ παιδίων προυνικῶν. In the Westermanniana, only MS O has the reading προυνικῶν, which is attested also in MS G (προνικῶν).[10] The sense of προύνικος as "lively, vivid" (for the meaning "fast, quick," see Hesychius 4034.1, *EM* 483.49) is also attested, among others, in Diogenes Laertius (*Vit. phil.* 4.7.1). Instead of this, MS M has the reading ἀνήβων, a word attested in ancient and Byzantine Greek (see LSJ, *DGE*, MGS, s.v. "ἄνηβος").[11] It may be assumed that the reading of M is the effort of a scribe (or of Libadenos himself) to replace the word προυνικῶν because it was no longer comprehensible. Since the word προυνικῶν is attested also in G, it should be adopted as the reading of the MORN recension as the *lectio difficilior* that also fits the context better.

16.4. ἕτοιμον ὠνήσω μορμολύκιον. The reading μορμολύκιον comes from MSS PWλ and is suggested by Perry in the Westermanniana version. MS M

---

10. On the word, see Stamoulakis 2016, 73–74, 371–72, with further bibliography.
11. Other manuscripts of the Westermanniana have νηπίων (P), κλαιόντων (B), or both (W).

has μόρμυκα and MS O μέρμυκα. Papathomopoulos adopts the unattested word of MS M (μόρμυκα) and translates it as μυρμήγκι (= ant), which, however, does not provide a satisfactory meaning in this context: "Aesop said to the merchant: 'You now have the proof of my promise, that you have bought a ready ant against mischievous children.'" In the first place, Aesop had not promised the merchant any such thing (that he would be an ant); second, ants were not frightening creatures to children, since children at that time were quite familiar with nature. One could perhaps suggest that the word is an abbreviation of μορμολύκιον in this passage (see above the abbreviation of the word μητέρα in all codices) and that an ancestor of the scribe of MO misread it. The reading of Lo ("quia factus sum in figura rapacis lupi mittens timorem in pueris") confirms this suggestion.

16.6. Εἰσελθὼν οὖν εὑρίσκει παῖδας. This is the reading of MS O. MS M has δύο παῖδας πρῶτον εὑρίσκει. As for the other manuscripts of the Westermanniana, only B transmits the numeral "two" (καὶ εὑρηκὼς δύο παιδάρια). This cannot be the original reading, since, according to chapter 20 the merchant brought the slaves, and "three were left: a teacher, a lyre player, and Aesop." Moreover, Lo also mentions "plures servos," not just two. The erroneous reading in MB was probably caused by the proximity of the mention of two children (Δύο δὲ παιδία ὑπὸ μητέρα ὄντα) a few lines above.

16.8. Ὅτι οὐδέποτε. This is the reading of MS O, whereas M has ὅτι τὸ οὐδέπω instead. The phrase τὸ οὐδέπω is transmitted by no other manuscript of the Life, and, as a search in TLG shows, the combination of the definite article τὸ + οὐδέπω does not have a temporal meaning. It usually has the sense "by no means" (see examples in Lampe 1976, s.v. "οὐδέπω").

16.9. Πλὴν πρὸς βασκανίαν τοῦ σωματεμπορείου αὐτὸν ὠνήσατο. Even though both manuscripts (MO) have the reading βασκανίαν,[12] Papathomopoulos suggests ἀβασκανίαν. It is not necessary to correct the unanimous reading of the manuscripts, since the word βασκανία has the meaning of "evil eye, spell" (*DGE*, s.v. I.1) already in classical times (Plato, Aristotle), in contrast to the word ἀβασκανία, which is not found in standard lexica (e.g. LSJ, *DGE*, *LBG*).

---

12. All other manuscripts have either the same (BPF) or a very similar reading (W: βασκανίον, G: προβασκάνιον).

Chapter 18

18.6. Τὴν ἐπιθυμίαν αὐτοῦ πληρώσωμεν. MS O, as well as all other manuscripts of the Westermanniana, have the reading πληρώσωμεν. The reading of MS M, ποιήσωμεν, seems to be a *lectio facilior*, a misreading of πληρώσωμεν.

18.7. καὶ ἐκίνησε διακλονούμενος. The text tradition of this passage is problematic. MS M has the reading διακλώμενος instead of διακλονούμενος (the reading of MSS GSAW). The same reading (διακλώμενος) is also to be found in MS P, whereas MS O has διὰ κελόμενος. The lemma διακλάω in lexica has the sense of "break, weaken" (see LSJ, Lampe 1976, *DGE*, s.v.), which is inappropriate in this context. An obvious suggestion would be that the reading διακλώμενος constitutes a misreading of διακλονούμενος. However, a search in TLG reveals, among others, a well attested passage, Orus frag. 147b,[13] in which the meaning of the word διακλώμενος is probably neither "break" nor "weaken" but "with outstretched arms," which would be appropriate in the relevant passage in MORN.[14]

Chapter 19

19.1. Σύνδυο. The word is recorded in many sources (see LSJ, s.v.). In both manuscripts (MO) it is attested as two separate words: σὺν δύο.

19.3. ἀνεκύλει τὸν γόργαθον. MS M has the reading ἀνεκύλει, and the reading of MS B (BPThSA) has the same ending (ἐκύλει). MS O has the standard form ἀνεκύλιε (as in MSS SPW). However, as the metaplasm of the verbs with the suffix -ίω to -ῶ is attested since imperial times (Jannaris 1897, §§702, 857–60), one may accept the reading of M as representative of the MORN recension. The same applies to the next instance of the verb κυλίω, a line below (ἐκύλει/ἐκύλιεν).

---

13. "σκορδινᾶσθαι· τὸ παρὰ φύσιν τὰ μέλη ἐκτείνειν μετὰ τοῦ χασμᾶσθαι διακλώμενον σκορδινᾶσθαι λέγεται. γίνεται δὲ περὶ τοὺς ἐγειρομένους ἐξ ὕπνου, ὅταν χασμώδεις ὄντες ἐκτείνωσι τὰς χεῖρας ... ὅπερ καὶ περὶ τοὺς ἄλλως πως βασανιζομένους καὶ διαστρεφομένους τὰ μέλη" (ed. Alpers).

14. Another possibility is a connection with the modern dialectal verb διακλώθω, "wander, wander around," for which see ILNE, s.v. "διακλώθουμαι."

19.4. Εἰ δὲ εἰς κατάβασιν. MS M has the reading ἐάν instead of εἰ, which is the reading of MS O (and of MSS SB). MS W agrees with M. Even though ἐάν with the indicative can be admitted for this period (see Blass and Debrunner 1990, §373.2), it might be best to adopt the reading of O, as it is preceded by a conditional sentence with εἰ (note the particle δέ here).

Chapter 21

21.1. ὑπέδυσε. MS M has the reading ὑπέδησε and MS O ὑπενένδυσε. Perry corrected to ὑπενέδυσε, followed by Papathomopoulos. Because the lemma ὑπενδύω has the meaning "put on underneath," I think the reading of M can be preserved with a slight change of η to υ (a common error due to iotacism). The verb ὑποδύω seems to have a neutral meaning ("put on clothes, dress") in the postclassical period (see Lampe 1976, s.v. "ὑποδύω"), as here.

21.3. προσβλεπτέον. MS O makes no mention of the second slave, apparently due to haplography (the passage that begins and ends with the same word, πρατηρίου, is omitted). MS M has the reading πρόβλεπτον, the meaning of which ("provide against"; see LSJ, s.v.) is not appropriate here. The other manuscripts of the Westermanniana (Wλ) have the reading λεπτὸν ὄντα, which is closer to G (λεπτὸν ἀπὸ τῶν σφυρῶν τυγχάνοντα). Papathomopoulos's correction προσβλεπτέον seems to be more suitable in this context (see LSJ, s.v. "προσβλεπτέος," "to be looked upon"). Alternatively, the word may be considered as a gloss and athetized from the text.

21.5. ὅλως ἦν ἁμάρτημα. Since both manuscripts have the reading ὅλως, it is not necessary to correct to ὅλος, as Papathomopoulos suggested.

21.6. ἐνέδυσεν αὐτὸν σακκοχίτωνα. MS M has the reading σακκοχίτωνα and MS O σάκκον. The other manuscripts of the Westermanniana give χιτῶνα (W: χιτωνίσκον) ἐκ σάκκου (SBWλ). Perry and Papathomopoulos adopted the reading of M, which is close to G's reading (σάκκον χιτῶνα). The lemma σακκοχίτων is found only in *LBG* (s.v.), which lists as its only attestation this passage from the Life. A search in TLG reveals no other source for this word.[15]

---

15. On σακκοχίτων, see Stamoulakis 2016, 242–43.

Chapter 24

24.7. ἐξ ὄπισθεν. Both manuscripts (MO) transmit two separate words, and perhaps this spelling should be preserved. In LSJ (s.v. ἐξόπισθεν) as well in the editions of Perry and Papathomopoulos it is written as one word.

Chapter 25

25.11. Οὐκ ἔστιν γὰρ ἄνθρωπος πάντα εἰδώς. Only MS M has the infinitive εἰδέναι instead of the participle εἰδώς. Since the verb ἔστιν in this context has an existential meaning and is not impersonal, the reading of O (εἰδώς) is much preferable.

Chapter 26

26.3. λύσας θύρας βαλαντίου. Instead of the participle λύσας, MS M has the reading λύσαι. No other manuscript of the Westermanniana version has this reading, according to Perry's *apparatus criticus*. Moreover, /i/ instead of /c/ is a common paleographic error. Consequently, it is better to adopt the reading of MS O (λύσας).

26.4. μή με σκώπτῃ. Version G and the other manuscripts of the Westermanniana have the imperative, except for MSS MO, which have the ending /-i/ (M: σκώπτῃ, O: σκόπτει). The hortatory and prohibitive subjunctive is attested since classical times (Schwyzer 1988, 314), so the retention of the reading of the subjunctive is justifiable in this passage.[16]

26.5. εἰ πτηνὸν λαλοῦν πολύτιμον εὑρίσκεται, τί με ἐξουθενεῖς;. The textual problem in this passage already existed in the archetype, as the modern editions of version G and of the Westermanniana indicate. Perry proposes εἰ πετεινὸν λαλεῖ, πολύτιμον εὑρίσκεται· τί με ἐξουθενεῖς; for the Westermanniana. The manuscripts of recension MORN provide the following readings: ἀπό τινων λάλων πολύτιμον εὑρίσκεται. Τί με ἐξουθενεῖς; (M); εἰ πτηνὸν λαλοῦν, πολύτιμον εὑρίσκεται, τι ἐμὲ ἐξουθενεῖς (O); and the Latin translation "gallus qui cantor est valde et carus; in me autem forsitan inve-

---

16. See Blass and Debrunner 1990, §364; Jannaris 1897.

nies hoc" (Lolliniana). Thus, the word πτηνόν (LSJ, s.v.) appears in MOR,[17] and the reading of MS O (εἰ πτηνὸν λαλοῦν πολύτιμον εὑρίσκεται) seems to be representative of the MOR recension. In this passage, the participle is attributive, and the conditional clause (εἰ πτηνὸν λαλοῦν πολύτιμον εὑρίσκεται) has, as an apodosis, the direct question τί με ἐξουθενεῖς;

26.9–10. Ἐὰν γὰρ ᾖς καλόδουλος, οὐ δραπετεύσω· ἐὰν δὲ κακόδουλος καὶ φθορὰν ἐργάζῃ. The omission of the phrase καλόδουλος, οὐ δραπετεύσω· ἐὰν δὲ in MS M is clearly due to haplography during the copying of MS M or one of its ancestors.

26.10. καὶ φθορὰν ἐργάζῃ. It is important that MS O has the reading παρεργάζει instead of ἐργάζῃ. However, the word παρεργάζομαι seems to occur only in Byzantine times (*LBG*, s.v.).

Chapter 27

27.2. σκῶψαί μου πάρει τὴν ἐμπορίαν; In the question of the merchant, "Are you here to mock my business," MSS MO have the readings παρῇ (M) and παρεῖς (O). Perry suggests πάρει with MSS Wλ and Papathomopoulos the reading of MS S πάρεις. Alternatively, it would be possible to keep the reading of MS O, correcting the /ei/ to /ē/: παρῇς (cf. BP), *i.e.* as a second person subjunctive of the verb πάρειμι (s.v. LSJ), functioning as a deliberative subjunctive. The reading of MS O would then be a common error of itacism.

27.9 σιωπῶσιν. MS M adds σκοπῶσι καὶ before σιωπῶσιν. Since only MS M in the Westermanniana has this reading, which is problematic from both a morphological and a semantic aspect, it would be better to consider it as not pertaining to the MORN recension.

Chapter 28

28.7. ἐξουσιαστὴς ὤν. MSS MO (and W of the Westermanniana) have this phrase; the Lolliniana also has "(Tu, qui es dominus) et potestatem habes." Consequently, even though it could be viewed as a gloss from a

---

17. On πετεινὸν–πτηνόν, see Thomas Magister, *Ecl. nom.*, letter pi 272.6: πτηνὸν λέγε· τὸ δὲ πετεινὸν ἀδόκιμον.

time before the archetype of the MORN recension,[18] the agreement of all three manuscripts demonstrates that the phrase ἐξουσιαστὴς ὤν existed in the archetype of MORN.

28.8. ταχῦναι. The reading of M ταχεῖναι may be regarded as the usual error of iotacism. MS W has the correct form ταχῦναι (O: ταχύνη), which is accepted by both editors (Perry, Papathomopoulos).

Chapter 29

29.3. ἐγκώμιόν τι γελοίου. In this passage all manuscripts (including those of Westermanniana) have a genitive (γελοίου). Perry also keeps a genitive in his Westermanniana edition, expressing doubts in the *apparatus criticus* (*malim* γελοῖον). Papathomopoulos, quoting Perry in his apparatus (γελοῖον Perry), inserts an accusative in the text of MORN. Since all manuscripts have a genitive and the meaning ("encomium of a ridiculous fellow") is acceptable (LSJ, *DGE*, s.v.), there is no reason to correct the unanimous reading.

29.6. ὑπὸ σῶν δουλεύομαι παιδαρισκαρίων. In this passage both manuscripts of the MORN recension transmit forms otherwise unattested in lexica: MS M has the reading παιδαρισκαρίων (and not παιδισκαρίων, as Papathomopoulos read) and MS O φωνισκαρίων (and not ψωνισκαρίων, as Papathomopoulos read). Neither form is found in a TLG search. Consequently, one may either adopt in the text the otherwise-unattested form παιδαρισκαρίων as a *hapax*, with a note in the *apparatus criticus* "παιδισκαρίων corr. Perry, Papath. fort. recte," or insert in the text the form παιδισκαρίων, a correction suggested by Perry and Papathomopoulos (see Karla 2019b, 174).

Chapter 30

30.3. τὰ κενά σου εἰς τὴν ὄψιν σοι. This is the reading of MS M and of MSS λW. Instead of this, MS O has κενή σοι ἡ χαρά, Lolliniana omits it entirely, and this is also the case with the BPThSA recension and MS G. The mean-

---

18. Because of the possibility of its being a gloss, perhaps as synonym to δεσπότης ὤν, both editors (Perry and Papathomopoulos) athetized it.

ing of the adjective κενός (see LSJ, Bauer 1988, Lampe 1976, s.v.) as "empty, destitute, bereft" does not fit the context of the passage in M. It is more appropriate to the context of MS O ("your joy is vain"). However, taking into consideration that the word κενόω has already in Galen the meaning "evacuate, defecate" (see Demetrakos 1936–1952, s.v. "κενόω"), that the word "κενώματα" (see LSJ, s.v. "κενόω," 3) also has the meaning of "evacuations, *excrement*" in Stobaeus, *Ecl.* 4.37.27, and that the words κενώνω and κένωση in Modern Greek mean the same thing as in Stobaeus (see Babiniotes 2012, s.v.), it is possible that the slave's utterance τὰ κενά σου εἰς τὴν ὄψιν σοι is equivalent to the common Modern Greek abusive expression σκατά στα μούτρα σου (see Babiniotes 2012, s.v. "σκατό," 1γ). In the dialogues between female slaves, as in the dialogue between them and Aesop, the language in the Life is in the "plain style" in order to transmit the vividness of spoken exchange (see the double meaning of the word κέρκος in G, ch. 30 with a sexual allusion, or the phrase μή μοι κολλῶ below). Moreover, the omission of this phrase from the Latin Lolliniana indicates that the translator, who had in front of him a Greek text that included it, chose to omit it because of its scatological content. This tendency can also be observed, for example, in chapter 67 (the etiological story about people looking at their own excrement), which the Latin translator also left out (see introduction on pp. 27 and 33).

30.8. καὶ ἀρραβωνήσομαι αὐτόν. It is important that almost all manuscripts of the Westermanniana give the form ἀρραβωνήσομαι from the assumed verb ἀρραβωνέομαι, which is attested only in the Life, according to *DGE* (s.v.).[19] The word here may have the meaning of "make a deposit" (see LSJ, s.v. "ἀρραβών").[20] However, it may also mean "become engaged to him," and in fact this sense fits the context much better, since just previously in the same chapter the female slaves claimed that «'Εμοὶ γὰρ εἰς ὕπνους τοῦτον συνέθετο.» Ἄλλη δὲ ἔφη «ἐγὼ ἐν ὀνείροις ἐνυμφευόμην.» Consequently, this passage of the Life (MORN recension) may constitute the earliest attestation of the words ἀρραβωνέομαι/ἀρραβών in their modern sense of "to be engaged/engagement." Another early attestation of this sense is to be found in Herodian (second century CE), where the follow-

---

19. Only MS B has the phrase ἀρραβῶνα λήψομαι.
20. See the translation of Papathomopoulos "καὶ θὰ τὸν καπαρώσω" (make a deposit on him).

ing definition is given: "μνηστεία, ὁ ἀρραβών· μνήστωρ· μνηστή, ἐπὶ τῆς γυναικός" (*Part.* 86.14).²¹

30.11. ἀβάσκαντα. On this form, see *DGE*, s.v. I (neuter plural as adverb ἀβάσκαντα, without the curse of the evil eye; see also y. Ber. 9.13c).

30.14–15. καὶ μή μοι κολλῶ. The phrase is attested in MS M (in G and W as well); MS O has the reading ἀκολύτως. The verb κολλῶ has the meaning of "join together" (see LSJ s.v. κολλάω, etc.). However, in this context it seems to have a similar sense to the Modern Greek phrase (μη μου κολλάς) "get off my case, leave me alone," which usually expresses displeasure (see Babiniotes 2012, s.v. κολλώ 2).

Chapter 31

31.7–8. «ἵνα <μὴ> εἰς τὴν ὁδὸν περιπατῶν οὐρήσω τοιαῦτά μοι ἔφης ῥήματα». MS M has the reading ἵνα εἰς τὴν ὁδὸν περιπατῶν οὐρήσω, which can hardly be correct. The opposite would have been expected in this context: "so that I would *not* pee while walking on the road." Therefore, it seems necessary to accept the Westermann's correction ἵνα μή, which is also accepted by Perry. However, it is notable that the same mistake (omission of μή) appears also in G, which means that probably this error already existed in the archetype. MS O (like MSS SB) has a participial construction: ἵνα τί εἰς τὴν ὁδὸν περιπατοῦντι καὶ οὐροῦντι, a reading adopted by Papathomopoulos (1999a) in his edition.

31.11. ἀνακέκραγε. This is the reading of MS M. MS O (as well as λ) has ἀνέκραγεν instead, adopted by Perry and Papathomopoulos for the edition of Westermanniana and MORNLo, respectively. The form ἀνέκραγεν is in use in classical times (see LSJ, s.v. "ἀνακράζω"). The past perfect form, however, is frequently attested in the postclassical period (see TLG). ἀνακέκραγε(ν) also occurs in chapter 27 (adopted by both the above-mentioned editors), as well as in two Aesopic fables (128 aliter, 319 aliter, ed. Chambry).

---

21. This conclusion relies on a textual search of TLG. A search of the papyri corpus could prove illuminating as to the earliest attestations of this meaning of the word.

Commentary 181

Chapter 32

32.5. ὅτε ἔλεγες. MS O reads ὅτε, whereas MS M has ὅτι. Since /i/ in place of /e/ is a common scribal error and ὅτε is more appropriate to the meaning, it is best to adopt here the reading of O.

Chapter 34

34.5. ἀσπαράγγους. The lemma τὸ ἀσπάραγγον appears in *LBG*; LSJ and *DGE* have ἀσφάραγος, with a reference in *DGE* to the variant ἀσπάρ-.

34.6. ἀρτύματα. Before the word ἀρτύματα, Papathomopoulos adds the word λοιπά, apparently because it occurs in G. However, there is no reason to correct the reading of the manuscripts, since the word means "condiment" (see LSJ, s.v.); ἀρτύματα are in this case herbs (like dill, parsley, spearmint, etc.) that add taste to food.[22] Before ἀρτύματα the text mentions ἀσπαράγγους, σεῦτλα, and μαλάχας (asparagus, beets, mallow), vegetables for cooking but not specifically for adding flavor to food (like ἀρτύματα).

Chapter 35

35.1. κύριε. It is remarkable that MS O has κύριε (as do all manuscripts of the Westermanniana) and MS M the reading κῦρι, which is the vocative of κῦρις (not listed in lexica; see Gignac 1976, 302). The form κῦρι was perhaps a feature of oral speech before the sixth century CE, as papyri attest (for example P.Apoll. 18.1; P.Apoll. 36.2; P.Col. 11300.1).[23] The question is whether the reading κῦρι is that of MORN or of a Byzantine scribe (like Libadenos). An argument in favor of the first possibility is the language used by the gardener, even though his style is not "plain," except for some words such as αὐτοματί and οὐαί. He is depicted as someone who has philosophical concerns and who is trying to speak in a "grand" linguistic style. However, if the author/redactor wished to parody this attempt, lexical fea-

---

22. Compare πέπερι καὶ ὀρίγανον καὶ θρύμβον καὶ βλισκούνην καὶ σίνηπι εὔζωμον, σέλινα, πετροσέλινα, ῥεφάνια, ἡδύοσμον, πεντάρτυμα, ἄνηθον, κύμινον, ἄνισσον, δαυκία, πήγανον· ταῦτα πάντα ἀρτύματα ἔχει τῶν εἰρημένων τροφῶν (Anonymi Medici, *De alimentis* 2.61–65 [Ideler 1963, 2:257–81]).

23. Search in https://papyri.info. According to Gignac (1981, 27), the vocative κῦρι is attested in papyri since the second century CE.

tures of oral speech would be a good vehicle.[24] Nevertheless, given that this reading appears only in MS M and nowhere else and that the evidence of the papyri is dubious, the second option seems more likely.

35.6. διοικεῖται. The fact that MS O has the reading οἰκεῖται here and the Latin translation (Lo) the reading "est locutus" favors the conclusion that the common ancestor of OLo had οἰκεῖται. But since all manuscripts of the Westermanniana and MS G have διοικεῖται, which is more appropriate in this context, there is no reason to correct the reading of MS M. Moreover, in chapter 36 Aesop's comment on Xanthus's answer contains the same verb (in the form of the participle διοικούμενα).

Chapter 37

37.2–3. αἰνίγματα διαλύειν. MS M has the reading διαλαλεῖν instead of διαλύειν (MS O). MS B also has διαλαλεῖν in this passage, with a sense that could potentially fit the context (see LSJ, s.v. II; *DGE*, s.v. 2). However, it seems to be a paleographical error, since in what follows the only verb used within the context of this story is διαλύω.

37.10. εὑρίσκει μητρυιά. It is interesting to note μητρ(ε)ία as an alternative reading of the manuscripts for the word μητρυιά. The form μητρία is attested since the twelfth century (see *LBG*, s.v.)

Chapter 40

40.3. δυσωδίας ληφθείς. MS O has δυσωδία, and both Perry and Papathomopoulos accepted this reading as dative. However, since all the other manuscripts of the Westermanniana, like MS M, have the genitive and verbs denoting "smelling of" govern the genitive (Blass and Debrunner 1990, §174), just like verbs with the meaning "to touch, to take hold of" (1990, §170), there is no reason to adopt the dative, which is attested in only one manuscript.

---

24. In ch. 37, Xanthus calls the gardener κομψότατε, a word that could allude to his "skillful" linguistic technique with a slight irony. See LSJ, s.v. "κομψός," 2: "but in Pl. and Arist., usu. clever, esp. skilful in technique, with at most a slight irony (κομψοὺς Πλάτων οὐ τοὺς πανούργους, ἀλλὰ τοὺς βελτίστους Moer.p.206 P.)"

Chapter 41

41.2. Δὸς φαγώμεθα. The word φαγώμεθα seems to be a hortatory subjunctive in the first-person plural (Schwyzer 1988, 339–42; Blass and Debrunner 1990, §335, with bibliography), and for this reason Perry adds a comma after δός. In the same chapter, a few lines below (41.4), there is κόμιζε καὶ φαγώμεθα, where καί indicates the hortatory function of φαγώμεθα. However, in the first case the subjunctive may correspond to the infinitive or clause of purpose (δὸς φαγεῖν or δὸς ἵνα φαγώμεθα), as the translators—Konstan here and Papathomopoloulos in his 1999 edition—accept.[25]

41.6. φακὸν γὰρ εἶπας καὶ οὐ φακούς. In this passage MS M has εἴρηκας instead of εἶπας. Since it is the only manuscript to show this reading, it probably was not in MORN.

Chapter 42

42.2. Ὁ δὲ Αἴσωπος λαβὼν ἕψει. Only MS M has the reading ἕψησεν (aorist) instead of ἕψει (imperfect). But since Aesop's action must be progressive/durative, thus enabling Xanthus to find an opportunity to interfere, the imperfect is required (Blass and Debrunner 1990, §327). This linear *Aktionsart* differentiates the imperfect sharply from the indicative aorist (1990, §324, with references), and this is one of the rare instances where imperfect and aorist appear to be interchanged (on this, see Mayser 1926, 137; Horrocks 2010, 174).

42.6. ἐνέδρα. It is strange that both manuscripts (MO) have the reading ἔνεδρα, like MS L of the Westermanniana. The scribe of MS W has corrected the reading ἔνεδρον, adding an "α super -ον" (Perry 1952, 156). There are two possibilities: either the form ἔνεδρα was common (at least in everyday speech), even though nowhere attested in the sources, or it was derived from ἔνεδρον by mistake.

42.6. τὸ περίαυλον. Only MS M has the masculine accusative form τὸν περίαυλον. The manuscripts of the Westermanniana (WBPV) have neuter τὸ περίαυλον and MS O (like L, F) the diminutive form τὸ περιαύλιον.

---

25. "Give us some to eat" (Konstan); "δῶσε μας νὰ φᾶμε" (Papathomopoulos).

According to LSJSup (s.v. "περίαυλον"), the form ὁ περίαυλος is attested in *Etymologicum Magnum*, and the sources (Vilinskij 1911, 126,31) for the masculine form in *LBG* (s.v. "περίαυλος ὁ") are also later. The neuter form is attested only in the first centuries CE (see LSJ, s.v.). It is possible that the masculine form is later and that it is due to a Byzantine scribe (perhaps Libadenos himself); otherwise, the reading of MS M constitutes the earliest evidence for the masculine form of the word περίαυλος.

Chapter 43

43.7. διηκόνησά σοι. Only MS M omits ἄν. The omission of irrealis ἄν may be justified, because it is observed already in MS G (and in other manuscripts) of the Life as well as in authors of the fifth/sixth century, such as Malalas (Karla 2001, 110).

Chapter 48[26]

48.1. ἑλκόμενον εἰς θυσίαν. This is the reading of MS O, whereas MS M has εἰς θυσίαν ἐρχόμενον. All manuscripts of the Westermanniana have ἑλκόμενον, and the Latin translation also has *portatur* (Lo). Moreover, a few lines below all manuscripts have ἑλκόμενον. Consequently, it is clear that the reading of M is a paleographic error, a *lectio facilior*.

48.8. ἀνέλυσαν ἐκ τοῦ δείπνου. In contrast to MS O, MS M omits the preposition ἐκ, similarly to MS W. Even though the verb ἀναλύω with genitive (see *DGE*, s.v. "ἀναλύω," I.2) is used with the meaning of "unloose, set free" (see LSJ, s.v. "ἀναλύω," B.2), it seems that in postclassical times ἀναλύω with a preposition (ἀπό, ἐκ, etc.) was much more common.[27]

Chapter 50

50.1. Ἐλθόντος δὲ αὐτοῦ. Instead of a *genitivus absolutus*, MS M has the reading ἐλθόντι δὲ αὐτῷ, which is not found in other manuscripts of the

---

26. In MS M of this chapter there are some readings that appear only in it.

27. According to a search in the TLG. See also Sophocles 1900, s.v. "ἀναλύω," 3, but with prepositions. Fitzgerald (pers. comm.) has observed that Luke 12:36 may be held as an instance of ἀναλύω with the preposition ἐκ: "depart/return from the wedding banquet.

Westermanniana. This case alternation in a participial construction is frequent since classical times (see Kühner, Blass, and Gerth 1904, §§493–96) and becomes even more common in the Koine period, but the *genitivus absolutus* seems to be here the MORN-reading.

50.2. οὐδὲν ἔλαβε. At this point, Xanthus has realized that the cause of the misunderstanding with his wife is Aesop, and therefore he summons him in order to interrogate him. There follows a dialogue with short questions and answers between Xanthus and Aesop, with occasional interpolations by Xanthus's wife, as in the following passage: Xanthus asked Aesop: "To whom did you give the pieces?" Aesop replied, "To the female who is devoted to you." Xanthus said, "She got nothing," and his wife declared, "I for one got nothing." MS M (like MSS λSW) has the reading οὐδὲν ἔλαβε, whereas MS O (the MSS BP) has the second-person singular (οὐδὲν ἔλαβες). Paleographically the two readings are quite close, and an interchange between them is easy. However, there is a narratological differentiation. In the first case (οὐδὲν ἔλαβε) Xanthus is sure that his wife got nothing, and his wife thought it necessary to declare, "I for one got nothing," interrupting almost rudely the dialogue between Xanthus and Aesop. In the second case (οὐδὲν ἔλαβες) we must add a question mark and imagine that Xanthus addressed his wife. In my opinion, in the first version the exchange is more lively and comic, whereas in the second Xanthus simply confirms information that he already had. The readings of the manuscripts following directly after this passage also differ, again not accidentally. Consistent with the first version, MS M has Καὶ ἡ γυνὴ ἐφώνησεν to emphasize her exasperation,[28] whereas MS O has Καὶ ἡ γυνὴ φησί, which is normal for a simple reply.[29]

50.4. αὕτη σου εὐνοεῖ. Instead of the genitive σου, which is the reading of MS M (like WPSA), MS O (like λ) has a dative, which is to be expected with the verb εὐνοέω in classical times (see LSJ, s.v.). But given that the genitive instead of the dative occurs often in Koine and in the text of the *Life*,[30] the reading of MS M should be preserved.

---

28. See LSJ, s.v. "φωνέω," 1: "(prop. of men, *speak loud*...) and 3 (as law term, *affirm, testify* in court...)."

29. Papathomopoulos in his edition of MORN kept the reading of MS M (Καὶ ἡ γυνὴ ἐφώνησεν), even though he preferred the reading of MS O (οὐδὲν ἔλαβες;).

30. See also in BPThSA (Karla 2001, 88–89).

50.4–5. ὁ δέ· «ἀλλὰ τίς, δραπέτα;». The omission of the phrase ὁ δέ by MS M is justifiable, if it is viewed as enhancing the vividness of the dialogue. However, because the change of speaker is usually signaled in the text for reasons of clarity, perhaps ὁ δέ should be added here.

Chapter 50a

This chapter is attested only by MS M (as in the recension BPThSA); MSS OLo (like version G) do not include this story. Consequently, the edition of this chapter for the MORN version can be based only on MS M. However, it must be noted that the reading of this manuscript was not easy even *in loco*, because of damage due to the passage of time. In comparison with the reports of this manuscript by Perry and Papathomopoulos, as can be seen from the *apparatus criticus*, the legibility of M has in the meantime clearly deteriorated.

Chapter 51

51.4. τὸ μάκελλον. The word appears in the manuscripts either as masculine or neuter, as indicated in LSJ (s.v.).

51.7. σὺν ὀξογάρῳ. The manuscripts of the MORN recension (in this case M and O), and the Westermanniana in general, display an interchange between the forms ὀξύγαρον and ὀξόγαρον (see LSJ, s.v. "ὀξύγαρον").

51.9. φιλολογία εἰσπέμπεται. This phrase appears in MS M; MS O has φιλοσοφία ἐκπέμπεται, which is accepted by Perry and Papathomopoulos. However, it seems that the latter is the reading exclusively of MS O, since ἐκπέμπεται is found only in O; φιλολογία occurs in MSS MWV and εἰσπέμπεται in MλW, according to Perry's *apparatus criticus*. The meaning of εἰσπέμπω "send, instruct" (LSJ, s.v.) is more adequate in this context.

Chapter 52

52.4. ἠκόνηται. The reading of MS O, εἰκόνηται (see LSJ, s.v. "εἰκονίζω," 3), is interesting, as it reveals the meaning of the passage: the tongue as a symbol is the depiction of fire.[31]

52.4. Τὸ γὰρ ἁλυκόν. This is a correction inserted from version G by Perry. The otherwise-unattested form ἀλυκτὸν is found in MS M and the reading ἑλικτὸν in MS O (as Wλ); the meaning of ἑλικτός (see LSJ, s.v.), however, is not suitable in the context.

52.5. συγκέκραται. This is again a correction from version G suggested by Perry. MS M has συγκροτεῖ and MS O συγκρᾶται. The reading of MS M is not totally unacceptable, since the metaphorical meaning "weld together" (see LSJ, s.v. "συγκροτέω," II.2) is appropriate. However, the sentence as it stands in MS M (Τὸ γὰρ ἀλυκ[τ]ὸν τῷ δριμεῖ συγκροτεῖ καὶ τῷ δάκνοντι ἐπειδὰν ἑνωθῇ) is syntactically and semantically problematic. Its meaning would be, "that which is salty is welded together with that which is sour and that which is spicy,[32] after being merged together," where the dependent clause (ἐπειδὰν ἑνωθῇ) repeats tautologically the sense of the verb συγκροτεῖ.

52.11. τι ἕτερον. The reading of MS O ἄλλο τίποτε is worth noting, as it is in fact identical with the corresponding Modern Greek phrase (see Babiniotes, s.v. "τίποτε/-α [η]").

Chapter 53

53.5–6. καὶ πάλιν καταβάλλονται. Only MS M has the reading πόλεις instead of πάλιν, probably a paleographical mistake. MS O and all other manuscripts of the Westermanniana have πάλιν. This reading is confirmed by Lo: *regitur civitas et coronatur, et pro lingua iterum traditur*.

---

31. Fitzgerald (pers. comm.) suggests comparing Acts 2:3 and its "tongues as of fire" and Jas 3:6: "The tongue is a fire."

32. Δάκνον has here the meaning "spicy" (see *DGE*, s.v. "δάκνω," I.2, with reference to the Life as the unique source with this sense).

Chapter 54

54.6. γλώσσας ἐπαγοράσας. The word ἐπαγοράζω with the meaning "to buy" is well attested (see Montanari, s.v.; *LBG*, s.v., with reference among others to the Aesopic fable 23 II 2, ed. Hausrath 1959).

Chapter 55

55.2–3. διὰ γὰρ ταύτης πολλοὶ ἀπόλλωντο (sic) καὶ εἰς πενίαν ἐσχάτην κατήντησαν (because of it many were destroyed and became destitute). MS O adds this sentence after καὶ τί ἐστι χεῖρον γλώσσης. It is also found in the BPThSA recension instead of διὰ γὰρ γλώσσης ἔχθραι, διαβολαί, μέμψεις, ἔριδες, φθόνοι, ζηλοτυπίαι, ἀφανισμοὶ πόλεων and in other manuscripts of the Westermanniana (Wλ).[33] However, this sentence is not found either in MS G or in Lo or M, so it cannot have been part of the MORN recension.

55.5–6. τούτῳ ἐὰν πρόσσχῃς, εἰς μανίαν σε περιτρέψει. This passage seems to be defective in the MORN tradition. It is a warning addressed to Xanthus by one of his guests after the dinner in the episode of the tongues. MS M has the reading προσχῇς (from the verb προέχω) and MS O the reading (τοῦτο) προσέχει. The correction πρόσσχῃς suggested by Perry on the basis of MS λ is plausible; however, Papathomopoulos's correction, μὴ πρόσσχῃς, from MS B, could also be acceptable in this context. Version G has τούτῳ ἐὰν πρόσσχῃς, which agrees with Perry's correction. However, the English and the Italian translations of G (by Wills and Ferrari, respectively) each give a different meaning. The first translates, "if you pay attention to him (he will soon drive you crazy)," and the second, "if you give him a free hand."[34] The latter meaning of the verb προσέχω is perhaps more appropriate in the context, but it does not seem to be recorded in the lexica, while the former is possible but far from perfect. In my opinion, there are two further possibilities: on the one hand, it can be viewed either as a warning (similar to Aristophanes, *Nub.* 1122)

---

33. On the encomium on the tongue in ch. 53 and the censure of the tongue in ch. 55, John Fitzgerald (pers. comm.) has suggested to see Jas 3:1–12, where both the positive and the negative aspects of the tongue are given.

34. Ferrari 1997, 153: "… se continui a dargli corda, presto ti condurrà alla follia."

in the sense of "let him take heed" (see LSJ, s.v. "προσέχω," 3), which is, however, problematic within a conditional clause, while Papathomopoulos's correction with μή seems in this case suitable; on the other hand, one may preserve the reading τοῦτο of G and O and in this case προσέχω means "continue" (see LSJ, s.v. "προσέχω," 5). The reading of MS O, τοῦτο ἐὰν προσέχῃ, εἰς μανίαν περιτρέπει ("if it continues, it drives you mad"), makes sense, even though the fifteen-syllable meter might indicate a late date for the O reading.

Chapter 56

56.4. τῶν ἰδίων οὐ μνημονεύοντες. This reading is given by MS M. The verb μνημονεύω can be construed with the accusative or the genitive (see LSJ, s.v. "μνημονεύω," 1), but the genitive object seems to be later.

Chapter 57

57.6. After πυλῶνος, MS O adds: μὴ περιεργασάμενος διὰ ποίαν αἰτίαν κέκληκε ("he did not express any curiosity as to why he was being invited"). In line 9, after φίλων, MS O adds: σὺν τοῖς ὑποδήμασι καὶ τῷ πηλῷ · ὁ δὲ Ξάνθος, «τίς ἐστιν οὗτος;» Αἴσωπός φησι· «ἄνθρωπος ἀπερίεργος» ("with his muddy boots on and Xanthus asked, 'Who is this fellow?' Aesop replied, 'A nonmeddler'"). As Perry already observed, both readings seem to derive from chapter 61. They are absent from all other manuscripts of the Westermanniana (M and Lo included).

Chapter 58

58.1. (οἰνόμελι) πιεῖν. The infinitive πιεῖν is transmitted only by MS M. Considering the context, it is not necessary; moreover, it is not found in any other manuscript of the Westermanniana.

58.2. ἡμεῖς οἱ φίλοι σου. The syntax whereby a noun is followed by the weak form of the genitive of the possessive pronoun (σου) is a noteworthy innovative feature.

58.3. Καὶ πῶς ἐφαίνετο ἀπερίεργος;. All manuscripts (MO and the other manuscripts of the Westermanniana) have this phrase. Both Perry and Papathomopoulos take Xanthus's ἔχω ἅπαξ as an independent clause and delete the /a/ of the word ἀπερίεργος.³⁵ In his edition of Lolliniana, Perry gives the following text: "Ecce, modo videam de quali re [in]obedientem invenisti" ("There now, let me see about what kind of thing you found him disobedient"), and it is significant that this phrase is linked to Xanthus's response. MS G has a lacuna in this episode. One might consider this phrase as a gloss, a comment *in margine* that was introduced in the text of MORN, or a rhetorical or even an ironical question by Xanthus in order to tease Aesop. In the last case, it should be translated as "And how did he measure up as a nonmeddler?" (Konstan).

58.4. Ξάνθος ἐπαφορμιζόμενος. The participle ἐπαφορμιζόμενος, which is the reading of all manuscripts of Westermanniana, is attested only in the Life, according to standard lexica. It is listed in the LSJ Sup (s.v. "ἐπαφορμίζομαι") with unique reference to this passage of the Life (translated as "look for a pretext"). The same word is also listed in *LBG* with references to later sources (eighth century).

58.5–6. οὔτε ὁ ζωμὸς σύγχυλος. The word σύγχυλος is a correction from Wλ suggested by Perry and adopted by Papathomopoulos. MS M has the reading σύγχειλος and MS O σύχολος. The reading σύγχυλος is quite close to both manuscripts readings. The reading of M is a common iotacism error, and the reading of MS O can be explained as a paleographical error. However, it must be noted that the word σύγχυλος is listed only in *LBG* with reference to the Life (the Westermanniana edition by Perry, ch. 58); *LBG* refers to Boned Colera and Rodríguez Somolinos 1998 and to the verb συγχυλόομαι in LSJ. Apparently, the meaning is "to be converted into chyle" (LSJ, s.vv. "συγχυλόομαι," "χυλός," "χυλόω").³⁶

58.8. Εἶτα εἰσφέρεται πλακοῦς πολυσήσαμος. MS M (and W) reads πολυσήσαμος, while MS O has the corrupt reading πολυσισάμους. The word πολυσήσαμος is a *hapax* and is recorded only in the LSJ Sup (translated

---

35. Both editors have καί πως ἐφαίνετο [ἀ]περίεργος. The comma at the end of this sentence in Papathomopoulos' edition is probably a typo.

36. A search in the TLG came up with only two results, one in Life and the other in Dioscorides, *Eup.* 2.141 (quoted in LSJ, s.v. "συγχυλόομαι"): συκῆς φύλλα λεῖα, χαμαίπιτυς καλῶς ποιεῖ, ὀρίγανος ὀνῖτις, πολύκνημον σὺν οἴνῳ, ὄρνιθος καθηψημένης συγχυλωθείσης ζωμός, κρέως λιπαροῦ ὁμοίως.

as "containing plenty of sesame") with unique reference to this passage of the Life.

In general, it is interesting to note that there are several uniquely attested words in this chapter.

Chapter 59

59.2. τῇ μὲν θέᾳ ἄγροικον. Instead of ἄγροικον, MS M has the reading ἄγριον (see LSJ, s.v. "ἄγριος," I; *DGE*, s.v. "ἄγριος," II.1), which seems to be found only in this manuscript. Nowhere in the following passages does MS M have the reading ἄγριον again. Like all the other manuscripts, it employs the word ἄγροικος.

59.3. ὀνάριον ἐλαύνοντα. All manuscripts that transmit the story of the nonmeddler (MλW and G) have ἐλαύνοντα, except MS O, which has the reading ἐπικαθήμενον. In version G a few lines later one finds ὁ ἄγροικος τῷ ὀναρίῳ ἐπικαθήμενος, which perhaps justifies the reading of MS O. However, in the specific context the reading ἐλαύνοντα is more appropriate both syntactically and semantically, since just below the same manuscript (O) reads ἱστάμενον (καὶ πρὸς τὸ ὀνάριον λαλοῦντα), like all other manuscripts. It must be noted that Perry (followed by Papathomopoulos) corrected the reading ἱστάμενον with ὑπεσταλμένον from version G and renders the passage: καὶ τῆς λεωφόρου ὁδοῦ ἐκνενευκότα καὶ τὴν τῶν πολλῶν ἀπάντησιν ὑπεσταλμένον καὶ πρὸς τὸ ὀνάριον λαλοῦντα ("he made a detour away from the high road in order to avoid meeting people, and he said to the donkey"). Even though the meaning is satisfactory, I do not believe that it represents the MORN version. The reading of all manuscripts of the Westermanniana ἱστάμενον can be preserved, if we consider that the participle ἐκνενευκότα has two objects, one in the genitive and one with the preposition πρός plus the accusative (see LSJ, s.v. "ἐκνεύω," II).

Chapter 61

61.11. φησὶ πρὸς ἑαυτόν. After φησί, MS O adds πρὸς ἑαυτόν, and Lo also has "et ait intra se." Perhaps the addition is necessary for the clarification of the meaning. What the country-fellow utters at this point is an esoteric monologue. There are many instances of monologues in the Life, such as those at chapters 10, 44, 49, 51, 57, 60, 62, 64, 77a, and 83–85.

61.11. πάντως τιμῆσαί με θέλει. After this phrase, MS O adds καὶ διὰ τοῦτο αὐτοχείρως νίπτει μου τοὺς πόδας ("this is why she washes my feet with her own hands"). MSS Lo and M omit it; consequently, one can suppose that the MORN recension did not include the supplementary phrase found in MS O.

Chapter 62

62.3. Ἀριστούντων. Perry suggested the corrected form ἀριστώντων, which Papathomopoulos also accepts. However, since all manuscripts of the Westermanniana have the same reading, and taking into consideration that in the postclassical period the interchange of the suffixes -άω and -έω is commonly found in papyri, in inscriptions, and in literature as well,[37] we should keep the reading ἀριστούντων.

62.3. παρετέθη ἰχθύς. In the Westermanniana version, only MS O has the reading ἰχθύων λοπὰς παρετέθη ("plate of fish was served"). Since version G and P.Oxy. 2083 also have this reading (λοπὰς ἰχθύων), Perry and Papathomopoulos edit the Westermanniana and MORN correspondingly in the same way. However, since Lo has "pisces," like all other manuscripts of the Westermanniana, we may suppose that the MORN version originally had the reading ἰχθύς and not ἰχθύων λοπάς.

Chapter 63

63.7. ὡς τὸ δοκεῖν καυθῆναι. Instead of ὡς τό, MS O has ὥστε. But since other manuscripts of the Westermanniana (LV) have the same reading as MS M (ὡς τό) and the use of ὡς as a conjunction "expressing consequence, like ὥστε," has been established since classical times (see LSJ, s.v. "ὡς," B.III.1),[38] we may accept the reading of MS M as representative of the MORN recension.

---

37. Moulton 1904, 110; Gignac 1981, 363–64; Dieterich 1898, 228–31; Jannaris 1897, §850b; Helbing 1928, 111–12; Wyss 1942, 84–87. See also the same interchange in version G (Tallmadge 1938, 31; Hostetter 1955, 47–51; Stamoulakis 2016, 208–9) and in BPThSA (Karla 2001, 78–79).

38. See also Blass and Debrunner 1990, §391.1; Jannaris 1897, §1757; Bartolo 2020.

Commentary 193

Chapter 64

64.1–2. τί οὗτος θυμοῦται. The reading of MS M, θαμβεῖται, does not produce a satisfactory meaning (see LSJ, s.v. "θαμβόομαι": "to be terrified") in this context. Lo has "tanto furore est repletus" ("he has filled with so much rage").

Chapter 65

65.2. ἐὰν οὐ πολυοχλῇ. This is the reading of MS M (and of MSS LFW). MS O has the *lectio facilior* ἐὰν οὐ πολλοὶ ὄχλοι (similarly to recension BPThSA). Papathomopoulos suggests the correction "ἐὰν οὐ πολυοχλῆται." However, it is not necessary to change the active voice to middle, since the active form of the verb πολυοχλέω occurs several times in the TLG (see for example Dionysius Halicarn. *Hist. et Rhet. Antiquit. Roman.* 5.6.4.2; Olympiodorus Diac. *Commentarii in Jeremiam* vol. 93 (p. 661.15); John Chrysostom *in Joannem* vol. 59, p. 167, 7).

65.6–7. Μὴ προσδοκῶν γὰρ ὑπηντηκέναι σοι. The infinitive ὑπηντηκέναι is the reading of MS M, whereas MS O (like LV) has a participle (ὑπηντηκώς). Since the construction of the verb προσδοκάω with a perfect infinitive is well attested (LSJ s.v. "προσδοκάω," 2), the reading of MS M can be retained.

65.7–8. εἰς τὸ εὐαπολόγητον. The reading of MS M, ἐπὶ τῷ εὐαπολογήτῳ, may be also adopted, even if not supported by any other manuscript.

Chapter 66

66.2. πρὸς τὸ μέσον τῆς εἰσόδου. MS O has the reading ὁδοῦ instead of εἰσόδου (MS M). MS Lo has "in medio ianue," which indicates that εἰσόδου is the reading of the MORN recension.

66.3. κατηρᾶτο τὸν τεθεικότα. The reading τὸν τεθεικότα is a correction by Perry from MS G, also accepted by Papathomopoulos. MS M has τῶν τεθεικότων, which is not suitable in the context (only one agent was necessary in order to move the stone) nor in respect to syntax (the verb καταράομαι does not govern the genitive). The corresponding reading of MS O ὥστε πάντας σχεδὸν τοὺς εἰσερχομένους καὶ ἐξερχομένους ἐπὶ τὸν λίθον προσκόπτοντας καὶ οὐδεὶς τήλοθεν τοῦτον ῥίξας ("so almost all of those who went in or out stumbled on the rock, but no one kicked it away") seems to be an interpolation of the scribe, since it is absent from all other manuscripts and since such interpolations belong to the *usus scribendi* of the specific scribe, who often introduces words or phrases of his own.[39]

Chapter 67

67.6. καθεζόμενος. Papathomopoulos's correction ἐπιλαθόμενος (from MS G) instead of καθεζόμενος is not necessary, since all manuscripts of the Westermanniana have the reading καθεζόμενος, which produces a satisfactory sense.

Chapter 68

68.4–5. δέσποτα, Διόνυσος <εὑρὼν> τὸ οἰνικὸν πόμα †τρεῖς κράσεις τῷ ἀνθρώπῳ διὰ πόματος χρήσασθαι εἶπεν†. Perhaps the *cruces* are not necessary, since the passage becomes meaningful with the addition of the participle εὑρὼν from G, which Perry suggested (and Papathomopoulos adopted). Here, as some lines later, Διό, δέσποτα, πιόντες καὶ εὐφρανθέντες, παραχωρήσατε […]ἐν οἷς δεδώκατε ἀπόδειξιν (68.6–7), the text seems to have been problematic in the archetype of the Westermanniana, since this passage makes no sense in all manuscripts of this version, and the meaning can be restored only by taking the phrase from MS G and adapting it in the context of the Westermanniana (Perry: τὴν τῆς ὕβρεως τοῖς νέοις· ἔχεις γὰρ ἀκροατήρια). My suggestion is that there is a lacuna in the archetype of the Westermanniana and therefore in the MORN recension.

Chapter 69

69.7–8. προσβαλόντες τοὺς δακτυλίους. This is based on the reading of MS M (προσβαλλόντες, like S), whereas MS O has προβάλλοντες (like W). Perry (followed by Papathomopoulos) suggested προβαλόντες from LV, which looks reasonable because the interchange between πρό and πρός is a common paleographical error. The same applies to the readings προεβάλου (MS M) and προσεβάλου (MS O) in chapter 70. However, since the reading

---

39. In fact, we observe the same phenomenon in the following sentence, where MS O reads: Εἷς δὲ ἐξ αὐτῶν ἐχέφρων ὢν καὶ μήπω προσκόψας λαβὼν τὸν λίθον ἑκὰς ἔβαλλε.

προσβαλόντες gives a meaning suitable for the context (see LSJ, s.v. "προσβάλλω," 2c), it may be taken as the reading of MORN.

Chapter 70

70.7. εἰ δυνατὸν ᾖ. This is the reading of MS M; MS O has εἶ (indicative) instead of ᾖ (subjunctive) in this passage, which, as a second-person singular, is syntactically problematic. The syntax of εἰ with the subjunctive (MS M) is perhaps acceptable, since it is attested in classical times, in later prose, and in the papyri.[40]

Chapter 71

71.2-3. ἅπερ παρ' οἴνῳ συνέθου. MS M has the reading παροιν (the last letter is no longer legible); MS O has παροῖνον. Perry and Papathomopoulos read παροινω. Both editors adopt the correction παροινῶν, which is analogous to the participle νήφων that follows (ταῦτα καὶ νήφων λέγε), and it is found in version G. Nevertheless, no manuscript of the Westermanniana (according to Perry's *apparatus criticus* on p. 172) has a participle in this passage as MS G does. Therefore, it is preferable to print a prepositional construction such as παρ' οἴνῳ (from MS M), which is already attested.[41]

71.4. πιγκέρνας. This is a correction from MS W, suggested by Perry and adopted by Papathomopoulos. The word πιγκέρνης is found not only in papyri (as recorded in LSJ, s.v.) but also in the Alexander Romance and in many Byzantine sources (including lexica such as the Suda, Photius, etc.), as a search in the TLG confirms. On the contrary, neither the reading of MS M πιγκερνίους nor that of MS O κέρνας is attested anywhere else.

Chapter 72

72.1. γέγονεν. This is the reading of MS M, while MS O has ἐγένετο, and the rest of the manuscripts of the Westermanniana have an aorist participle (γενόμενος).

---

40. See Blass and Debrunner 1990, § 372, 3, with many references.
41. The exact phrase occurs in Sophocles, *Oed. tyr.* 780 (see LSJ, s.v. "παρά," B.I)

72.6–7. τὸ δὲ πλῆθος τῆς πόλεως συνέδραμον. MS O has the reading συνέδραμεν instead of συνέδραμον. Because the plural can be accepted as a *constructio ad sensum* and other manuscripts of the Westermanniana have the same rhetorical figure (MS B also has συνέδραμον and MSS LV συνήχθησαν), the reading of MS M can be adopted as representative of the MORN recension.

Chapter 73

73.1. πῶς ἐθήκαμεν. The aorist transmitted by MS M is also found in MS G (ἔθηκα) at the same place in the story. Consequently, it is not necessary to adopt Perry's correction based on τεθείκαμεν of MS W, even though it is closer to the reading of MS O τεθήκαμεν.

Chapter 75

75.13–14. εἰ μὴ τὰ δέκα πληρώσῃς. MS O has a subjunctive at this place, which was corrected to an indicative by Perry (a correction adopted by Papathomopoulos). However, since the construction εἰ μή with the subjunctive is already attested (see Blass and Debrunner 1990, §376, with references and bibliography) and there are also several other passages of the text where a subjunctive is indicated instead of the indicative (see chs. 27, 70, 133) in conditional sentences, there is no reason to correct the reading of MS O in this case.

75.15. τὸ μηρόν. This is the reading of MS O. Perry corrected it to a masculine τὸν μηρόν, a form adopted also by Papathomopoulos. Perhaps the neuter can be preserved in the text. Since gender variation in the second declension is common in the period (see Blass and Debrunner 1990, §49 with many examples and bibliography) one cannot reject the reading of MS O (τὸ μηρόν, neuter instead of masculine) outright.

Chapter 76

76.1–2. κριθῆναί <με> μετὰ τῆς κυρίας μου. The pronominal object με in the accusative is a correction suggested by Perry. The omission of με from the text may be due to an error of haplography, since the following word (μετά) begins with με.

76.4–5. ἔναν λίθον βαλεῖν μοι δέκα κοκκύμηλα. Here MS O has an accusative instead of a dative (ἐνὶ λίθῳ, instrumental dative), and Perry, followed by Papathomopoulos, corrects accordingly. In the very next sentence we encounter the dative in the same construction: Βαλὼν οὖν ἐγὼ εὐστόχως ἐνὶ λίθῳ. But given that the accusative instead of the dative is usual in postclassical times,[42] the reading of MS O may be preserved, noting, however, that one would expect the dative here in the place of the accusative.

76.7. Ἐρίσασα. MS O has the reading ἐρήσασα, and Papathomopoulos's correction to ἐρίσασα is reasonable. Perry proposed ἀκούσασα from the reading of MS Lo "audiens." The verb ἐρίζω is often transitive, while the construction without an object is found in the sense of *sophistical disputations* (see LSJ, s.v. "ἐρίζω," 1). However, the Life often contains words with unusual syntax and innovative meanings. Consequently, one cannot exclude that in this case the word ἐρίσασα is construed absolutely (cf. Romanus Melodus, *Cant. dub.* 71.21.6) and has the meaning "wrangle, be furious."[43]

76.12. νωχελεύω. MS O has the reading νοχλεύω, which is not recorded in lexica or found in the TLG. Perry suggested νωχλεύω, which is also unattested. Papathomopoulos corrected to νωχελεύομαι, which has the sense of "be slothful" (see LSJ, s.v.; *LBG*, s.v.). Kriaras has an entry ενοχλεύω, 'νοχλεύω, but the meaning (for animals: harass) is totally inappropriate in the context (see Kriaras 1968–, s.v.). Moreover, even if the meaning of the word ἐνοχλέω fits this passage (LSJSup, s.v. "ἐνοχλέω"; also *LBG*, s.v. "ἐνοχλείω," "ὀχλέω"), this verb cannot be adopted, as the deletion of unstressed initial vowels is a later phenomenon not established for this period. A possible correction is νωχελεύω in the sense of "be bored," which is close to the reading of MS O (νοχλεύω) paleographically but is also unattested; another possibility would be to accept the correction of Papathomopoulos: νωχελεύομαι with the meaning "be bored."

76.13. μὴ θέλῃς, κῦρι, ἵνα σοι βάλῃ ἐξ αὐτῶν. MS O has the reading μὴ θέλῃ, κῦρι, ἵνα σοι βάλει ἐξ αὐτῶν. Perry deleted the whole phrase and inserted instead οὕτως ποιείτω, κύριε, translating the phrase of MS Lo "ita faciat, domine." Papathomopoulos suggested the correction adopted here (θέλῃς

---

42. In particular in the Life (recension BPThSA), one also finds the accusative instead of *dativus instrumentalis* (see Karla 2001, 87).

43. See Bauer s.v. "ἐρίζω," with the meaning of "quarrel."

instead of θέλῃ and βάλῃ instead of βάλει), which seems to carry the right meaning, is syntactically correct, and is close to the reading of MS O.

Chapter 77

77.1. Ὁ Ξάνθος λέγει τῷ Αἰσώπῳ «δεδῶναι ἑστῶσαί εἰσι….» The phrase δεδῶναι ἑστῶσαί εἰσι is my correction (Karla 2006). MS O (and λ[44]) has the reading δεδόνιστος εἰμί. No other manuscript of the Westermanniana (nor the Latin MS Lo) has this reading, but MS G has at this locus the reading συνεόνητος εἶ, which is meaningless in the context. Perry, taking into consideration the readings of Oλ and G, suggested the correction οἰωνιστής εἰμι for both versions (G and Westermanniana), which is, however, contradicted by chapter 85 of the Westermanniana, where Xanthus claims that "'I am not an omen interpreter or a bird augur." I have argued (Karla 2006, 86) that the reading that stood in the archetype of the Life was δεδῶναι ἑστῶσαί εἰσι, which would justify the erroneous readings in MSS OλG from a paleographic viewpoint.

77.5. ἡ μία ἀνέπτη. The ἀνεπετάσθη reading of MS M, unique to this manuscript, is correct grammatically (see LSJ and *DGE*, s.v. "ἀνίπταμαι") and also occurs in contemporary texts.

Chapter 77a

77a.11. ἀνακομβώσας. The lemma ἀνακομβόω is listed in LSJSup and in *DGE* with reference to the Life and to Geop. 10.83.1, while further quotations from Byzantine times are found in *LBG* (s.v.).

Chapter 77b

77b.5. κρούσαντος τὸν πυλῶνα. Papathomopoulos's correction <εἰς> τὸν πυλῶνα is superfluous, as the syntax of κρούω with the accusative in the meaning of "knock at the door" is well attested since classical times (see, e.g., LSJ, s.v. "κρούω," 6). On the other hand, some lines later we find εἰς τὸν πυλῶνα κρούσας and at the end of the story τῷ γὰρ πυλῶνι τῷ σῷ προσκεκρουκότων, which can be explained as variants.

---

44. λ has δεδώνιστός εἰμι Αἴσωπε.

77b.7. Οὕτως οὖν πολλοὺς <ἀπολεγουμένου>. MS M is torn in the locus of ἀπολογουμένου/ἀπολεγομένου. Perry likewise saw this (see the *apparatus criticus* at Perry 1952, 177), whereas Papathomopoulos read ἀπολογουμένου in MS M (see *apparatus criticus* of MORNLo) and suggested the correction ἀπολεγομένου. Perry preferred the reading of MS B, τοῦ Αἰσώπου πολλοὺς ἀπολογουμένου, but added the preposition <πρὸς> before πολλοὺς because the verb ἀπολογέομαι with πρός and accusative has the meaning "in reference or in answer to" (see LSJ, s.v. "ἀπολογέομαι," 1), which is appropriate here. Otherwise, the correction by Papathomopoulos, ἀπολεγομένου with the meaning of "decline" (see LSJ "ἀπολέγω," II), which the word has in later Greek, seems reasonable. However, if MS M did have the reading ἀπολογουμένου, it can be retained, either by correcting πολλοὺς to πολλοῖς (cf. MSS LV) or by keeping the accusative πολλούς, since the replacement of the dative by the accusative is common in this time. The same participle is found twice in this story: in the first passage, τοῦτον ἀκούσας καλῶς ἀπολογησάμενον (77b.10), it refers to the guest, it is without object (absolute), and it means "to answer"; in the second, οὕτως τοῦ Αἰσώπου ἀπολογηθέντος (77b.29), it refers to Aesop, it is again absolute, and it means "speak in defense, defend oneself" (see LSJ, s.v. "ἀπολογέομαι," 1).

77b.24. μορμολύκειον. It is not necessary to correct either to μορμολύκιον (Perry) or to μορμολυκεῖον (Papathomopoulos), since the orthographical variant μορμολύκειον, attested by the older codices, is found also in Byzantine works (see *LBG*, s.v. "μορμολύκειον").

77b.28. τὸν σαφῶς ἀνταποκριθέντα μοι. The reading of MS M (and also of W), σαφῶς, is not completely inapplicable (in the sense of "distinctly," see LSJ, s.v. "σαφής," II.1), but in the context the reading σοφῶς (see MSS SBPλ) could be preferable, since Xanthus's invitation was only for wise men (σοφούς),[45] and the whole story is about the antithesis wise/fool. The /a/ instead of /o/ (σαφῶς instead of σοφῶς) is easy to explain paleographically.

---

45. Xanthus's order to Aesop is μὴ ἐάσῃς τινα τῶν ἰδιωτῶν ἀνδρῶν εἰσελθεῖν ἐν τῷ οἴκῳ μου, ἀλλ' ἢ μόνον σοφούς (don't let any of the ordinary men enter my house, but only the sages).

Chapter 78

78.7–8. τί μοι χαρίζεις. The reading of MS M χαρίζεις is justifiable, since the active forms of deponent verbs are also found in the papyri of this period (see Gignac 1981, 325–26). Furthermore, the active form of the verb is already attested in the first centuries CE (see Lampe 1976, s.v. "χαρίζω," I) as well as in the BPThSA recension, in 80.14 (Karla 2001, 209).[46]

Chapter 79

79.1–2. ἀνεπόδισεν ἀπὸ τῆς στήλης βήματα τέσσαρα. The reading of MS M, ἀναπηδήσας (see also SBW ἀνεπήδησεν), seems to be a *lectio facilior*.

79.12. ἐνθάδε. The ἐνταῦθα reading of MS M is equally good.

Chapter 80

80.2. τὸ ἥμισυ τοῦ εὑρέματος. The χρυσίου reading of MS M is equally acceptable, even though it is found only in this manuscript. The same is true of the reading ἐκέλευσε τὸν Αἴσωπον (M) instead of αὐτόν (80.7) and εἰς τὸν οἶκον (M) instead of εἰς τὴν οἰκίαν (80.5).

Chapter 81

81.2. Πανδήμου γὰρ ἀγομένου. Both manuscripts (MO) of the MORN recension have this reading. Πανδήμου γὰρ ἑορτῆς ἀγομένης is the reading of MSS SBPλW, which previous editors preferred. The problem is that the word πάνδημος is listed in modern lexica (see LSJ, Lampe 1976, etc.) as an adjective. A search in the TLG has shown that actually in most examples the word is used as a noun. In the Suda, for example, the word is explained as "Πανδήμου: παντὸς τοῦ πλήθους, ἢ παντὸς τοῦ δημώδους καὶ ἀγελαίου ὄχλου..." (pi 176). Further, in Joannes Malalas (a chronicler of the fifth/sixth century CE) there are two phrases quite close to the reading of MO in two different passages, where the word πάνδημον is used as a noun: "ἦν γὰρ μῖμος δεύτερος καὶ εἰσῆλθεν εἰς τὸ παιγνίδιν πανδήμου ἀγομένου" (12.50.4: "He was second mime and came on to give a comic turn during

---

46. Lampe (1976, s.v. "χαρίζω," I) gives only the sense "show favour to."

a popular festival"; "…πεμφθείσης ᾔτησεν πᾶς ὁ δῆμος τοῦ ἀχθῆναι πάνδημον· καὶ τοῦ πανδήμου ἀχθέντος καὶ τάπητος ἁπλωθέντος ἕκαστος καθ' ὃ ηὐπόρει ἔρριπτεν ἐν τῷ τάπητι" (18.59.14–15: "… and when the petition sent … the whole population asked for a public meeting to be summoned. When the public meeting was summoned and a carpet stretched out, each threw what he could afford on the carpet" [both trans. Jeffreys et al. 1986). Consequently, the reading πανδήμου γὰρ ἀγομένου can be preserved in the MORN recension.

Chapter 82

82.1. διαπορῶν καὶ αἰτήσας διωρίαν. Perry noted that MS M gives the conjunction καὶ in this passage, and Papathomopoulos did not see a conjunction in either manuscript. However, in my opinion καί is discernible in MS O.

82.1. διωρίαν. It is worth noting that both orthographic variants διωρίαν (MS M) and διορίαν (MS O) are transmitted.

Chapters 83–85

83–85.2. ἤδη σοφός. Oddly, Papathomopoulos suggests the reading ἡδύσοφος, which is to be found neither in modern lexica nor in the TLG.

Chapter 86

86.3. ἐλθεῖν τὸν οἰκέτην αὐτοῦ. In this place, only MS M has the reading συνιδεῖν τὸν Αἴσωπον, the meaning of which is not appropriate to the context. What Xanthus had said above was that a very experienced slave of his would interpret the omen, without naming him. Therefore, the Samians did not yet know the name of the slave.

Chapter 88

88.4. οἱ ὄχλοι διεπόππυζον. The lemma διαποππύζω is attested only in *DGE* (s.v.: "*chistar para hacer callar*") and in *LBG* (s.v.: "*zurufen*"), with the only reference to this passage of the Life. A lemma ποππύζω is recorded in LSJ (s.v.) in the sense of "smack the lips or cluck."

Chapter 92

92.5. Βασιλεὺς Λυδῶν. The king of the Lydians is the famous Croesus, who reigned circa 560–546 BCE. He is identified by name in chapters 95–96 and 98.

Chapter 95

95.7. πέμψαι πρεσβευτάς. The reading πρεσβευτάς of MS M (and of the BPThSA recension) is correct and makes good sense (see LSJ, s.v. "πρεσβευτάς," 1), but since all other manuscripts of the MORN recension have πρεσβύτας (see LSJ, s.v. "πρεσβύτης [ῡ]"), it is probable that the latter is the reading of the MORN recension. The same occurs in chapter 98.

Chapter 96

At the end of chapter 96 (96.5) MSS ORN add οἱ δέ, λέγε, and OR continue καὶ ὁ Αἴσωπος. MS M does not contain this phrase. It is hard to say whether MS M represents the reading of the MORN recension and the addition in the remaining manuscripts is simply the reading of the ORN family or whether the reading of ORN is that of MORN and the omission of MS M is due to contamination with the BPThSA recension.[47]

Chapter 97

97.4. ἐὰν θέλετε. In this phrase, the lettering of MS M is faded and illegible. MS O has the reading εἰ θέλετε, and all other manuscripts (RNWL) have ἐὰν θέλετε. The syntax ἐάν + indicative is attested from the second century CE onward (see Blass and Debrunner 1990, §372.1) and can be accepted also in this case.[48]

Chapter 98

98.10. Τοὺς γὰρ φίλους σου. MS M has a dative (τοῖς γὰρ φίλοις σου), which makes no sense syntactically, as in that case the meaning would be not

---

47. Neither recension BPThSA nor Wλ have the additional phrase of MSS ORN at this passage.

48. See also in BPThSA (Karla 2001, 114–15).

"since you will force your friends to give you advice that is contrary to your interests," but "you will force someone to give advice that is contrary to your friends," which is contradicted by the following sentence.[49] Consequently, the correction by Perry to an accusative is defensible.

98.12–14. Οἱ δὲ ταχὺ ἐμπιστεύοντες λόγοις ὥσπερ τὰ κενὰ τῶν ἀγγείων τοῖς ὠταρίοις εὐβάστακτοι εὑρίσκονται. In this passage MS M omits the words τοῖς ὠταρίοις given by MS W.[50] Perry adopted the reading of W, followed by Papathomopoulos. The whole phrase seems to be a Pythagorean sentence (*Gnom. Sententiae Pythagoreorum*, ed. Elter 41a): Οἱ ἐλαφροὶ τῶν ἀνθρώπων ὥσπερ τὰ κενὰ τῶν ἀγγείων, εὐβάστακτοι τοῖς ὠτίοις εἰσίν. The presence of the word τοῖς ὠταρίοις in W shows that it existed in the textual tradition of MORN, but only some traces were preserved in contaminated manuscripts such as W and L.

Chapter 99

99.2. τὴν εὔλαλον τερετίστριαν τέττιγα. Perry's correction to τερετιστρίαν seems to be unnecessary, since in all codices the word is accentuated on the third syllable from the end (antepenultimate). The same accentuation is preserved in the edition of the fables (Hausrath and Hunger 1956, fable 298). It is noteworthy that this word is attested only here (in the MORN recension and in MSS WL), since it does not occur in any other text (see LSJSup, s.v. "τερετίστρια"), as a search in TLG shows. There is also a verb τερετίζω occurring many times and in some cases specifically expressing the sound of the cicada.[51] One may wonder whether the word in this passage is a noun or an adjective. It is more likely that it is an adjective modifying the noun τέττιγα (as reflected in Konstan's translation "chirping cicada") than a noun; in the latter case, τέττιγα would be a gloss for τερετίστριαν (Karla 2019b, 174).

---

49. In G (ch. 98) the meaning is similar to the restored text: the friends of the king must be free to express their opinions and advice.
50. MS L has the corrupt reading τοῖς ἀνταρίοις, which apparently comes from τοῖς ὠταρίοις.
51. See, e.g., Pollux Grammaticus, *Onom.* 5.89.7: καὶ κοψίχους σίζειν, καὶ τέττιγας τερετίζειν, καὶ μελίττας βομβεῖν, καὶ ἔποπας πιπίζειν.

99.5. Φωνῆς δὲ πλείω. MS M reads πλείω. The reading ποίω of MS O is perhaps a misunderstanding of πλείω. MS R has the reading πλεῖον, which is a variant of the form πλείω (see LSJ, s.v. "πλείων, πλέων," II.2.d) and is preferred by Perry and Papathomopoulos.

Chapter 100

100.2. αἴτησαί μοι. Since all manuscripts have a dative, it is not necessary to correct it to an accusative (Perry, Papathomopoulos). The middle verb has the same syntax as the active one (see LSJ, s.v. "αἰτέω," I.2 and II.1).[52]

100.6-7. ὡς ἕνεκεν Αἰσώπου καταλλαχθῆναι αὐτοῖς. MS R has the reading κατηλλάχθαι, and most likely so does MS M (this is what Perry and Papathomopoulos read). MS O has the similar form κατήλλαχθαι. Perry corrected to κατηλλάχθη on the basis of L, and Papathomopoulos agreed. However, since the conjunction ὡς can be construed with an infinitive (Jannaris 1897, 570.7c), one may retain the reading of the manuscripts (perfect infinitive). Moreover, this form of the infinitive is found in the corresponding passage in G (ch. 100.9–10, Ferrari 1997).

100.8-9. χορείαν ἤγειραν. The form ἤγειραν must correspond to the verb ἐγείρω, meaning "organize, arrange, celebrate."

Chapter 101

This chapter marks the beginning of the Life's use of the Ahiqar story, which continues through chapter 123. In the older Aramaic version of the story found at Elephantine in Egypt, Ahiqar is an official in Assyria in the time of Sennacherib (705–681 BCE). He is childless but adopts and rears his nephew Nadin (Nadan). Soon after Sennacherib's death and Esarhaddon's accession to the throne (681–669 BCE), Ahiqar retires from his position at the court and is succeeded by his foster son Nadin. The latter proves ungrateful and frames Ahiqar by portraying him as a traitor who was fomenting rebellion against the new Assyrian king, Esarhaddon. Enraged, Esarhaddon orders one of his officials to execute Ahiqar.

---

52. For John Fitzgerald (pers. comm.), the αἴτησαί καὶ λήψει combination points to Matt 7:8/Luke 11:10.

But instead of killing Ahiqar, the official spares his life because Ahiqar had earlier rescued him when he was falsely accused. The official agrees to conspire with Ahiqar and to harbor him until the time for his restoration is right. Unfortunately, the extant Aramaic version breaks off at this point, but other extant ancient versions indicate that the occasion for Ahiqar's restoration to favor comes when Pharaoh, the king of Egypt, hears that Ahiqar is dead. He writes to the Assyrian king demanding that he send a sage who can answer his riddles and supervise the construction of a palace in the sky, "between heaven and earth." It is at this opportune time that the official reveals to the king that Ahiqar is alive and brings him to the court, where he is vindicated and restored to favor. Subsequently he is sent to Egypt and succeeds in answering the Pharaoh's riddles, including the enigma concerning the celestial palace. He returns in triumph to Assyria, where he admonishes and punishes his foster son, Nadin, who swells up and dies.

The Aramaic version was extremely popular, with even the book of Tobit reflecting a knowledge of its story (Tob 1:21–22; 2:10; 11:18; 14:10). It was ultimately translated into many different languages, including Greek. The author of the Life of Aesop used a Greek version of the tale of Ahiqar, but how that Greek version related to the Aramaic version from Elephantine cannot be determined with certainty. For the Aramaic version and an English translation, see Porten and Yardeni 1993; see also Cowley 1923, 204–48; and Lindenberger 1983–1985. On the incorporation of the Ahiqar tale into the Life, see Konstantakos 2013; and Zafiropoulos 2014. On its use more broadly in ancient prose fiction, see Marinčič 2003.[53]

101.2-3. Παραγενομένου δὲ αὐτοῦ ἐν Βαβυλῶνι καὶ τὴν αὐτοῦ ἐπιδειξαμένου σοφίαν μέγας ἐγένετο παρὰ Λυκούργῳ τῷ βασιλεῖ. The syntax of this clause is remarkable: it involves two consecutive absolute genitives (παραγενομένου, ἐπιδειξαμένου) whose subject is the same as the subject of the main verb. This is partly explicable in view of the fact that in MS M immediately after the participial constructions there follows the sentence μέγα τὸ τούτου ὄνομα ἦν. On the other hand, MSS OR give the participles in the accusative or nominative (as variants), something that would legitimize

---

53. I owe the information and the bibliography on the Aramaic version of the Ahiqar story to J. Fitzgerald (pers. comm.).

this construction. Consequently, the coexistence of *genitivus absolutus* and a verb with coreferential subject is quite likely a false reading in this case and should probably be corrected.

In the Life of Aesop, Lycurus, the fictional king of Babylon, takes the place that Sennacherib, the king of Assyria, had in the Aramaic story of Ahiqar. In chapter 103, Aenus is adopted by Aesop and thus assumes the role played by Nadin in the Aramaic tale of Ahiqar. In addition to changing the cast of characters, the author of the Life of Aesop (or its Greek *Vorlage*) also simplifies the story. In the Aramaic version, there are two Assyrian kings, Sennacherib and Esarhaddon, and the adopted son Nadin betrays Ahiqar after the death of Sennacherib; it is Esarhaddon who is deceived by Nadin and becomes angry. In the Life there is only one king, Lycurus, throughout the story.

Chapter 103

103.2–3. προπαιδείαν καὶ πᾶσαν διδάξας σοφίαν. The reading of MSS OR πρὸς παιδείαν demonstrates that the correct accentuation is on the penultimate syllable. However, the reading of MS M προπαίδειαν seems to be attested at least since Byzantine times (see *LBG*, s.v. "προπαίδεια").

Chapter 105

Nectenabo (Nectanebo, Nektanebo) is the Greek name of two kings from the Thirtieth Egyptian Dynasty: Nakhtnebef (Nectenabo I) and Nakhthorheb (Nectenabo II). The Alexander Romance (1.1–13) depicts the latter as the biological father of Alexander the Great. Inasmuch as both kings reigned in the fourth century BCE, and the Life of Aesop depicts Aesop as a contemporary of Croesus, king of Lydia (sixth century BCE), Nectenabo is an obvious anachronism.

105.7–8. Εἰ δ' ἀπορεῖς, πέμψον μοι ὑπὲρ πάσης τῆς ὑπὸ σὲ γῆς φόρους ἐτῶν δέκα. In this passage it is said that, if Lycurus manages to send people who will build a tower that touches neither the earth nor the sky, along with someone who can answer everything that Nectenabo asks him, he will receive a tribute for ten years. If he fails, he is the one who must pay Nectenabo the tribute for ten years. The second condition is transmitted by MS R (as well as BWV), while it is absent from MS M (and LPSA). It is worth noting that MS G has only the first condition, and after that it has a corrupt passage (see the *apparatus criticus* of the relevant editions). The narrative rendering the second condition is necessary, as it comes to pass in chapter 123: "He [Nectenabo] gave Aesop a tribute for ten years and sent him off." Alternatively, one could suppose that, because of the corrupt passage in the archetype of the Life, the MORN recension omitted it, and later someone (scribe, redactor) added what he considered to be a necessary clarification.

Chapter 106

106.2–3. εἰ δύνασθε τοῦ πύργου λῦσαι τὸ ζήτημα;. This is the reading of MS M (and LW). The conjunction εἰ introducing direct questions is found especially in inscriptions and in the text of the Bible (see *DGE*, s.v. "εἰ," D.II). The claim that this use of εἰ should be considered a Hebraism (see Blass and Debrunner 1990, §440.3) needs to be reconsidered in the light of this passage from the Life and the corresponding inscriptional evidence.

Chapter 107

107.2. τὸ αὑτοῦ ἁμάρτημα. My correction αὑτοῦ is just an orthographic variant of reading αὐτοῦ found in MS R, easily justifiable paleographically. Since the beginning of the word in M is illegible, it could be either ἑαυτοῦ (as in MSS WL)[54] or αὐτοῦ (as in R). Consequently, the MORN recension may have had either ἑαυτοῦ or αὐτοῦ.

107.3. μὴ οὕτω κατάλυπος γίνου. After this sentence MS R adds the following: ἵνα τί περίλυπος εἶ καὶ ἵνα τί συνταράττει; ὁ δὲ βασιλεὺς ἔφη· οἴμοι ἕρμιππε τῶν συμβάντων ἀπώλεσα τὸν εὔλαλον αἴσωπον. Τότε ἕρμιππος ἔφη. Καὶ οὕτως πράττε ὦ βασιλεῦ ("Why are you sad, and what is upsetting you?" The king said, "Oh, Hermippus, what a catastrophe! I have lost the sweet-speaking Aesop." Then Hermippus said, "Then, O king, you must do this.")

107.4. ὅτι μετάμελον εἶχεν. This is the reading of M(L), whereas MS R has μεταμεληθῆναι ἔχεις. Perry suggested μετάμελον ἔχεις from MS W (fol-

---

54. There are many instances where MSS M, W, and L agree with each other (see Perry 1933, 215, 221–22).

lowed by Papathomopoulos). The reading of MS M can be retained, if the subject of the verb is ἡ ἀπόφασις, in which case the meaning would be: "(the decision) would be changed/regretted."

107.10. ἐν ῥύπῳ καὶ κόμῃ δυσώδει. This is again the reading of MS M(L), while MS R has καὶ πολλῇ τῇ κόνι δυσειδοὺς ὄντως. Perry proposed the correction ἐν ῥύπῳ καὶ κόμῃ δυσειδεῖ, adopted by Papathomopoulos. No other manuscript of the Westermanniana refers to hair; in MS G there is a mention of hair (ῥυπῶντος καὶ κομῶντος καὶ ὠχρῶντος) without further comment. It is more probable that the MORN recension also makes mention of hair, as MSS MR demonstrate. The question is whether Aesop's hair was ugly (δυσειδεῖ) or dirty-sticky (δυσώδει). Perry's correction is based on version G (κομῶντος), and the interchange between δυσώδει and δυσειδεῖ is common. However, since the reading of MS M δυσώδει is not problematic (morphologically, syntactically, and semantically), it can be kept in the text (with some reservations).

Chapter 109

109.2. κἂν μέχρι τοῦ νῦν. This is the reading of MS R. The conjunction κἂν does not occur in MS M (or L), while instead of νῦν MS M (like L) has ζῆν. If we keep the reading of MS M(L), then a different punctuation is required: Ἐπάκουσον τῶν ἐμῶν λόγων, τέκνον, καὶ φύλαξον ἐν τῇ καρδίᾳ σου μέχρι τοῦ ζῆν· οὐ δικαίας μοι χάριτας ἀνταπέδωκας ("Listen to my words, my son, and guard them in your heart as long as you live. You have not paid me back justly," 109.1–2). In this case the last sentence is not connected with the previous sentences. As for the other manuscripts, the BPThSA recension omits the passage κἂν ... ἀνταπέδωκας; apart from MSS MR the sentence is also found in MSS WL; version G as well as Codex Vindob. theol. gr. 128 (Perry 1952) connect these sentences with each other: ἄκουσον τῶν ἐμῶν λόγων, Ἥλιε, <δι' ὧν> καὶ πρότερον παιδευθεὶς οὐκ ἀληθῆ μοι τὰς χάριτας ἀπέδωκας (ch. 109.1–3, Ferrari 1997); ἐπάκουσον τῶν ἐμῶν λόγων, τέκνον Λῖνε, δι' ὧν καὶ πρότερον παιδευθεὶς οὐκ δικαίας μοι χάριτας ἀποδέδωκας (ch. 109.1–2, Perry 1952). Consequently, if we accept that the initial sentences are connected in MOR, as in G and in Codex Vindob. theol. gr. 128, then we must adopt the readings of MS R(W).

109.12. κοῦφον γὰρ τὸ γυναικεῖον γένος. The reading of MS R ζοῦφον instead of κοῦφον (MS M) is interesting. If it is not an error of MS R, with a simple substitution of /z/ for /k/, then this constitutes one more *testimonium* for the medieval word ζοφός (see *LBG* and Kriaras 1968–, s.v.; also Eustathius, *Comm. ad Hom. Il.* 3.595.21) in MS R (of the fourteenth century), involving the change of /o/ to /u/, which is found only much later in Modern Greek colloquial language, with the meaning "empty, light, metaphorically of persons" (see Babiniotes 2012, s.v. "τζούφιος," 2).

109.12–13. καὶ κολακευόμενον ἐλάττω φρονεῖ καὶ κακά. Papathomopoulos's correction κακίω instead of κακά is unnecessary, since the conjunction καί need not connect adjectives of the same grade of comparison. It may also connect the simplex with the comparative, as in this case.

109.13. Πάντα δεινὸν ἄνδρα φεῦγε. It is worth noting that MS M (as well L) has πᾶν instead of πάντα. This indicates that by this time the endings of third declension adjectives such as πᾶς were fluid, and perhaps there was a tendency for πᾶν to become fossilized (like πάντων; see Blass and Debrunner 1990, §164.1).

109.22–23. ἀεὶ γὰρ ὁπλίζεται πῶς σου κυριεύσει. Papathomopoulos suggested the addition of the participle μηχανωμένη after ὁπλίζεται, on the basis of Codex Vindob. theol. gr. 128 and P.Oxy. 3720.[55] However the addition is superfluous, since the verb ὁπλίζομαι can have the meaning "make oneself ready, prepare, get ready" in the middle voice (see LSJ, s.v. "ὁπλίζω," 3) and since μηχανωμένη is found neither in manuscripts of the MORN recension nor in the Westermanniana in general.

Chapter 110

110.1–2. Τὸν καθημερινὸν ζήτει προσλαμβάνειν ἄρτον καὶ εἰς τὴν αὔριον [μὴ] ἀποθησαύριζε. Papathomopoulos proposed the addition of the pronoun τι after προσλαμβάνειν, which, however, is not indispensable semantically (see the translation by Konstan "Seek to acquire your daily bread" in the sense of being frugal), and moreover is not attested by any manuscript. The negation in μὴ ἀποθησαύριζε, attested only in MS M, should perhaps be

---

55. Papathomopoulos claims that it also occurs in MS G, but according to Ferrari's edition the participle μηχανωμένη is not found there.

corrected since it clashes with the following advice ("it is better to die and leave it to your enemies than to live and be in need of friends").

110.4. Αἰσχρὸν ἀτυχοῦντα ἐπιγελᾶν. Only MSS ML read ἀτυχοῦντα; all other manuscripts of the Westermanniana (WBPS) have the dative (ἀτυχοῦντι). The appearance of an accusative in this construction may be justified, since from this period onwards the use of the dative recedes in favour of the accusative (Horrocks 2010, 184–85). Thus the accusative can stand in the text, with a note in the *apparatus criticus* that one would have expected the form ἀτυχοῦντι.

110.13–14. ὃς χάριτας καλὰς ἐκτιννύειν οἶδεν. MS M (L) reads ἐκτιννύειν. R has ἐκτείνειν, and both Perry and Papathomopoulos prefer the reading of MS W, ἐκτίνειν, which is close to that of R. However, the reading of M is satisfactory and well attested at this time (see *DGE*, s.v. "ἐκτιννύω").

110.17. ἀποκρημνισάμενος. MS R adds the reading ἑαυτόν, which is absent from M(λ). Since the boundaries between middle and passive voice are fluid,[56] ἑαυτόν can be omitted.

Chapter 111

111.3–4. οὕτως τε αὐτοὺς διδάξας τρέφεσθαι καὶ μανθάνειν παῖδας διὰ θυλακίων βαστάζειν. MS R reads διδάξας, which is absent from M and the other manuscripts of the Westermanniana. It seems that in this passage there is a problem of syntax in the Westermanniana version in general, since in all probability a verb has been omitted. Perry tried to correct it by proposing the verb ἐκέλευσε instead of διδάξας on the basis of MS G, and Papathomopoulos concurred with Perry's correction. However, the adoption of readings from different versions, while it is a solution, is not the best editorial practice. The participle διδάξας attested by MS R is possible, since the participle in the Koine occasionally has the function of a verb. An alternative is to change the punctuation, placing a raised dot after ἔσχατα πτερά and forming the sentence οὕτως … καλῶς (111.3–5).

---

56. On *passivi aoristi* in Koine, see Radermacher 1947, 28–29; Mihevc-Gabrovec 1960, 58–59.

Commentary 211

111.5. ἀνίπταντο εἰς ὕψος δεδεμένοι καλῶς. Westermann's correction κάλῳς ("rope") instead of the *lectio facilior* καλῶς, which is found in all manuscripts of the Westermanniana version, is ingenious and accepted by Perry and Papathomopoulos. It is most probably based on the corresponding passage of version G, ἀνίπταντο εἰς τὸν ἀέρα δεδεμένοι καλῳδίοις, and may be correct. The reading ἐν κάλῳ in P.Oxy. 3720 confirms the correction. However, since both manuscripts (MR) of MORN (as well as λ; MS W bears no accent according to Perry's *apparatus criticus*) have the reading καλῶς, which makes sense in the context, it is doubtful whether the reading κάλῳς originally stood in MORN.

111.6–7. ὅταν γὰρ ἤθελον οἱ παῖδες. MS M (as well L) reads ὅταν and can be retained in the text, since "ὅταν with the indicative denotes in the first place indefinite repetition in past time" (Blass and Debrunner 1990, §382.4).

Chapter 112

112.7. διὰ λίθων. This is the reading of MS M (λS as well). Διά with genitive is attested in later prose, and its function is to express the material out of which a thing is made (see LSJ, s.v. "διά," III.2).

Chapter 113

113.3. σὲ μὲν τὴν σεληνιακὴν διχομηνίαν ἔχοντα. Papathomopoulos saw a syntactical problem here as a reply to the question, "What do I and those around me look like to you?" and suggested: σὲ μὲν τῇ σελήνῃ τῇ διχομηνίαν ἐχούσῃ (vel ἀγούσῃ), which, however, cannot be justified from the manuscript tradition. If the verb ἔχω has the meaning "hold, wear" (LSJ s.v. "ἔχω," II.3), and considering that Nectenabo had put on "a diadem that had horns set with gems" (see Konstan's translation) in the previous chapter, then the syntax and the meaning here are comprehensible. Likewise, Papathomopoulos's addition of ἰκέλους or ἴκελοί εἰσι in this chapter is unnecessary because they can easily be supplied by the reader.

Chapter 115

115.6–7. κατὰ τὴν ἐμὴν βασιλείαν οὐδὲν εἶναι Λυκοῦρον. MS M reads οὐδὲν, whereas MS R has μηδέν, which is preferred by both editors (Perry, Papathomopoulos). However, the phrase οὐδὲν εἶναι for persons in the sense of "he

Chapter 116

116.5. στήσας κατὰ γωνίαν τοῦ δειχθέντος τόπου τοὺς ἀετούς. All manuscripts (MR and the other manuscripts of the Westermanniana except B) read κατὰ γωνίαν. It is clear that Aesop placed the eagles not at one corner only but at the four corners; if we consider that the singular can stand for the plural, then κατὰ γωνίαν can be kept. Otherwise, one must accept Papathomopoulos's correction κατὰ γωνίας, which is found in MS B. In the latter case, it is easy to explain it paleographically as an abbreviated suffix /-as/ that was read as /-an/. As for the reading δειχθέντος, it is that of MS M (as well as of λBPW), whereas MS R has δοθέντος (like MS S). Both readings are possible, since both verbs (δείξῃς, ἔδωκεν) were mentioned immediately above. As long as MS M is considered the *Leithandschrift*, its reading is preferable.

116.5–6. διὰ τῶν ἡμιτελῶν θυλάκων. The reading ἡμιτελῶν of MSS MR(LS), referring to θυλάκων ("bags"), is not suitable in this context, if the word ἡμιτελής has the literal meaning "half-finished" (see LSJ, s.v.). Perry put it in brackets ([ ]) and deleted it from the text; Papathomopoulos wondered in the *apparatus criticus "an ἡμιφανῶν scribendum?,"* suggesting a reading that does not fit well semantically or paleographically. He translated the phrase with μισοσάκκουλα, a word that does not exist in Modern Greek. Maybe it means "half-bags," that is, indicating that the bags had been cut in two, shortened in order to fit the size of the children. Another possibility is that ἡμιτελής here means "half-open" or has the metaphorical meaning "provisional" (cf. Hippocrates, *Epid.* 1.5.32: εἰ δ' οὖν προχείρως, ἡμιτελέα).

116.8. ὅσα πρὸς οἰκοδομὴν χρειώδη κομίσατε. MS M (as well as L) reads χρειώδη; MS R has the *lectio facilior* χρὴ ὧδε. But since χρειώδη gives adequate sense in the context ("needful"; see LSJ, s.v. "χρειώδης") and is well attested in the period (first centuries CE), it can be taken as the reading of the MORN recension.

116.11. ἴσα θεῷ ἐρίζειν βασιλεῖ. MS M (and LV) reads ἴσα θεῷ; MS R (and WB) has the *lectio facilior* ἰσοθέῳ. The meaning is the same, but the phrase ἴσα θεῷ seems to have a long literary history (see, for example, Homer, *Od.* 15.520; Phil 2:6) and should be preferred as the original for the MORN recension.

Chapter 117

117.5. Συλλαβόντες δὲ ἕνα παμμεγέθη, ἤρξαντο δημοσίᾳ μαστίζειν. MS R (and WSPV) reads ἤρξαντο; MS M (LB) has ἤρξατο. In the first case, the subject of the verb is the slaves of Aesop, who have caught the cat (συλλαβόντες), and there is no syntactic problem since the subject of the participle is coreferential with that of the main clause verb; in the second case, the subject of the verb is Aesop. He ordered the slaves to catch the cat, and he himself beat it. Because of this, he is accused and brought to the king Nectenabo. Paleographically, the two readings are quite close. As far as the meaning is concerned, both could be correct, and MS G cannot help, since it has a lacuna at this point. The syntactic problem (in the second case a *genitivus absolutus* would be expected) is perhaps an argument against the reading ἤρξατο, even though ἤρξαντο describes something not reasonably expected: Aesop ordered his slaves only to bring a cat and not to beat it.

117.9. ὦ παῖ. This is the reading of MS M(L); MS R has εἰς τὸν αἴλουρον at this point. The sense of παῖς as "slave, servant" (see LSJ, s.v. "παῖς," III) does not fit here, since Aesop is not a slave in this context but an ambassador of King Lycurus. However, the word also has the meaning "boy, young man" in relation to age (see LSJ, s.v. "παῖς," II), and understood this way this reading is preferred.

117.9. Θεοῦ γὰρ Βουβάστεως. Because of the difficulty of the phrase (Βούβαστις, -εως is not a frequently attested word; ca. fifteen times in the whole TLG corpus), there is a problem in the textual tradition. Perry's correction (Βουβάστεως) based on MS S is suitable. Boubastis was the Greek name for the ancient Egyptian city Per-Bastet ("House of Bastet," modern Tell-Basta) located along the Nile in the eastern Delta region of Lower Egypt. It is often identified with the Pi-beseth of Ezek 30:17. Boubastis was the home of the feline goddess Bastet, here and elsewhere eponymously called Boubastis. Herodotus (*Hist.* 2.59–60) equates her with Artemis and says that her festival was the most celebrated in the whole of Egypt. In Hellenistic and Roman times she was occasionally equated with Isis, so that in the Isis aretalogy Isis says that the city of Boubastis was built for her. A beautiful temple to her (a *boubasteion*) was built in Boubastis (*Hist.* 2.137) and was a popular site for pilgrimages, with Herodotus claiming that 700,000 pilgrims visited there (*Hist.* 2.60; see Rutherford 2005). The cat was one of Egypt's sacred animals, and to kill one, even by accident, was considered a capital offense (Diodorus Siculus, *Bib. hist.* 1.83.6–9).[57]

Chapter 119

119.3–4. τὶς τῶν Ἡλιοπολιτῶν. MS M has Ἡλιοπολιτῶν and MS R(L) two separate words: ἡλίου πολιτῶν. Even though all other manuscripts of the Westermanniana have the reading Ἡλιουπολιτῶν,[58] the reading of the MS M can be considered a variant and kept in the text.

Chapter 121

121.3–4. ἐπερωτήσωμεν αὐτῷ προβλήματα. Both manuscripts (MR) have a dative at this *locus*, and so do all other manuscripts of the Westermanniana (except MS P, which has an accusative). The verb ἐπερωτάω is construed with accusative (see LSJ, s.v.), but since all manuscripts have a dative and there are also other attestations in Greek works in which the verb is found with a dative (see, e.g., Vit. Euth. 14.93.1: αὐτοῖς ἐπερώτα), the dative αὐτῷ can be retained in the text. Besides, it illustrates the variation between accusative and dative: the interchange is not only from dative to accusative but also the reverse, perhaps as hypercorrection.

Chapter 123

123.5. ἀνατεθῆναι τῷ Αἰσώπῳ. This is a difficult case because the passage in MS M is illegible. Probably the reading is not ἀνατεθῆναι, even though that is the reading of most manuscripts of the Westermanniana (RWSBPV). I could detect (like Perry and Papathomopoulos) the beginning ἀνε- in MS M (by autopsy); both previous editors suppose the existence of the reading ἀνεγεῖραι, perhaps based on the reading of L (ἀνεγεῖραι).[59] After this word, MS R has a genitive (τοῦ Αἰσώπου), whereas in MS M I could read ᾧ (most

---

57. I thank John Fitzgerald for his comments on Boubastis in this chapter.
58. On Heliopolis, see Healey 2003; and Seidlmayer 2006.
59. It is noteworthy that there are many agreements between the two manuscripts (ML); for agreements between Μλ, see Perry 1933, 216–17.

probably the ending of the article τῷ) and then Αἰσώπῳ. Consequently, in the MORN recension there stood either ἀνατεθῆναι τοῦ Αἰσώπου (MS R) or ἀνεγεῖραι τῷ Αἰσώπῳ (MS M).

123.5. καὶ ἐτίμησε μεγάλως εὐφημοῦντα αὐτόν (he honored and praised him greatly). This is the reading of MS R, added at the end of the chapter. Both editors retain the sentence in their edition, Perry exactly in this form and Papathomopoulos with a correction (εὐφημούντων ἁπάντων), in order to resolve the syntactic problem. However, it is significant that all other manuscripts of the Westermanniana do not include this sentence. Moreover, in version G the text reads καὶ ἐποίησεν ἑορτὴν μεγάλην ὁ βασιλεὺς ἐπὶ τῇ τοῦ Αἰσώπου σοφίᾳ ("The king organized a great festival to celebrate Aesop's wisdom") (Perry 1952).[60] This could be an argument in favor of retaining the reading of MS R; however, considering that the MORN recension is abridged in content in comparison to version G and that no other manuscript of the Westermanniana has this reading, perhaps it should be omitted from the text of the present edition.

Chapter 125

125.7. Οὐδὲν ἄξιον ποιεῖτε τῶν προγόνων ὑμῶν. MS R reads Οὐδὲν ἄξιον. This passage is absent from MS M, so R becomes the unique source of the MORN recension at this point. All other manuscripts of the Westermanniana also have ἄξιον (W) or ἄξια (S); only MS L has οὐδὲν ἀνάξιον,[61] which is more suitable in this case, since Aesop castigates the Delphians and their behavior and points out that they are doing nothing unworthy of their ancestors, because in what follows he will claim that their ancestors were slaves, so the Delphians are not free and will become slaves of the Greeks. Perry and Papathomopoulos print οὐδὲν ἀνάξιον in their editions based on the MS L and G, respectively.

Chapter 126

126.3. ἐὰν πόλις καταβάληται, τῶν λαφύρων τὸ δέκατον μέρος πέμπειν. MS M (as well L) has the reading πόλις καταβαλῆται; καταβαλῆται as a vari-

---

60. Ferrari 1997: καὶ ἐποίησεν ἑορτὴν μεγάλην [ὁ βασιλεὺς] ἐπὶ τῇ τοῦ Αἰσώπου σοφίᾳ.
61. MS G also has ἀνάξιον.

ant form of the third-person singular subjunctive aorist (καταβάληται) is found twice in TLG, in Byzantine texts of the twelfth/thirteenth century (Euthymius Tornikes, *Or.* 3.26.15; Acta Monast. Lemb. 16). MS R and the other manuscripts of the Westermanianna have a plural: πόλεις καταβάλλοντε (R), πόλεις καταβάλωνται (W), πόλεις καταβάλλωνται (S). Perry and Papathomopoulos prefer the reading of W in their editions. G has the middle voice and πόλις in singular (ἐὰν πόλιν καταλάβωνται). The question is whether the reading of MORN is πόλις καταβάληται/πόλις καταβαλῆται (M) or πόλεις καταβάλωνται (both paleographically close to the reading of R). Another deviation of MS M(L) is the reading τὸ δωδέκατον μέρος; MS R has τὸ δέκατον μέρος, and so do MSS WS of the Westermanniana, MS G of version G, and P.Golenischeff. Since historically the customary tax was one tenth and not one twelfth, and since paleographically δέκατον and δωδέκατον are easily interchangeable and most witnesses of the text's tradition have δέκατον, the reading δέκατον should be considered as representative of the MORN recension.

126.6. καθίστασθε. Again M(L) have καθίστασθε and all other manuscripts καθεστήκατε. Both readings are linguistically correct, the first as a historical present and the second as a past tense.

Chapter 127

127.1–2. λογισάμενοι ὅτι καὶ εἰς ἑτέρας πόλεις ἀπελθὼν Αἴσωπος χεῖρον αὐτοὺς κακολογήσει. This is the reading of MS M(L), whereas MS R has the reading λογισάμενοι ὅτι, ἐὰν εἰς ἑτέρας πόλεις ἀπέλθῃ ὁ Αἴσωπος, χεῖρον αὐτοὺς κακολογήσει. The BPThSA recension (see Karla 2001) and P.Golenischeff are close to the reading of R, whereas version G has direct speech at this point.[62]

---

62. Ferrari 1997: οἱ δὲ ἄρχοντες ἰδόντες αὐτοῦ τὸ κακόλογον ἐλογίζοντο· "ἐὰν αὐτὸν ἀφῶμεν ἀποδημῆσαι, περιελθὼν εἰς τὰς ἑτέρας πόλεις πλεῖον ἀτιμοτέρους ἡμᾶς ποιήσει" ("But the city officials, smarting at his abuse, reasoned among themselves: 'If we allow him to depart, he will make a round of the other cities saying even worse things about us'").

Chapter 128

128.4. ἐκτινάξαντες ἐκεῖνοι τὸ στρῶμα. MS M(L) has the reading τὸ στρῶμα, whereas MS R and all other manuscripts (including G) have τὰ σκεύη. In the previous chapter the Delphians "hid in his bedding a golden bowl," so the reading of MS M seems correct.

128.7-9. οὐχ εὑρίσκων μηχανὴν τῆς πονηρᾶς τύχης, ὡς θνητὸς ὢν οὐ δυνήσεται τὸ μέλλον ἐκφυγεῖν, ἐπένθει. The negation οὐ is given by MS M(LS); MS R has καὶ πῶς instead. Perry and Papathomopoulos omitted the particles in their editions at this point, following MSS WV.[63] In Papathomopoulos's edition the subordinate clause is translated as an indirect interrogative, most probably in apposition. However, if it is considered a causal clause, translatable as "since, as a mortal, he would not be able to escape what was coming, [Aesop] began to mourn" (Konstan), the negation may be kept.

Chapter 129

129.11-12. καὶ λύσας τοὺς βόας ἀπήλασεν. The reading of M(L) is ἀπέλυσεν. MS R(SW) has ἀπήλασεν, like MS G. The reading ἀπήλασεν seems to be the *lectio difficilior* (see LSJ, s.v. "ἀπελαύνω") and most probably constitutes the reading of the MORN recension. Moreover, the participle λύσας contains the meaning of ἀπέλυσεν and was probably what caused the interchange between ἀπέλυσεν and ἀπήλασεν.

Chapter 130

130.2. ἡ τοιαύτη σου σοφία εἰς τὸ ἀτιμάζειν πολίτας κατήντησεν ("your great wisdom has led you to such a low point, to insult citizens"): After Δελφοὺς, MS R (as well as WBP) adds this sentence, which is absent from MS M(LS). Perry preserves it in his edition with reservations (*nescio an recte*); Papathomopoulos considers the phrase as belonging to the MORN recension. The text of MS G at this point takes the form of rhetorical questions, which are appropriate in this context, as they evoke the corresponding rhe-

---

63. Version G switches to direct speech here: Αἴσωπος μὴ εὑρίσκων μηχανὴν τῆς σωτηρίας ἔφη· νῦν ἐγὼ θνητὸς ἄνθρωπος ὢν πῶς δυνήσομαι τὸ μέλλον ἐκφυγεῖν; (Ferrari 1997) (Aesop found himself unable to devise any means of escape and said, "If I am but a mortal man, how shall I be able to escape what is about to happen?").

torical questions in chapter 85 that were addressed by Aesop himself to his master Xanthus in order to prevent him from committing suicide. In this way, Aesop's tragic situation is highlighted.[64] A possible explanation is that the redactor of MORN wished to replace the corresponding passage of version G with that sentence, which, however, is insulting to Aesop and is discordant from a narratological point of view.

130.2. ἐν τῇ ἰδίᾳ πατρίδι. Papathomopoulos added αὐτῶν between ἰδίᾳ and πατρίδι based on the corresponding reading of MS G and P.Golenischeff. However, it is unnecessary, since the meaning of αὐτῶν is already contained in ἰδίᾳ; moreover, it is methodologically unsound to adopt readings from other versions when they are not indispensable.

Chapter 131

131.2. Εὐχομένης δὲ αὐτῆς παρρησίᾳ. All manuscripts of the Westermanniana (including MR) have the reading παρρησίᾳ. Reiske suggested the correction παριοῦσα or παροῦσα (see the *apparatus criticus* in Perry's and Papathomopoulos' editions). Since, however, the word παρρησία has the meaning "speaking freely or openly" (see LSJ, s.v.), it fits the context, giving the sense that "the mother prayed openly" so that the daughter could hear her prayer.[65]

131.3. τὸν λόγον κατέσχε. MS R has τῶν λόγων, and MS M is illegible at this point. The reading τὸν λόγον of MSS LS, which is accepted by both Perry and Papathomopoulos, seems more suitable syntactically and is just an orthographical variant of the reading of R (ω instead of ο).[66]

---

64. See Karla 2009a, 450. On Aesop as a tragic person, see Compton 1990, 342–44; Holzberg 1992a, 71.

65. For παρρησίᾳ in the sense of "openly" as opposed to "privately" or "secretly," see John 7:4, 13; 10:24; 11:14, 54; 16:25; 18:20. Cf. 11:10; 16:29 (suggested to me by John Fitzgerald, pers. comm.).

66. On the interchange between ο and ω, see Gignac 1976, 275–77, especially on ο > ω (277). The identification shows the loss of quantitative distinctions that "came about elsewhere in the Koine by the beginning of the Roman period."

131.4. καὶ τῆς προαυλίου προκύψασα θύρας. The word προαύλιος is attested in both orthographic variants (/i/ or /ei/).⁶⁷ Since it is found as an adjective with the ending –ιος (see Lampe 1976, s.v. "προαύλιος"), there is no reason to change it to –ειος, as Papathomopoulos suggested.

Chapter 133

133.10–11. νόμῳ ἐκδικηθήσομαι. All manuscripts of the Westermanniana (including MSS MR) have the reading νόμῳ here. Papathomopoulos wondered whether it should be corrected to λοιμῷ (see *apparatus criticus* in Papathomopoulos 1999a). However, it is not necessary to correct the reading of the manuscripts, if the dative νόμῳ is taken in the sense "according to the custom, justly, deservedly."

133.11. τὸν ἐμὸν ἐκδικήσωσι θάνατον. MS R(P) has the reading ἐκδικήσωσι; MS M has ἐκδικήσει(ε). Papathomopoulos suggested the correction ἐκδικήσουσι based on the reading of MS R, while Perry preferred the reading ἐκζητήσουσι from SBW. However, since the subjunctive aorist in Late Greek expresses future action (Blass and Debrunner 1990, §363), the reading ἐκδικήσωσι can be kept in the text of the MORN recension.

Chapter 137

137.7–8. ῥίψας αὐτὰ κατήρραξε. MS M has the reading κατήρραξε (κατέρραξε LS); MS R(W) has κατέαξε, and so does MS G. The reading κατήρραξε can be regarded as the original reading of MORN, since the meaning of the verb καταρρήγνυμι is suitable in this context (see LSJ, s.v. "καταρρήγνυμι," II.3), and the form κατήρραξε is attested in the TLG three times, with the earliest evidence in the fourth-century author Themistius ('Επὶ τῆς εἰρήνης Οὐάλεντι, 16.1 ed. Schamp).

Chapter 138

138.1. Γνοὺς δὲ ὁ Ζεὺς τὴν ἀδικίαν καὶ παρασπόνδησιν τοῦ κανθάρου. MS M has παρασπόνδησιν (S: παραπόνδησιν), the meaning of which is appropriate in this context (see LSJ, s.v. "παρασπόνδησις," breaking of faith). Instead of

---

67. See Lampe 1976 (s.v. "προαύλιος") and in *LBG* (s.v. "προαύλειος") as a noun.

παρασπόνδησιν, MS R (LW) has παραπόνησιν, which seems to be the *lectio facilior*. The word παραπόνησις is not recorded in LSJ, only in *LBG* (s.v.), and appears twice in the TLG, in the Life and in Sophronius (*Thaum* 45.3, p. 350).[68]

Chapter 141

141.6. ὑφ' ὑμῶν ἀποθανεῖν. The ὑφ' ὑμ- is illegible in MS M; the passage is absent from MS R because it ends just before that. Consequently, one must choose between ὑφ' ὑμῶν, which is the reading of MSS WL, adopted by Perry in his edition of the Westermanniana, and παρ' ὑμῶν, the reading of MSS BP, adopted by Papathomopoulos in his edition of MORN. Taking into consideration the fact that MS M frequently displays the same readings as MS L and that BP is a different recension, I regard the reading ὑφ' ὑμῶν as more likely to be that of the MORN recension.

---

68. See *LBG*, s.v., where it is recorded that the word is listed also in other lexica of Late Greek (such as Demetrakos 1936–1952, Lexicon of the Chronicle of Moreas, Somavera, and Andriotis 1974).

BIBLIOGRAPHY

Adrados, Francisco Rodríguez. 1979. "The Life of Aesop and the Origins of Novel in Antiquity." *QUCC* NS 1:93–112.

———. 1999. *Introduction and from the Origins to the Hellenistic Age*. Vol. 1 of *History of the Graeco-Latin Fable*. Translated by L. A. Ray. Revised and updated by the author and G.-J. van Dijk. Leiden: Brill.

Alpers, Klaus. 1981. *Das attizistische Lexikon des Oros: Untersuchung und kritische Ausgabe der Fragmente*. Sammlung griechischer und lateinischer Grammatiker 4. Berlin: De Gruyter.

Andreassi, Mario. 2015. "The Life of Aesop and the Gospels: Literary Motifs and Narrative Mechanisms." Pages 151–66 in *Holy Men and Charlatans in the Ancient Novel*. Edited by S. Panayotakis, G. Schmeling, and M. Paschalis. ANS 19. Eelde, the Netherlands: Barkhuis.

Andriotis, Nikolaos P. 1974. *Lexikon der Archaismen in neugriechischen Dialekten*. Vienna: Österreichische Akademie der Wissenschaften.

Avlamis, Pavlos. 2011. "Isis and the People in the Life of Aesop." Pages 65–101 in *Revelation, Literature, and Community in Late Antiquity*. Edited by P. Townsend and M. Vidas. Tübingen: Mohr Siebeck.

———. 2013. "Does Triviality Translate? The *Life of Aesop* Travels East." Pages 261–84 in *The Romance between Greece and the East*. Edited by T. Whitmarsh and S. Thomson. Cambridge: Cambridge University Press.

Babiniotes, Georgios. 2012. *Λεξικό της Νέας Ελληνικής Γλώσσας: Με σχόλια για τη σωστή χρήση των λέξεων*, 4th ed. Athens: Lexicology Centre.

Bancroft-Marcus, Rosemary E. 1982. "Literary Cryptograms and the Cretan Academies." *Byzantine and Modern Greek Studies* 8:47–76.

Bartolo, Giuseppina di. 2020. "Purpose and Result Clauses: ἵνα-hína and ὥστε-hō'ste in the Greek Documentary Papyri of the Roman Period." Pages 19–38 in *Postclassical Greek: Contemporary Approaches to Philology and Linguistics*. Edited by Dariya Rafiyenko and Ilja A. Seržant. Berlin: De Gruyter.

Bauer, Walter, et al. 1988. *Griechisch-deutsches Wörterbuch zu den Schriften des Neuen Testaments und der frühchristlichen Literatur*. 6th ed. Berlin: De Gruyter.

Beavis, Mary Ann. 1990. "Parable and Fable." *CBQ* 52:473–98.

———. 1992. "Ancient Slavery as an Interpretive Context for the New Testament Servant Parables with Special Reference to the Unjust Steward (Luke 16:1–8)." *JBL* 111:37–54.

Beschorner, Andreas. 1992. "Zu Arnolt Bronnens 'Aisopos.'" Pages 155–61 in Holzberg 1992b.

Beschorner, Andreas, and Niklas Holzberg. 1992. "A Bibliography of the *Aesop Romance*." Pages 165–87 in Holzberg 1992b.

Blass, Friedrich, and Albert Debrunner. 1990. *Grammatik des neutestamentlichen Griechisch*. Edited by Friendrich Rehkopf. 17th ed. Göttingen: Vandenhoeck & Ruprecht.

Boned Colera, Pilar, and Juan Rodríguez Somolinos, eds. 1998. *Repertorio bibliográfico de la lexicografía griega*. Madrid: Consejo Superior de Investigaciones Científicas, Instituto de Filología.

Bronnen, Arnolt. 1956. *Aisopos, Sieben Berichte Hellas: Der antike Aisopos-Roman*. Hamburg: Rowohlt.

Bühler, Winfried. 1987. *Zenobii Athoi proverbia*. Vol. 1. Göttingen: Vandenhoeck & Ruprecht.

Chambry, Emile. 1925–1926. *Aesopi Fabulae*. Paris: Belles Lettres.

Colonna, Aristide. 1951. *Himerii declamationes et orationes cum deperditarum fragmentis*. Rome: Typis Publicae officinae polygraphicae.

Compton, Todd. 1990. "The Trial of the Satirist: Poetic *Vitae* (Aesop, Archilochus, Homer) as a Background for Plato's *Apology*." *AJP* 111:330–47.

Cowley, A. E. 1923. *Aramaic Papyri of the Fifth Century B.C.* Oxford: Clarendon.

Cuddon, J. A. 2013. *A Dictionary of Literary Terms and Literary Theory*. 5th ed. Rev. by M. A. R. Habib. Chichester: Wiley-Blackwell.

Daly, Lloyd W. 1961. *Aesop without Morals: The Famous Fables, and a Life of Aesop*. New York: Yoseloff.

Demetrakos, Demetrios. 1936–1952. *Μέγα Λεξικὸν ὅλης τῆς ἑλληνικῆς γλώσσης*. 15 vols. Repr., Athens: Ekdotikos Organismos N. Asemakopoulos, 1964–1978.

Dicke, Gerde. 1994. *Heinrich Steinhöwels Esopus und seine Fortsetzer: Untersuchungen zu einem Bucherfolg der Frühdruckzeit*. Tübingen: Niemeyer.

Dieterich, Karl. 1898. *Untersuchungen zur Geschichte der griechischen Sprache von der hellenistischen Zeit bis zum 10. Jahrhundert nach Christus.* Leipzig: Teubner. Repr., Hildesheim: Olms, 1970.

Dillery, John. 1999. "Aesop, Isis, and the Heliconian Muses." *CP* 94:268–80

Eberhardt, Alfred. 1872. *De Syntipa et de Aesopo narrationes fabulosae partim ineditae.* Vol. 1 of *Fabulae Romanenses Graece conscriptae.* Leipzig: Teubner.

Eideneier, Hans. 2011. *Äsop – Der Frühneugriechische Roman: Einführung, Übersetzung, Kommentar, Kritische Ausgabe.* Wiesbaden: Reichert.

Elliott, Scott S. 2005. "'Witless in Your Own Cause': Divine Plots and Fractured Characters in the *Life of Aesop* and the Gospel of Mark." *R&T* 12:397–418.

Elter, Anton. 1905. *Gnomica homoeomata.* Bonn: Georg.

Ferrari, Franco. 1995. "'P. Oxy.' 3331 e 'Vita Aesopi' 18." *ZPE* 107:296.

———. 1997. *Romanzo di Esopo.* Introduction and critical text by Franco Ferrari; translation and notes by Guido Bonelli and Giorgio Sandrolini. Milan: Biblioteca Universale Rizzoli.

Froelich, Margaret, and Thomas E. Phillips. 2019. "Throw the Blasphemer off a Cliff: Luke 4.16–30 in Light of the *Life of Aesop.*" *NTS* 65:21–32.

Fusillo, Massimo. 1994. "Letteratura di consumo e romanzesca." Pages 233–73 in *I Greci e Roma.* Part 3 of *La produzione e la circolazione del testo.* Vol. 1 of *Lo spazio letterario della Grecia antica.* Edited by G. Cambiano, L. Canfora, and D. Lanza. Rome: Salerno.

———. 1996. "Modern Critical Theories and the Ancient Novel." Pages 277–305 in *The Novel in the Ancient World.* Edited by Gareth Schmeling. Leiden: Brill.

Gignac, Francis T. 1976. *Phonology.* Vol. 1 of *A Grammar of the Greek Papyri of the Roman and Byzantine Periods.* Milan: Cisalpino.

———. 1981. *Morphology.* Vol. 2 of *A Grammar of the Greek Papyri of the Roman and Byzantine Periods.* Milan: Cisalpino.

Goodwin, William Watson. 1893. *Syntax of the Moods and Tenses of the Greek Verb.* Boston: Ginn & Heath.

Grottanelli, Cristiano. 1987. "The Ancient Novel and Biblical Narrative." *Quaderni Urbinati di Cultura Classica* NS 27:7–34.

Guilland, Rodolphe. 1927. *Correspondance de Nicéphore Grégoras.* Paris: Belles Lettres.

Hägg, Tomas. 1997. "A Professor and His Slave: Conventions and Values in the Life of Aesop." Pages 177–203 in *Conventional Values of the Hel-*

lenistic Greeks. Edited by Per Bilde et al. Aarhus: Aarhus University Press.

———. 2012. *The Art of Biography in Antiquity*. Cambridge: Cambridge University Press.

Hansen, William F. 1998. *Anthology of Ancient Greek Popular Literature*. Bloomington: Indiana University Press.

Harnisch, Wolfgang. 1985. *Die Gleichniserzählungen Jesu: Eine hermeneutische Einführung*. Göttingen: Vandenhoeck & Ruprecht.

Haslam, M. W. 1980. "3331. Life of Aesop." Pages 53–56 in *The Oxyrhynchus Papyri, Part XLVIII*. London: Egypt Exploration Society for the British Academy.

———. 1986. "3720. Life of Aesop (Addendum to 3331)." Pages 149–72 in *The Oxyrhynchus Papyri, Part LIII*. London: Egypt Exploration Society for the British Academy.

Hauge, Matthew Ryan. 2016. "Fabulous Parables: The Storytelling Tradition in the Synoptic Gospels." Pages 89–105 in *Ancient Education and Early Christianity*. Edited by M. R. Hauge and A. W. Pitts. LNTS 533. New York: Bloomsbury.

Hausrath, August. 1959. *Corpus Fabularum Aesopicarum I I.2*. Leipzig: Teubner.

Hausrath, August, and Herbert Hunger. 1956. *Fabulae Aesopicae soluta oratione conscriptae*. Vol. 1 of *Corpus Fabularum Aesopicarum*. 2 fasc. 2. Leipzig: Teubner.

Hawthorn, Jeremy. 2000. *A Glossary of Contemporary Literary Theory*. 4th ed. New York: Oxford University Press.

Healey, John F. 2003. "Heliopolis." *OCD*, 676.

Hedrick, Charles W. 2004. *Many Things in Parables: Jesus and His Modern Critics*. Louisville: Westminster John Knox.

Helbing, Robert. 1928. *Die Kasussyntax der Verba bei den Septuaginta*. Göttingen: Vandenhoeck & Ruprecht.

Hilpert, Regine. 1992. "Bild und Text in Heinrich Steinhöwels 'Leben des hochberümten Fabeldichters Esopi.'" Pages 131–54 in Holzberg 1992b.

Hinterberger, Martin. 2005. "Ο Ανδρέας Λιβαδηνός, συγγραφέας/γραφέας λογίων κειμένων, αναγνώστης/γραφέας δημωδών κειμένων: Ο ελληνικός κώδικας 525 του Μονάχου." Pages 25–42 in *Copyists, Collectors, Redactors and Editors: Manuscripts and Editions of Late Byzantine and Early Modern Greek Literature*. Edited by D. Holton et al. Herakleion: Crete University Press.

Holton, David. 1991. *Literature and Society in the Renaissance Crete.* Cambridge: Cambridge University Press.

Holzberg, Niklas. 1992a. "Der Äsop-Roman: Eine strukturanalytische Interpretation." Pages 33–75 in Holzberg 1992b.

———, ed. 1992b. *Der Äsop-Roman: Motivgeschichte und Erzählstruktur.* Tübingen: Narr.

———. 1993. "A Lesser Known 'Picaresque' Novel of Greek Origin: The Aesop Romance and Its Influence." *Groningen Colloquia on the Novel* 5:1–16.

———. 2021. *Leben und Fabeln Äsops: Griechisch-deutsch.* Berlin: De Gruyter.

Horrocks, Geoffrey C. 2010. *Greek: A History of the Language and Its Speakers.* 2nd ed. Oxford: Wiley-Blackwell.

Hostetter, Winifred Hager. 1955. "A Linguistic Study of the Vulgar Greek *Life of Aesop.*" PhD diss., University of Illinois.

Husselman, Elinor Mullett. 1935. "A Lost Manuscript of the Fables of Babrius." *TAPA* 66:104–26.

Ideler, Julian L. 1963. *Physici et Medici Graeci Minores.* 2 vols. in 1. Repr., Amsterdam: Hakkert.

Jannaris, Antonius N. 1897. *An Historical Greek Grammar Chiefly of the Attic Dialect as Written and Spoken from Classical Antiquity down to the Present Time Founded upon the Ancient Texts, Inscriptions, Papyri and Present Popular Greek.* London: Macmillan. Repr., Hildesheim: Olms, 1968.

Jedrkiewicz, Stefano. 1989. *Sapere e Paradosso nell'Antichità: Esopo e la favola.* Rome: Edizioni dell'Ateneo.

———. 2009. "Aesop and the Gods: Divine Characters in the Vita Aesopi." *Métis* NS 7:171–201.

Jeffreys, Elizabeth, et al. 1986. *The Chronicle of John Malalas.* Melbourne: Australian Association for Byzantine Studies.

Jong, Irene de. 2001. *A Narratological Commentary on the Odyssey.* Cambridge: Cambridge University Press.

Jouanno, Corinne. 2005. "La Vie d'Ésope: Une biographie comique." *REG* 118:391–425.

———. 2006. *Vie d'Ésope: Livre du philosophe Xanthos et son esclave Ésope; du mode de vie d'Ésope,* Paris: Belles lettres.

Karla, Grammatiki A. 2001. *Vita Aesopi: Überlieferung, Sprache und Edition einer frühbyzantinischen Fassung des Äsopromans.* Wiesbaden: Reichert.

———. 2003. "Die Redactio Accursiana der *Vita Aesopi:* Ein Werk des Maximos Planudes?" *ByzZ* 96:661–69.

———. 2006. "Maximos Planudes: Dr. Bowdler in Byzanz? Zensur und Innovation im späten Byzanz." *Classica et Mediaevalia* 57:213–38.

———. 2009a. "Die älteste Version des Äsopromans." Pages 442–52 in Ἀντιφίλησις: *Studies on Classical, Byzantine and Modern Greek Literature and Culture.* Edited by E. Karamalengou and E. Makrygianni. Stuttgart: Steiner.

———. 2009b. "Fictional Biography vis-à-vis Romance: Affinity and Differentiation." Pages 13–32 in *Fiction on the Fringe: Novelistic Writing in the Post-Classical Age.* Edited by G. A. Karla. Leiden: Brill.

———. 2011. "A Parody of the *Odyssey* in the *Life of Aesop.*" *Cambridge Classical Journal* 57:55–69

———. 2014. "Isis-Epiphany in the *Life of Aesop*: A Structural Analytic Approach." Pages 83–102 in *The Ancient Novel: Frontiers of Genre.* Edited by M. P. Futre Pinheiro, G. Schmeling, and E. Cueva. Eelde, the Netherlands: Barkhuis.

———. 2016a. "*Life of Aesop*: Fictional Biography as Popular Literature?" Pages 47–64 in *Writing Biography in Greece and Rome: Narrative Technique and Fictionalization.* Edited by K. De Temmerman and K. Demoen. Cambridge: Cambridge University Press.

———. 2016b. "*The Literary Life of a Fictional Life:* Aesop in Antiquity and Byzantium." Pages 313–37 in *Fictional Storytelling in the Medieval Eastern Mediterranean and Beyond.* Edited by C. Cupane and B. Krönung. Leiden: Brill.

———. 2019a. "*Locus amoenus* in the *Life of Aesop*: Mirroring (Re)birth and Death." Pages 99–107 in *Des dieux et des plantes: Monde végétal et religion en Grèce ancienne.* Edited by A. Gartziou-Tatti and A. Zografou. Liège: Presses Universitaires de Liège.

———. 2019b. "Το λεξιλόγιο της αρχαίας λαϊκής λογοτεχνίας και η νέα ελληνική γλώσσα." Pages 171–88 in *Λέξεις: Τιμητικός τόμος για την Χριστίνα Μπασέα-Μπεζαντάκου.* Edited by G. Karla, I. Manolessou, and N. Pantelidis. Athens: Καρδαμίτσα.

Konstan, David. 1998. "The Alexander Romance: The Cunning of the Open Text." *Lexis* 16:123–38.

Konstan, David, and Robyn Walsh. 2016. "Civic and Subversive Biography in Antiquity." Pages 26–44 in *Writing Biography in Greece and Rome: Narrative Technique and Fictionalization.* Edited by K. De Temmerman and K. Demoen. Cambridge: Cambridge University Press.

Konstantakos, Ioannis M. 2004. "Trial by Riddle: The Testing of the Counsellor and the Contest of Kings in the Legend of Amasis and Bias." *Classica et Mediaevalia* 55:85–137.

———. 2006. "Aesop Adulterer and Trickster: A Study of *Vita Aesopi* Ch. 75-76." *Athenaeum* 94:563–600.

———. 2008a. *Γένεση καὶ ἀφηγηματικὸ ὑλικό*. Vol. 1 of Ἀκίχαρος: Ἡ Διήγηση τοῦ Ἀχικὰρ στὴν ἀρχαία Ἑλλάδα. Athens: Stigmi.

———. 2008b. *Ἀπὸ τὸν Δημόκριτο στοὺς Περιπατητικούς*. Vol. 2 of Ἀκίχαρος: Ἡ Διήγηση τοῦ Ἀχικὰρ στὴν ἀρχαία Ἑλλάδα: Athens: Stigmi.

———. 2013. *Ἡ Διήγηση τοῦ Ἀχικὰρ καὶ ἡ Μυθιστορία τοῦ Αἰσώπου*. Vol. 3 of Ἀκίχαρος. Athens: Stigmi.

Kriaras, Emmanouel. 1968–. *Λεξικὸ τῆς μεσαιωνικῆς δημώδους γραμματείας 1100–1669*. Thessaloniki: Centre for the Greek Language.

Kühner, Raphael, Friedrich Blass, and Bernhard Gerth. 1904. *Ausführliche Grammatik der griechischen Sprache*. 3rd ed. 4 parts in 2 vols. Hannover: Hahnsche Buchhandlung.

Kurke, Leslie. 2011. *Aesopic Conversations: Popular Tradition, Cultural Dialogue, and the Invention of Greek Prose*. Princeton: Princeton University Press.

Kussl, Ralf. 1992. "Achikar, Tinuphis und Äsop." Pages 23–30 in Holzberg 1992b.

Lampe, Geoffrey W. H. 1976. *A Patristic Greek Lexicon*. 4th ed. Oxford: Clarendon.

La Penna, Antonio. 1962. "Il Romanzo di Esopo." *Athenaeum* NS 40:264–314.

Le Coq, Albert von. 1922. *Nebst einem christlichen Bruchstück aus Bulayïq*. Vol. 3 of *Türkische Manichaica aus Chotscho*. Berlin: Verlag der Königlichen Akademie der Wissenschaften.

Leone, Pietro Luigi. 1982–1983. *Nicephori Gregorae epistulae*. Matino: Tipografia di Matino.

Lindenberger, James M. 1983–1985. "Ahiqar (Seventh to Sixth Century B.C.): A New Translation and Introduction." Pages 479–507 in vol. 2 of *The Old Testament Pseudepigrapha*. Edited by James H. Charlesworth. 2 vols. Garden City, NY: Doubleday.

Ludwig, Claudia. 1997. *Sonderformen byzantinischer Hagiographie und ihr literarisches Vorbild: Untersuchungen zu den Viten des Äsop, des Philaretos, des Symeon Salos und des Andreas Salos*. Frankfurt am Main: Lang.

Luzzatto, Maria Jagoda. 1996. "Aisop-Roman." *DNP* 1:359–60.

Macray, William Dunn. 1890. *Annals of the Bodleian Library, Oxford: With a Notice of the Earlier Library of the University*. 2nd ed. Oxford: Clarendon.

Madan, Falconer, and H. H. E. Craster. 1922. *A Summary Catalogue of Western Manuscripts in the Bodleian Library at Oxford*. Vol. 2. Oxford: Clarendon.

Marinčič, Marko. 2003. "The Grand Vizier, the Prophet, and the Satirist. Transformations of the Oriental *Ahiqar Romance* in Ancient Prose Fiction." Pages 53–70 in *The Ancient Novel and Beyond*. Edited by Stelios Panayotakis, Maaike Zimmerman, and Wytse Keulen. Leiden: Brill.

Mayser, Edwin. 1926. *Analytischer*. Part 1 of *Satzlehre*. Vol. 2 of *Grammatik der griechischen Papyri aus der Ptolemäerzeit mit Einschluss der gleichzeitigen Ostraka und der in Ägypten verfassten Inschriften*. Berlin: De Gruyter.

Mazzatinti, Giancarlo. 1892. *Inventari dei manoscritti delle biblioteche d'Italia*. Vol. 2. Florence: Olschki.

Merkle, Stefan. 1996. "Fable, 'Anecdote' and 'Novella' in the *Vita Aesopi*: The Ingredients of a 'Popular Novel.'" Pages 209–34 in *La letteratura di consumo nel mondo greco-latino: Atti del convegno internazionale; Cassino, 14–17 settembre 1994*. Edited by Oronzo Pecere and Antonio Stramaglia. Cassino: Università degli Studi di Cassino.

Mignogna, Elisa. 1992. "Aesopus Bucolicus: Come si 'mette in scena' un miracolo (*Vita Aesopi* c. 6)." Pages 76–84 in Holzberg 1992b.

Mihevc-Gabrovec, Erika. 1960. *Études sur la syntaxe de Ioannes Moschos*. Ljubljana: Filozofska fakultet Univerze.

Moulton, James H. 1904. "Grammatical Notes from the Papyri." *CR* 18:106–12, 151–55.

Nagy, Gregory. 1979. *The Best of the Achaeans: Concepts of the Hero in Archaic Greek Poetry*. Baltimore: Johns Hopkins University Press. Rev. ed., 1999.

Omont, Henri Auguste. 1888. *Inventaire sommaire de manuscrits grecs de la Bibliothèque Nationale*. 4 vols. Paris: Leroux.

Panagiotakis, Nikolaos M. 1974. "Ὁ Francesco Barozzi καὶ ἡ Ἀκαδημία τῶν Vivi τοῦ Ρεθύμνου." Pages 232–51 in vol. 2 of *Πεπραγμένα τοῦ Γ΄ Διεθνοῦς Κρητολογικοῦ Συνεδρίου*. Athens: n.p.

Papademetriou, Ioannes-Theophanes A. 1989. *Αἰσώπεια καὶ Αἰσωπικά*, Athens: n.p.

———. 1997. *Aesop as an Archetypal Hero*. Athens: Hellenic Society for Humanistic Studies.

Papathomopoulos, Manolis, ed. 1990. Ὁ Βίος τοῦ Αἰσώπου: Ἡ παραλλαγὴ G. Edited with introduction and translation. Athens: Ioannina.

———, ed. 1999a. Ὁ Βίος τοῦ Αἰσώπου: Ἡ Παραλλαγὴ W. Edited with introduction, translation, and commentary. Athens: Ioannina.

———, ed. 1999b. Πέντε δημώδεις μεταφράσεις τοῦ Βίου τοῦ Αἰσώπου, Athens: Papadēma.

———, ed. 2009. Βίβλος Ξάνθου φιλοσόφου καὶ Αἰσώπου δούλου αὐτοῦ: Περὶ τῆς ἀναστροφῆς Αἰσώπου. Critical edition with introduction and Modern Greek translation. Athens: Aletheia.

Parsons, Mikael C. 2007. *Luke: Storyteller, Interpreter, Evangelist*. Peabody, MA: Hendrickson.

Parsons, Mikael, and Michael W. Martin. 2018. *Ancient Rhetoric and the New Testament: The Influence of Elementary Greek Composition*. Waco, TX: Baylor University Press.

Perry, Ben Edwin. 1933. "The Text Tradition of the Greek Life of Aesop." *Transactions and Proceedings of the American Philological Association* 64:198–244.

———. 1934. "The Greek Source of Rinuccio's Aesop." *CP* 29:53–62.

———. 1936. *Studies in the Text History of the Life and Fables of Aesop*. Haverford, PA: American Philological Association.

———. 1952. *Greek and Latin Texts*. Vol. 1 of *Aesopica: A Series of Texts Relating to Aesop or Ascribed to Him or Closely Connected with the Literary Tradition That Bears His Name*. Urbana: University of Illinois Press.

———. 1959. "The Origin of the Book of Sindbad." *Fabula* 3:1–94.

———. 1966. "Some Addenda to the Life of Aesop." *ByzZ* 59:285–304.

Pervo, Richard I. 1998. "A Nihilist Fabula: Introducing the *Life of Aesop*." Pages 77–120 in *Ancient Fiction and Early Christian Narrative*. Edited by Ronald F. Hock, J. Bradley Chance, and Judith Perkins. SymS 6. Atlanta: Society of Biblical Literature.

Pesce, Mauro, and Adriana Destro. 1999. "La lavanda dei piedi di Gv 13,1–20, il Romanzo di Esopo e i Saturnalia di Macrobio." *Bib* 80:240–49.

Pontani, Filippomaria. 2005. *Sguardi su Ulisse: La tradizione esegetica greca all'Odissea*. Rome: Edizioni di storia e letteratura.

Porten, Bezalel, and Ada Yardeni, eds. 1993. *Literature, Accounts, Lists*. Vol. 3 of *Textbook of Aramaic Documents from Ancient Egypt*. Texts and Studies for Students. Jerusalem: Hebrew University, Department of the History of the Jewish People.

Radermacher, Ludwig. 1947. *Koine.* Sitzungsberichte / Akademie der Wissenschaften in Wien, Philosophisch-Historische Klasse 224. Vienna: Rohrer.

Rásonyi Nagy, László. 1930. "Das uigurische Aesop-Josipas-Fragment." *Byzantinisch-Neugriechische Jahrbücher* 7:429–43.

Reece, Steve. 2016. "'Aesop,' 'Q' and 'Luke.'" *NTS* 62:357–77.

Rigopoulou, Anastasia. 2012. "Λαϊκότροπες μυθιστορικές αφηγήσεις: Βίος Ομήρου – Αγών Ομήρου και Ησιόδου – Βίος Αισώπου: Συγκριτική θεώρηση." PhD diss., National and Kapodistrian University of Athens.

Robertson, Noel. 2003. "Aesop's Encounter with Isis and the Muses and the Origins of the Life of Aesop." Pages 247–66 in *Poetry, Theory, Praxis: The Social Life of Myth, Word and Image in Ancient Greece; Essays in Honour of William J. Slater.* Edited by Eric Csapo and Margaret C. Miller. Oxford: Oxbow.

Ross, William A. 2016. "'Ὢ ἀνόητοι καὶ βραδεῖς τῇ καρδίᾳ': Luke, Aesop, and Reading Scripture." *NovT* 58:369–79.

Ruiz Montero, Consuelo. 2010. "La *Vida de Esopo* (rec. G): Niveles de lengua y aspectos de estilo." Pages 605–12 in *Dic mihi, Musa, uirum: Homenaje al profesor A. López Eire.* Edited by Francisco Cortés Gabaudan and Julián Víctor Méndez Dosuna. Salamanca: Universidad de La Laguna.

———. 2014. "The Life of Aesop (rec. G): The Composition of the Text." Pages 257–71 in *A Companion to the Ancient Novel.* Edited by Edmund P. Cueva and Shannon N. Byrne. Hoboken, NJ: Wiley.

Rutherford, Ian. 2005. "Down-Stream to the Cat-Goddess: Herodotus on Egyptian Pilgrimage." Pages 131–50 in *Pilgrimage in Graeco-Roman and Early Christian Antiquity: Seeing the Gods.* Edited by Jaś Elsner, Ian Rutherford. Oxford: Oxford University Press.

Rydbeck, Lars. 1967. *Fachprosa, vermeintliche Volkssprache und Neues Testament: Zur Beurteilung der sprachlichen Niveauunterschiede im nachklassischen Griechisch.* Uppsala: Universitet.

Schädlich, Hans Joachim. 1999. *Gib ihm Sprache: Leben und Tod des Dichters Äsop; Eine Nacherzählung.* Hamburg: Rowohlt.

Schamp, Jacques. 2023. *Discours V–XIII: Les Empereurs Illyrien et Pannonien.* Vol. 2 of *Thémistios.* Paris: Belles Lettres.

Schwyzer, Eduard. 1988. *Syntax und syntaktische Stilistik.* Vol. 2 of *Griechische Grammatik: Auf der Grundlage von Karl Brugmanns Griechischer Grammatik.* Completed and edited by Albert Debrunner. 5th ed. Munich: Beck.

Scott, Bernard Brandon. 1989. *Hear Then the Parable: A Commentary on the Parables of Jesus*. Minneapolis: Fortress.

Seidlmayer, Stephan J. 2006. "Heliopolis, Heliupolis." *BNP*. http://dx.doi.org/10.1163/1574-9347_bnp_e506530.

Shiner, Whitney. 1998. "Creating Plot in Episodic Narratives: *The Life of Aesop* and the Gospel of Mark." Pages 155–76 in *Ancient Fiction and Early Christian Narrative*. Edited by Ronald F. Hock, J. Bradley Chance, and Judith Perkins. SymS 6. Atlanta: Society of Biblical Literature.

Sophocles, E. A. 1900. *Greek Lexicon of the Roman and Byzantine Periods (from B.C. 146 to A.D. 1100)*. New York: Charles Scribner's Sons.

Stamoulakis, Ioannis P. 2016. *Το λεξιλόγιο της Μυθιστορίας του Αισώπου*. Athens: National and Kapodistrian University of Athens.

Stigall, Joshua J. 2012. "The Progymnasmata and Characterization in Luke's Parables: The Parable of the Rich Fool as a Test Case." *PRSt* 39:349–60.

Strong, Justin David. 2021. *The Fables of Jesus in the Gospel of Luke: A New Foundation for the Study of Parables*. Paderborn: Brill Schöningh.

———. 2022. "How to Interpret Parables in Light of the Fable: Lessons from the Promythium and the Epimythium." Pages 327–52 in *Overcoming Dichotomies: Parables, Fables, and Similes in the Graeco-Roman World*. Edited by Albertina Oegema, Jonathan Pater, and Martijn Stoutjesdijk. WUNT 483. Tübingen: Mohr Siebeck.

Talbot, Alice-Mary. 1991a. "Gregoras Nikephoros." Pages 874–75 in vol. 2 of *The Oxford Dictionary of Byzantium*. Edited by Alexander P. Kazhdan et al. 3 vols. Oxford: Oxford University Press.

———. 1991b. "Libadenos Andrew." Page 1222 in vol. 2 of *The Oxford Dictionary of Byzantium*. Edited by Alexander P. Kazhdan et al. 3 vols. Oxford: Oxford University Press.

Tallmadge, Edwin R. 1938. "A Grammatical Study of the Greek Life of Aesop." PhD diss., University of Illinois.

Thomas, Christine M. 1998. "Stories without Texts and without Authors: The Problem of Fluidity in Ancient Novelistic Texts and Early Christian Literature." Pages 273–91 in *Ancient Fiction and Early Christian Narrative*. Edited by Ronald F. Hock, J. Bradley Chance, and Judith Perkins. SymS 6. Atlanta: Society of Biblical Literature.

Toth, Ida. 2005. "*The Story of Iosop the Wise and How He Lived*: A Medieval Slavonic Translation of the *Life of Aesop*." Pages 115–27 in *Approaches to Texts in Early Modern Greek: Papers from the Conference Neograeca Medii Aevi V, Exeter College, University of Oxford, September 2000*. Edited by Elizabeth Jeffreys and Michael Jeffreys. Oxford: Sub-faculty

of Modern Greek, Faculty of Medieval and Modern Languages, University of Oxford.
Tronci, Liana. 2020. "Future Forms in Postclassical Greek: Some Remarks on the Septuagint and the New Testament." Pages 111–44 in *Postclassical Greek: Contemporary Approaches to Philology and Linguistics*. Edited by Dariya Rafiyenko and Ilja A. Seržant. Berlin: De Gruyter.
Van Dijk, Gert-Jan. 1995. "The Fables in the Greek *Life of Aesop*." *Reinardus* 8:131–83.
Vilinskij, Sergej G. 1911. *Žitie sv. Vasilija Novago v russkoj literatuře*. Odessa: Technik.
Vouga, François. 1992. "Formgeschichtliche Überlegungen zu den Gleichnissen und zu den Fabeln der Jesus-Tradition auf dem Hintergrund der hellenistischen Literaturgeschichte." Pages 173–87 in vol. 1 of *The Four Gospels: Festschrift for Frans Neirynck*. Edited by Frans van Segroeck et al. 3 vols. Leuven: Leuven University Press.
———. 1999. "Zur form- und redaktionsgeschichtlichen Definition der Gattungen: Gleichnis, Parabel/Fabel, Beispielerzählungen." Pages 75–95 in *Die Gleichnisreden Jesu 1899–1999: Beiträge zum Dialog mit Adolf Jülicher*. Edited by Ulrich Mell. Berlin: De Gruyter.
———. 2001. "Die Parabeln Jesu und die Fabeln Äsops. Ein Beitrag zur Gleichnisforschung und zur Problematik der Literalisierung der Erzählungen der Jesus-Tradition." *WD* 26:149–64.
Watson, Duane F. 2010. "The 'Life of Aesop' and the Gospel of Mark: Two Ancient Approaches to Elite Values Author(s)." *JBL* 129:699–716.
Westermann, Anton. 1845. *Vita Aesopi ex Vratislaviensi ac partim Monacensi et Vindobonensi codicibus*. London: Williams & Norgate.
Wheatley, Edward. 2000. *Mastering Aesop: Medieval Education, Chaucer, and His Followers*, Gainesville: University Press of Florida.
Wiechers, Anton. 1961. *Aesop in Delphi*. Meisenheim-Glan: Hain.
Wilkens, Jens. 2000. *Manichäisch-Türkische Texte der Berliner Turfansammlung*. Alttürkische Handschriften. Stuttgart: Steiner.
Wills, Lawrence M. 1997. *The Quest of the Historical Gospel: Mark, John, and the Origins of the Gospel Genre*. London: Routledge.
———. 2008. "The Aesop Tradition." Pages 222–37 in *The Historical Jesus in Context*. Edited by Amy-Jill Levine, Dale C. Allison, and John Dominic Crossan. Princeton: Princeton University Press.
Wojciechowski, Michael. 2008. "Aesopic Tradition in the New Testament." *JGRChJ* 5:99–109.

Wyss, Karl. 1942. *Untersuchungen zur Sprache des Alexanderromans von Pseudo-Kallisthenes (Laut- und Formenlehre des Codex A)*. Fribourg: Paulusdruckerei.

Zafiropoulos, Christos A. 2014. "Ahiqar, His Tale and the *Vita Aesopi*." Review of Ἡ Διήγησῃ τοῦ Ἀχικὰρ καὶ ἡ Μυθιστορία τοῦ Αἰσώπου, vol. 3 of Ἀχίχαρος, by Ioannis Konstantakos. *Scrinium* 10:479–95.

Zeitz, Heinrich. 1935. "Die Fragmente des Äsopromans in Papyrushandschriften." PhD diss. Giessen.

Zieme, Peter. 1968. "Die türkische Yosīpas-Fragmente." *MIOF* 14:45–67.

Zimmermann, Ruben. 2014. "Fable. III New Testament." *EBR* 8:650–51.

GENERAL INDEX

Acts of the Apostles, 2, 58, 187
Accursiana (version), 7, 10. *See also* Planudean
Accursius, Bonus, 7, 11
Aenus, 48, 206
Aesopeum, 3, 38, 48
Ahiqar, 1, 5, 8, 204–6
Alexander Romance, 2, 8, 195, 206
Amorion, 29
anecdote(s), 1, 8
antihero, 9, 33, 61
apocrypha, 17
Aphrodite, 39
Apollo, 4, 28, 34, 37, 38, 56
Apuleius, 2, 5
Aramaic, 1, 5, 204–6
archetype, 6–7, 20, 25, 33–34, 45–47, 58–59, 61, 169, 176, 178, 180, 194, 198, 207
Aristophanes, 1, 188
Aristotle, 1, 173
Asia Minor, 36
Babylon/Babylonian, 1, 3–5, 36, 47, 206
Balzac's *Contes Drolatiques*, 12
Barocci, Giacommo, 16
Bertoldo (*Le sottilissime astuzie di Bertoldo*), 12. *See also* Cesare, Giulio (dalla) Croce
Bible 207. *See also* Acts of the Apostles; New Testament
biography, 2, 8
 civic biography, 2
 fictional biography, 2
 subversive biography, 2
Boccaccio's *Decameron*, 12
Byzantine(s), 47

Cappadocia, 29
Cato, *Distichs* or *Sententiae*, 16–17
Caxton, William, 12
Cervantes, Miguel de, *Don Quixote*, 12
Cesare, Giulio (dalla) Croce, 12. *See also Bertoldo*
closed texts, 8. *See also* open texts
comedy, 35, 170
Constantine Porphyrogennitus, 10
contamination, 21, 24–25, 46, 202
Croesus, 3, 5, 38, 41–42, 48, 202, 206
Cyranides, 19
Delphi/Delphian(s), 1, 4–5, 8, 36, 38, 46, 56, 215, 217
Demosthenes, 36 (Δημοσθένης)
Dexicrates, 47
Digenis, 12
Digin (emperor), 12
Diocles (philosopher), 15
Diogenes, 1, 8, 172
Dionysios Periegetes, 16
Dionysius, 47
Dionysius of Halicarnassus, 193
Dionysus 28
Egypt/Egyptian(s), 3, 5, 204–6, 213–14
Elephantine, 1, 204–5
Empedocles, 11
Ephesus, 8
 widow of (story), 8, 56
epimythium, 48
Etymologicum Magnum, 172, 184
Euripides, 29
Eustathius, bishop of Thessalonike, 16, 209
fable(s), 1, 3, 5–10, 13, 15, 17–18, 38–39, 44, 46, 48, 59, 180, 188, 203

-235-

florilegium, 44
genre (literary), 2, 5, 12
George, bishop of the Arab tribes, 13
gloss, 171, 175, 177–78, 190, 203
gnomae, 44
gospels, 2, 3, 18, 58. *See also* Acts of the Apostles; Bible; New Testament
Greece, 36, 56, 58
Greek, Modern, 7, 11, 179–80, 187, 209, 212
haplography, 175, 177, 196
Hellenistic (period), 1, 169, 213
Hera, 47
Herodian, 179
Herodotus, 1, 213–14
Hesiod, 1, 8
Hesychius, 172
Himerius, 10, 34
Historia Apollonii regis Tyri, 8
Homer
    Iliad, 19, 56
    Odyssey, 19, 213
    Life of Homer, 2, 8
Hurus, Johann or Hans, 12
interpolation(s), 56, 62, 168–69, 185, 194
Iosop, the Story of, 12–13
iotacism, 175, 177–78, 190
Isis, 2–4, 28, 37, 38, 169, 213
itacism, 177. *See also* iotacism
John Chrysostom, 193
John, the Stylite of Litarb, 13
joke(s), 1, 35, 43
Julian, 10
Kamp, Johann, 12
Koine, 35, 61, 167, 170, 185, 210, 218
lacuna(e), 16, 30, 54, 190, 194, 213
Lazarillo de Tormes, 12
lectio facilior/difficilior, 172, 174, 184, 193, 200, 211–12, 217, 220
legend(s), 8
Leithandschrift (copy-text), 61–62, 212
Leon Grammatikos, 16
Libadenos, Andreas, 11, 15–16, 62, 168, 172, 181, 184
Libanius, 18, 19, 34

Libanius Alchemista, *De hominis generatione*, 19
locus amoenus, 38–39
Lolliniana (Latin translation), 7, 11, 17, 19, 25–26, 28–29, 33, 177–79, 190
Lycur(g)us, /-os, 3–5, 38–39, 41, 45, 47–48, 55–56, 206, 213
Lydian(s), 36, 202
Macho, Julien, 12
Malalas Joannes, 184, 200
Mark, Gospel of, 3, 9. *See also* gospels
Marsyas, 38
Maximos Planudes, 7, 10, 16, 32
Memphis, 5, 36
metaphrases, 7
Modern Greek. *See* Greek, Modern
Moschos, *Europa*, 16
motivation, 43
    actorial, 41
Muses, 2, 5, 34, 37–38, 56
narrative, 8–10, 26–27, 31–34, 37, 39–40, 45–46, 49, 58, 207
    comic-picaresque narrative, 5
    episodic narrative, 9
    structure, 8, 42, 47
Nectenabo, 4–5, 45, 206, 211, 213
New Testament, 170–71. *See also* Bible
Nicephoros Gregoras, 11
Nonnus (Pseudo-Nonnus), *Scholia mythologica*, 17
novella(s), 1, 12
Olympiodorus, 193
Olympus, 38
open text(s), 8, 61. *See also* closed texts
    open tradition, 58
parables, 18. *See also* gospels
Persian, 1
Petronius, 5
Phoenicia, 36
Phrygia(n), 1, 10–11, 29
pharmakos, 6
Philoxenia, 28
Photius (Patriarch), 10, 195
Planudean (version), 2, 7, 10–11, 18. *See also* Accursiana

Plato, 11, 173
Plutarch, 2
prolepsis, 39
Prometheus, 39
proverb(s), 15–16
Ptochoprodromos, 16
Ptolemaic (period), 5
Pythagoras/Pythagorean, 11, 16–17, 203
Qočo, 13
riddle(s), 1, 4, 12, 43, 45, 49, 205
Rinuccio da Castiglione of Arezzo, 7, 11–12
Samian(s), 3, 5, 38–39, 41, 45, 48, 201
Seven Sages, 1, 8
Sicily, 36, 58
Socrates, 1, 8,
Sorg, Anton, 12
Spanos, 171
Stephanites and Ichnelates, 15
Stobaeus,179
Suda, 10, 195, 200
Symeon, 15 (Συμεών). *See also Stephanites and Ichnelates*
Syntipas, 15–16
Tyche, 3, 28, 37, 39, 169
usus scribendi, 26, 194
Uyghur (Book), 13
Westermann, 7, 171
Westermanniana (version or version W), 2, 7, 15, 24–25, 34, 54, 56, 58–59, 61, 169–70, 172–92, 194–96, 198, 208–12, 214–16, 218–20
Yosipas, 13
Zainer, Günter, 12
Zainer, Johann, 11

www.ingramcontent.com/pod-product-compliance
Lightning Source LLC
Chambersburg PA
CBHW021352300426
44114CB00012B/1188